T0245589

THE DESIGN BOOK

THE DESIGN

BOOK

Φ

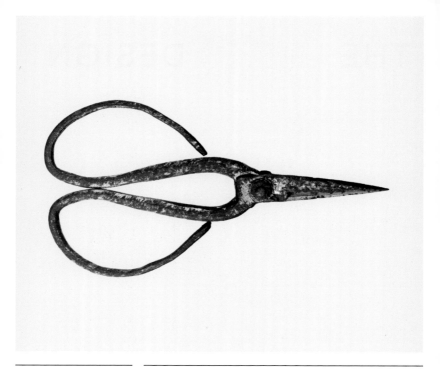

**ZHANG XIAOQUAN
HOUSEHOLD
SCISSORS (1663)**
Zhang Xiaoquan
(c.1643–83)
Hangzhou Zhang
Xiaoquan
1663 to present

In China, the Zhang Xiaoquan brand represents not only a pair of scissors but also a part of Chinese culture. The Hangzhou Zhang Xiaoquan scissors factory has been in operation for over 300 years and now sells 120 types of scissors in 360 specifications. The original scissors are a beautiful example of simple, functional design; they are lightweight, comfortable in the hand and extremely hard wearing. In 1663, the Zhang Dalong scissors factory in Hangzhou, Zhejiang province, was taken over by the son of its founder and took on its inheritor's name, Zhang Xiaoquan. Since then, the company has grown enormously and enjoyed

the patronage of China's emperors. Chairman Mao, in his 1956 writings focussing on the socialist recon-struction of the handicraft industry, cited Zhang Xiaoquan scissors for their contribution to the nation and advised that the industry be developed. With government backing, the new enterprise began to build larger premises and was state-run from 1958 until 2000, when it was transformed into a limited company. The company is now continually ranked first in national quality evaluations and Zhang Xiaoquan Household Scissors sales make up 40 per cent of the Chinese scissors market.

ARARE TEAPOT
(1700s)
Designer Unknown
Various
1700s to present
Iwachu
1914 to present

It is not necessary to have visited Japan to be familiar with the Arare Teapot. The ubiquitous presence of the teapot throughout the country has elevated this purposeful design into an international standard. Made from cast iron, Arare – which means 'hail' in Japanese – takes its name from the traditional hobnail design on the top of the pot's black body and on the outer edges of its lid. Arare's rise to prominence has its roots in eighteenth-century Japan, when the literati adopted the Sencha tea ceremony method as a symbolic revolt against the more gilded Chanoya ceremony favoured by the ruling classes.

As the Sencha method encouraged more people to partake in the pleasure of the tea ceremony, a market opened up for a less expensive teapot. The Arare is an adaptation of earlier teapot designs that arose during this period and it emerged in its contemporary form in 1914. The Arare's most popular manufacturer, the Iwachu Company of Morioko, is now Japan's largest and foremost producer of cast iron kitchenware, with a history that is over 100 years old. Today the Iwachu Arare Teapot is exported in vast quantities all over the world.

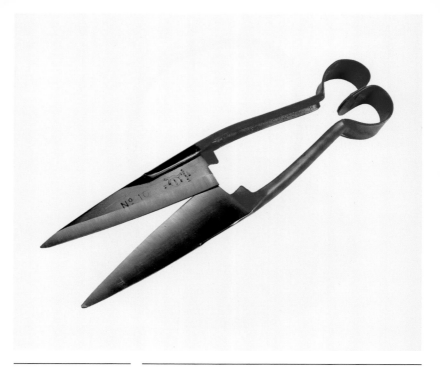

SHEEP SHEARS
(1730)
Designer Unknown
Various
1700s to present
Burgon & Ball
1730 to present

Sheep shears, which have been around in the same basic shape for thousands of years, form part of the anonymous crowd of neglected masterpieces of design. They are known to have existed from 300 BC in Egypt and there are also records of their existence from Roman times. The manual shears developed in a variety of sizes and patterns suitable for different kinds of breed and fleece. The reason for their enduring success lies in the perfection of the design, which ensures the maximum performance in the simplest shape. The mechanism of the shears allows the user to put the hand right over the blades, concentrating all the energy into the cut. 'Maximum possible cutting control, plus maximum energy efficiency', say Burgon & Ball of Sheffield, established in 1730 and one of the largest sheep shears manufacturers in the world. Today the company produces over sixty different patterns, but its bestseller remains the Red Drummer Boy, which is noticeable for its peculiar double-bow pattern and red painted handles.

SACK-BACK
WINDSOR CHAIR
(c.1760s)
Designer Unknown
Various
c.1760s to present

Early versions of Windsor-like chairs date back to the Gothic period, but the true development of the Windsor began during the 1700s. Initially conceived in Britain as a rural chair (supposedly by wheelwrights) the Windsor was used in farms, taverns and gardens. The chair's name may have derived from the fact that, early on, many makers originated in Windsor, England, peddling their chairs from farm wagons. The Sack-Back Windsor is a superior example of the form. Its comfortable, lightweight back and broad oval seat compose a beautiful whole. The name 'sack-back' is thought to have

originated from the shape and height of the back, suited to allow a 'sack' to be pulled over to deflect winter drafts. Windsors took advantage of the unique attributes of different wood species: seats were pine or chestnut; stretchers and legs were maple; bent parts were hickory, white oak or ash. The Windsor Chair exemplifies principles of good design: its form and structure embody centuries of craftsmanship, material ingenuity, simple yet sophisticated engineering and aesthetic beauty, while fulfilling the complex requirements of comfort and durable construction.

TRADITIONAL WHITE CHINA (c.1796)
Josiah Wedgwood & Sons
Wedgwood 1796 to 1830, c.1930 to 2004, 2005 to present

The initial development of bone china, a form of porcelain made from china clay, feldspathic rock, flint and calcined animal bone, is attributed to Josiah Spode. Adding bone to the compound was found to give the ceramic body both its strength and durability and contributed to the translucency of the material, creating an ivory white appearance. Wedgwood, founded in 1759, first put bone china into production in 1812 at its factory near Stoke-on-Trent. Although bone china production was discontinued between 1828 and 1875 due to the company's dire economic situation, it returned to become an important part of

Wedgwood production. Traditional White was an undecorated range in bone china and earthenware. It was not specifically a range of its own until the 1930s, although the shapes of many of the pieces date back to c.1796. At the beginning of the 1800s the fashion was for highly decorated wares, brilliantly coloured and lavishly gilded, often with Oriental motifs, and Traditional White was used as a basis for these pieces. Today, Traditional White has achieved its own status because of its simplicity and sophistication. Its strength, durability, whiteness and translucency have ensured its enduring quality and lasting appeal.

LE PARFAIT JARS
(c.1825)
Designer Unknown
Various
c.1825 to present

These jars have quietly become a fixture in the domestic landscape, rising from the ranks of anonymous canning and preserving jars to become something like the equivalent of the Chair No.14 by Thonet, now a universal standard. Early examples of this type of clip-top preserving jar have been made since at least the beginning of the nineteenth century, and used for storage of conserves, fruits, terrines and, of course, foie gras. Modern French-made Le Parfait Preserve Jars are constructed in pressed glass to form a perfect seal. The jars are available in a variety of sizes, from 50 ml to 3 litres (0.1 to 5.25 pt) and each

has a glass lid that flips closed using a wire bail and is sealed by the distinctive orange rubber gasket. When the jar is heated a vacuum forms inside, making the seal airtight. The flat lid is designed for easy stacking, and the wide mouth for easy filling. The openings vary in size from 7 to 10 cm (2.75 to 4 in). The jars have been repeatedly patented, imitated and distributed, but none quite equals the distinctive orange-sealed original.

GALVANIZED METAL DUSTBIN (c.1830)
Designer Unknown
Various
c.1830 to present

The origins of the galvanized metal dustbin have faded in the memory of long-standing manufacturers such as Garrods of Barking in East London. The company has been manufacturing dustbins for more than 200 years and is the oldest bin manufacturer in the country. In the 1700s, rubbish, which was previously stored indoors, was moved to external containers, and the need arose for a vessel that could withstand weathering. Garrods' management saw the first examples of industrial machinery that could be used to manufacture metal dustbins at the 1851 Great Exhibition in London, and began industrial

production shortly afterwards. Today, half of the company's production still runs off the same Victorian machinery. Production is divided into two main families of machinery: corrugators and rimming tools. Thin sheets of galvanized steel, appropriate for its resistance to corrosion and rust due to its zinc coating, are passed through the corrugating machine. Next, the dustbin is finished in all its details with the aid of the rimming machines. Garrods is one of the last remaining manufacturers of a mass-produced, low-cost product to have resisted relocating its facilities to countries with cheap labour.

HURRICANE LANTERN (1840)
Designer Unknown
R. E. Dietz Company
1840 to present
Various
1840s to present

Hurricane lanterns, or storm lanterns, were named after their ability to remain lit even in high winds. The title 'Hurricane' normally refers to a tubular lantern whose flame is generated by air supplied via metal side-tubes. The air feeds into the kerosene-based burning mixture to create a bright flame. The main types of tubular lanterns are the hot- and cold-blast systems, both invented by John Irwin in 1868 and 1874, respectively. Hot-blast allows fresh air to enter the main body of the lantern – the glass 'globe' – at its base. A mixture of heated air and spent gases then rises up into the canopy, from where a significant percentage descends back through the side tubes to resupply the flame. The cold-blast principle does not allow the heated by-products of combustion to re-enter the system. Instead, these escape via a chimney-like opening; an air chamber surrounding the 'chimney' brings fresh air into the tubes and straight to the flame. The American lamp and lantern manufacturer, R. E. Dietz Company, produced the first hot-blast lantern in 1868 and the first cold-blast in 1880. Shown here is a Dietz Hot-Blast Lantern, originally intended to demarcate barricades or road hazards.

SAFETY PIN (1849)
Walter Hunt
(1785–1869)
Various
1849 to present

Sometimes a design is so commonplace that it seems as if it has always been in existence. Such is the case with the safety pin, the ubiquitous household helpmate that was designed by the New Yorker Walter Hunt. Hunt, it seems, was frustrated by the flimsiness and pernicious pricking of straight pins. Working with a 20 cm (8 in) piece of brass wire, he conceived a simple solution by fashioning a coil at one end to provide spring action, and a simple catch at the other end. Hunt's 1849 patent application included drawings of variations on the 'Dress-Pin', which included simple round, elliptical and flat spiral coils.

Hunt's Dress-Pin 'is equally ornamental, and at the same time more secure and durable than any other plan of a clasp pin heretofore in use, there being no joint to break or pivot to wear or get loose' he wrote in the patent application. Hunt received all the historical kudos for designing the safety pin, but none of the money. After acquiring the patent for his creation on 10 April 1849, he sold the idea to his friend for a paltry $400.

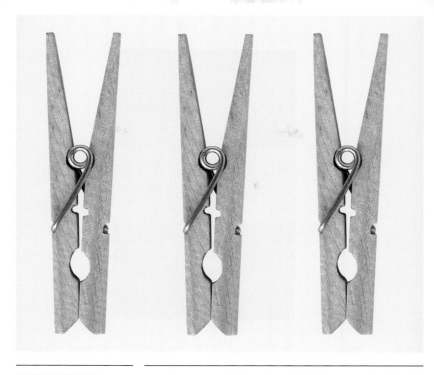

CLOTHES PEG
(1850s)
Designer Unknown
Various
1850s to present

We like to be able to attribute every product to an individual genius, but some of our most useful products have developed more organically. The credit for the original clothes peg is often ascribed to the Shakers, the religious sect founded in the US in 1772 by Ann Lee. The furniture and products they crafted were completely pared down, and their peg was simply a piece of wood with a split in it to fasten the clothes to the line. But no one can really claim credit for designing the clothes peg. Indeed between 1852 and 1887, the US Patent Office granted patents to 146 different pegs, although

it seems likely that most of them were based on the same premise as the Shaker two-prong clothes pin. The classic peg shown here – created by D. M. Smith of Springfield, Vermont, in 1853 – consists of two wooden pins fastened by a steel spring that clamps them firmly together. In 1944 Mario Maccaferri produced a hard-wearing plastic version. The clothes peg was firmly fixed as an icon in 1976 by the artist Claes Oldenburg, who installed a giant model bluntly titled *Clothespin* in Centre Square, Philadelphia.

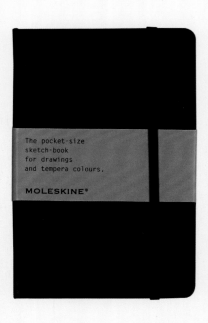

MOLESKINE NOTEBOOK (c.1850)
Designer Unknown
Anonymous firm
(Tours) c.1850 to 1985
Modo & Modo
1997 to 2006
Moleskine
2006 to present

Moleskine Notebooks are oilcloth-covered notebooks based on a legendary 200-year-old product. The first manufacturer was a small family-run firm in Tours, France, which closed in 1985. Reissued by the Italian company Modo & Modo in 1997, the design has been the beneficiary of a strong advertising campaign, which builds on the original's literary and artistic mystique. The small, pocket-sized notebook has developed a remarkable following due to Modo & Modo's claim that the product is 'the legendary notebook of Hemingway, Picasso and Chatwin'. The standard Moleskine Notebook measures 14 × 9 cm (5.5 × 3.5 in)

and contains lightweight, acid-free paper within its covers. The product's name derives from the French spelling of 'moleskin', which the notebook's oilcloth covering resembles. By the time the original French notebooks were phased out, the term 'moleskine' had become something of a generic brand name. That familiarity made it a 'brand of fact', according to the Italian government, allowing Modo & Modo to resurrect the product legally, raise its status to an uppercase M and inherit its legacy. The famous name is now found on over three million upmarket notebooks and related stationery sold every year.

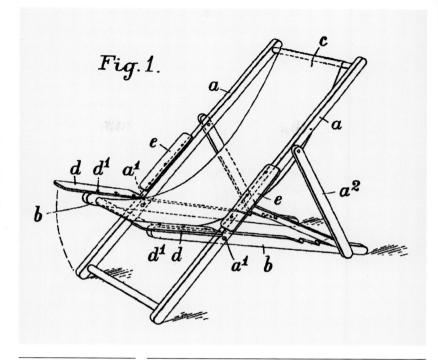

Fig. 1.

**TEXTILE GARDEN
FOLDING CHAIR
(1850s)**
Designer Unknown
Various
1850s to present

There is no mistaking the nautical origins of the textile garden folding chair, first used on the decks of cruise ships. Its debt to the hammock, the traditional space-saving berth for sailors, is clear, and its canvas seat is commonly printed in bold-coloured stripes, taking its visual cue from sails; ranks of unfolded but unoccupied deck chairs, their seats blown out by the breeze, can resemble a flotilla on the move. As well as strong pointers to the sea and seaside, the design is informed by maritime practicality. As an outdoors item, the chair is seasonal and not needed in bad weather or the colder months when it can be folded flat and stored without taking up a great deal of space – a premium commodity both below deck on a ship and in the garden shed. By happy accident, it seems ideally designed for enforced relaxation. Being impossible to sit up straight in a textile chair, the occupant has to recline. For all its no-nonsense roots and practicality, the textile chair is the ultimate labour-saving device – a machine for maximizing idleness.

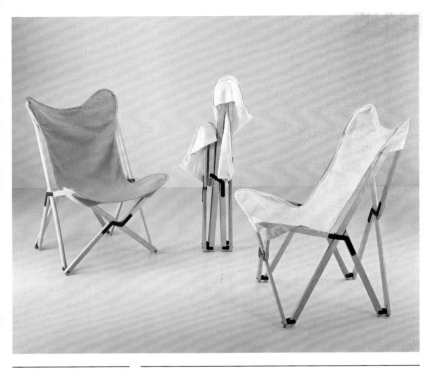

**TRIPOLINA
FOLDING CHAIR
(c.1855)**
Joseph Beverly
Fenby (nd)
Various
1930s to present

This icon in the world of folding chairs was devised by Joseph Beverly Fenby in England around 1855 for use by officers during British Army campaigns. Fenby went on to patent the chair in 1877. Its utilitarian appearance and lack of any extraneous decoration give it a sense of modernity not usually found in nineteenth-century furniture intended for the upper classes. This 'modern spirit' was most likely born out of a requirement for lightness and robustness, to allow it to function on the battlefield, and was what made it a fitting chair to put into production approximately sixty

years later. A slightly developed version, using leather instead of canvas, was manufactured for domestic use throughout the 1930s in Italy, under the name Tripolina. The Tripolina uses a much more complex, three-dimensional folding structure than the famously unsupportive X-framed deck chair, as its canvas or leather sling is supported from four points. However, it is still lacking in good lumber support, a problem associated with many slung seats. Its presence is a reminder of another time and usage, while its style survives its origins and it continues to stand out in any given environment.

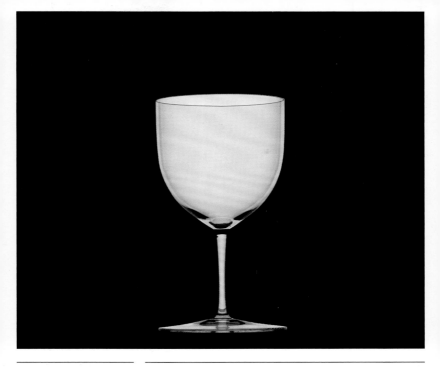

LOBMEYR CRYSTAL DRINKING SET
(1856)
Ludwig Lobmeyr
(1829–1917)
Lobmeyr
1856 to present

Ludwig Lobmeyr was part of a family firm of Austrian glassware sellers, and added his own design legacy by creating an innovative and highly sought after range of crystal glasses. Lobmeyr had a good understanding of glass design and it was one of his passions. Inspired by the Eastern, Greek, Roman and Venetian glass he saw at the Great Exhibition of 1851 in London, he began experimenting with enamelling and painting glass. By 1856 he had developed what came to be known as 'muslin' glass. This crystal, patterned glass, mere millimetres thick, was difficult to manufacture.

It had to be hand-blown, cut, engraved and polished by hand – a process involving more than a dozen skilled craftsmen to ensure every last detail was exact. A whole range of muslin glass was produced, from decanters and goblets to the Lobmeyr Crystal Drinking Set. Wine aficionados loved it because it created the thinnest possible surface between the liquid and one's mouth. Unadorned and fragile, the glass has a timeless appeal that would not look out of place had it been designed a century later. The hand-produced range continues to be bought by collectors and fine restaurants today.

CHAIR NO. 14 (1859)
Michael Thonet
(1796–1871)
Gebrüder Thonet
1859 to present

No name just a number. An unassuming entry in the extensive catalogue of Michael Thonet and Sons cabinetmakers. This modest anonymity belies the fact that little No. 14 is a giant presence in the history of furniture. Designed by Thonet in 1859, what set this chair apart was not its general form but its manufacture. In the 1850s, Thonet pioneered a process of steam-bending wooden rods and strips. This 'bentwood' method was hugely liberating in terms of time and skilled labour, permitting simplified versions of the styles of the period. It allowed furniture to be mass-produced, shipped as parts and assembled at destination at very low cost, setting a precedent in the production of furniture. No. 14 and its retinue anticipated by more than fifty years the essential themes and axioms that would come to define Modernism. Michael Thonet died in 1871, but by that time Gebrüder Thonet was the largest furniture factory in the world. The success of No. 14, probably the single most commercially successful chair ever produced, has done nothing to diminish its enduring formal and conceptual charm. Today, this manifestation of nineteenth-century high technology still retains a fresh and elegant utility.

YALE CYLINDER LOCK (1861)
Linus Yale Jr.
(1821–68)
Yale 1862 to present

Linus Yale Jr was the son of a locksmith and invented locks whose basic principles are still in use. Yale created his first lock in 1851, and named it, with all the flair of a circus ringmaster, the Yale Magic Infallible Bank Lock. The lock avoided the use of springs and other components that had a tendency to fail. Yale devised a mechanism that made the lock inaccessible to picking tools, and, he claimed, impervious to attack by gunpowder. His second lock, the Yale Infallible Safe Lock, was an improvement on this first model. In the 1860s, Yale developed the Monitor Bank Lock, the first combination bank

lock, and the Yale Double Dial Bank Lock. He then began to rework the pin-tumbler mechanisms of the ancient Egyptians as a basis for his Cylinder Lock, for which he received patents in 1861 and 1865. In 1868, Yale set up the Yale Lock Manufacturing Company in Philadelphia, with Henry Towne. He died just three months after construction began on the plant. But in 1879, padlocks, chain hoists and trucks were added to the locks, and the Yale name became the most established manufacturer of locks.

PEUGEOT PEPPER MILL (1874)
Jean-Frédéric
Peugeot (1770–1822)
Jean-Pierre Peugeot
(1768–1852)
Peugeot
1874 to present

The 17.5 cm (7 in) Provence model may be only one of the eighty currently available options of Peugeot Pepper Mill, established in 1810 in eastern France, but it is unquestionably the most recognized. This model, produced since 1874, is the most popular of Peugeot's two million annual sales. It appears traditional, but the simple logic of its design, the technical innovation and the construction of the grinding mechanism all transcend style. Its patented adjustable mechanism uses double rows of spiral teeth that channel and feed the peppercorns – first through a cracking stage and then to fine grinding. Mechanisms are fabricated out of steel that is case-hardened to assure reliability and durability. The lion, the emblem of Peugeot first used in 1850, was adopted because of the association of the strong jaws of the beast with the cast steel blades originally used. Today, the internal mechanism is made of heavy-gauge processed steel, which is practically indestructible. In 1810, the Peugeot brothers converted a family grain mill into a steel mill and, by 1818, had been awarded a patent for tool production. Since 1874, Peugeot has remained the leading manufacturer of pepper mills.

TOAST RACK (1878)
Christopher Dresser
(1834–1904)
Hukin & Heath
1881 to 1883
Alessi 1991 to 2013

Although it might look like an object to come out of Germany's Bauhaus, this toast rack was designed by the British designer, Christopher Dresser, over forty years prior to the school's opening. Dresser's work was championed by Modernists of the early twentieth century, but though he often designed with sparse aesthetics, using simple geometric forms, Dresser was not an advocate of one style or rigid doctrine. In his silverware, however, he concentrated upon economical use of materials and the majority of his surfaces remained unadorned. In the toast rack this economy is plain to see. Ten cylindrical pegs

pierce through an oblong plate: four extend to make the feet, and the other six are hammered over like rivets on the underside of the rack, a detail likely to have been inspired by the exposed rivets on Japanese metalwork. The T-shaped handle is another Japanese motif Dresser borrowed for a number of his designs; he was the first European designer to visit Japan, which he did in 1876. Originally manufactured in silver by the British company Hukin & Heath, for whom Dresser worked for many years, the piece was reissued in polished stainless steel by Alessi in 1991.

WAITER'S FRIEND CORKSCREW (1882)
Karl F. A. Wienke (nd)
Various
1882 to present

Patented in Rostock, Germany, in 1882, the original design of Karl F. A. Wienke's Waiter's Friend has remained more or less the same ever since. Unassailable in its combination of simplicity, practicality and affordability, this single-lever corkscrew is still mass-produced around the world. The Waiter's or Butler's Friend was so-called because it could be easily collapsed and, at 11.5 cm (4 in) in length, kept in a pocket, winning many fans among waiters. Wienke's patent drawings describe a steel handle-lever with three retractable appendages: a knife for cutting the foil seal, a wire helix corkscrew and a fulcrum that grips the rim of the bottle, allowing the lever action to remove the cork. Several German companies, notably Eduard Becker of Solingen, initially manufactured the Waiter's Friend. Despite the success of rival designs, Wienke's corkscrew continues to enjoy favour with wine connoisseurs as well as waiters. A plethora of facsimile Waiter's Friends – ranging from cheap steel versions to state-of-the-art models with solid ABS plastic handles, stainless steel micro-serrated knives and five-turn Teflon-coated worms – is available, yet all bear the same basic Wienke patent design and function in exactly the same way.

WÜSTHOF CLASSIC KNIVES (1886)
Ed Wüsthof Dreizackwerk Design Team
Ed Wüsthof Dreizackwerk
1886 to present

The Wüsthof Classic Knife design has changed very little since it first appeared in 1886. Designed and manufactured by Ed Wüsthof Dreizackwerk of Solingen, Germany, the Classic series was created for both professional and domestic cooks worldwide. The beauty and success of the design lies in its simplicity of form and ease of use, combined with high standards in craftsmanship and materials. Launched during the early days of the Industrial Revolution, the Wüsthof Classic Knife is forged from a single piece of stainless steel, eliminating the common failing of the blade coming away or breaking off from the handle.

The tang is fully visible, forming blade and handle core. There is no need for stamping, welding, or short cuts, thus eliminating any weak points in the form and construction of the knife. The characteristic three rivets along the handle provide a simple method for secure attachment, and the three-piece construction presents a knife that is cleverly designed for maximum strength, safety, balance and heft. The Wüsthof Classic is still in production today and owes its enduring popularity to the minimal and unpretentious nature of its form and materials.

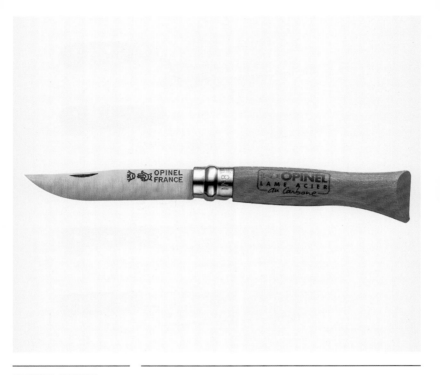

OPINEL KNIFE
(1890)
Joseph Opinel
(1872–1960)
Opinel
1890 to present

This pocketknife, made of pearwood and carbon stainless steel, could be described as a wolf in sheep's clothing. It is compact, has a graceful form with a pleasing tactile quality, and has a high-quality blade that really cuts – a surprise when it is extracted from its innocent hiding place. Joseph Opinel was nineteen when he designed the knife. He was the son of a toolmaker from the Savoie region in France, an area locally renowned for its axes, billhooks and pruning knives. Initially, Opinel produced the knives for a few friends; when they became successful, he put them into production. He solved the problem of how to create a split in the handle to house the blade without weakening it, by inventing a machine to cut out the precise amount of wood required. The resulting tool with its organic form fits perfectly into the hand and comes in eleven sizes, from the no.2 with a blade of 3.5 cm (1.4 in) to the no.12 with a blade of 12 cm (4 in). As with any good tool, this knife needs maintenance and care – an interesting requirement in this day of disposable obsolescence.

TIFFIN (c.1890)
Designer Unknown
Various
c.1890 to present

'Tiffin' is an Anglo-Indian word describing a light luncheon. In the days before microwaves and fast food restaurants, the Tiffin was the only means by which Indian workers could enjoy hot, fresh, home-cooked meals at their place of work. The traditional Tiffin consists of three or four round, stainless-steel containers that slot one on top of the other to form a compact stack. Each container is fitted with metal lugs that allow it to slip onto a frame with a handle on top. The metal containers are extremely good conductors of heat, and consequently help keep each other warm. But the system is particularly

successful in that it allows for a variety of different foods to be transported without their mixing. The delivery system of the Tiffin began under the British Raj over a century ago, and the *dhabawal-lah* (delivery man) evolved as a result of lunches being delivered to the British workers. That the Tiffin box has survived and prospered in India is due both to the efficiency of its design and the work of *dhabawallahs*. In Mumbai alone almost 200,000 meals are delivered by this system every day.

**SWISS ARMY
KNIFE (1891)**
Karl Elsener
(1860–1918)
Victorinox
1891 to present

The renowned outline of the Swiss Army Knife began life as a utilitarian tool for soldiers. The contemporary range using the recognizable motif of the Swiss cross is synonymous with a superior, functional, multipurpose tool. Karl Elsener trained as a cutler and provided the Swiss Army with its first delivery of soldier's knives in 1891. He founded the Swiss Cutlers' Association, with twenty-five fellow cutlers, to facilitate production by sharing resources. However, the soldier's knife was not successful, leaving Elsener heavily in debt. Undeterred, he redressed the problems of weight and limited function and registered the developed design in 1897. The functionality and aesthetic of the small, pocket-sized knife was well received by the Swiss Army and soon found favour in the public marketplace. The redesigned knife had a more elegant outline than the original and employed only two springs for six tools. Elsener named the growing company after his mother, Victoria, and in 1921 added the international designation for stainless steel, 'inox', to create the brand name Victorinox. Today, the Victorinox brand has a range of nearly 100 products that share the original ideals of quality of design and function.

HUTTER STOPPER
(1893)
Karl Hutter (nd)
Various
c.1893 to present

Initially invented by Charles de Quillfeldt in 1875, the Lightning Stopper revolutionized the beer and soft drinks bottling industry, which until then had tended to employ corks. The earliest attempt at creating closures for these bottles was by Henry William Putnam, who invented a heavy wire bail in 1859 that would swing over the cork to secure it. Charles de Quillfeldt's design simply leveraged a rubber disc around a cork into the lip of the bottle. The key improvement to de Quillfeldt's patent came in 1893, when Karl Hutter added a tapered porcelain plug, fitted with a rubber washer. As well as being extremely easy to refit, Hutter's improved Hutter Stopper, or 'swing-top', meant that bottles no longer needed to have long, swan-like, necks to protect the cork. By the 1920s, the Hutter Stopper had been usurped by the simple metal Crown Cap. However, by then, it had already made an indelible mark on the mass consciousness. A form of the Hutter Stopper is still used by the Dutch brewer, Grolsch. The company has been employing the swing top since 1897 and has effectively made it a part of the brand experience.

BLOEMENWERF CHAIR (1895)

Henry van de Velde
(1863–1957)
Société Henry
van de Velde
1895 to 1900
Van de Velde
1900 to 1903
Adelta
2002 to c.2005

Derision greeted Henry van de Velde at the unveiling of his Bloemenwerf House in the Brussels suburb of Uccle in 1895. But this was an important articulation of a new ideal of the house as a single work of art, prefiguring the Gesamtkunstwerk exploits of the Vienna Workshop as well as providing an early marker for Art Nouveau. Backed by his wealthy mother-in-law, the former painter van de Velde turned to decorative and applied arts in the early 1890s. His concept kicked against both the low quality of mass production and the embellishment of basic forms with gratuitous decoration. The furniture was guided by this

rational perspective: the sideboard and centre element of the dining table featured brass plates to prevent hot dishes marking the surfaces. The beechwood dining chairs, meanwhile, evoked harmony and comfort, echoing English 'rustic' designs of the eighteenth century but also suggesting a distinctive contemporary departure. From 1895 the furniture was produced by the Société Henry van de Velde and formed the basis of van de Velde's reputation. The Bloemenwerf Chair was resurrected in 2002 when the German company Adelta launched a series of eleven van de Velde reproductions.

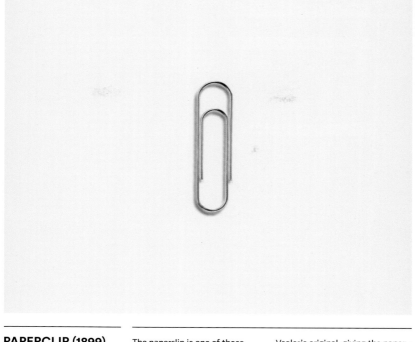

PAPERCLIP (1899)
Johan Vaaler
(1866–1910)
Various
1899 to present

The paperclip is one of those low-tech inventions that support the cliché that the simplest ideas are often the best. Today's paperclip has been honed to the optimum dimensions – a length of steel wire 9.85 cm (3.9 in) long and 0.08 cm (0.31 in) in diameter provides just the right tension of firmness and give. It is the work of Johan Vaaler, a Norwegian inventor, who developed the clip in 1899. In 1900, American inventor Cornelius J. Brosnan filed for his own paperclip, the 'Konaclip.' Gem Manufacturing of England designed the double oval-shaped clip that we recognize today. It has one extra corner from

Vaaler's original, giving the paper added protection from scratches by the metal. Other designs proliferated, among them the non-tangling 'owl', the 'ideal' (for thick wads of paper) and the self-explanatory 'non-skid'. Norway is still the spiritual home of the clip, and one story of defiance proves it. When, during World War II, the occupying Nazi forces banned Norwegians from wearing any buttons bearing the likeness of their king, the Norwegians started wearing paperclips, even though the flaunting of such peaceful mechanical superiority brought the risk of arrest.

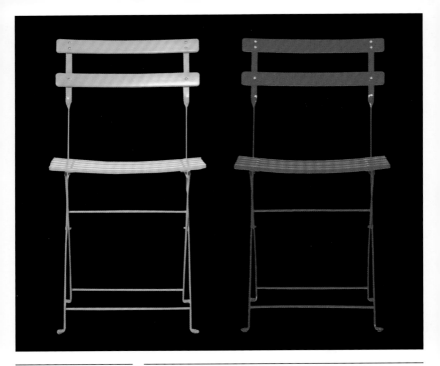

GARDEN CHAIR
(1900s)
Designer Unknown
Various 1900s
Habitat
1998 to present

This now ubiquitous garden chair first appeared in the public spaces of Paris around the turn of the twentieth century. The chair is still used in gardens, parks and bistros and its popularity is related to the success of the design, in terms of its functionality and style. The folding chair first appeared shortly before the Renaissance. As it became more common, the folding variety and its technical achievement followed naturally. By the nineteenth century folding chairs were a widespread utilitarian feature of public spaces where there was a need to rearrange or regularly remove seating.

Folding chairs also allowed for storage in a small space when not in use. The folding design of this garden chair has a simple side X-pivot mechanism, positioned below the seat level. The chair's slender metal frame made it noticeably lighter than its predecessor, which was made entirely of wood. Furthermore, its narrow metal structure allowed for reduced dimensions, imbuing the chair with a previously unseen elegance and space-saving benefits. The design is flawless, as is proved by its adoption as the archetypal form of outdoor chair with its understated style and highly practical design.

CALVET CHAIR (1902)
Antoni Gaudí
(1852–1926)
Casa y Bardés 1902
BD Ediciones
de Diseño
1974 to present

The remarkable Catalan architect Antoni Gaudí's first foray into furniture design was a desk for his own use, designed in 1878. Subsequent furniture designs were always specifically for the interiors of his own buildings. The Casa Calvet was built between 1898 and 1904 for Don Pedro Mártir Calvet, a Barcelona textile manufacturer. Oak furniture, including desks and this armchair, was designed in 1902 for offices in the building and made by the firm of Casa y Bardés. Gaudí's previous furniture had overtones of the Gothic Revival derived from designers such as Viollet-le-Duc, and even incorporated naturalistic decoration. This chair marks a departure from reproductions of historic precedents, which Gaudí achieved by synthesizing the decoration with the structure of the chair. Most notable is the organic, plastic character of the design, whereby the elements appear to grow out of one another. There are references to architectural motifs, 'C' scrolls and a suggestion of a cabriole leg, for example. But these baroque elements are subsumed into the overall coherent vegetative form of Gaudí's exuberant chair, in the same way that the building for which it was designed expressed organic principles of design.

HILL HOUSE LADDER BACK CHAIR (1902)
Charles Rennie Mackintosh (1868–1928)
Cassina
1973 to present

Charles Rennie Mackintosh enjoyed an influential career as one of Britain's most important contributors to twentieth-century design. As his Glasgow School of Art unfolded at the turn of the century, publisher Walter Blackie approached Mackintosh to design his home, The Hill House, in Helensburgh outside Glasgow. Blackie was drawn towards Mackintosh's approach to designing, whereby one person created everything from the building to the cutlery and door handles. It was for Blackie's bedroom that Mackintosh designed the Ladder Back Chair. Turning away from the organic naturalism of Art Nouveau, Mackintosh adopted abstract geometry inspired by the rectilinear patterns of Japanese design. He was interested in balancing opposites, choosing a dark ebonized ash wood frame in contrast to the white wall behind. The seemingly unnecessary height of the chair enhanced the spatial qualities of the room. For Mackintosh, the visual effects of a wholly integrated scheme was more important than the quality of craftsmanship and truth to materials advocated by his Arts and Crafts contemporaries.

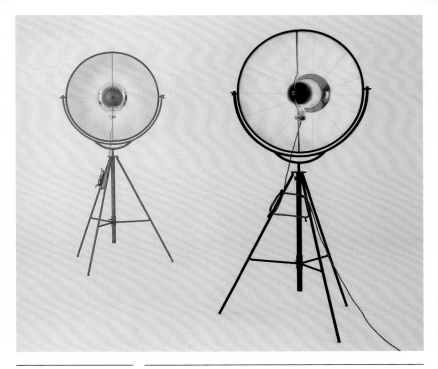

FORTUNY MODA LAMP (1903)
Mariano Fortuny y Madrazo (1871–1949)
Pallucco Italia
1985 to present

While experimenting with the newly invented electric light bulb, Mariano Fortuny y Madrazo created the Fortuny Moda Lamp. Sometimes technology, science, materials and the designer's interests come together to create an ingenious design. This is the case with the Fortuny Moda Lamp. Fortuny y Madrazo's insights into the way light could transform stage sets led to his experiments with indirect lighting in interiors. By reflecting light off fabric he was able to create whatever mood he wished. Fortuny y Madrazo patented his system of indirect lighting in 1901. The refinements of the system lead him to design

the Fortuny Moda Lamp, which was patented in 1903. The lamp's form speaks to the designer's varied interests: camera tripods probably influenced the lamp's base, with its adjustable central column and swivelling head. The lamp's shade is a simple inversion of traditional shades of the time, with the added function of tilting. Fortuny y Madrazo's genius is in his combination of these elements into the form, which continues to remain contemporary. Conceptually, Fortuny y Madrazo's Lamp was clearly ahead of its time, and when seen, either in a studio or the home, it is still distinctive.

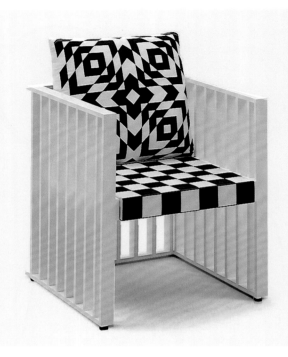

PURKERSDORF CHAIR (1903)
Josef Hoffmann
(1870–1956)
Koloman Moser
(1896–1918)
Franz Wittmann
Möbelwerkstätten
1973 to present

This chair by Josef Hoffmann and Koloman Moser, was designed for the lobby of the Purkersdorf Sanatorium, an elegant, spa-like resort on the outskirts of Vienna designed by Hoffman and the Wiener Werkstätte. The Purkersdorf, an almost perfect cube, is the ideal complement to the strong rectilinear quality of the building. The use of black and white and the geometric motif also enhances the sense of order and calm that one might expect from a visit to a sanatorium. The chair's strong, underlying geometry suggests rationalism and an encouragement of contemplation, while the use of white also reflects the contemporary fascination with new ideas about hygiene. The Josef Hoffmann Foundation has granted the sole rights to Franz Wittmann Möbelwerkstätten to reproduce his furniture, and the Purkersdorf has been reproduced since 1973. Both Moser and Hoffman were members of the Vienna Secession, a group opposed to the excessive ornamentation of the time. The austere architecture of the sanatorium contrasts with an interior of adornment and detail, such as the checkerboard pattern used for the seat, representing a departure from the overly decorative styles of Art Nouveau and the Victorian era.

SANTOS WRISTWATCH (1904)
Louis Cartier
(1875–1942)
Cartier
1904 to present

The history of the watch goes back to the sixteenth century, but wristwatches date from little over a century ago, and the Cartier Santos Wristwatch has a good claim to being the first commercial model. It was among the first 'true' wristwatches and its design, which has endured unchanged to this day, has been extremely influential and much imitated. It was devised by Louis Cartier, grandson of the Cartier establishment's founder and the driving force behind the company becoming an international name and its cultivation of blue-blooded clients. It was with good reason that Edward VII dubbed Cartier the 'jeweller of kings, king among jewellers'. The client behind the Santos (and the watch's name) was the Brazilian pilot Alberto Santos-Dumont, who wanted a timepiece he could see easily while engaged in airborne daredevilry. He first donned the watch for a 220 m (720 ft) flight in 1907. The Santos's origins explain its robust, masculine appearance and the pronounced screw-like rivets that punctuate the steel strap and quadratic face. This has surprisingly added to its unisex appeal, and the company continues to make numerous versions for women.

ARMCHAIR FOR THE POSTSPARKASSE (1904–6)
Otto Wagner
(1841–1918)
Gebrüder Thonet
1906 to 1915
Gebrüder Thonet
Germany
1987 to present
Gebrüder Thonet
Vienna
2003 to present

Austrian architect Otto Wagner won a competition for the Postsparkasse, the Austrian postal savings bank, in 1893. The Postsparkasse was designed as a unified work, with a glass ceiling in the entrance, detachable office walls, and an exterior wall, interior fittings and furniture made of aluminium. This project allowed Wagner to apply his philosophy of moving towards a modern, rational style. In 1904, Wagner slightly modified his Zeit Chair (c.1902) for the Postsparkasse, and Thonet produced the design. The chair was the first to use a single length of bentwood to form the back, arms and front

legs. U-shaped braces were added to support the D-shaped seat and back legs. It came with or without arms, and is still recognized for its efficient use of material and the great comfort it provides. Metal decorative details, like studs, sabots and plates to prevent the chair from wear, were used to customize the chair for specific uses. The most luxurious version, embellished with then-rare aluminium, was used for the directors' offices. The chair's popularity was such that by 1911 many versions, produced by various companies, were on the market, and are still being produced today.

SITZMASCHINE (1905)
Josef Hoffmann (1870–1956)
Jacob & Joseph Kohn 1905 to 1916
Franz Wittmann Möbelwerkstätten 1997 to present

The Sitzmaschine, or Sitting Machine, was designed by the leading Viennese designer of the early twentieth century, Josef Hoffmann. Every part of this chair was designed to tell us that it was machine made and that, in fact, we are to regard it as a machine itself. The mechanical impression is achieved through the absence of any historical or traditional decorations. Geometry and the play of lines, curves and planes, solids and voids, appear to govern the form of the chair. The back and seat are two oblongs (echoed in the side panels) suspended between simple D-shaped runners. The machine-like character is reinforced by the mechanism to raise and lower the back. A rod, fitted against domes mounted on the frame, dictates the slope of the back. This chair appears to be the epitome of logic and functionalism. Kohn, its manufacturer, was one of the leading pioneers of mass-produced bentwood furniture. The design clearly exploits the potential for repetitive production of simple units that bentwood technology embodied. Perhaps influenced by the geometric patterns of Charles Rennie Mackintosh, Hoffmann championed a similar style that could be easily translated to mass-production processes.

CONTINENTAL SILVER CUTLERY
(1906)
Georg Jensen
(1866–1935)
Georg Jensen
1906 to present

The Continental Silver Cutlery range was the first major cutlery pattern to emerge from the workshop of Danish silversmith Georg Jensen. Jensen's meticulously handcrafted silverware has become synonymous with the global luxury goods market, yet when he first set up his silversmith studio in Copenhagen in 1904, his business was both niche and radical. The Continental range has been one of the company's most popular and enduring silver cutlery patterns. Characteristically understated in its refinement, the range uses simple decoration and delicately beaten surfaces to create silverware that is sensual and sculptural and pays homage to traditional Danish wooden utensils. Jensen was instrumental in defining the character of twentieth-century Scandinavian design by drawing on indigenous traditions and infusing them with a progressive design rationale. He was also pivotal in the transition from Art Nouveau to Art Deco, adding crisp geometric forms to his existing repertoire of undulating organic forms as early as 1915. Jensen's work caught the eye of tycoon William Randolph Hearst at the Panama-Pacific International Exposition in San Francisco in 1915. Hearst was so impressed he bought the entire exhibit.

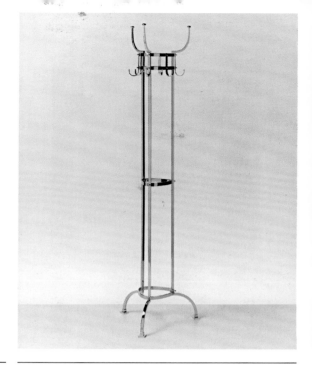

NYMPHENBURG COAT STAND (1908)
Otto Blümel
(1881–1973)
Vereinigte Werkstätte
1984 to 1990
ClassiCon
1990 to present

Designed by Munich-based Otto Blümel, the Nymphenburg Coat Stand is a classic example of Jugendstil, the German Art Nouveau style. Avoiding the fussy excess of some Art Nouveau decoration, the coat stand favours a more restrained approach, anticipating the crisper rectilinear ornament of Art Deco and the pared-down simplicity of the Modern movement. The refinement, simplicity and clean lines of Blümel's brass and nickel-plated coat stand, which stands at 180 cm (71 in) high, lend themselves to mass production – these 'contemporary' design credentials have ensured its continued popularity.

Blümel studied both architecture and painting, and in 1907 became head of the design department at the Vereinigte Werkstätte für Kunst im Handwerk (Unified Workshops for Art in Handicraft) in Munich. His relationship with craft, which is explored at its most stylized, rationalized form in the Nymphenburg Coat Stand, took on a more literal aspect for the designer, when after World War I he helped establish the Heimatmuseum branch of the Museumsverein Werdenfels, a museum dedicated to the celebration and promotion of indigenous German arts and handicrafts designs.

KUBUS ARMCHAIR
(1910)
Josef Hoffmann
(1870–1956)
Franz Wittmann
Möbelwerkstätten
1973 to present

Looking at the Kubus Armchair, one could be forgiven for assuming it was produced later than 1910, the year it was exhibited in Buenos Aires. Its designer Josef Hoffmann played an important part in shaping Viennese Modernism. He co-founded the Wiener Werkstätte in 1903 out of a desire to save the decorative arts from their aesthetic devaluation through mass production. Hoffmann had been influenced by Otto Wagner's idea of the 'complete work of art', whereby the architect was involved in all aspects of design. The chair is composed of polyurethane foam over a wooden frame and is upholstered in black leather. Its square pads and austere, straight form are a true representation of Hoffmann, who preferred the plain cube form. The Wiener Werkstätte's primary aim of bringing good design into every part of people's lives was at odds with its commitment to the high-quality production of unique, handcrafted designs and emphasis on artistic experimentation. The projects were necessarily costly and exclusive, but they were the precursors of Modernism. In 1969 the Josef Hoffmann Foundation granted the manufacturer Franz Wittmann Möbelwerkstätten sole rights to recreate the Kubus Armchair.

BINDER CLIP (1911)
Louis E. Baltzley
(1895–1946)
LEB Manufacturing
1911
Various to present

The binder clip, invented by Louis E. Baltzley in 1911, is a simple but inspired design for holding loose paper together. The inspiration for this elegent fastener came from Baltzley's father Edwin, who was a prolific writer. The traditional method of the time for keeping manuscript pages in order involved punching holes along the pages and sewing them together with needle and thread. This meant that inserting or removing pages involved a laborious rebind. Louis came up with the perfect solution in the binder clip. The clip's hollow, triangular-shaped black base is made of a sturdy but flexible metal. Attached to it are two moveable metal handles that slot like hinges into the top. These can flex back flat, becoming strong levers to prise open the base and firmly clamp the paper. Baltzley began manufacturing the clip at his own company, LEB Manufacturing, and later licensed the design out to other companies. He also revised and modified his 1911 design a further five times between 1915 and 1932. Baltzley could not have predicted the lasting ubiquity of his binder clip in today's workplace.

CHESTER ARMCHAIR AND SOFA (1912)
Designer Unknown
Poltrona Frau
1912 to 1960,
1962 to present
Various
1912 to present

The Chester Armchair and Sofa looks back to the classical armchairs of Edwardian England's clubs and country houses for its inspiration. However, its design strips away all unnecessary materials and decoration to focus exclusively on the fabric, structure and construction of the chair. The leather covering is folded into a series of pleats, or plissés, on the bulbous arms to create the range's trademark look. The backrest and arms are hand-quilted to create the distinctive Chesterfield diamond-pattern motif. The upholstery and construction are equally important. A suspension system of steel springs, which are tied by hand on jute belts, helps create the structure and shaping for the hand-moulded horsehair padding, ensuring the correct amount of weight absorption and very small movement of the seat. The result is a sofa whose contours are perfectly attuned to the human body. Such attention to detail makes the Chester an enduring design; every element of it – from its solid, seasoned beech-wood frame to its goose-feather-filled seat cushions and hand-selected hides cut with a shoemaker's knife – is lovingly crafted. The Chester has consistently remained Poltrona Frau's best-known model.

SERIES 'B' GLASSWARE (1912)
Josef Hoffmann
(1870–1956)
Lobmeyr
1914 to present

Josef Hoffmann enjoyed a lengthy relationship with the Viennese glassmaker J. & L. Lobmeyr and its head, Stefan Rath. The Series 'B' Glassware was an early product of this partnership, which began in 1910. Lobmeyr was one of the most enthusiastic supporters of Hoffmann's strict forms, and still makes Series 'B' today. In its modernity, simplicity of form and deployment of black and white, the design carries the hallmarks both of Hoffmann's work and the output of the Wiener Werkstätte, which Hoffmann and Koloman Moser founded in 1903 as a co-operative of applied arts. The Series 'B', in common with several other designs from the Hoffmann-Lobmeyr partnership, is made from blown crystal, decorated with black bronzite and frosted. The technique it used, developed just two years earlier in Bohemia, involved coating the glass with a layer of bronzite, on to which the decorative design was painted with varnish. Any unvarnished bronzite was then removed with acid, leaving a decorative pattern with a metallic sheen. Lobmeyr sustained a lofty reputation, with its products included as early as the 1920s in New York's Museum of Modern Art and London's Victoria and Albert Museum.

ZIP FASTENER (1913)
Gideon Sundback
(1880–1954)
Hookless Fastener
(Talon)
1913 to present
Various
1930s to present

The zip began life as Whitcomb Judson's 'clasp locker': a fastener intended for shoes using parallel rows of vicious-looking metal hooks, patented in 1893. The credit for perfecting the zip goes to Swedish immigrant Gideon Sundback of the Universal Fastener Company of Chicago. Over the course of five years Sundback miniaturized and refined Judson's design, increasing the number of 'teeth' per inch to ten, and developed a method for mass-manufacturing the result.
His 'hookless fastener' moved from novelty to widespread use in 1923, when the BF Goodrich Company used it for its galoshes.

One of Goodrich's marketing people suggested the name 'zipper' based on how quickly it closed and the sound it made. The zip spread into clothing in the 1930s via childrenswear and men's trousers, and then on to its current global omnipresence. It has gone beyond being a simple fastener; it has made a deep impression on fashion and social consciousness itself. Certain iconic fashions such as biker chic and the 1970s punk designs of Malcolm McLaren and Vivienne Westwood are almost impossible to imagine without numerous, often purposeless, zips.

DIXON TICONDEROGA PENCIL (1913)

Dixon Ticonderoga
Design Team
Dixon Ticonderoga
1913 to present

In 1860, most people still wrote using quills; by 1872 the Joseph Dixon Crucible Company was producing 86,000 pencils a day, and by 1892 Dixon Crucible had manufactured more than 30 million pencils. Dixon did not invent the first pencil or design its classic characteristics, (history points to Nicolas-Jacques Conté [1755–1805] as the inventor of the process to make pencil leads from powdered graphite) but Dixon is associated with the dry, clean, portable writing instrument for the superior mass-production and quality it developed. Joseph Dixon (1799–1869) produced his first pencils in 1829; by the 1890s

his company was a leading producer. The ingenious design of his tooling included a wood-planing machine for shaping pencils that produced 132 pencils a minute. The sustained high quality of Dixon's pencils have ensured their status as timeless objects. The name 'Ticonderoga' was added in 1913 on a brass (now green plastic) ferrule with two yellow bands, establishing the trademark and giving us the archetypal yellow pencil we recognize today.

ORIGINAL SIEGER CAN OPENER (1913)
Gustav Kracht (nd)
Sieger (formerly
August Reutershan)
1913 to present

The Sieger Can Opener is an object with a functionalist appeal that has endured throughout its history. The Sieger, which translates as 'victor', was invented in 1913 and has changed little since its incarnation. Before World War I, tins were opened with a hook-like stick. The Sieger transformed this task and became instantly popular. Its ratchet, a shiny nickel-plated surface, now has a riveted plastic layer in the middle. Tempered steel is used for the cutter blade, the transport wheels and the cap lifter, making an impenetrable surface. The device is a compact 15 cm (6 in) long, 5 cm (2 in) wide, with the

handle a slim 2.2 cm (0.8 in), and weighs just 86 g (3 oz). The Can Opener became the driving force behind the August Reutershan Company, founded in 1864 in Solingen. Various styles were added to the original design – the Eminent in 1949, the Gigant in 1952, the Zangen-Sieger in 1961, and the wall-mounted Der große Sieger in 1964. Despite these variations, the original remains an international bestseller. August Reutershan even changed its name to Sieger, in order to connect the famous brand to its manufacturer.

US TUNNEL MAILBOX (1915)
Roy J. Joroleman (nd)
Various
1915 to present

Roy J. Joroleman's Tunnel Mailbox originated as a model to standardize US mail delivery on rural routes, which began in 1896. At that time, mailboxes were homemade, usually from some sort of discarded container slapped onto a pole. In 1901 the US Postal Service created a commission for a standardized mailbox. The committee eventually turned to postal engineer Joroleman, whose proposal for a tunnel-shaped box became the standard. The design was approved by the postmaster general in 1915, and was not patented in order to encourage competition between manufacturers. In 1928 a larger version was approved, the No.2 Size Box, which could also accommodate parcels. Both models have remained in production ever since. Its effortlessly simple design is not very different from the cans that preceded it. It grew in depth to accommodate both letters and newspapers, yet still remained a 'can', although one with a flattened side, a hinged end, and flag signaling incoming or outgoing mail. Its structurally efficient shape could be easily manufactured at competitive prices. In today's digital world, the Tunnel Mailbox has been appropriated as the symbol for email and thus its iconic status is assured.

CLÁSICA WATER BOTTLE (1916)
Gregorio Montesinos
(1880–1943)
Laken 1916 to present

Top of any expedition equipment list is a Laken water bottle. The Laken company pioneered the design of aluminium drinking-water bottles with the Clásica model in 1916 and remains a market leader in Spain today. Gregorio Montesinos became aware of the emerging aluminium industry when he was working in France. Returning to Spain in 1912, he established the company Laken in Murcia and began to design water bottles as an alternative to ceramic and glass drinking bottles. Aluminium is strong, lightweight and resistant to oxidation, properties that Montesinos was keen to harness.

Designing for the armed forces, he came up with the Clásica made from 99.7 per cent pure isotope aluminium. An external felt or cotton cover keeps the water fresh, protects the bottle from breakage, and can be soaked in order to cool the water inside by evaporation. The Clásica stands at 18.5 cm (7 in) high and comes in two diameters of 13.8 cm (5.4 in) and 8.2 cm (3 in). Resilient to extremes of temperature, the Laken water bottle has been taken on expeditions to the North Pole, Antarctica, the Sahara and the Amazon, and is still favoured by armed forces around the world.

**TANK
WRISTWATCH
(1917)**
Louis Cartier
(1875–1942)
Cartier
1919 to present

Cartier's first wristwatch collection, launched in 1888, was aimed only at the women's market. The wristwatch was only an acceptable form of timepiece for men when it was realized how invaluable it was for reading the time during warfare, motoring or aviation, when one's hands were not able to access a pocket watch. Pocket watches were typically geometric in shape and included models that were square with rounded corners, or pure circles, rectangles, hexagons or octagons. In this context, the design of the Tank Wristwatch was revolutionary. Its rectangular case is based on the plan of armoured World War I tanks while its sides represent the tank's straight-line caterpillar tracks. These extend beyond the main body and so provide the lugs for the wristband. Developed in 1917, the Tank's launch was delayed until 1919, when it became an immediate success. It remains in production, although now with a quartz movement. The Tank is in some ways a victim of its own esteem: it has earned the unfortunate accolade of most imitated wristwatch of all time.

RED AND BLUE ARMCHAIR (c.1918)
Gerrit Rietveld
(1888–1964)
Gerard van de
Groenekan
1924 to 1973
Cassina
1973 to present

The Red and Blue Armchair is one of a handful of seating designs that is universally recognizable. With no direct precedents, the chair is symbolic of Gerrit Rietveld's career and epitomizes his theories. The construction of the chair is simply and clearly defined through the standardized wood components meeting and overlapping. In the first model the oak remained unpainted and was suggestive of a stripped-down sculptural version of a traditional armchair. Within a year Rietveld had slightly modified the design and painted the components. The geometry and structure were defined by colour: black was used for the frame, yellow for the cut ends and red and blue for the back and seat. Rietveld was only twenty-nine when he created this seminal piece and began his search for furniture designs that translated the two-dimensional painting system, Neoplasticism. The Rietveld chair has always been a key reference point in the design of furniture and applied art, as well as their teaching. Although produced only intermittently until 1973, when Cassina made a licensed reproduction, the Red and Blue Armchair remains in production today – a mark of its importance and influence in the history of Modernism.

BROWN BETTY
TEAPOT (1919)
Designer Unknown
Various
1919 to present

The Brown Betty has the archetypal teapot form. It originated in the seventeenth century, when British potters copied the spherical designs of teapots imported from China. The deep brown Rockingham-glazed Brown Betty evolved from unglazed teapots made from red clay discovered by the Dutch Elers brothers at Bradwell Wood in Staffordshire. Its chubby form and sturdy feel have made it a much-loved icon of the British tea table despite 'finer' china becoming available. Alcock, Lindley and Bloore, a small factory in Stoke-on-Trent, put the Brown Betty into production from 1919 to 1979. Royal Doulton took over this company in 1974 and manufactured a similar version. Since then a number of other companies have brought out their own interpretations. Not all have the original features. A high-quality Brown Betty has a grid of holes pierced in the body, behind the spout, to catch the tea leaves. The lid does not fall when the pot is poured and the tip of the spout is sharpened to reduce drips. Available in sizes from two to eight cups, the Brown Betty has conquered the mass market by striking a perfect balance between elegance and utility.

PITCHER NO. 432
(1920)
Johan Rohde
(1856–1935)
Georg Jensen
1925 to c.2015

Johan Rohde was an architect, painter and writer who created a range of high-quality silverware for Georg Jensen in Copenhagen. In 1906, Rohde asked Jensen to execute various designs for his own use; he was later given permanent employment at the workshop as a designer. Pitcher No. 432, designed in 1920, is one of Rohde's finest works. Rohde's designs were often characterized by curving lines, and flower, fruit and animal forms appear in tight clusters on his tea services, bowls and candlesticks. By contrast, the Pitcher shows a remarkable simplicity of form and functionalism of design that anticipates the

development of a more streamlined style in the 1930s. The pitcher did not enter production until 1925, as it was felt to be too avant-garde to appeal to consumers. It was originally produced with a silver handle but later versions incorporated an ivory handle to add a much sought-after touch of luxury. During the Art Deco period, only a few Danish silver workshops, such as that of Georg Jensen, maintained the traditions of their craft. Many of Rohde's designs are still in production by Jensen's studio, which has been part of Royal Copenhagen since 1985.

WHISKEY FLASK
(1920s)
Designer Unknown
Various
1920s to present

Flasks to carry whiskey or other spirits had been popular accessories since the eighteenth century. Changing social circumstances and the introduction of Prohibition in the United States, however, made their use and ownership common practice in the 1920s. Before that time, flasks were usually made of silver, designed to be carried in a pocket and held with one hand. Most had a hinged, bayonet-fit lid, but some had a pull-off cup or screw-off lid attached with a security chain. They came in sizes ranging from 0.03L to 1.14L (1 fl oz to 2 pt) and were shaped to the contours of the human body. Most were

relatively unadorned but, depending upon the styles of the era, some were engraved or shaped to resemble animals or objects. For today's collectors, such novelty flasks are the most valuable. In the 1920s, a slim version of the flask that could be hidden in a hip pocket or handbag or held by a garter became the preferred standard. Because of its ease of production, the two-part, twist-off lidded hip flask became a common and elegant example of the period's metalwork.

OPAQUE GLOBE
PENDANT LAMP
(1920)
Designer Unknown
Bauhaus
Metallwerkstatt 1920
Tecnolumen
1980 to present

The Opaque Globe Pendant Lamp is often referenced as an unattributed design by someone attending the Bauhaus between 1919 and 1933. Although the creator is still unknown, the simple suspended opaque glass globe can be traced to the first decade of the twentieth century. With the advent of electricity, the need to devise new fittings to hide or decorate the light source was quickly addressed. The Opaque Globe appears as an almost Minimalist design, without decoration and in the purest geometric form, the sphere. It diffuses the light evenly and its size can easily be adapted to suit the space in which it is hung. The

design works equally well singularly or en masse, in rows or a grid. This low-cost, mass-produced design has been specified in large numbers in pre-war schools and factories. As with many classic designs, particularly those without attributed designers and licences, it has been widely produced to various levels of quality. The simplicity of the Opaque Globe Pendant Lamp has been highly influential as a template for similar lighting designs, from early Marianne Brandt table and pendant lights to the more contemporary Glo-Ball series by Jasper Morrison.

INSULATED TEAPOT (1920s)
Designer Unknown
Various
1920s to present

Now a standard feature in any home decor that acknowledges retro influences and kitsch styling, the insulated teapot is designed as much for practicality as for style. When first launched in the late 1920s, the insulated stoneware tea service was adopted as the standard for a high tea service at hotels and restaurants across Europe. The styling was in keeping with the desire for a modern look, and the integrated tea cosy would keep tea warm for up to an hour. Like many of the most successful classic designs, the idea and construction is simple. The product consists of a stoneware teapot and a brushed stainless steel 'cosy', lined with an insulating fabric, that either sits over the pot or surrounds its body. This design embraced the burgeoning popularity for Art Deco style and the adoption of a machine aesthetic. Teapots are classically either stoneware or porcelain, and, until this design, heat-preserving covers were usually quilted fabric or knitted, making them more part of a craft sensibility than a design process. The insulated teapot with its chrome-looking cover challenged this tradition and allowed the beauty of the modern design to be uncompromised.

AGA STOVE (1922)
Gustaf Dalén
(1869–1937)
Aga 1922 to present

An object of affection, and sometimes obsession, since its introduction in 1922, the enamelled cast-iron Aga Stove has become a symbolic lifestyle appurtenance for generations of people in northern climes for its dual-purpose as an oven and heating source. The Aga's inventor, Gustaf Dalén, a Swedish physicist and managing director of Svenska Aktiebolaget Gasaccumulator (AGA), lost his eyesight from an explosion, which left him house-bound and restless. He honed his attention on constructing an oven that would burn more steadily with less intervention. Constructed of cast iron coated with three layers of enamel, the burner unit was placed next to two stacked cooking chambers, the lower for slow cooking and the upper for roasting and baking. He designed the cooker's surface with two hotplates insulated by lids that give off warmth when not in use. With an even transfer of heat from the inner core to the ovens and covered surface areas, the Aga does away with knobs or dials with an internal thermostat that regulates the temperature, making the cooker both sleekly uncluttered and unconditionally yielding in its readiness to serve; a warm, maternal figure for even the chilliest and busiest of households.

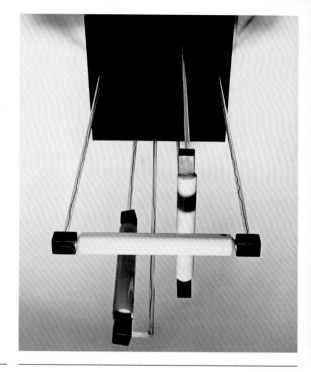

HANGING LAMP
(1922)
Gerrit Rietveld
(1888–1964)
Van Ommen
Electricien
1922 to 1923
Tecta (licensed
by Cassina)
1986 to present

The Hanging Lamp was designed by Gerrit Rietveld for one of his most important early commissions: an interior for Dr A. M. Hartog, a general practitioner in Maarssen, near Utrecht. The lamp comprised four standard incandescent lighting tubes, which were manufactured by Philips, arranged in a spatial composition rather like that of Rietveld's slat furniture. The tubes were fixed at either end into small blocks of wood, suspended from rods attached to a ceiling plate. The light hung over the desk in Hartog's office. The Hanging Lamp was redesigned with three tubular lamps for the interior of the Rietveld-Schröder House in 1924, and another version with only two tubes appeared in the Elling interior a year later. Rietveld's explanation for the different configurations was pragmatic: the number of tubes was due to the fact that different regions of Holland used different voltages. The interplay of lines and the clear articulation of individual elements is characteristic of the De Stijl movement to which Rietveld belonged. The lamp form was highly influential: it was a likely source for the tube lamp that hung in the office of Walter Gropius at the Bauhaus.

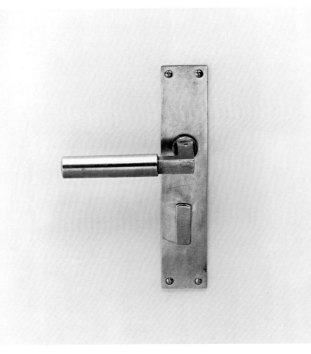

GRO D23 E NI DOOR HANDLE (1923)
Walter Gropius
(1883–1969)
Adolf Meyer
(1881–1929)
Bauhaus
Metallwerkstatt
1923 to 1933
S. A Loevy
1923 to 1933
Tecnoline
1984 to present

The Gro D23 E NI Door Handle, designed by Walter Gropius and Adolf Meyer, is one of the first mass-produced door handles with a clear, distinctive design and one of the defining fittings of Modernism. It is a direct expression of the Modernist ideals of Gropius, who was a founder of the Bauhaus in Dessau, Germany. The door handle was created in 1923 to be part of Gropius and Meyers' Fagus Factory in Alfeld on the Leine, Germany and went on to feature in the Bauhaus building itself. Its geometric, abstract design consisted of a cylindrical handle, which joined an orthogonal section and a small square door plate. German historian Siegfried Gronert called it 'the first mass-produced handle consciously designed with a primary stereo-metric form.' The material was polished nickel-plated steel, and the Berlin company S. A. Loevy began manufacturing it in 1923. Versions were also available with long door plates, and with a lock. The handle swiftly became well known and is still manufactured under license by Tecnoline. It is now present in important design collections all over the world, including the permanent collection of the Victoria and Albert Museum in London.

MT 8 TABLE LAMP
(1923–4)
Wilhelm Wagenfeld
(1900–90)
Bauhaus
Metallwerkstatt 1924,
1925 to 1927
Schwintzer and Gräff
1928 to 1930
Wilhelm Wagenfeld
& Architekturbedorf
1930 to 1933
Tecnolumen
1980 to present

The MT 8 Table Lamp, often referred to as the Bauhaus Table Lamp, was produced in the metal workshops of the Weimar Bauhaus under the guidance of László Moholy-Nagy. It was made of metal with an opaque glass shade, circular base and a glass shaft through which the electrical cable is visible. This distinctive design feature had been used by Carl Jacob Jucker (1907–97) in a number of lamp prototypes of 1923. Wagenfeld developed the idea for the opaque glass shade edged with nickel-plated brass. The two design ideas were fused into one, and in some subsequent versions Wagenfeld replaced

Jucker's glass shaft with a nickel-plated metal shaft, set into a metal base. The first versions of the lamps were handmade, using traditional craft techniques such as burnishing the metal plates by hand. With modifications, the lamp continued to be produced by the Bauhaus, Dessau, until the late 1920s. The subsequent history of the copyrighted design is highly complex. The original MT 8 was never produced in large quantities, and its enduring history is as a museum piece and collector's item. An exclusive licensed nickel-plated version is now produced by Tecnolumen.

MONTBLANC MEISTERSTÜCK 149 (1924)
Montblanc Design Team
Montblanc
1924 to present

In Germany, a Meisterstück is a final-year project for a young craftsman, marking the transition from apprentice to master. The Montblanc Meisterstück 149 has managed to fulfil the prophecy of its name to become a powerful global icon representing luxury, tradition, culture and power. Each pen is individually crafted and can be specially tailored with various point sizes and ranges of flexibility in the nib. The pen is 148 mm (5.8 in) long by 16 mm (0.63 in) in diameter. A white star on the tip of the cap represents the snowcap and six glacial valleys of Mont Blanc: the height of the mountain in metres, 4810, is inscribed on the pen's 18 carat hand-ground gold nib. The name of the pen is also etched into the widest gold-plated band of the three iconic gold rings found on the cap. The name Montblanc was registered in 1911, although it was not until 1924 that the company began producing lines of pens and the Meisterstück 149 was issued. The pen has changed little over the years – a specially developed resin has replaced the original celluloid – but functionally and aesthetically the design has endured.

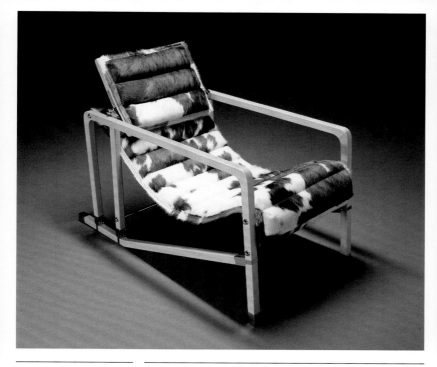

TRANSAT
ARMCHAIR
(c.1924)
Eileen Gray
(1879–1976)
Jean Désert
1924 to 1930
Écart International
1986 to present

Irish-born, Paris-based designer Eileen Gray took an interest in the Dutch De Stijl movement's pure geometric forms. For her Modernist house, E. 1027, on the shores of the Mediterranean at Roquebrune, she conceived a number of items of furniture, including the Transat Armchair. The Transat plays with the form of the deckchair – known as a *transatlantique* in French – and demonstrates an idiosyncratic fusion of the then-popular Art Deco style and the functionalism espoused by the Bauhaus and De Stijl. Functionalism is suggested by the angular frame, whose lacquered wood provides the

illusion of various layers. The frame could be disassembled, and its wooden rods were joined with chromed metal fittings. The headrest was adjustable and the seat was pliable, slung low and suspended from the lacquered wooden frame. Black leather and lacquer were used for the Transats appearing in E. 1027, though versions in other colours were sold through Gray's Paris shop, Galerie Jean Désert. The chair was patented in 1930, yet it was not until 1986 that it received wider attention through a reproduction from Écart International, triggering a renewed interest in Gray's work.

ASHTRAY (1924)
Marianne Brandt
(1893–1983)
Bauhaus
Metallwerkstatt 1924
Tecnolumen
1987 to present

Marianne Brandt is best remembered for the numerous designs that she produced at the metal workshop at the Bauhaus, where she worked under László Moholy-Nagy. Brandt thrived in the creative environment of the workshop, producing nearly seventy products at the Bauhaus's Weimar and Dessau sites. She began experimenting with geometric forms as the creative starting point for her tableware and lighting designs, inspired by Cubism, De Stijl and Constructivism. Elementary forms such as spheres, cylinders, circles, and hemispheres were considered easy to mass produce at a time when industrial processes were still insufficiently understood. Conceived as sections of circles and spheres, the base, body, lid, and cigarette balance of this ashtray are each clearly defined and constructed with mathematical exactitude. Brandt was passionate about metal, especially steel, aluminium and silver, and her energetic experimentation gave rise to the unusual combination of different metals in the same product, as this brass and part nickel-plated ashtray exemplifies. Her name and designs only became well known when manufacturers such as Alessi and Tecnolumen reissued certain products, including this ashtray.

TEA INFUSERS AND STAND (1924)
Otto Rittweger
(1904–65)
Josef Knau
(1897–1945)
Bauhaus
Metallwerkstatt 1924
Alessi 1995 to 2013

The early twentieth century witnessed a tension in German manufacturing between goods imbued with the artist's personality and craftsmanship and those dedicated to rational blueprints for mass manufacturing. This dichotomy would spill over into the workshops of the Bauhaus, and the arrival of the Hungarian László Moholy-Nagy to run the metal workshop in 1923 signalled an abrupt change of direction. Otto Rittweger and Josef Knau's design is a good example of the results. Out went predecessor Johannes Itten's preoccupation with spirituality and philosophy, along with handicraft materials

like silver, wood and clay, and in came an emphasis on functionality and pragmatism, expressed in materials such as tubular and sheeted steel, plywood and industrial glass. Moholy-Nagy saw the machine as a democratizing force, rather than the threat to humanity perceived by the Bauhaus's artists. The clean-lined, simple shape of Rittweger and Knau's Tea Infusers and Stand, which was nickel-plated, expresses the new sobriety. This would help the school generate much-needed income through commissions and by selling designs and patents rather than by producing expensive one-offs.

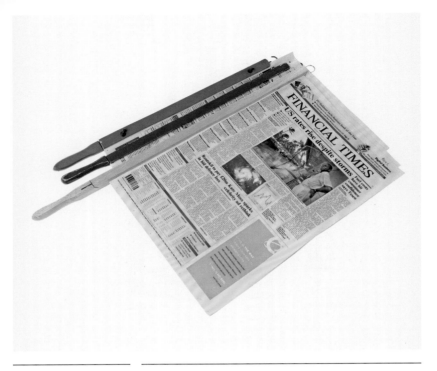

NEWSPAPER HOLDER (1924)
Fritz Hahne
(1897–1986)
Fritz Hahne
1924 to present
Alessi
1996 to 2016

The newspaper holder initially appeared more than two centuries ago in coffee houses in Germany and Switzerland, but became forever associated with the Viennese coffee house culture in Austria at the end of the nineteenth and the beginning of the twentieth century. It was a ubiquitous object and therefore numerous designs were patented in the early part of the twentieth century. This version, by Fritz Hahne, one of the earliest and only manufacturers still producing holders, is based on a variety of designs. Each design over the years has been slightly different: some have two wing-nut screws at either end, which open

to allow a small gap; others have a hinge at one end so that one side opens. The company, founded by Fritz Hahne, is a family-run business and still produces the holders in pine. They are sold almost exclusively to newspaper publishers in Germany, Switzerland, Austria, the Netherlands and Belgium. Recently, Kuno Prey revisited the design and came up with a model that holds either magazines or newspapers between three round bars.

WASSILY CHAIR
(1925)
Marcel Breuer
(1902–81)
Standard-Möbel
1926 to 1928
Gebrüder Thonet
1928 to 1932
Gavina/Knoll
1962 to present

The Wassily Chair is Marcel Breuer's most important and iconic design. The sitter is offered all-encompassing support whilst being virtually suspended within this tubular frame, which acts as a Modernist interpretation of the club chair. The relatively complex tubular steel frame was designed to provide comfort without the traditional timber, spring and horsehair seating construction of the period. The use of Eisengarn upholstery 'straps' and tubular steel was part of a revolutionary movement to create mass-produced 'equipment' for modern living: designs that were to be affordable, hygienic, light and strong. Marcel

Breuer designed the Wassily in 1925, apparently inspired by the fine frame of a newly purchased bicycle. The result followed studies in timber furniture at the Bauhaus and formed part of his project to furnish the apartment of painter Wassily Kandinsky. The Wassily was reintroduced in 1962 by Gavina, which was taken over by Knoll in 1968 and produced as part of Knoll International's collection of classics. It remains part of the Knoll collection today. With its origins, often confused with the high-tech movement of the late 1970s, the Wassily continues to maintain a highly relevant position in modern seating.

STARR 'X' BOTTLE OPENER (1925)
Thomas C. Hamilton (nd)
Brown Manufacturing Company
1926 to present

As a man who had made his fortune bottling and distributing Coca Cola, Raymond Brown would have been familiar with one of the main drawbacks of glass containers: they chip and break, especially while being opened. When a failed attempt to manufacture recording equipment left him with some spare factory capacity, he offered it to Thomas C. Hamilton, who had developed a wall-mounted bottle opener that was guaranteed not to chip the bottle neck. Hamilton's opener consisted of a small plaque with a hole for it to be screwed to the wall. Over this was an eyelid-like hood that gripped the outer edge of the bottle cap. The bottle was inserted under the hood and then pushed towards the vertical; as the hood gripped the edge of the cap and levered it against the central protuberance, the cap was prised off. The design is simple enough, requiring only one cast and containing no moving parts. The hood provided a perfect eye-level space for branding, and over the years the logos and devices embossed onto the opener have included beer and soda companies, patriotic imagery, college sports teams, proverbs, witticisms and the simple instruction, 'open here.'

MARTINI GLASS
(c.1925)
Designer Unknown
Various
1920s to present

Made from clear, colourless glass, the geometrically inspired shape of the Martini glass is a drinking vessel as iconic as the cocktail it was designed to celebrate. The decisive outline of the glass, comprising a straight-flared V-shaped cup supported by a tall stem and an elegantly proportioned base, is now the kingpin of cocktail motifs. The precise origins of the Martini glass remain difficult to establish, yet it is known to have originated during the mid-1920s, born from the changing currents influencing both high-class entertaining and the glassware designed to maintain it. Around this time, tastes in cocktails were moving away from the extravagances of the early 1920s towards a refined simplicity exemplified by Martinis and Manhattans. As these cocktails reflected the shift in taste, decorative glassware gave way to a streamlined Modernism. These new glasses were decidedly avant-garde, and, specifically, the Martini glass was a geometrically refined variation on the saucer-shaped champagne glass, which had replaced the flute at the turn of the century. The Martini glass remains cemented as an icon of 1920s glassware: accessible, instantly recognizable and endlessly revisited by illustrators, artists, filmmakers and the like.

BAUHAUS COCKTAIL SHAKER (1925)
Sylvia Stave
(1908–94)
C. G. Hallbergs
Company
1925 to 1930
Alessi
1989 to 2013

The Bauhaus Cocktail Shaker, a perfect sphere with a looped arc handle, was commonly believed to be designed by Marianne Brandt, but, after much research by Peter Hahn, director of the Bauhaus Archiv, it is now attributed to Sylvia Stave. It is as far from the traditional form of the cocktail shaker as it is possible to achieve. Horizontal rather than vertical, and uncompromising and geometric in its form, this was a wildly innovative piece that pushed the limits of metal manufacturing. In 1989 it was reintroduced by Alessi under licence from the Bauhaus Archive. Its seamless metal sphere, now produced in mirror-polished

18/10 stainless steel instead of the original nickel-plated version, is still a difficult object to produce, requiring two halves of the orb to be stamped separately then welded together and polished by hand. While there is a removable strainer hidden under the stopper for ease of pouring, it suffers from a common Bauhaus flaw in that it confuses geometry with functionality. Objects such as this opened the Bauhaus up to accusations of being 'just another style', although this shaker's style has gained momentum through the years.

LE CREUSET CAST IRON COOKWARE (1925)
Le Creuset Design Team
Le Creuset
1925 to present

Following a tradition that dates back to the Middle Ages, all Le Creuset Cast Iron Cookware is made from enamelled cast iron. Based at Fresnoy-Le-Grand, in northern France, the Le Creuset factory began producing cast iron in 1925. This was originally done by hand-casting molten iron in sand moulds. Even when using a similar technique today, each mould is destroyed prior to the cookware being polished and sanded by hand. The cast iron has a double enamel coating that, due to its extreme firing process of 800°C (1470° F), makes the pans hard and durable and virtually resistant to damage.

The porcelain-enamelled cast iron spreads heat evenly, retains heat and does not react to acidic foods. This, combined with the precise, tight-fitting lid, forms a blanket of heat that cooks food gently. The material allows the pans to be used on all heat sources. The cast iron is energy-efficient, and, as much of the finishing is done by hand, each piece is unique. Available in a range of colours, Le Creuset Cookware has become a symbol for home cooking, quality and the culture of the kitchen as central to domestic life.

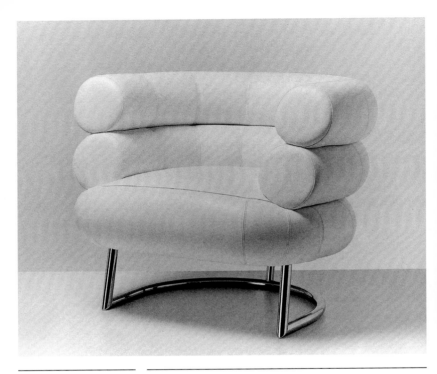

BIBENDUM CHAIR
(1925–6)
Eileen Gray
(1879–1976)
Aram Designs
1975 to present
Vereinigte
Werkstätten
1984 to 1990
ClassiCon
1990 to present

Eileen Gray designed custom-made furniture, hand-woven carpets and lighting to create exclusive interiors for wealthy, forward-thinking clients. Her iconic designs possessed an almost alchemical flair with materials and structure. Her Bibendum Chair was created in 1925–6 to furnish Madame Mathieu-Lévy's apartment in Paris, and finally achieved the recognition it deserved when Aram Designs, a London-based furniture company, put some of Gray's archive back into production in the 1970s. The chair was named after the mascot created in 1898 for the tyre company Michelin. The rounded form of the cheerful giant was echoed in the armchair. The leather-clad chair, with its distinctive tubular upholstered form housed within a chrome-plated tubular steel frame, was an opulent approach to Modernist aesthetic concerns. Unlike her contemporaries, Gray did not share a rigid aesthetic preoccupation with machine-age Functionalism. Instead, she fused Functionalism with the more sumptuous materiality of Art Deco. Unfairly neglected for most of her considerable career, Gray is now recognized as one of the most influential – and one of the few successful female – designers and architects of the twentieth century.

TEA AND COFFEE SERVICE (1925–6)
Marianne Brandt
(1893–1983)
Bauhaus
Metallwerkstatt 1926
Tecnolumen
1984 to present

Marianne Brandt's Tea and Coffee Service is an iconic example of the progressive teachings of the Bauhaus. University lecturers and curators pay regular homage to it, and collectors are frustrated by the fact that there remains only one complete original set. Comprising kettle, teapot, coffee pot, sugar bowl, cream jug and tray, the set is made from 925/1000 silver with ebony details. The ensemble's basic geometric forms of the circle and the square lend the design a feeling of strength, born of a well-defined profile. The teapot – with its stand of two straight cross members, elegantly polished bowl, circular lid and tall silver handle with an inlaid ebony grip – gives an initial impression of stoicism mixed with serious intent, which in turn yields an almost accidental beauty. The only woman to work in the Bauhaus metal workshop, Marianne Brandt was a versatile designer who became known for her adjustable metal lamps, paintings and witty photo-montages. Her Tea and Coffee Service is a classic example of the Bauhaus philosophy that emphasizes manual working practices and where form is determined by the intended use of the piece.

LACCIO TABLE
(1925)
Marcel Breuer
(1902–81)
Gebrüder Thonet
1929 to 1945,
1978 to present
Gavina 1962 to 1968
Knoll 1968 to present

Marcel Breuer's Laccio side and coffee table combines a satin-finished, plastic laminate top with polished chrome-plated tubular-steel frame and legs. While heading the Bauhaus furniture workshop in the 1920s, Hungarian born Breuer started to experiment with tubular steel to produce chairs, stools and tables, creating some of the most influential furniture to come out of the school. He conceived the low Laccio as a companion to the Wassily Chair. Breuer's linear, multipurpose nesting tables reflect his rationalist aesthetic and accomplished technique. The construction is extremely stable,

the materials are of exceptional quality and the forms are sculptural. The tubular-metal technology used in Laccio embodies the impact of the Bauhaus on the development of modern design and architecture in the twentieth century. For Breuer, metal was the material with which he could change the image of furniture. As he said, 'In my studies on mass production and standardization I very quickly discovered polished metal, luminous lines and spatial purity as new constructional elements for our furnishings. In these luminous, curved lines I saw not only symbols of modern technique, but technique in general.'

**E. 1027 DAYBED
(1925)**
Eileen Gray
(1879–1976)
Aram Designs
1984 to present
Vereinigte
Werkstätten
1984 to 1990
ClassiCon
1990 to present

For many years designer Eileen Gray collaborated with the Romanian architect Jean Badovici. One of their first and most important projects was E. 1027, a 1929 house on the coast of Roquebrune near Cap Martin in the south of France. Gray designed many pieces of furniture, including the E. 1027 Daybed, for its multipurpose living room. The daybed is made of a double, padded, rectangular leather mattress supported by a chrome-plated frame. Here Gray does not use the tube for mere construction, but also as a decorative line that pops up at the back to serve as a support for a cushion, a rug or a fur. Its asymmetric shape carries echoes of the past and is reminiscent of a classic Biedermeier chaise longue. In contrast to other Modernist designers, Gray liked the combination of opposites; of hard and soft materials and of machine-made and hand-crafted parts. In the early 1980s Aram Designs took the prototype of the daybed and introduced it into their collection of classics. They granted the Munich-based company Vereinigte Werkstätten the rights to reproduce it in 1984, and ClassiCon took over the production when the company closed down.

HAEFELI 1-790 CHAIR (1926)
Max Ernst Haefeli
(1901–76)
horgenglarus
1926 to present

Max Ernst Haefeli was a founding member of the Federation of Swiss Architects together with luminaries Karl Moser, Werner M Moser, Rudolf Steiger and Emil Roth. He developed a design language that brought together technological innovation and artistic tradition. It is no surprise, therefore, that he developed a partnership with Swiss furniture manufacturer horgenglarus. Established in 1882, horgenglarus adhered to the highest standards in craft tradition, using only hand methods in its furniture production. The Haefeli 1-790 Chair was a product of this union and illustrates the designer's and the manufacturer's shared creative ideologies. The chair is made in accordance with the high standards of the craft tradition. With its frame and gently curved legs constructed in solid wood and its flat, wide back and seat machined in ply, the chair stands out from the bentwood ply and tubular steel designs of the time. It references Haefeli's architectural training in its simple form, perfect proportions and clean lines. The ergonomic seat and back form a chair that combines traditional shapes with a craft sensibility and results in a timeless, practical and comfortable seating solution.

PYRAMID CUTLERY
(1926)
Harald Nielsen
(1892–1977)
Georg Jensen
1926 to present

Pyramid Cutlery, designed by Harald Nielsen for the silversmith Georg Jensen, epitomizes the look and essence of Art Deco, yet also represents an early example of Modernist cutlery. It was designed and first produced in 1926 and has since proven to be one of Jensen's most popular silver designs. Jensen had a skill for creating designs based on contemporary and historical sources and for setting standards in form and design. He recruited associates and family members, among them his brother-in-law, Harald Nielsen, to work for his firm as designers. Nielsen's work played a major part in defining the Jensen style between the wars. His Pyramid Cutlery illustrates the restrained Art Deco aesthetic that was to become prevalent in the 1930s. Of his designs, Nielsen remarked, 'The cutlery's ornamentation is designed to accentuate the overall harmony of the piece but at the same time exists completely for its own sake and must never dominate.' The design's simplicity allied it with Modernism and was a forerunner of the era of Functionalism. The combination of organic and geometric forms streamlined Jensen's more naturalistic forms, and became characteristic of Nielsen's work for the firm.

TEA DOSER (1926)
Hans Przyrembel
(1900–45)
Bauhaus
Metallwerkstatt 1926
Alessi 1995 to 2013

This cylindrical Tea Doser is simple in form yet invites the user to partake in the ritual of tea drinking. It appears to be nothing more than a narrow cylinder 20.5 cm (8 in) tall and 6 cm (2 in) in diameter, with a reflective surface without decoration. Yet the cap slides off to reveal a spout fashioned in an arc around the inner sleeve. This spout acts as a spoon to measure the tea leaves. When closed it is quite enigmatic; when open it is practical and useful. The Bauhaus metal workshop, under László Moholy-Nagy, developed a range of prototypes intended for industrial production. Wilhelm Wagenfeld was an assistant instructor in the workshop, and his inspiration was a critical catalyst for this work, as he said, 'every object has to find its formal solution in its functional use'. It was in this spirit that Hans Przyrembel developed his tea doser. Like so many other designs from the Bauhaus, it never reached production until 1995, when it was issued by Alessi along with eight other Bauhaus designs. Przyrembel's prototype was made of silver; the Alessi version is fabricated from stainless steel.

OYSTER
WRISTWATCH
(1926)
Rolex Design Team
Rolex 1926 to present

The Rolex brand name was registered in 1908 to feature on the dials of the watches distributed by a young Bavarian entrepreneur since 1905. The Oyster Wristwatch created by Rolex in 1926 was the first truly water-resistant and dustproof wristwatch. Its rapid success was assured by the perfect time-keeping of the model worn by Mercedes Gleitze when she swam the English Channel the following year. The Oyster was heralded as the 'Wonder Watch that Defies the Elements.' It is truly waterproof thanks to a screw-down waterproof case back and winding crown.

The case is crafted from a solid piece of stainless steel, 18ct gold or platinum. The crystal is cut from synthetic sapphire, making it highly shatter- and scratch-resistant. By introducing a self-winding mechanism in 1931, Rolex made the Oyster case even more resistant. The watch has long maintained its status as one of the most revered wristwatches in the world. Epitomizing the values that have made the brand world famous, the Oyster is first and foremost an archetype, a symbol of a way of life and a benchmark for style.

CLUB CHAIR
(c.1926)
Jean-Michel Frank
(1895–1941)
Chanaux & Co
1926 to 1936
Écart International
1986 to present

The rectangular Club Chair is one of the most familiar products from the Art Deco period and has avoided becoming outdated thanks to its angular form. Parisian designer Jean-Michel Frank created this timeless design, the simplicity of which is characteristic of his influential aesthetic, as part of a series of upholstered cubic seating. For each of his high-profile interior designs, the chair would be adapted and reworked. Frank had a penchant for applying unexpected materials to his designs, with bleached leather and sharkskin being particular favourites. His well-documented style, which he claimed was influenced by Neo-Classicism, Primitive Arts and Modernism, was marked by spare, rectilinear details and elegant, pared-down forms. Much of what we now recognize as Art Deco style is widely credited to Frank and his original designs of the 1930s. So popular were these designs that Frank was propelled into the upper echelons of European creative society, for whom he designed extravagant interiors and sophisticated products. His designs retain some of that sophistication, which might explain the continued popularity of one of his most basic but necessary pieces, the Club Chair.

E. 1027 ADJUSTABLE TABLE (1927)
Eileen Gray
(1879–1976)
Aram Designs
1975 to present
Vereinigte
Werkstätten
1984 to 1990
ClassiCon
1990 to present

The E. 1027 Adjustable Table is constructed from stainless steel and glass, with circular steel tubes forming the base and boundary for a disc-shaped glass top. The table leg is telescopic, controlled by a key in the back so that the table's height can be altered. This table must be one of the most plagiarized pieces of furniture of our time. While it is rigorously Modernist in form and materials, it avoids the cold rationalism of the movement with its grace and flexibility. Legendary architect Le Corbusier described it as 'enchanting and refined.' The table was part of a revolutionary furniture series Eileen Gray designed for her house, E. 1027, in Roquebrune on the French Riviera. The 'E' stands for Eileen, while the numbers correspond to their sequence in the alphabet: '10' and '2' for 'JB,' Jean Badovici (1892–1956), the Romanian architect who was her friend and mentor, and '7' for 'G' in Gray. Gray is among only a handful of women to get a mention in the male-dominated Modern Movement. Her output ranged from luxury decorative items in her early years to simpler, Modernist pieces of furniture as she grew older.

MR10 CHAIR AND MR20 CHAIR (1927)
Ludwig Mies van der Rohe (1886–1969)
Berliner Metallgewerbe Josef Müller 1927 to 1931
Bamberg Metallwerkstätten 1931
Gebrüder Thonet 1932 to present
Knoll 1967 to present

The apparent simplicity of Ludwig Mies van der Rohe's MR10 Chair makes it appear as a single, continuous piece of tubular steel. The 'free-floating' seat, supported by the front legs alone, was a revelation when the chair was shown in Stuttgart at the 1927 exhibition, 'Die Wohnung' (The Dwelling). Also on show was the Dutch architect Mart Stam's S33. Stam had drawn Mies a sketch of his idea for a cantilevered chair the previous year. Mies immediately saw its potential and, by the time of the exhibition, had come up with his own version. Where Stam's was rigid and heavy in construction, Mies's chair was

lighter and had a springy resilience aided by the graceful curve of its legs. Mies added arms to the chair with a simple cuff joint to create the MR20. Both chairs met with critical success and were soon selling in large numbers. Variations included separate leather or iron-yarn slings for the back and seat or a one-piece upholstery in woven cane designed by Mies's partner Lilly Reich. Originally the chairs were available with a red or black lacquered finish as well as the nickel-plated version that remains so popular today.

TUBE LIGHT
(1927)
Eileen Gray
(1879–1976)
Aram Designs
1984 to present
Vereinigte
Werkstätten
1984 to 1990
ClassiCon
1990 to present

The 1927 Tube Light was the creation of the early Modernist designer Eileen Gray. Gray studied fine art at the Slade School of Fine Art in London, but moved into interior design shortly after her studies. The light was arguably the most radical of a number of iconic objects that were designed for E. 1027, the hugely influential Modernist house she had built for her close friend, the architect Jean Badovici, in 1925 on the French Riviera. Rejecting the notion of a shade for the recently invented fluorescent filament, it took the then unheard-of step of proudly displaying a naked light, revelling in its manufactured inherent beauty. The Tube Light's perpendicular form, enhanced by the elegant chrome-plated steel upright, created a wholly new minimalist form of floor lamp. Today's designers owe much to the work of their pioneering predecessor, Eileen Gray, whose breaking of convention by using naked lights inspired the likes of Ingo Maurer and the Castiglionis. The leading furniture manufacturer Aram Designs reissued the design in 1984 and sub-licensed Gray's work to other manufacturers.

DOOR HANDLE
(1927–8)
Ludwig Wittgenstein
(1889–1951)
Tecnoline
2001 to present

What is now known as the Wittgenstein House in Vienna (1926–8), is a unique chapter in the remarkable life of Ludwig Wittgenstein, the enigmatic philosopher. Wittgenstein's sister, Margarethe Stonborough, had originally assigned the house to another architect, however, her brother's ideas on a consistent sense of space became more interesting to her. The exact spaces of the rooms, with tall, thin doors, influenced the design of the door handles so that their shape would not disturb the overall harmony of the architecture. Wittgenstein's handle for the metal and glass doors shows an excellent understanding of mechanics (from his initial training as an engineer) and a sensitive use of proportion and scale. The two main elements, inserted through the doorframe without a mount, are held together by a screw and washer, and are cast in brass, which was a Viennese standard. This reduces the handle to four components and leads to a seamless transition between handle and door. Each handle was a unique production and was lost when the house was abandoned between 1972–5. Today, Tecnoline is producing a handle based on the original, though greatly reworked using polished nickel plate.

LC4 CHAISE LONGUE (1928)

Le Corbusier
(1887–1965)
Pierre Jeanneret
(1896–1967)
Charlotte Perriand
(1903–99)
Gebrüder Thonet
1930 to 1932
Heidi Weber
1959 to 1964
Cassina
1965 to present

The now-familiar outline of the Le Corbusier LC4 Chaise Longue, model B306, dates from 1928. The H-shaped base and separate seating element, with hide upholstery and head cushion, are inherently linked with high-design interiors. The chaise originated from Le Corbusier's concept of functional furniture as equipment for the home, a 'machine for living'. It incorporates flexibility of movement with the rocking, adjustable seat, while the base borrows its outline from the wings of aeroplanes. The design pays strong attention to ergonomics, with its adjustable neck roll and the free positioning of the seat on its frame. It offered comfort, flexibility and a progressive aesthetic that immediately found favour in the international high-design market. Le Corbusier worked with his cousin Pierre Jeanneret and young designer Charlotte Perriand on the tubular steel designs that included the LC4, the LC1 Basculant Chair and the LC2 Grand Confort Chair. Cassina, the current producer of the licensed product, used Perriand as a consultant for its version. It is perhaps one of the most familiar icons of twentieth-century furniture design, to the extent that it is known affectionately in the design community as the 'Corb chaise'.

**TUGENDHAT
COFFEE TABLE
(1928)**
Ludwig Mies van
der Rohe
(1886–1969)
Berliner
Metallgewerbe
Joseph Müller
1927 to 1931
Bamberg
Metallwerkstätten
1931
Knoll 1952 to present

In 1928–30, Mies van der Rohe designed a Modernist villa for Grete Weiss Löw-Beer and Fritz Tugendhat in Brno, Czechoslovakia. The Tugendhat Coffee Table, often mistakenly called the Barcelona Table, was designed for the entrance hall of the villa. This low table, like the famous Barcelona Chair, uses an X-shaped frame. The table uses the X-shape as both a decorative element and a structural solution. Its hand-polished steel is set vertically to give stability. The X-shaped frame combines with a glass tabletop, 18 mm (0.75 in) thick and 100 cm (40 in) square, with

bevelled edges, to create a solid, symmetrical structure. The table was first produced by Berliner Metallgewerbe Joseph Müller and named 'Dessau Table.' In 1931, a tall version was produced by Bamberg Metallwerkstätten, Berlin, in nickel-plated steel. Knoll took over the production in 1952 and from 1964 produced the table in stainless steel with a glass top, and referred to it as the 'Barcelona Table'. The table received awards from the Museum of Modern Art in New York in 1977, and the Design Centre in Stuttgart in 1978, many years after its initial production.

THONET NO. 8751 (1928)/TRIC CHAIR (1965)
Gebrüder Thonet
Design Team
Achille Castiglioni
(1918–2002)
Pier Giacomo
Castiglioni (1913–68)
Gebrüder Thonet
1928
Bernini 1965 to 1975
BBB Bonacina
1975 to 2017

As well as producing close to 150 original designs and championing 'ready-made' furniture, Achille Castiglioni was concerned with 'redesigning' – updating existing designs to suit the needs of modern life. The Tric Chair from 1965 was one such redesign, which took its influence from a simple beechwood folding chair designed by Thonet in 1928, known as No. 8751. Castiglioni made two changes: he raised the back for better support and he added red felt to the backrest and seat for increased comfort. Folded, the chair is only 4 cm (1.6 in) deep. Despite its status as a reworked piece, the Tric Chair is

commonly credited to Castiglioni. In an interview released in 1988 he said, 'Sometimes the manufacturer asks the designer to restyle an old object. The designer can just reinvent the object or choose to limit the intervention to a new interpretation of the old object. This is what happened when I redesigned the Thonet chair.' Originally produced by Bernini in 1965, the Tric Chair was manufactured between 1975 and 2017 by BBB Bonacina. Yet it must be acknowledged that the Thonet No. 8751 set a standard as one of the first, most uncomplicated designs for folding chairs.

DOUBLE-LEVER CORKSCREW (1928)
Dominick Rosati (nd)
Various
1930 to present

The ubiquitous corkscrew with twin arms and central screw may appear as an uncelebrated object, however Dominick Rosati's design has been little altered since it was patented in 1928. Anyone who has opened a bottle of wine will without doubt have used a double-lever corkscrew, and variations on the design can be purchased virtually anywhere. The patent drawings lodged by Rosati on 29 October 1928 show two arms cut with cogs to lift the central 'Archimedean worm' topped with a turning key. The key facilitates easy entry of the worm into the cork, with minor damage to the cork's internal structure. When

the raised arms are lowered, the cork is smoothly drawn into the central cavity of the corkscrew. The original version has seen many adaptations, from whimsical to decorative to functional. A common reworking of the original adds a bottle opener to Rosati's top screw. Wine storage in corked bottles is a relatively recent phenomenon, but by the 1880s the straight-sided cork was being commonly used internationally. Between this time and that of Rosati's design over 300 corkscrew patents were registered, but it is his that remains the most readily copied.

DOOR HANDLE WD (1928)
Wilhelm Wagenfeld
(1900–90)
S. A. Loevy
1928 to 1933
Tecnolumen
1982 to present

Wilhelm Wagenfeld designed the Door Handle WD in 1928 and it was put into production by S. A. Loevy in Berlin that same year. It became well known after the architect Erich Mendelsohn chose it for the Columbushaus Building, Berlin, built between 1930 and 1932. It is believed that over 1,000 of the door handles were used in this building and also in many of Mendelsohn's commissions for private houses. In 1984 the German company Tecnolumen (known as Tecnoline from 2002) reissued the door handle. The handle is manufactured today using a traditional die-casting technique, which requires labour-intensive sanding and polishing by hand. The fact that this door handle is still available is because of the high production standards and the use of expensive materials such as brass. Wagenfeld's semi-industrial icon has been able to survive, despite mediocre copies. Wagenfeld was one of the first heroes of industrial design in Germany, an early Minimalist who saw the connection between good design and industry. He not only created successful products, but also provoked discussions with manufacturers. His Door Handle WD is a timeless example of elegance.

LC2 GRAND CONFORT ARMCHAIR (1928)

Le Corbusier
(1887–1965)
Pierre Jeanneret
(1896–1967)
Charlotte Perriand
(1903–99)
Thonet Frères
1928 to 1929
Heidi Weber
1959 to 1964
Cassina
1965 to present

The LC2 Grand Confort Armchair was part of a short-lived but fruitful collaboration between Le Corbusier, Pierre Jeanneret and Charlotte Perriand that also produced the LC1 Basculant Chair and the LC4 Chaise Longue. It is constructed from a welded chromium-plated steel frame comprised of a mitred tubular top frame and legs, a thinner solid retaining bar and thinner-still L-section bottom frame, which supports five upholstered leather cushions with tensile straps. Once in place, the cushions complete a compact cube shape. This novel design was first shown at the 1929 Salon d'Automne

in Paris. Following a favourable public reception, production was taken up by the Thonet furniture company. There have been various incarnations of the Grand Confort Armchair, with and without the ball foot, as a sofa and as a wider 'female' version (the LC3), which compromised the original cube form but allowed sitters to cross their legs. Since 1965 it has been produced by Cassina in Italy, who also make a two- and three-seater sofa in the same style. This model has become a byword for respectability and gravity and as such remains in huge demand.

LC7 REVOLVING ARMCHAIR (1928)
Le Corbusier
(1887–1965)
Pierre Jeanneret
(1896–1967)
Charlotte Perriand
(1903–99)
Gebrüder Thonet
1930 to c.1932
Cassina
1978 to present

Although he is best known as an architect and planner, Le Corbusier was also active in the fields of theory, painting and furniture design. The Swiss designer's LC7 Revolving Armchair and LC8 Stool were first unveiled at the 1929 Salon d'Automne in Paris, as part of a display called 'Equipment for the Home', which he designed with Pierre Jeanneret and Charlotte Perriand. It is based on a traditional typist's chair and is intended to be used with a desk. The four chrome tubular legs, which are produced as shiny or matt polished chrome, bend at right angles and meet in the centre under the seat. As with the majority of

Le Corbusier's work, the LC7's elegance and beauty are a result of the lines generated by its structure. Because the metal tubing was similar to that used in the manufacture of bicycles, Le Corbusier attempted to persuade Peugeot to manufacture his furniture. They declined, and Thonet Frères stepped in. In 1964, the Italian manufacturer Cassina acquired exclusive rights to Le Corbusier's furniture designs and continues to produce them. They are stamped with the official Corbusier logo and numbered to ensure their authenticity.

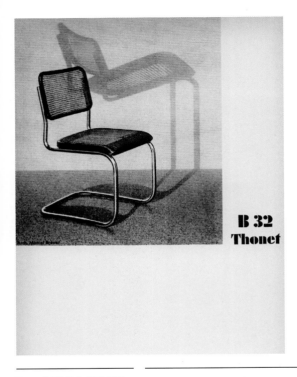

B 32
Thonet

B32 CESCA CHAIR (1928)
Marcel Breuer
(1902–81)
Gebrüder Thonet
1929 to present
Gavina/Knoll
1962 to present

The B32 Cesca Chair may be considered a familiar and even unworthy seating form. It does, however, mark an important cornerstone as a cantilever chair. Unlike precedents made of timber or tubular steel that required support at both front and back, the Cesca allowed the sitter to 'rest on air.' The originator of this concept remains a contentious issue, but Dutch architect Mart Stam's 1926 design is believed to have been the first. Hundreds of designers soon took to designing chairs with two legs. However, elements beyond the cantilever mark the B32 as an elegant design, as it is a sensitive understanding of comfort, resilience and appreciation of materials. The design illustrates sophistication and is unique in its mixture of Modernist shining steel, wood and cane, which soften and offer a humane warmth to the B32 that many hard-edged and clinical Modernist designs could not attain. The armchair version, the B64, enjoyed similar success. When both designs were relaunched by Gavina/Knoll in the early 1960s they were renamed 'Cesca' after Breuer's daughter. The host of clear imitations of this graceful cantilever design are a credit to Marcel Breuer's perceptive balance of form and materials.

CITÉ ARMCHAIR (1929–30)
Jean Prouvé
(1901–84)
Ateliers Jean Prouvé
1930
Tecta 1990 to 2000
Vitra 2002 to present

The Cité Armchair is a remarkable seating design that quietly encapsulates many of Jean Prouvé's theories and processes. Its mixture of materials – canvas 'stocking' upholstery stretched over a tubular frame, steel sled base suggesting engineered machine parts, and leather straps fastened with buckles to create taut armrests – provides for a wholly functional design. The chair's design, engineering and manufacturing make it a reference point for important seating designs. Originally a competition entry for the Cité Universitaire in Nancy, France, for use in student dormitories, the Cité is an early

work by Prouvé and establishes a design vocabulary for his later works. Prouvé began his illustrious career as a *ferronier d'art* (art metalworker) in Nancy in 1923. He pursued creative solutions for an enormous range of designs, from door furniture, lighting, seating, tables and storage, through to architectural facades and prefabricated building designs. Prouvé's furniture designs have always maintained a cult following among enthusiasts and collectors. Vitra recognized a growing enthusiasm and market for Prouvé's designs and in 2002 relaunched the Cité as part of a wider collection of his work.

ST14 CHAIR (1929)
Hans Luckhardt
(1890–1954)
Wassili Luckhardt
(1889–1972)
Desta 1930 to 1932
Gebrüder Thonet
1932 to 1940
Gebrüder Thonet
Germany
2003 (now ceased)

The sinuous profile of the ST14 Chair suggests a design more recent than 1929. The sweeping arc of the cantilevered frame is echoed and balanced by the moulded plywood sheets, which offer support through the seat and back. The seat itself seems to float in mid-air with minimal structural support. The frame is uncomplicated and the support does not rely on upholstery for comfort: the plywood elements meet the contours of the user, without the need to offer soft, relatively short-lived fabrics or upholstery. The Luckhardt brothers successfully practised architecture and were

active theorists as part of the Novembergruppe. They worked together in Berlin from 1921, gaining a strong reputation as leading architectural exponents of Expressionism. Their designs, such as the Hygiene Museum in Dresden, illustrated individualistic flair. However, when this style proved unforgiving in a post-war period of shortages, poverty and escalating inflation, they adopted a more sensitive and democratic approach in their designs. This change of ideology was evident in the remarkable ST14 Chair, which embraces the demands of mass production.

LOOS DRINKING SET (1929)
Adolf Loos
(1870–1933)
Lobmeyr
1929 to present

The Viennese company Lobmeyr has been successfully building on its international reputation for glass-making since Josef Lobmeyr founded the business in 1823. Today, the company boasts nearly 300 drinking sets, including this bar set designed by the Austrian architect Adolf Loos in 1929. From 1897 Loos worked as an independent architect in Vienna, where he introduced a more rational and often geometric style than that of the Vienna Secession group of artists and architects. Loos's 1908 essay titled 'Ornament und Verbrechen' ('Ornament and Crime') challenged the value of decoration, claiming it was a waste of energy and represented cultural degeneracy. Indeed, this drinking set for Lobmeyr captures a refined, sturdy sophistication that is free from period-specific patterning or ornamentation. Today the glasses are hand-blown from lead-free crystal, made in Germany to Austrian specifications. Each glass is then cut and engraved by a copper wheel, creating the simple, geometric grid. The set, including a finger bowl, beer glass, water pitcher, white wine glass and liqueur glass, has sustained successful market positioning for the specialist glass maker and retains a timeless appeal for customers today.

BARCELONA™ CHAIR (1929)
Ludwig Mies van der Rohe (1886–1969)
Berliner Metallgewerbe Joseph Müller 1929 to 1931
Bamberg Metallwerkstätten 1931
Knoll 1948 to present

The design for this graceful chair arose from the commission for the German Pavilion (1928–9) for the Barcelona International Exhibition in 1929. Ludwig Mies van der Rohe designed a building of horizontal and vertical planes built of marble and onyx walls, tinted glass and chrome-plated columns. He then designed the Barcelona™ Chair so it would not appear too solid nor affect the flow of space. Mies was determined to produce a chair that was 'important, elegant, monumental.' Using a scissor frame – with two flawless, curving, chrome-plated steel legs like slashes of Chinese calligraphy – each side

was joined by a cross-bar with bolts, and the entire frame was welded and hand filed. Leather straps, which were stretched over the frame, cleverly concealed the bolts. Knoll began to produce the chair with an entirely singular-welded frame to reduce the necessity for polishing and sanding. In 1964, the thin chrome-plated steel was replaced with polished stainless steel. The Barcelona™ Chair was never intended for mass production, but its designer began using it in the reception areas of his influential buildings – which explains why it is particularly seen in the lobbies of today's office buildings.

BRNO CHAIR
(1929–30)
Ludwig Mies van der
Rohe (1886–1969)
Berliner
Metallgewerbe
Joseph Müller
1929 to 1931
Bamberg
Metallwerkstätten
1931
Knoll 1960 to present

In 1928, Ludwig Mies van der Rohe designed the Tugendhat Villa, situated in Brno in the Czech Republic, for Grete Weiss Löw-Beer and Fritz Tugendhat. The fame of some of the furniture he created for the villa has far exceeded that of the building itself. The Brno Chair is one such example. For the dining room, Mies initially intended to use his MR20 Chair with elbow rests, designed in 1927, however it did not fit into the space, and a less spacious alternative was therefore needed. His adapted version, the Brno Chair, is one of his most elegant chair designs. It contrasts the elegantly tensed line of the frame and the angularity

of the back and seat. The first Brno Chairs were made in nickel-plated tubular steel and were produced in 1929 by Josef Müller in Berlin. In 1931, a variation called the MR50 was introduced and produced by Bamberg Metallwerkstätten, also in Berlin. The American company Knoll reintroduced the Brno Chair in 1960 in chrome-plated tubular steel, and then from 1977 in flat steel bands. Both steel versions were used throughout the Tugendhat Villa, in either red or white leather.

STACKING CHAIR
(1930)
Robert Mallet-
Stevens (1886–1945)
Tubor 1930s
De Causse
c.1935 to 1939
Écart International
1980 (now ceased)

The Stacking Chair by Robert
Mallet-Stevens symbolizes
a philosophical shift from the
leading Art Déco style of its time.
In strong opposition to what
he referred to as the prevalent
'arbitrary' nature of decoration,
Robert Mallet-Stevens emulated
more closely the principles
of functionality and simplicity.
He helped to form the Union
des Artistes Modernes (UAM),
a group of Modernist designers
who emphasized geometric
form, pleasing proportions,
economy of manufacture and
the absence of ornament. The
Stacking Chair, constructed of
tubular and sheet steel, originally
lacquered or nickel-plated,
exemplified Mallet-Stevens's
ideology and appeared in several
of his interiors. It was particularly
suited to mass production and
available with either metal or
upholstery seats. The dominant
plane created by the back and rear
legs suggests a minimal wall from
which the seat and front legs are
suspended, adding implied visual
strength to this diminutive chair.
Some controversy exists about its
design origins, but most historians
attribute it to Mallet-Stevens.
The chair has been reissued by
Écart International and is available
in white, black, blue, hammered
grey and aluminium.

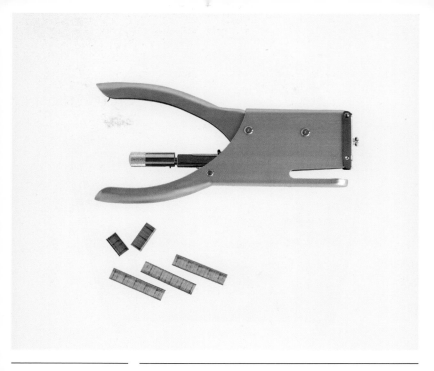

JUWEL GRIP
STAPLER (1930s)
Elastic Design Team
Elastic 1930s to 1986
Gutenberg
1986 to 2002
Isaberg Rapid
2002 to present

Within the context of the twenty-first-century office, the Juwel Grip Stapler appears defiantly sober. This manually operated device is devoid of any of the technical advances lauded by today's automated office workers; it remains all the more attractive for it. Branding is understated to the point of passiveness and superfluous detail is non-existent. And yet this unassuming design and Elastic, the Mainz-based manufacturer that originated it, have become icons within their field. The slab-sided, nickel-plated Juwel Grip Stapler was designed in the 1930s and takes its name from the spring-loaded, ergonomically shaped handle that fits the hand as would a pair of pliers. The mouthpiece is left agape, and the staples are dispensed from a rear-loaded magazine. The design is acknowledged as being one of the most reliable staplers on the market, rarely jamming and delivering staples with a precise, firmly closed grip. The quality of its design and its consequent longevity mean the Juwel Grip Stapler is yet to be superseded by novel devices incorporating modern, lightweight materials.

MODEL 904 (VANITY FAIR) CHAIR (1930)
Poltrona Frau
Design Team
Poltrona Frau
1930 to 1940,
1982 to present

Many of the world's classic chairs have been designed by architects, but Renzo Frau learned about chair construction through the artisanal route of upholstery. He set up the manufacturing company Poltrona Frau in Turin and staffed it with car-leather workers. Using traditional tools and skills to achieve a high level of craftsmanship, Frau created strikingly modern designs of divans and armchairs. He originally conceived the Vanity Fair Chair around 1910 as the Model 904 Chair; it was not until the 1930s that it saw the light of day. It was a timely entrance. The chair graced the Italian navy's glamorous transatlantic liner the Rex. With its bulbous, plump leather form stuffed with goose down and padded with horsehair, balanced on seasoned beechwood glides and finished with leather piping and a long row of leather-covered nails, the chair offered a louche, languid and graceful seating experience that was a perfect metaphor for the era. It was discontinued in 1940, but was reintroduced in 1982 and made available in its now trademark bright red leather. Since then it has been carving out a niche in the movies, starring in *The Last Emperor*, *La Famiglia* and *The Bodyguard*.

BESTLITE (1930)
Robert Dudley Best
(1892–1984)
Best & Lloyd
1930 to 2004
GUBI
2004 to present

In 1930, the lighting manufacturer Best & Lloyd took a gamble on its latest design: Robert Dudley Best's plain, black BestLite. The design was not well received, as it stood in stark contrast with the trend for the highly decorative. Indeed, its initial appeal was industrial, and it became indispensable in car mechanic shops and aircraft hangars during World War II. It came to the attention of the design world only when its use in architects' studios made it the lamp of choice for cutting-edge buildings. The BestLite became a favourite of Winston Churchill, who gave the lamp pride of place on his desk at Whitehall. Temporarily forgotten after the war, the lamp was rediscovered by Danish designer Gubi Olsen, who spotted it in a shoe shop in Copenhagen and set about obtaining distribution rights. The sales of the lamp have increased steadily since 1989, and in 2004 GUBI took over the BestLite collection, which today includes floor lamps, pendants and wall fixtures. Few lamps have been in continuous production for seventy-five years, but the BestLite, characterized by its simple, elegant design, has proved to be a timeless focal point in any setting.

WEYLUX QUEEN KITCHEN SCALE (1930s)
Cyril Fereday
(1904–72)
David Fereday
(1938–2017)
H. Fereday & Sons
1930s to present

By the 1930s, when H. Fereday & Sons introduced its domestic versions, cast-iron kitchen scales had become a prestige product as a result of their simplicity of design, weighing accuracy and longevity. The scales were not, however, without problems: the rough iron castings negatively affected the smooth flow of the mechanism and weighing accuracy, and created a look that was clunky and unwieldy. The Weylux Queen, developed by David Fereday seventy years after his grandfather, Henry, founded the company in 1862, addressed these problems. The iron bearings and beam edges were replaced with modern alloys to allow smoother movement and greater accuracy on lower weights, a wider brass or stainless steel pan was introduced and a range of colours were added to the cast-iron body. The resulting scales are a rare success: an old-fashioned mechanical piece of engineering that sits well in a contemporary space. The low-slung, fluid lines of the platform and dish are modern but stand out for their obvious pre-machine age aesthetics. So confident is Fereday of the Queen's durability that it offers a lifetime guarantee on it.

FORM 1382 DINNER SERVICE (1931)
Dr Hermann Gretsch
(1895–1950)
Arzberg
1931 to present

Form 1382 was not the first modern porcelain collection, but it was the most influential. Arzberg needed to produce a dinner service that was modern yet affordable and so turned to Dr Hermann Gretsch, an architect and designer who went on to become head of the Deutscher Werkbund. In 1931 Gretsch created a simple, elegant and eminently functional dinner service. He was determined 'to create shapes that meet real daily needs.' The dimensions of his teapot, for example, are generous enough for a family. Its globe shape is geometrical but not severe and its handle is broad enough to be easily grasped. The entire sixteen-piece dinner service is similarly plain and yet possesses a lyrical quality. Form 1382 was the first dinner service available to purchase by the piece, which meant that less well-to-do families could assemble a collection over time. Originally produced in white, in a platinum colour or with a blue rim and handles, today there is a much broader range. Arzberg updated the collection in 1954 with Form 2000, which was rimless and more biomorphic in design and that is still used today by Germany's Federal Chancellery for entertaining dignitaries.

REVERSO WRISTWATCH (1931)
César de Trey
(1876–1934)
Jacques-David LeCoultre
(1875–1948)
René Alfred Chauvot
(nd)
Jaeger-LeCoultre
1931 to present

Once the wristwatch came of age in the interwar period, it started to be worn while out driving or playing sport. However, few dress wristwatches could genuinely withstand the rigours of such sports as polo, skiing or car racing. The watch house of Jaeger-LeCoultre thus introduced the Reverso Wristwatch in 1931, with polo-playing British officers of the Indian army particularly in mind. The Reverso was designed by César de Trey, Jacques-David LeCoultre and René Alfred Chauvot with the rectangular movement and dial within a self-contained case, which was itself mounted in a robust oblong carriage so that it could be turned over to protect the glass and dial. Its sleek lines, the easy sliding and rotating action of the reversible case and its durability meant that the Reverso caught on immediately and was never successfully imitated. The original concept was so well engineered that it remained completely unchanged until 1985, when technical advances resulted in the introduction of an improved version. Despite numerous variations and elaborations, the unadorned, Art Deco model remains the mainstay of production today and one of the world's most enduring wristwatches.

ARMCHAIR 41 PAIMIO (1931–2)
Alvar Aalto
(1898–1976)
Artek 1932 to present

Of all Alvar Aalto's furniture designs, the Armchair 41 Paimio is probably his most famous, recognized for its structural ingenuity and novel use of materials in a combination of almost spare perfection. It was designed for the Paimio Tuberculosis Sanatorium in western Finland, the building that brought Aalto's architectural work to an international audience, and then marketed as part of a range of plywood furniture. The Paimio made a virtue of its rather hard seat, and the consequent alertness of the sitter meant it was an ideal chair for reading. Aalto began experimenting with wooden laminates in collaboration with the furniture manufacturer Otto Korhonen in the late 1920s. Aalto used wooden laminates because of their low cost, but he also felt that wood had a number of advantages over tubular steel: it conducted heat less well, it did not reflect glare and it tended to absorb rather than propagate sound. The success of Aalto's furniture abroad followed on almost immediately from the launch of the range in London in 1933. The Paimio indicated the apparently simple but widely unrecognized potential of plywood to be bent into shapes of considerable resilience, strength and beauty.

ESAGONALI GLASSWARE (1932)

Carlo Scarpa
(1906–78)
Paolo Venini
(1895–1959)
Venini
1932 to present

Paolo Venini was a lawyer from Milan until 1921, when his career changed quite suddenly. Entering into partnership with Giacomo Cappellin, he acquired a glassworks on the Venetian island of Murano. Although nothing in Venini's background suggested a career in glassmaking, he would make a significant contribution to the revitalization of the Venetian glass industry. Venini became involved with the artistic direction of his company and worked with some key figures of the architecture and design world. It was from one such collaboration with the Venetian architect Carlo Scarpa that Esagonali Glassware was created.

This work was in stark contrast to the old Venetian style. It made use of thinly blown glass and translucent colours, which allowed for a greater visual priority to the subtley modern form including a hexagonal flattening of sides and a vertical elongation. The shape clearly demonstrated the technical virtuosity of their manufacture. The partnership of Cappellin Venini & C. lasted only five years, but during this time it created a revival in glass production. The work continued after Paolo Venini's death in 1959, and the company, now called Venini, is part of the Royal Scandinavia group.

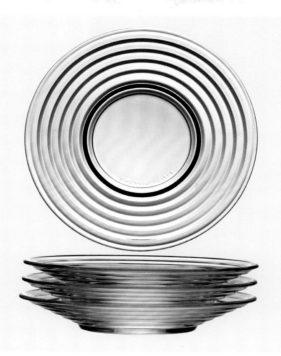

**PRESSED GLASS
4644 (1932)**
Aino Aalto
(1894–1949)
Karhula 1932 to 1982
Riihimäki
1988 to 1993
iittala 1994 to present

In 1932, the manufacturing firm of Karhula – which later merged with iittala - held a competition for affordable utility glass. The design that came in second, the Pressed Glass 4644 by Aino Aalto, is now represented in museum collections throughout the world and has proved enduringly popular in its home market. The success of this design lies in the way Aalto produced an integrated solution to complex practical and aesthetic considerations. To keep the cost down – essential for achieving Karhula's aim and for satisfying Aalto's social concerns – all the pieces have a smooth interior surface and a simple ribbed exterior

that allows them to be produced from moulds in a mechanized pressing process. The underlying forms of the pieces and the corresponding annular ribbed bands satisfy Modernist preferences for straight lines and simple geometric shapes. The banding fulfils both decorative and structural functions, giving a static and balanced appearance to each piece and unity to the set and providing strength and rigidity, making the pieces robust enough for family use. If there was just one word to sum up what was important about this design, it would be economy.

STOOL 60 (1932–3)
Alvar Aalto
(1898–1976)
Artek 1933 to present

Aalto's simple stacking stool – a circular seat supported by three bent, L-shaped legs – is one of his most straightforward pieces of furniture. Since its release in 1933, Stool 60 has been one of his bestselling designs: according to Artek, its Helsinki-based producers, well in excess of one million examples have been sold. In the 1930s, most European purchasers were attracted by the space-saving practicality of the stacked stools and their remark-ably low cost. They might also have been drawn by the striking spirals created by the legs of the stack, a device that Aalto was keen to exploit. Aalto regarded the L-shaped leg as his most significant contribution to furniture design. His solution to the problem of producing a sufficiently strong joint between the horizontal and vertical elements was to cut staggered vertical slots in the end of a section of birch and inserting glued sections of veneer. The dampened result was then bent under stress. When the glue set, it left a permanently fixed right angle, which he called the 'bent-knee.' The result was innovative, successful and unobtrusive. The stool is still being produced in birch veneer, as well as linoleum, laminate and upholstered versions.

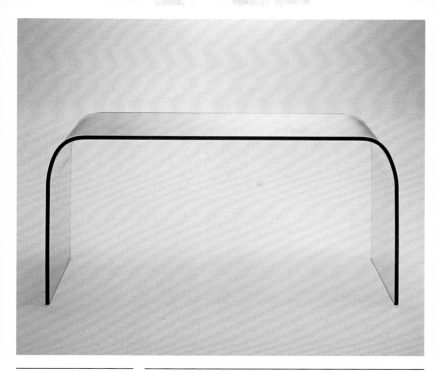

FONTANA TABLE (1932)
Pietro Chiesa
(1892–1948)
FontanaArte
1932 to present

Glass has always played an important role in the work of Italian furniture and lighting company FontanaArte, and nowhere is this better illustrated than in Pietro Chiesa's Fontana Table of 1932. As artistic director of the company, Chiesa was fascinated by the properties of this fluid, versatile material. He utilized a number of techniques, including cutting, moulding and grinding, to design a range of furniture, lamps and objects using glass. The clay-moulded Fontana Table is one of the earliest of these. The curved float-glass table is an object of subtle and understated beauty, displaying perfect proportions in its shape and luminescent line, but its most staggering feature is that it is constructed of one continuous sheet of 15 mm (0.59 in) crystal. Bending such a sheet was – and remains – an extraordinary engineering and manufacturing feat, particularly when the largest table in the series is 1.4 m (55 in) long and 70 cm (28 in) wide. Since its debut at the 1934 Bari Fair, the Fontana Table has remained an elegant piece of Minimalist glass that has never been improved upon, nor will it lose its sense of timelessness.

OMEGA DRAWING PIN (1932)
A. Schild S.A.
Design Team
Lüdi Swiss AG
c.1947 to present

The provenance of this unpretentious little drawing pin is quickly established: 'Swiss Made' reads the engraving stamped into the top of the thumbnail-sized pinhead. The head sits atop three sharp pins cut with one edge straight and one slanted, which come to meet at a sharp point. Architects have been using Omega Pins since the late 1940s. The design has remained unchanged since it was patented by A. Schild S.A. of Grenchen, Switzerland in 1932 as the ASSA Pin. Lüdi Swiss AG, which established itself in the 1930s as a supplier of paper clips and expanded into the office equipment market during the 1940s, first manufactured the pin as 'Omega' in 1947. The Omega Drawing Pin was marketed as a precision implement for professional draughtsmen who required their drawings to be held firmly in place. Once secured, the pin's grip is so effective that a specially designed lever device, included with each box, is needed for extraction. Despite the prevailing proliferation of computer-aided design, a market remains for the Omega Drawing Pin, ensuring that the family-owned company is likely to prosper beyond the third generation who currently administer the brand.

MK FOLDING CHAIR (1932)

Mogens Koch
(1898–1992)
Interna 1960 to 1971
Cadovius 1971 to 1981
Rud Rasmussen
1981 to 2011
Carl Hansen & Sons
2011 to present

The Danish architect Mogens Koch was strongly influenced by the furniture design of Kaare Klint. Like Klint, he was careful to avoid superficial tricks, preferring a sober approach often based on the improvement of already existing furniture types and the use of traditional materials. Koch's MK Folding Chair, like Klint's Propeller Folding Stool (1930), is modelled on military campaign furniture. A folding stool with a canvas seat forms the central section of the chair and is enclosed by four poles, two of which, slightly longer than the others, have canvas between them to provide a backrest. Metal rings loop around each of the four poles and are fixed just below the seat. These allow the chair to be folded up, but restrict the seat from collapsing under weight when in use. Koch's chair was designed in 1932 for a competition to provide church furniture but was not made in any quantity until the model was released by Interna in 1960, along with matching tables, and marketed for outdoor use. The additional pieces were designed to fit together when folded, minimizing storage space.

CALATRAVA WRISTWATCH (1932)
Patek Philippe
Design Team
Patek Philippe
1932 to present

By the 1920s Patek Philippe had established its reputation as the world's finest maker of both pocket- and wristwatches. Its 1932 wristwatch model, the Calatrava, has more than stood the test of time. The name is derived from the fortress of Calatrava in Spain, which was successfully defended against the Moors by a religious order in 1138. The order's symbol of a cross formed from four fleurs-de-lis had already been adopted in the late nineteenth century by Patek Philippe as its trademark, but the name has also become associated with the characteristic flat-rim bezel of this watch model. The Calatrava is unquestionably Art Deco in inspiration, but its circular shape was unusual among watches of that era, when rectangular or square cases were in vogue. The flat-rim bezel set back from the ring holding the crystal in place is classically Art Deco. The gentleman's model, with its sleek masculine lines, became an instant success and has endured as Patek's longest-standing design; the Model 96, featured here, was introduced in 1946. The range has been extended to include hobnail-cut or diamond-set examples in white, yellow or rose gold. The rarest of all are in steel.

ZIG-ZAG CHAIR
(1932–3)
Gerrit Rietveld
(1888–1964)
Van de Groenekan
1934 to 1973
Meltz & Co
1935 to c.1955
Cassina
1973 to present

With the Zig-Zag, Gerrit Rietveld successfully broke with the conventional geometry of the chair by introducing a diagonal support. The Zig-Zag Chair is angular and rigid, consisting of just four flat rectangular planes of wood – back, seat, support and base – of identical width and thickness. Rietveld had been experimenting since the late 1920s with designs for a chair that could be cut from one piece of material, or 'pop out of a machine, just like that.' Early drawings suggest a chair that could be bent to shape from a single steel plate. In 1938 a version was produced that appears to be made from a single

piece of moulded five-ply wood. However, it proved more practical to join together four separate planes of solid 2.5 cm (1 in) wood. The eye is drawn to its construction methods: the dovetail joints between seat and back and the triangular wedges fitted to reinforce the forty-five degree angles. First made in Holland by Van de Groenekan, and also put into production by the Dutch manufacturers Metz & Co in 1935, the Zig-Zag established itself as a historical point in terms of its design.

ZIPPO LIGHTER (1933)
George G. Blaisdell
(1895–1978)
Zippo
1933 to present

The Zippo Lighter is legendary, retaining its credibility and remaining virtually unchanged since its origins in 1933. The Zippo made its reputation in World War II when the US government ordered the entire production for army and navy issue. It reportedly deflected potentially fatal bullets, acted as a signalling device in rescue operations and even heated soup in upturned helmets. Its designer, George Blaisdell, was a former oil company executive who purchased the US distribution rights to an Austrian lighter. When it proved to be as clumsy as it looked, he embarked on a redesign. First, he streamlined

the chrome-plated brass case, fashioning a smooth, rectangular shape that fitted comfortably in the hand. Then he used a spring-loaded hinge enabling users to flick open the top. Finally, he surrounded the wick with a perforated screen to shield it from gusts of wind, yet still allow sufficient airflow for the spark to take. A striking wheel spins against a tiny piece of flint to create a spark that ignites the wick. In a clever piece of marketing, Blaisdell offered a lifetime warranty and free repair for any defects – a bold policy that still holds today.

MOKA EXPRESS COFFEE MAKER (1933)
Alfonso Bialetti
(1888–1970)
Bialetti Industrie
1933 to present

The Bialetti Moka Express is, according to its manufacturers, the only industrial object that has remained unchanged since its first appearance in 1933. The stove-top coffee maker echoes a traditional tall coffee pot in its basic form, yet has a distinctive Art Deco styling. Its octagonal shape is cinched before tilting outwards in eight facets of shiny metal. The pot consists of three metal parts, the base compartment for boiling the water, the filter section that holds the coffee and an upper coffee-collecting compartment with an integral spout. Alfonso Bialetti, grandfather of the Italian manufacturer Alberto Alessi, was responsible for the design. He trained as a metalworker in Paris before opening a small metalworking shop in 1918. It is said that his Moka Express was inspired by early washing machines consisting of a boiler base and tub above. He used aluminium for the body because it both retains and transmits heat well, and because its porosity allows it to absorb the flavour of the coffee. The knob of the lid and the handle were designed in heat-resistant Bakelite to prevent burnt hands. An impressive 200 million Moka Express coffee makers have been sold since 1933.

**BENT PLYWOOD
ARMCHAIR (1933)**
Gerald Summers
(1899–1967)
Makers of Simple
Furniture
1934 to 1939
Mvsevm
1984 to present

The introduction of the Bent
Plywood Armchair by Gerald
Summers transformed a simple
piece of furniture into a seminal
moment in the history of furniture
design. Produced from a single
piece of plywood, bent and held
in place without the use of screws,
bolts or joints, it questioned the
manufacturing techniques that
preceded it. The chair is one of the
earliest examples of single unit
construction – a technique that
would not be achieved in metal or
plastic design for several decades.
Its unique organic profile is easy to
appreciate. The chair's undulating
landscape of smooth curves,
rounded silhouettes and sweeping

surfaces sitting close to the
floor in a low-slung, almost
laid-back manner – an early test
bed for ergonomics – presented
a profound contrast to the typical
linear furniture format. Summers
manufactured the chair under his
own Makers of Simple Furniture
brand. Although the design offered
inspiration to an optimistic 1930s
design scene, commercially its
success was cut short when the
British government imposed
restrictions on importing plywood
into the UK. As a result, Summers's
company was forced to close
in 1939, having produced only 120
chairs. As such, original examples
have become highly collectable.

4699 DECK CHAIR (1933)
Kaare Klint
(1888–1954)
Rud Rasmussen
1933 to 2011

The 4699 Deck Chair epitomizes Kaare Klint's highly influential approach to modernity. This reinterpretation of a nineteenth-century design demonstrates his study of human proportion aligned with meticulous detailing and high-quality construction. The dynamic teak frame reveals the form of the structure. The brass fixings are carefully detailed and exposed to illustrate their relevance in the construction of the chair. The elegantly arched, cane-inlaid seat and back and the full-length removable canvas upholstery pad with head-cushion support the user. Klint's preoccupation with updating historical designs to suit contemporary requirements had enormous impact on future generations of designers. His furniture designs were internationally exhibited as early as 1929 in Barcelona, and were shown at the 1937 Paris exhibition. They provided the basis for an era of international dominance by Danish designers, such as Hans Wegner, Ole Wanscher and Børge Mogensen. Klint's theories on the marriage between traditional furniture types and the requirements of twentieth-century lifestyles provided designs of lasting importance.

LUMINATOR FLOOR LAMP (1933)
Pietro Chiesa
(1892–1948)
FontanaArte
1933 to present

The name 'luminator' is associated with Achille and Pier Giacomo Castiglioni, who designed their version of the uplighter in 1954. The duo named their lamp in tribute to this piece, designed more than twenty years earlier by Pietro Chiesa. An even earlier version exists, designed by Luciano Baldessari in 1929 but it is Chiesa's uplighter that hindsight has shown to be the most innovative. Chiesa worked principally on glasswork and *novecento* style furniture before merging his workshop with Gio Ponti and Luigi Fontana's newly established FontanaArte in 1933.

As artistic director, he was responsible for around 1,500 prototypes in all areas of design. His Luminator Floor Lamp – the first domestic uplighter – is a product whose simplicity results in a grand expression of form. Chiesa took the idea of indirect lighting from the studio equipment of photographers and realized that it could produce a gentle, softly diffused light. He housed the lamp in an elegant and simple brass tube, fixed to a base that flared out like a champagne flute at its top. The honesty of its form belies the time during which it was designed.

STANDARD CHAIR (1934)
Jean Prouvé
(1901–84)
Ateliers Jean Prouvé
1934 to 1956
Galerie Steph Simon
1956 to 1965
Vitra 2002 to present

Jean Prouvé's Standard Chair, with its solid structure and simple aesthetics, is an understated design. It evolved from Prouvé's work for a furniture competition run by the University of Nancy in France and used a combination of sheet and tubular steel with rubber feet. Prouvé conceived the chair for mass production and during the war created a version that could be dismantled. The Standard was conceived for the institutional and contract markets, although today its logical form and strong functionality make it a versatile chair that can be used in domestic environments as well as public

areas such as restaurants, cafes and offices. It reflected Prouvé's belief that design should be a populist form of modern Functionalism. In 2002, Vitra reissued the Standard Chair almost seventy years after its initial conception. Vitra already had a collection of original Prouvé pieces, including the Standard Chair, in its Design Museum Collection, so it made sense for the manufacturer to produce what it regarded as a design icon. Vitra's endorsement brought Prouvé's chair beyond design collectors' circles and places it on a par with designs by the Eameses and George Nelson.

LOLA BRUSH (1934)
Herbert Schmidt
(1904–80)
A. Schmidt
1934 to 1980
Lola (formerly
Schmidt-Lola)
1981 to present

A staple addition to any German worktop, the LOLA Brush is one of those understated items that people take to their hearts. The LOLA is as coveted for its familiar form as it is for its function of washing vegetables or dishes. The brush's natural fibre bristles are secured into a circular wooden head, which is connected to a slender arm by a metal clasp. This not only allows for a certain freedom of movement but also means that the head can be easily detached. The brush is efficient, agile and hard wearing. Its design has required no updating: the LOLA Brush available today is manufactured using the same blueprint as

those first produced in 1934. The product still bears the original logo, which is a great example of German graphic design. Schmidt, its manufacturer, has specialized in brushes since its inception and has been in the hands of the Schmidt family since 1929. LOLA's unusual name is an abbreviation for 'Lockstedter Lager', where the brushes were stored before transportation across Germany. This simple, functional, everyday object is one of Germany's most celebrated and democratic design items.

SCAGNO CHAIR
(1934–6)
Giuseppe Terragni
(1904–43)
Zanotta
1972 to present

As was common among architects before the rise of a distinct design industry, Giuseppe Terragni did not separate his plans for the Scagno Chair from any of the other elements for his enduring masterpiece, Casa del Fascio, in Como. The project was designed as a single, unified whole. Unfortunately, the Scagno Chair remained only as a series of sketches during Terragni's lifetime. Nearly four decades passed before its initial limited production in 1971 by Zanotta, followed in 1983 by the production model available today, and poorly renamed 'Follia', meaning madness. Unlike the other chairs designed for the Casa del Fascio, with their tubular steel frames and padded seats, the Scagno Chair avoids soft curves in favour of the sculptural and architectural. The black lacquered beechwood seat of the Scagno joins four similarly imposing legs to create a structural cube. Twin cantilevered, semicircular supports – originally designed with a chrome-plated metal finish, but manufactured in 18/8 chrome-plated stainless steel – join the seat to the modestly curved backrest. The design is a testament to Terragni's perfectionism and fruitful rejection of orthodoxy, playing with symmetry, rotation and subtraction, and is an early example of a uniquely Italian Modernism.

ANGLEPOISE®
1227 LAMP (1935)
George Carwardine
(1887–1947)
Anglepoise®
1935 to present

The Anglepoise 1227 Lamp is all about function – a supreme piece of rational design that is still manufactured by the same British company as when it was launched. Originally manufactured in lacquered metal with a solid Bakelite base, it has the shiny industrial aesthetic of the burgeoning 1930s machine age. There is elegance in its long, narrow, angular body and its bonnet-like shade gives it a strangely touching, human posture. Its designer, George Carwardine, was a specialist in vehicle suspension systems. Carwardine set about developing a frictionless mechanism that could balance and direct light to any position. He wanted to create a lamp that was as versatile as a human arm – with instant flexibility and, more elusively, the ability to hold the chosen position. Carwardine based the mechanics of the lamp on the tension principle of muscles in limbs. He used springs, instead of the more traditional counterweights, to keep the arm in position, necessitating complex mathematical equations to create the optimum tension in the springs. The lamp was originally intended for commercial applications, but the market for home and office use soon became apparent.

ICE CREAM SCOOP
(1935)
Sherman L. Kelly
(1869–1952)
Zeroll
1935 to present

The Zeroll Ice Cream Scoop is a beautiful object: elegant, shiny and sculptural. Its design is perfect for its task, and thus it has remained unchanged since it first came on the market in 1935. At that time, ice cream was changing from being a luxury product into one that was widely available, thanks to advances in freezing technology. However, ice cream fresh from the freezer is often very hard, and scraping it from its tub with a spoon is difficult. Sherman L. Kelly's innovation, which is literally at the heart of the Zeroll Scoop, is a hollow handle core that contains antifreeze. This antifreeze conducts body heat from the scooper's hand and delivers it to the blade of the scoop, helping it to cut a path through the ice cream. The handle is intentionally thick for the antifreeze chamber, but it also permits a far better grip than a spoon. Other advantages of the 18.5 cm (7.3 in) long Zeroll Scoop are that it produces more standard portions and is easy to clean and keep in good condition. Smooth, wonderful, and perpetually necessary, a timeless appeal may honour a nostalgic emotion towards this scoop.

ARMCHAIR 400 (TANK CHAIR) (1935–6)
Alvar Aalto
(1898–1976)
Artek 1936 to present

Among Finnish architect Alvar Aalto's designs for seating furniture, which are notable for being pared down and lightweight, the Armchair 400 (also known as the Tank Chair) is unusual. In this chair Aalto makes a much more robust statement, emphasizing mass and solidity and thus a different possibility for his laminated wooden furniture. In this model, thin sheets of birch veneer have been glued together and set around a mould to produce the wide, curved and cantilevered strips that provide the open frames either side of the mattress-type seat and back. These laminated strips are wider than in other

models, partly to support the bulky aesthetic of the piece and partly to give added strength. At the junction of the arm and the back, the downward-pointing terminals of the laminated strips help give an overall rigidity to the design. This is one detail in which the Armchair 400 differs from its close relative, the 406, where the arm terminates in an upward curl. Although this is a small difference, it indicates the aesthetic function of such an element – which in the 400 helps to complete the picture of muscular, weight-bearing capacity.

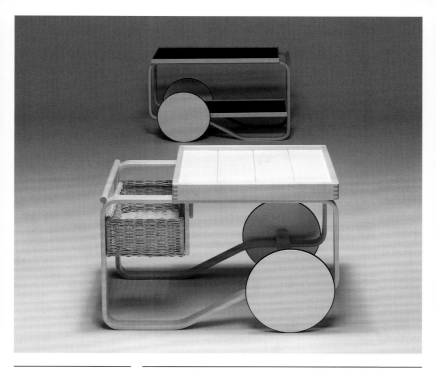

TEA TROLLEY 901
(1935–6)
Alvar Aalto
(1898–1976)
Artek 1936 to present

In 1929, Alvar Aalto submitted a number of designs to a competition that the Berlin-based company Thonet was sponsoring. These included a low-slung serving table that boasted three levels of surface space and curvilinear runners that were reminiscent of a sled. The configuration was adapted over the following seven years to become the Tea Trolley 901, which was manufactured by Artek, the industrial arts company Aalto set up with Modernist colleagues in 1935. Replacing the sled runners with a curvilinear chassis that had planar wheels, Aalto's birch, ceramic and rattan trolley is indicative of the Finnish designer's innovative but humane aesthetic, combining a gridded tile serving surface with an adjacent storage basket. The trolley's bentwood birch structure is typically Aalto. Although a linoleum-covered version with no basket was first displayed in Artek's showroom in 1936, Aalto's Tea Trolley 901 had its international debut at the Milan Triennale later that year. A second model called the Tea Trolley 900 was revealed at the 1937 Paris Expo. Thanks to its robust design, the continuing existence of Artek and special arrangements with Herman Miller, the 901 and 900 models are manufactured to this day.

FIESTAWARE (1936)
Frederick Hurton
Rhead (1880–1942)
Homer Laughlin
China 1936 to 1973,
1986 to present

In 1936, when the Homer Laughlin China Company released its Fiestaware range of ceramic tableware, America was still in the grip of the Depression. Fiestaware made itself an essential purchase by appealing to middle-class notions of domestic propriety. Although manufactured in Ohio, Fiestaware was designed by an Englishman, Frederick Hurton Rhead. At a time when dinnerware was still echoing Victorian and Art Nouveau designs, Rhead introduced bold colours and simple Art Deco styling, with five concentric ridges serving as the only ornamentation. Colour was the keynote. Originally released in red,

medium green, cobalt blue, yellow and ivory, Fiestaware ('the dinnerware that turns your table into a celebration') helped transform the domestic interior. The red range became somewhat notorious for being one of the most radioactive products on the market, because of the depleted uranium oxide used in the glaze. Fiestaware was discontinued in 1973 but reissued in 1986 in a new range of colours to mark its fiftieth anniversary. The design has changed little in seventy years except to reflect countless shifts in colour fashion. Even today, the release of a new colour is something of an event for collectors and aficionados.

AIRSTREAM CLIPPER (1936)
Wallance Merle Byam (1896–1962)
Airstream 1936 to 1939, 1945 to present

As the Airstream literature reads, 'Wallace Merle Byam was practically born a traveller.' As a child he travelled on a mule train in Oregon, and later he moved around as a shepherd and merchant marine. Byam finally settled in Los Angeles where he owned his own advertising and publishing companies. Byam's first trailer was built as a response to complaints from his readers about plans for building a travel trailer published in one of his magazines. He set about designing an improved version. By simply introducing two basic changes – dropping the trailer's floor between the wheels and raising the height of the roof – he transformed the trailer into a mobile home. After the first designs, Byam began to look at aircraft construction technology. This culminated in 1936 with the design of the Clipper, which incorporated an innovative aluminium monocoque with an aerodynamic teardrop design, so light that it could be pulled by a man-powered bicycle. Restrictions on use of aluminium during World War II led the company to close. Airstream reopened after the war and resumed the production of the Clipper. Even today, 60 per cent of all Airstreams ever built are still in use.

LOUNGE CHAIR 36 (1936)
Bruno Mathsson
(1907–88)
Bruno Mathsson
International
1936 to 1950s,
1990s to present

During the 1930s, designer Bruno Mathsson began research into what he termed 'the business of sitting.' Mathsson's Lounge Chair 36 was the result of these studies and remains an enduring legacy of his career. From 1933, he had designed pressed laminate chair frames with the seat and back forming one sweeping unit, which was clad with plaited strips of saddle girth. The Lounge Chair 36 evolved from an earlier design: the Grasshopper Chair of 1933. The Lounge is striking because of a lightness conveyed by its simple structure. Mathsson based his designs on the physiology of sitting, with the need for support,

activity and repose. He wrote that 'comfortable sitting is an "art" – it ought not to be. Instead, the making of chairs has to be done with such an "art" that the sitting will not be any "art".' Taking his cue from the Swedish craft tradition, he explored organic, even anthropomorphic shapes in his popular wooden furniture. His father Karl, whose furniture business in Värnamo would later manufacture many of Bruno's designs, trained Mathsson as a cabinetmaker. Mathsson's furniture designs combine beauty with form, and were seen as innovations both in their day and at present.

FLATWARE (1936)
Gio Ponti (1891–1979)
Argenteria Krupp
1936 to 1969
Sambonet
1969 to 1990,
2003 to present

Gio Ponti did not limit himself in his architecture or interior design to any single material, technique or creative discipline, and the broad sweep of his attention to detail took in the smallest of scales, right down to cutlery. His Flatware was designed in 1936 and its style set it apart from the conventional insistence on decorated, clearly delineated handles. Ponti's softly undulating curves nearly disappear into the working ends of each piece and sit naturally in the hand. The flatware was originally produced by Argenteria Krupp in zama, an alloy using zinc rather than copper, which was in short supply during World War II. Production in stainless steel followed in 1942 – one of the earliest examples of stainless steel cutlery. During the 1960s, Sambonet acquired Krupp and continued to make Ponti Flatware until the early 1990s; it was reintroduced in 2003. Today, the still contemporary, simple lines of this range are produced in both 18/10 stainless steel and mille silver electroplated stainless steel with either a mirror or satin finish. Ponti continued to design cutlery throughout his career. Most of these designs were more strikingly self-conscious and 'modern' than the early, classic Ponti Flatware.

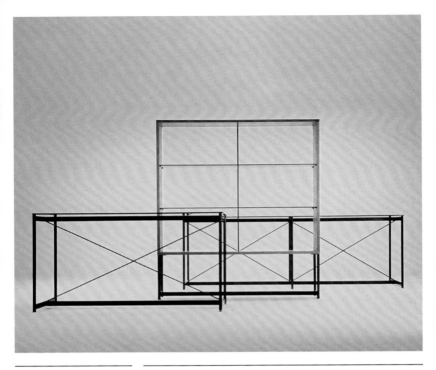

ASNAGO-VENDER TABLE (1936)
Mario Asnago
(1896–1981)
Claudio Vender
(1904–86)
Pallucco Italia
1982 to present

This steel and glass table was designed by Mario Asnago and Claudio Vender to update Bar Moka, a Milanese café. The bar opened in 1939, but the table was displayed at the VI Milan Triennale in 1936. The table is perhaps one of the purest and most enduring embodiments of Italian Rationalism – the short-lived design movement based on Modernism that flourished in Italy in the 1930s. While other designers of the period turned their attention to the nationalistic and monumental possibilities of Rationalism in order to promote the fascist cause, architects Asnago and Vender stayed independent and true to their own vision, which is perhaps best exemplified in this table. The table is composed of a simple, 10 mm (0.4 in) rectangular tempered crystal top supported by a drawn steel-rod frame, intersected by two diagonal rods. This structural cross is the only embellishment, albeit a stark one, to the strict section. Asnago and Vender applied their disciplined yet elegant Rationalist principles to a series of architectural projects, yet it is their unique table design in which their legacy is encapsulated. Indeed, this is the most rational example of Rationalism remaining in production today.

SANT'ELIA CHAIR
(1936)
Giuseppe Terragni
(1904–43)
Zanotta
1970 to present

The Benita Chair was designed by Giuseppe Terragni for his most acclaimed building, the Casa del Fascio, in Como, Italy. It was later renamed the Sant'Elia as a result of the unfortunate connection of its original name with that of the Italian dictator, Benito Mussolini. Terragni designed every element of the Casa del Fascio's interior – windows, doors, lamps, tables, desks, shelves and chairs – with the same experimental attitude that he had used throughout the building. This included a cantilevered chair, named Lariana, with a single, sinuous frame made from steel tubing supporting either leather

upholstery or a moulded wooden seat and back. For use in the executive boardroom, Terragni transformed the Lariana into the Benita by extending the frame into an elegant armrest. The various curves of both chairs give the structure of the seat, back and armrest an unusual and comfortable flexibility, while also combining beauty and function. The two chairs were intended to be manufactured by Columbus in Milan, who was starting to produce metal-tube furniture, however they were not mass-produced until the 1970s, when Zanotta re-edited both versions as part of its classic collection.

SAVOY VASE (1936)
Alvar Aalto
(1898–1976)
iittala 1937 to present

Alvar Aalto's Savoy Vase, his best-known glass design, has provoked considerable speculation about the inspiration for its unusual amoebic shape. Suggestions include the eccentric growth rings of trees, the fluidity of water and Finland's many lakes. Aalto remained tight-lipped about his sources. Even his original name for the Savoy Vase – 'An Eskimo Woman's Leather Breeches' (Eskimoerindern Skinnbuxa) – reveals more about his sense of humour than it does his inspiration. The vase represents one of the few occasions when Aalto came close to designing something ornamental. Empty of flowers, it can stand alone as a piece of sculpture. The shape also relates to the curves that Aalto was producing in his laminated wooden furniture. The vase was created for a competition at the Paris World Fair of 1937, sponsored by the manufacturer Karhula (later iittala). It won first prize. At the same time several were ordered to for Aalto's Savoy Restaurant in Helsinki, thus its name. Although the vase was originally blown into wooden moulds, a more durable cast-iron mould is now used. The vase has been in production, in a variety of colours and sizes, and in popular demand since its introduction.

KLISMOS CHAIR (1937)
Terence Robsjohn-Gibbings (1905–76)
Saridis
1961 to present

The Klismos Chair in walnut with woven leather thongs, a faithful reproduction drawn from ancient Greek representations, presents a particular ideal of beauty and perfection that has inspired artists and designers for well over 2,000 years. The elegant strength of the joinery combined with the delicacy of the tapering curves and the obvious consideration of the human body make this an early example of a comfortable household chair, long before ergonomics became a buzzword. Unlike other examples of ancient seating, the Klismos demonstrates an unprecedented level of sophistication. It is somewhat ironic that Terence Robsjohn-Gibbings, British-born interior and furniture designer, is best known for this chair because he was an ardent, if idiosyncratic, Modernist. In his 1944 book *Goodbye, Mr Chippendale*, he stated that 'the antique furniture cancer is a deeply rooted evil' and pressed the argument for Modernism. After a prolific period of work in his warm brand of Modernist style, he turned again to ancient Greece for inspiration. In 1961, he designed the Klismos line of furniture in collaboration with Saridis in Athens, extending the collection to include reproductions of several types of furniture from classical Greece.

MIRACLE MIXER (WARING BLENDOR) (1937)
Frederick Osius (nd)
Waring
1937 to present

The Waring Blendor revolutionized the way we make drinks. Fred Waring, a former architecture and engineering student who became leader of the successful big band, The Pennsylvanians, was the dedicated promoter and financial backer of the blender that would eventually bear his name. The blender was not the first of its kind (Stephen Poplawski had developed a precursor in 1922), but its inventor, Fred Osius, made significant improvements that he patented in 1933. The blender acquired its cloverleaf shape in 1937 and was introduced as the Miracle Mixer at the National Restaurant Show in Chicago.

By 1954, one million had been sold. Still manufactured by Waring and virtually unchanged since its introduction, the machine, with its round, gently undulating and tapered polished stainless-steel base, shows the influence of Art Deco. Coupled with its 40-oz cloverleaf glass bowl, the design is an icon of American pre-World War II design. Because of rationing, only a few blenders were made during World War II, and these were for scientific purposes. The efficacy and reliability of the Waring Blendor made it the scientists' blender of choice, and it was used by Dr Jonas Salk while working on the polio vaccine.

LUXO L-1 LAMP (1937–8)
Jacob Jacobsen (1901–96)
Luxo 1938 to present

Having been in production for over six decades, during which time over 25 million units have been sold, the multi-award-winning Luxo L-1 Lamp is widely regarded as the forerunner of all self-balancing desk lamps. Yet despite this, the L-1 owes a large part of its success to George Carwadine's 1934 Anglepoise Lamp. Jacob Jacobsen recognized the potential of the Anglepoise's spring-based balancing system and in 1937 acquired the production rights to the lamp. Consequently, Jacobsen's L-1 lamp uses a similar spring system derived from the constant tension principle of human limbs (undeniably,

both the L-1 and the Anglepoise look a lot like prosthetic limbs with a bulb attached), but harnesses it to a much more refined design – which is why the L-1 has become a definitive model. In particular, Jacobsen's design features a more elegant aluminium lampshade and is characterized by a formal harmony between shade, stand and the various articulated joints between them. Still manufactured today by Jacobsen's company, Luxo, the L-1 lamp comes in several versions, incorporating a selection of bases, mounts and shades. Despite many attempts to improve on it, it remains one of the world's leading task lights.

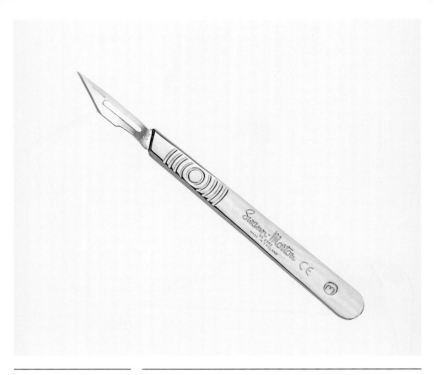

SWANN-MORTON SURGICAL SCALPEL (1937)
Swann-Morton
Design Team
Swann-Morton
1937 to present

Swann-Morton, based in the renowned steel-manufacturing town of Sheffield, England, first produced the sterilized surgical scalpel during the late 1930s. Mr W. R. Swann, Mr J. A. Morton and Miss D. Fairweather founded the business in August 1932 to produce razor blades. In 1937 the company's emphasis shifted to the burgeoning market for sterilized surgical blades when the original US patent filed by the company Bard Parker expired. The design's innovative bayonet fitting enables blades to be simply attached by being flexed onto the stainless steel slotted handle. Removal is a straightforward

process, and the design's intuitive qualities have helped establish the Swann-Morton Surgical Scalpel as the industry-defining product. The product has evolved into its current range of over sixty blade shapes and sizes, with twenty-seven different handle designs. There are specific products for surgeons, dentists, chiropodists and veterinary surgeons, as well as specialist scalpels for use in art, craft and design studios. Swann-Morton continues to dominate the global market for surgical and craft blades, producing 1.5 million each day, which are supplied to more than one hundred countries.

JERRY CAN (c.1937)
Designer Unknown
Various
1937 to present

The Jerry Can is a perfect example of innovation prompted by warfare. Although it is thought that the Italians first used it in Africa, it was the German army that first used it on a large scale in World War II. For this reason British troops dubbed it the Jerry Can. The name stuck, though not surprisingly the Germans used another term: *Wehrmachts-kanister*. Until its invention, the business of on-board fuel transportation was surprisingly hazardous. The five-gallon Jerry Can had several advantages that aided the Germans' Blitzkrieg tactics: its three handles made it easy to carry, the indentations in its sides allowed the contents to expand, an air pocket meant the can floated even when full, and its cam lever release mechanism worked better than the old screw caps. The can's design was considered so important that German units destroyed their fuel containers if in danger of being captured. But by 1942 the British were able to copy the design after the Eighth Army captured Jerry Cans from the Afrika Korps. The design has remained virtually unchanged since, though it is now made in plastic as well as pressed steel.

CACCIA CUTLERY (1938)
Luigi Caccia
Dominioni
(1913–2016)
Livio Castiglioni
(1911–79)
Pier Giacomo
Castiglioni
(1913–68)
R Miracoli & Figlio
1938
Alessi
1990 to present

Caccia Cutlery, which takes its name from one of its designers, was first created in 1938 as a collaborative project by a group of highly influential Italian designers: Livio and Pier Giacomo Castiglioni and Luigi Caccia Dominioni. They all trained as architects in Italy and worked together designing interiors, exhibition installations, furniture and products. The Caccia design was shown at the Milan Triennale in 1940 and was described by fellow Italian designer Gio Ponti as, 'the most beautiful cutlery in existence.' Ponti's opinion was widely shared. In its day the set was a consummate example

of how craftsmanship was embracing the industrial future of housewares. The profile is sleek and curved, while retaining an elegant and slender form, and there is a superb play on the thickness of the elements within the pieces. It is modern yet retains the essence of classicism. Caccia was originally available in sterling silver, however, Alessi relaunched it in 1990 using stainless steel. Luigi Caccia Dominioni completed the set using the original design drawings from the 1930s, with the addition of a four-pronged fork, as the original three-pronged design had been thought by many to be too unusual.

ARMCHAIR 406
(1938–9)
Alvar Aalto
(1898–1976)
Artek 1939 to present

The interlocking open curves of both the frame and seat of the Armchair 406 present one of Alvar Aalto's most elegant designs. In many ways, the 406 is similar to the 400, but whereas the 400 makes a forceful statement through its squat bulk, the 406 emphasizes slenderness. The 406 was a refinement of the plywood Paimio Chair and retains its technically innovative cantilever frame, but has a seat made from straps of webbing. Its final version was initially designed for the Villa Mairea, the home of Aalto's patron and business partner, Maire Gullichsen, but it is not clear whether she requested the seat's material. It is likely that the suggestion for the use of webbing came from Aalto's wife Aino, who had used it on a 1937 cantilevered reclining chair that was marketed as her husband's design. For Swedish Modernist designers in the 1930s, webbing was seen as an inexpensive and perfectly satisfactory material. For Aalto, webbing also had the advantage of being thin enough to prevent the lean profile of his design from being obscured, allowing the clearest possible expression of its structure.

ORGANIC CHAIR (1940)
Charles Eames
(1907–78)
Eero Saarinen
(1910–61)
Haskelite
Corporation,
Heywood-Wakefield,
and Marli Erhman
1940
Vitra 2005 to present

Highly celebrated for his architecture, the Finnish-born American Modernist Eero Saarinen is equally important for his furniture designs. For the outstanding Organic Chair, he collaborated with Charles Eames, both men being interested in the possibilities of moulded plywood. Saarinen and Eames's progressive ideas were inspired by their interest in organic form, by the possibilities of plastics and plywood laminates and by the technological advance of 'cycle-welding', a process developed by the Chrysler Corporation that enabled wood to be joined to rubber, glass or metal. The prototype for the Organic Chair's

seat and back was fractured and reset until an appropriate human form seating shape was found. This structural shell, designed to support layers of glue and wood veneer, had to be hand manufactured; only between ten and twelve prototypes were built. Despite being key to the Eameses' development of plywood furniture, the Organic Chair is fundamentally associated with Saarinen. It led towards the creation of his highly successful furniture designs for Knoll, most notably the No. 70 Womb Chair (1947–8), the Saarinen Collection of office seating (1951) and the Tulip Pedestal group of chairs and tables (1955–6).

**MILK BOTTLE
(1940s)**
Designer Unknown
Various
1940s to present

The design of the milk bottle is not in itself remarkable, but the way it symbolizes both its contents and a particularly British way of life is. The first milk bottles were produced in 1880 by the Express Dairy Company in London, and were gradually adopted in a variety of designs by dairies throughout the country. The bottles came in a number of sizes; the pint became the most common during the 1940s, when domestic electric refrigerators became more commonplace. By the 1980s, when the dairy industry was marketing its product with the slogan 'Milk Has Gotta Lotta Bottle', packaging and product seemed to have become one. While the consumption of milk was associated with good health, the bottle itself advertised cleanliness. Unlike wooden or metal churns, the clear glass gave customers a vision of the milk's impeccable whiteness, while bottle-top technology graduated from porcelain stoppers to cardboard tops to aluminium caps to achieve greater degrees of hygiene. Today, the glass milk bottle along with the cheaper and more practical plastic and cardboard containers is still used throughout the United Kingdom, with electric milk floats still delivering fresh milk daily.

GEDESS LEAD SHARPENER
(c.1940)
Georges Dessonnaz
(nd)
Hermann Kuhn
1944 to present

In 1941, Georges Dessonnaz patented his innovation for a pencil-lead sharpener that revolutionized the draughtsman's toolbox. It replaced the hand-held bladed sharpeners used to trim the pencil's wooden casing and the sandpaper for sharpening the lead. While some draughtsmen used finger-held bladed blocks and mechanical crank-operated sharpeners, they could force softer degree pencil leads to break, while the harder lead might not be suitably exposed. Dessonnaz's design solved these problems by ensuring the pencil was centred, thus reducing pressure on the delicate lead and ensuring a consistent level of abrasion, with a dramatically reduced breakage rate. The office-product firm Kuhn, based in Bassersdorf, bought the rights and began large-scale manufacture after World War II. The result was the Gedess Lead Sharpener, which featured individually replaceable parts and a novel, rotational case-hardened steel movement housed within a distinctive Bakelite shell. The Gedess, usually complemented by Swiss Caran d'Ache drafting pencils, became a ubiquitous sight throughout drawing offices in post-war Europe.

ROUND THERMOSTAT (1941)
Henry Dreyfuss
(1904–72)
Honeywell Regulator Company
1953 to present

The Round Thermostat was possibly the most ubiquitous domestic design of late-twentieth-century America. Its low price and ability to fit most situations has made the Round one of Dreyfuss's most successful designs. Conceived in the early 1940s from a simple circular sketch by the Honeywell Regulator Company's president H. W. Sweatt, the Round was developed by Dreyfuss and design engineer Carl Kronmiller. It finally made its debut in 1953. Although the project had been significantly delayed by World War II, it benefited from innovations developed during the war. A bimetal coiled thermometer and a scaled mercury switch prevent dust settling. Several versions have since followed, including units with air-conditioning control and digital display features. Unlike its rectangular competitors, the Round represented a more appropriate, less technical aesthetic for the domestic setting, and its form had an in-built logic, as it could never be mounted crooked. The removable cap was designed to be painted to match the interior decor. Over fifty years since its launch, the Round has sold over 85 million units and is still in production, representing Dreyfuss's ideal of a product that has successfully stood the test of time.

CHEMEX®
COFFEEMAKER
(1941)
Peter J. Schlumbohm
(1896–1962)
Chemex®
1941 to present

The Chemex Coffeemaker looks as if it belongs as much in the laboratory as in the kitchen. Every aspect of it, from its name to its design, is engineered to present a scientific approach to coffee brewing. Dr Peter J. Schlumbohm, the chemist who created it, started with a simple chemistry set: an Erlenmeyer flask and a glass laboratory funnel. That combination gives the finished Chemex – made of a single piece of heatproof, laboratory-grade, borosilicate glass – its distinctive hourglass shape. Schlumbohm made some practical modifications, such as adding an air channel and a pouring spout, a small 'belly button' on the side of the flask to mark the half-full level, and a wood and leather collar so it can be picked up when it is hot. His economic use of materials was partly a result of the need to use non-priority materials at a time of war, but it also reflected the Bauhaus principles of simplicity and honesty in design that he had brought with him from Germany. Ultimately his coffeemaker is the perfect fusion of science and art: it does what it looks like it does and it looks good as well.

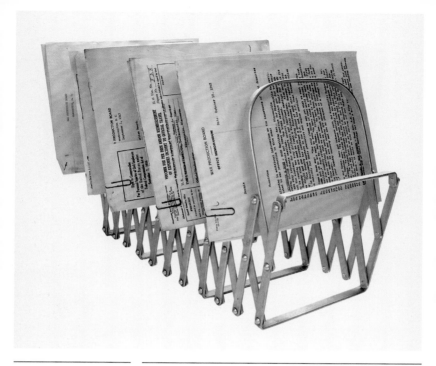

FLEXIFILE (1941)
Luther W. Evans (nd)
Evans Speciality
Company
1943 to 2001
Lee Products
1995 to present

The FlexiFile portable filing, collating and sorting system is cleverly flexible in its function and truly timeless in its design. It has changed little from its original 'Adjustable Rack' patent model of 1941. Its 'Lazy Tongs' system comprises a series of levers with simple rivet joints that are pivoted together like a pair of scissors. The file can expand quite extensively, and when not in use it can be folded into an extremely compact unit. The FlexiFile is currently available in twelve, eighteen or twenty-four slots, with each slot holding up to a ream of paper. The patent for the original

Adjustable Rack, designed by Luther W. Evans of Richmond, Virginia, described its suitability as a freestanding desk unit, shelf unit or inside element for drawer files. It also described the variety of materials that could be used for the rack bars, including wood, plastics or metal. A version of the FlexiFile, currently manufactured by Lee Products, has addressed twenty-first-century environmental concerns by using recycled aluminium. The FlexiFile is a successful design because it uses a straightforward mechanism simply and ingeniously, and in so doing provides an all-in-one office organizer.

666 WSP CHAIR (1941)
Jens Risom (1916–)
Knoll
1942 to 1958,
1995 to present

The simple wood and webbed construction of the 666 WSP Chair is the result of both the constraining circumstances of wartime and Jens Risom's Danish roots. Born and raised in Denmark, Risom studied under the important Modernist figure Kaare Klint, who advocated simple, straightforward forms designed with human proportions as the primary guide. In 1939 Risom immigrated to the United States and in 1941 he designed his first piece of furniture for the company headed by Hans Knoll. The 666 WSP Chair was first produced during World War II and as a result it could only be made of available, non-regulated materials. Risom soon followed this design with a number of variations, all using the same army surplus webbing – a material Risom described as, 'very basic, very simple, inexpensive.' Easy to clean, easy to replace and comfortable to use, the webbing made a perfect material for these everyday household chairs. In addition, the light, airy structure afforded by the material gave the chair a less weighty appearance and an informal quality consistent with the light-filled and flexible new, modern homes. The elegance and practicality of Risom's 666 WSP Chair has ensured its popularity.

BOOMERANG
CHAIR (1942)
Richard Neutra
(1892–1970)
Prospettiva
1990 to 1992
House Industries &
Otto Design Group
2002 (limited edition)
VS America
2013 to present

Richard Neutra developed the Boomerang Chair with his son Dion for the government-sponsored Channel Heights Housing Project in San Pedro, California in 1942. This garden community was designed to house shipyard workers employed for wartime industry. The use of low-cost materials and straightforward construction created a chair that these workers could assemble for use in their compact residences. The assertive yet softened raking lines of the chair create a striking and efficient structure, held together with simple pegged-through tenons and webbing. The plywood side panels economically eliminate the

need for separate back legs and support the side dowels, which form the front legs. The structure is thereby fashioned from two bold side profiles, two dowels, minimal cross rails and a webbed seat and back. Despite its name, the elegant shape that emerged as the chair's final form was not inspired by the Australian boomerang. Dion Neutra licensed Prospettiva to manufacture the chair with subtle changes in 1990. In 2002, with Otto Design Group, he again revisited the design and licensed House Industries to produce it in limited editions. The chair's continued popularity over a sixty-year span is evidence of its powerful and lasting appeal.

FRUIT LANTERN
(1943)
Kaare Klint
(1888–1954)
Le Klint
1943 to present

Kaare Klint's Fruit Lantern illustrates the grace and ingenuity of the best Danish design. The lanterns are made from paper, which makes them fragile, but also affordable. Indeed, since they first appeared on the market in 1943, they have sold in the millions. The influence of origami, a traditional Japanese discipline, can clearly be seen in the complex technique of paper folding used in these lamps. Although Klint was emboldened by his knowledge of origami to attempt such an ambitious design, it was his father, PV Jensen Klint, who first introduced him to the idea of using folded paper in lighting

design. Paper lanterns were something of an obsession within the Klint family; it is thought that the Fruit Lantern design was developed by Kaare Klint with the help of his son. Where PV Jensen Klint's experiments in folded paper were handmade in very small numbers, Kaare Klint insisted that his lamps should be available to everyone. Le Klint, a family company, soon went from being an artisanal industry to a mechanized manufacturer. Fruit Lanterns were, and still are, made from sheets of paper scored by machine and assembled by hand.

LUMINOR BASE WRISTWATCH
(1943)
Officine Panerai
Design Team
Officine Panerai
1943 to present

The Luminor Base Wristwatch is the simplest of all Officine Panerai models. The company was established by Giovanni Panerai in 1860 in Florence, and initially created professional timepieces more than pocket watches. It later capitalized on this experience to produce watches for the retail market, which became renowned for their accuracy and craftsmanship. In the early 1930s, Panerai began supplying the Royal Italian Navy with precision pocket watches and aiming sights for torpedoes. The first Luminor appeared around 1943 and has a Modernist style that defies its military origins.

The watch face features oversized sans serif numerals in keeping with the design aesthetic of the time. With the addition of a device that protects the hand-winding crown, the watch could descend to a depth of 200 m (656 ft). In 1949, the patent was approved for Luminor – a luminous substance based on tritium that replaced radiomir – which allowed the dial of the watch to be read in absolute darkness. Fifty years after the watch was developed exclusively for the navy, the Luminor Base was reissued for limited-edition retail, opening the market for this deft balance of Italian styling and Swiss technology.

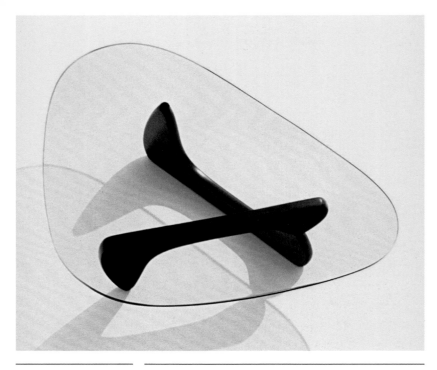

COFFEE TABLE
IN50 (1944)
Isamu Noguchi
(1904–88)
Herman Miller
1947 to 1973,
1984 to present
Vitra Design
Museum
2001 to present

The base of Coffee Table IN50 consists of two identical asymmetrical shapes, one inverted and glued to the other, arranged to form a steady three-sided leg structure. A glass top of a loosely triangular shape sits directly on this configuration. The result is a symmetrical structure with the appearance of a dynamic and asymmetrical form. The table is a striking example of the organic design being promoted in the United States in the early 1940s, yet the formal asymmetry also shows Isamu Noguchi's cultural heritage; much of the Japanese tradition in painting, ceramics and garden design emphasizes asymmetrical balance and carefully considered naturalness. In 1949, 631 tables were produced. From 1962 to 1970 the table was given a plate glass top and a base of solid walnut or ebony-finished poplar. The glass was originally 2.2 cm (0.87 in) thick, but was reduced to 1.9 cm (0.75 in) after 1965. A distinctive product at an accessible cost, the table proved to be very popular and was quickly established as an enduring icon of the period. In 2003, Herman Miller added Noguchi's signature to the table, because of the rapid increase of imitations.

1006 NAVY CHAIR (1944)
US Navy
Engineering Team
Emeco Design Team
Alcoa Design Team
Emeco
1944 to present

The 1006 Navy Chair's distinctive form and character arise from the wartime conditions surrounding its development. Emeco (Electric Machine and Equipment Company) was founded in 1944 by Wilton C Dinges, a master tool-and-die maker with an engineering background. He collaborated with the aluminium industry and naval engineers to create this chair for the US Navy. Aluminium was chosen because it is light and strong, easy to transport, durable in heavy use, resistant to corrosion and non-flammable – an essential consideration on board ship. The use of a single material predicts developments in moulded plastics

some twenty years later. However, whereas plastic chairs can be made in single mouldings, up to seventy-seven processes are required to weld, shape and finish the 1006 Navy Chair. Its appearance has sometimes been described as 'neutral', but this has ensured that it has become a classic piece of twentieth-century design. From the basic model, Emeco has developed a family of high chairs, stools and chairs with swivel bases and even upholstery. In 2000, Emeco began production of the Hudson Chair designed by Philippe Starck, an homage to the original 1006 by one of the best contemporary designers.

THREE-LEGGED CYLINDER LAMP (1944)
Isamu Noguchi
(1904–88)
Knoll 1944 to 1954
Vitra Design Museum
2001 (now ceased)

Isamu Noguchi's artistic vision combined Japanese cultural traditions with a strong Western Modernist idiom. He moved fluidly between the worlds of fine art and design, exhibiting in top New York galleries and international museums, while also designing for prominent companies, such as Knoll and Herman Miller. An early Three-Legged Cylinder Lamp design for Knoll in the 1940s was the precursor to a series of lighted sculptures Noguchi called 'lunars'. He first conceived of an illuminated sculpture in his Musical Weathervane of 1933. Initially using magnesite, Noguchi moulded organic forms over

electric light sources. These were eventually developed into lighting fixtures. The first example of the Cylinder Lamp was a gift made for his sister. It was constructed from opaque aluminium and had a paper shade. Knoll put the design into production in 1944, replacing the aluminium legs with cherry-wood and the paper with translucent plastic. The use of three legs and organic forms runs through many of Noguchi's pieces, such as Coffee Table IN50 (1944) and Prismatic Table (1957). Knoll stopped production of the Three-Legged Cylinder Lamp but it was reissued by Vitra Design Museum in 2001.

LCW CHAIR (1945)
Charles Eames
(1907–78)
Evans Products
1945 to 1946
Herman Miller
1946 to present
Vitra 1958 to present

In 1941, New York's Museum of Modern Art hosted a design competition entitled 'Organic Design in Home Furnishings'. Charles Eames and Eero Saarinen's prize-winning Organic Chair comprised a plywood shell form integrating seat, back and side. Although formally advanced it was technically difficult and expensive to produce. Eames, however, pursued three-dimensional moulded ply further to combine material economy with contoured comfort. In the end, his solution resulted from breaking the problem down into simpler parts and generated the LCW (Lounge Chair Wood) design of 1945. The

back, seat and leg frames are separate components linked by a third element. The connection between each component was mediated through elastic rubber shock mounts providing resilience. Breaking the chair into discrete components offered other possibilities and generated the LCM (Lounge Chair Metal) using the same LCW seat and back elements but, in this instance, mounted on to a welded steel frame. The LCW is a mid-century high point in furniture design, delivering organic, ergonomic comfort with visual lightness and economic viability.

TUPPERWARE
(1945)
Earl Silas Tupper
(1907–83)
Tupperware
1945 to present

Tupperware boxes, the pastel-coloured, soft plastic containers found in kitchens around the world, revolutionized lunchbox culture and food storage. New Hampshire-born Earl Silas Tupper worked as a chemist for DuPont in the 1930s. In the early 1940s, he heard of a new thermoplastic, polyethylene, that was soft and flexible at room temperature. Tupper worked with DuPont to produce a finer version of the plastic which he grandly called 'Poly T – Material of the Future.' He also developed a new injection moulding process in order to make products out of it. In 1945, Tupper Plastics launched its range of food containers. Ingeniously, the patented lid rim formed an airtight seal – as the lid was pressed down, it caused negative air pressure inside the container and thus the external atmospheric pressure kept the seal tight. Tupper was not only a great inventor, but also a great salesman. In 1951 he withdrew all Tupperware products from stores and began to sell them exclusively through gatherings held in customers' homes – the Tupperware Party was born. Tupper sold his company to the Rexall drug conglomerate in 1958, and retired to Costa Rica as a multimillionaire.

BA CHAIR (1945)
Ernest Race
(1913–64)
Race Furniture
1945 to present

The BA Chair occupies a unique place in British design of the late 1940s. Its innovation and style were symbolic of a new spirit in furniture design. The shortage of traditional furniture-making materials in post-war Britain motivated Ernest Race to design the BA Chair using cast recycled aluminium, which allowed mass production without the need for traditional skilled labour. The chair is made from five cast aluminium components, with the addition of two aluminium sheets for the back and seat. The seat was initially finished with rubberized padding covered with a cotton duck fabric. The legs

have a tapered T-section, giving them strength with minimal material use. Originally, the components were sand cast, but after 1946 a pressure die-cast technique was used which reduced materials and cost. From the outset the chair was available both with and without arms, and after 1947, as wood became more plentiful, mahogany, birch and walnut veneer finishes were introduced. Race was awarded the gold medal at the Milan Triennale for the BA Chair in 1954. Used in many public buildings throughout the 1950s, the chair is still in production, with in excess of 250,000 made to date.

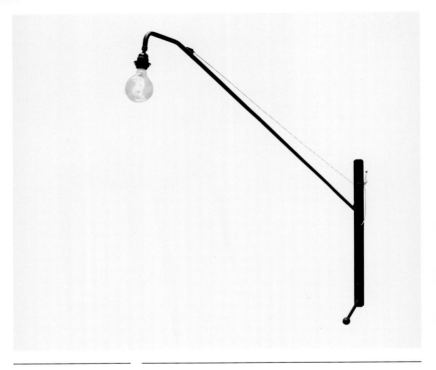

POTENCE LAMP
(c.1945)
Jean Prouvé
(1901–84)
Ateliers Jean Prouvé
c.1945 to 1956
Vitra 2002 to present

The pure, stripped-down elegance of the Potence Lamp has made it one of Jean Prouvé's emblematic works. The French architect originally designed it for his Maison Tropicale, an experiment in prefabricated housing, and it has all the qualities such a project would require. Consisting of little more than a metal rod, which extends approximately 2.25 m (7 ft), a light bulb and a wall-mounted bracket, the lamp can be rotated to cover a 180 degree arc. In addition to being simple and practical, the lamp does not take up valuable floor space or require electrical wiring through the ceiling. Prouvé had originally trained as a

blacksmith, and the sensitivity he developed is evident in the material elegance of his lamp. The perfect engineering in the lamp's bracket and wire support make this a sculptural object worth marvelling at. Prouvé's reputation was for a time overshadowed by that of Le Corbusier and his circle, but he returned to a more public prominence in 2002, when a number of his designs, including the Potence Lamp, were reissued by Vitra, and he became justly recognized internationally as one of the great designers of the twentieth century.

BOMBÉ TEA AND COFFEE SERVICE (1945)
Carlo Alessi (1916–)
Alessi 1945 to present

In many ways the Bombé Tea and Coffee Service can be seen as a symbol of the history of Alessi production. The service was designed by Carlo Alessi, who joined the company following studies as an industrial designer in Novara. He became general manager of the company in the 1930s and was responsible for designing most of the objects produced between the mid-1930s and 1945. In 1945 he launched his final project: the Bombé Tea and Coffee Service, which helped to establish the company's reputation for producing modern and innovative products. The enduring design, produced in four different sizes, is an unashamedly industrial product. It displays a purity of form that pays homage to modern design history. The service has clearly been inspired by the simple geometric forms and lack of adornment that characterize works by earlier designers. It was originally made from silver-plated and chrome-plated brass and has been produced in stainless steel since 1965. At the time of its production it was unashamedly modern and now sits comfortably alongside new designs. It is still one of the most successful tea and coffee sets sold by Alessi.

VARIO TOASTER (1946)
Max Gort-Barten
(1914–2003)
Dualit
1946 to present

The Vario Toaster, with its coolly functional modern styling, was the essential kitchen accessory in the 1980s. First designed in 1946, it has been harnessed to the cause of millennial Minimalism and retro home styling. Max Gort-Barten, the designer of the Vario Toaster, was primarily an engineer, which explains its innovative mode of function as well as its machine aesthetic. The first product he invented was the Dual-Light Fire, the manoeuvrable electric heater with a double element that gave the Dualit company its name. The key to the success of the toaster's design is the 'stay-warm' premise, the toast being cooked for a specified period by setting a time switch and then manually ejected rather than being automatically 'popped.' This allows the toast to be kept warm inside the machine, a concept that became hugely popular. Dualit responded to the surge in demand by keeping the clean-lined styling of its classic model but introducing chrome finishes and unbreakable elements that incorporated the same heatproof material used in the space shuttle. Each Dualit Vario Toaster is assembled by hand and includes the assembler's individual mark on the base plate.

PLATFORM BENCH (1946)
George Nelson
(1908–86)
Herman Miller
1946 to 1967,
1994 to present
Vitra 2002 to present

The strong architectural form of George Nelson's Platform Bench is a reflection of the post-war ethos promoted by American creative endeavour. North American designers in the 1940s began to enthusiastically embrace the philosophical and aesthetic tenets of European Modernism and uphold them as models for everyday living. Nelson joined Herman Miller in 1946 as director of design, and his Platform Bench was introduced in that same year. It was a flexible and useful piece of furniture, designed to accommodate both people and objects. Its purpose was not ambiguous, but rather it followed a Modernist

design imperative aligning function to form. Constructed in maple with metal levelling glides and strengthened by finger-jointed, ebonized legs, the rectilinear bench top is a plane of slats, purposely spaced to allow both light and air to pass through, expressing both transparency and elegance. The bench was part of Nelson's first collection for Herman Miller, and by 1955 it had proved to be one of the firm's most flexible and useful pieces. It was reintroduced in 1994, and its enduring legacy as an important piece of post-war furniture is a testament to the prophetic vision of its designer.

EAMES SCREEN (1946)
Charles Eames
(1907–78)
Ray Eames (1912–88)
Herman Miller
1946 to 1955,
1994 to present
Vitra 1990 to 2019

The folding screen that Charles and Ray Eames designed for Herman Miller in 1946 was an adaptation of a similar screen designed in Finland in the late 1930s by Alvar Aalto, made of flat strips of pine connected by canvas 'hinges.' The Eameses adapted Aalto's idea into something more practical, flexible and elegant. They widened the strips to 22.5 cm (9 in), used plywood moulded into a U-shape and then connected the strips of ply with full-length canvas hinges. These innovations gave the screen much greater stability. The screen could be folded up easily for shipping, carriage and storage, with each U-shape acting as a receptacle for its neighbour. The production process involved a lot of hand labour and considerably reduced the product's potential for mass production. Production ceased in 1955, but the Eames Screen was later reintroduced using a polypropylene mesh without compromising the integrity of the 1946 design. The Screen is the perfect example of an unselfconscious piece of practical design that allows room for personal statement, fitting Charles and Ray Eames's belief that anyone and everyone could, and indeed should, be an architect or a designer.

FREEFORM SOFA (1946)
Isamu Noguchi
(1904–88)
Herman Miller
1949 to 1951
Vitra Design Museum
2002 to present

Japanese-American sculptor-designer Isamu Noguchi's predilection for biomorphic language is well represented in his 1946 Freeform Sofa. His sculptural background informs the fluid shape of the piece, which looks as though it is made from two large, flat stones, yet has a dynamic, light appearance. The thin cushion and ottoman ensure comfort. Freeform is upholstered in wool and supported by a beechwood frame with maple feet. In all his design work, Noguchi combined a knowledge of contemporary sculptural forms with a mastery of technical skills. An assistant of Constantin Brancusi in 1927 and

an admirer of Alexander Calder, Noguchi drew on these influences in his work. As a sculptor, Noguchi was interested in materials and shapes as well as their interaction with space. He believed that every-day objects should be perceived as sculptures with a functional value, or 'things for everyone's pleasure.' The Freeform design, radically different from his other works of the time, was produced for only a few years and in small quantities by manufacturer Herman Miller, making the original a highly collectable piece. Vitra, in collaboration with the Isamu Noguchi Foundation, reissued the Freeform Sofa in 2002.

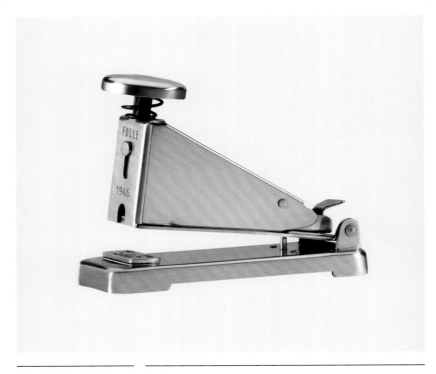

FOLLE CLASSIC STAPLER (1946)
Folmer Christensen
(1911–70)
Folle 1946 to present

When it was first produced, the Folle Classic Stapler so transcended the limits of its function that it was stocked by exclusive furniture stores as well as office-supply shops. Designed by Folmer Christensen, it was first produced in 1946 by Folle, a company that Christensen founded in the town of Vanløse. Instead of articulating the crocodile-like snapping action of most desk staplers, the Folle, with its large polished steel button, has been designed to perform a simple downward action. It is constructed of simple sheet steel beneath which is a more complex design based

around four spring mechanisms. The most obvious of these is coiled beneath the button; others allow the user to open the stapler head and select between settings that cause the staples to close either inwards or outwards. The classic 1946 Folle Classic Stapler is still manufactured using the original machines and tools, along with a number of variations, including a long-arm version and a side stapler for binding magazines. They are so sturdy, with a weight of approximately 290 g (10.22 oz), many retailers boast that the groove at the stapler's base can be used as a bottle opener.

BALL CLOCK (1947)
Irving Harper (1917–)
George Nelson
Associates
Howard Miller Clock
Company 1948 to 1952
Vitra Design Museum
1999 to present

Designed in 1947 and produced by the Howard Miller Clock Company, the Atomic or Ball Clock became an icon of the 1950s. Its original version featured a brass central hub, painted red, from which radiated twelve brass spokes terminated by red-painted wooden balls. Its black hands are punctuated by geometric forms: a triangle for the hour, an ellipse for minutes. Its design has been seen to represent an atom's structure, as though it was an effort to pacify nuclear energy. Lacking numbers, it reflects a metaphysical state in which time passes without reference.

Whether this was the designer's intention is questionable, as is whether Irving Harper even designed it. In *The Design of Modern Design*, Nelson denies that he or Harper designed the clock. He recalls that the design appeared on a roll of paper covered with drawings by Harper, Buckminster Fuller, Isamu Noguchi and himself, made during a night of too much drinking. Nelson contends that the drawings bear the signs of Noguchi, but the key attribution is given to Harper. Reissued by Vitra Design Museum, this clock is available in white, natural beech and multicoloured versions.

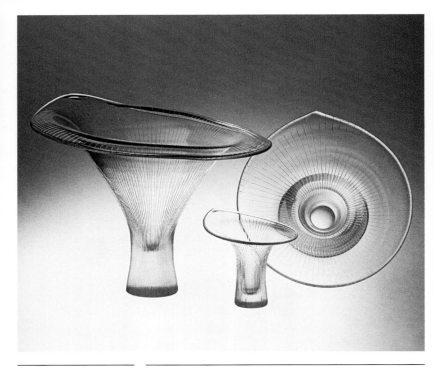

KANTARELLI VASE (1947)
Tapio Wirkkala
(1915–85)
iittala 1947 to present

Tapio Wirkkala's trumpet-shaped Kantarelli Vase, which gets its name and basic shape from a woodland fungi, was his entry for a competition by the Finnish glass-making firm iittala. The original model, in clear glass with a gently undulating and curled lip, carefully engraved with splaying vertical lines, was produced only in two short series of about fifty models each. A modified design, with a more regular lip that could be wheel-engraved, was conceived for serial production. It was not until the early 1950s, when both versions were included in a series of travelling exhibitions of Finnish design, that the Kantarelli began to attract international recognition. Since then the vase has become one of the most frequently illustrated pieces of Finnish design. Commentators have often remarked approvingly about the sculptural qualities of the piece, especially the flowing sense of balance that Wirkkala achieved between the undulating horizontal lip and the engraved vertical lines inspired by the gills of the fungus that enhance the waisted stem. Others have drawn comparison between the clarity of the glass and the frozen lakes of the Finnish winter.

WOMB CHAIR (1947)
Eero Saarinen
(1910–61)
Knoll 1948 to present

The Womb Chair, launched onto the American market in 1948 and in more or less continuous production ever since, represents one of the most commercially successful and popular outcomes of Eero Saarinen's experiments with organic shell-type seats. By the second half of the 1940s, Saarinen had begun to move away from the use of plywood, testing glass-fibre reinforced synthetic plastics, as used in his Womb Chair. In order to keep the design as light as possible the shell seat was supported on a frame with thin metal rod legs and given a slim but sufficient layer of padding for comfort. Saarinen

paid considerable attention to comfortable seating positions when working on his designs. He emphasized that people sat in many different ways and developed the form of his chair to allow people to draw their legs up on the seat, to slouch and to lounge. In this way, the Womb Chair was created as a modern chair for a modern way of living. But it was also a chair with an enfolding, comforting and cloak-like seat that allowed users a little space to withdraw and shelter themselves from the modern world.

MUSEUM WATCH (1947)
Nathan George
Horwitt (1889–1990)
Movado Group
1961 to present

Nathan George Horwitt was a Russian immigrant who settled in New York City in the 1930s and developed a range of products, including radios, lamps, furniture, refrigerators and digital clocks. His 1939 Cyclox design was the initial inspiration for a watch face devoid of any articulation save a gold dot at the top of a circular field, signifying 12:00, and thin, linear minute and hour hands endlessly dividing the orb geometrically. Horwitt considered the design as equal, in its essential nature, to the sundial. He had three prototypes made, one of which was accepted into the permanent collection of New York's Museum of Modern Art. Manufacturers remained unwilling to take on Horwitt's watch until 1961, when Movado decided to produce the timepiece in limited editions. Exploiting its exhibition in MoMA, the watch was dubbed the 'Museum Watch.' Initially Horwitt's watch face was applied to Movado's standard programme, but it was eventually given a flat, manually-wound movement, Calibre 245/246, in keeping with Horwitt's concept of the watch casing. Ironically, the watch that took nearly two decades to make its way onto the market has defined Movado's reputation.

PEACOCK CHAIR (1947)

Hans Wegner
(1914–2007)
Johannes Hansen
1947 to 1991
PP Møbler
1991 to present

The Peacock Chair was first shown as part of the 'Living Room for a Young Family' at the 1947 Cabinetmakers' Exhibition in Copenhagen. It is based on the English Windsor chair, one of the standard designs in the history of wooden furniture. Hans Wegner launched a number of spindle-back chairs inspired by the Windsor, often with a unique feature. For example, the Peacock Chair features distinctive back slats, which give the design its name. Wegner's ability to draw on historical reference is evident in the chair, which represents the Danish Modernist tradition of fusing time-honoured craft techniques with natural materials. Wegner developed a philosophy of 'stripping the old chairs of their outer style and letting them appear in their pure construction of four legs, a seat and combined top rail and armrest.' In 1943 he opened his own design office and since then designed more than 500 pieces of furniture. The Peacock Chair was originally produced by Johannes Hansen and has been produced since 1991 by PP Møbler, now the largest manufacturer of Wegner's furniture. It is available in solid ash with a laminated hoop and a choice of teak or ash arms.

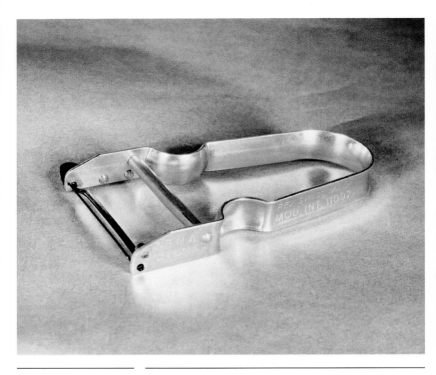

REX VEGETABLE PEELER (1947)
Alfred Neweczerzal
(1899–1958)
ZENA
1947 to present

For such a simple and unassuming object, the Rex Vegetable Peeler is a masterpiece of innovation, reduction and quality. The peeler is made from only six parts: an aluminium strip, 13 mm (0.5 in) wide and 1 mm (0.04 in) thick, is bent into a horseshoe shape with generous indents for thumb and forefinger; an innovative swivel blade is punched from sheet steel, a crossbar holds the utensil together and a potato-eye remover is riveted to the side. The remaining two parts are fixings. Designer Alfred Neweczerzal worked in partnership with businessman Engros Zweifel, and in 1931 they began manufacturing the peeler

with a mechanical die-cutting machine. In 1947 a patent was registered for the Rex and in the following year the company became known as ZENA-produkte (an acronym of the inventors' names). The Rex is still produced by the company, now known as ZENA, and duly sells 3 million pieces a year. Since 1984, the peeler has been available in plastic as well as in stainless steel. The peeler has been known to last thirty years in some households, although many meet their demise much earlier by accidentally ending up on the compost heap.

AARNE GLASSWARE (1948)
Göran Hongell
(1902–73)
iittala 1948 to present

Aarne Glassware, with its pure, minimalist lines, was designed by Göran Hongell. Primarily a decorative glass artist, he trained in the glassworks of Karhula and began working with Finnish glass manufacturer iittala after World War II. Today he is considered one of the pioneers of Finnish glassmaking. The glassware set consists of ten pieces, including eight different glasses (such as a pilsner, double old-fashioned, martini, cordial, old-fashioned universal, and champagne glass), pitcher and ice bucket, in various sizes, from the 5 cl shot glass to the 150 cl pitcher. The variations use the same basic profile: a thick, circular glass base, with a receptacle with straight glass sides that diverge from bottom to top. The glasses made their film debut in Alfred Hitchcock's The Birds (1963), in a scene in which Tippi Hedren elegantly drank a martini. This hand-turned and moulded-blown glassware set a trend for minimal design during the 1950s. The set was an instant success for Hongell and for iittala, winning the gold medal at the Milan Triennale in 1954. Aarne was chosen as iittala's symbol to mark the company's centenary in 1981, as it remains the company's best-selling glassware.

COMPAS DESK
(1948)
Jean Prouvé
(1901–84)
Ateliers Jean Prouvé
1948 to 1956
Galerie Steph Simon
1956 to 1965
Vitra 2003 to present

Jean Prouvé did not separate design from production, or architecture from furniture. The economy of materials, the means of assembly and the visibility of structure appear regardless of form or scale. Prouvé used materials appropriated from the automotive and aviation industries to create pieces that were affordable and easily mass-produced. The Compas Desk, with its namesake base, is an elegant illustration of his work. Built at his Maxéville factory, the structure is exposed, self-evident and in constant tension. The laminated-wood desk sits atop welded sheet-metal components made

using a folder-press, and initially finished with car body paint. The desk appeared in various versions over the years and occasionally came with a set of plastic drawers designed by Charlotte Perriand. The desk's production and elegantly bent metal was rooted in heavy industry. Its compass imagery surfaces on other Prouvé works: the veranda of the Sécurité Sociale Building, the interior of the École de Villejuif and the refreshment bar in Évian. The ease and versatility of the solution illustrates a vision of construction that needed only material, structure and assembly to create beauty independent of scale.

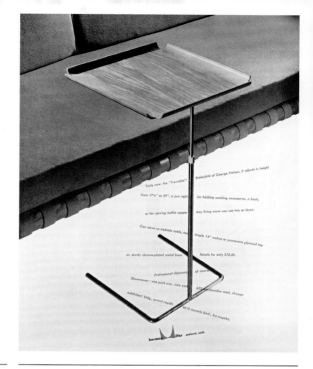

**TRAY TABLE
MODEL 4950 (1948)**
George Nelson
(1908–86)
Herman Miller
1949 to 1956,
2000 to 2004
Vitra Design Museum
2002 to 2016

George Nelson's Tray Table Model 4950 looks more like a product from the Bauhaus than an American product of the 1940s. In the early 1930s, Nelson had spurned what he saw as the shallow hypocrisy of American stylists such as Raymond Loewy, and travelled to Europe to immerse himself in the Modernist movement. The tray table's lineage can clearly be traced to the tubular steel furniture of the likes of Marcel Breuer and Eileen Gray. A tray table in name alone – as its square, moulded plywood surface is not removable – the piece adjusts in height via a metal collet that holds the two yokes of the steel frame

together. This adjustability, along with the offset stem, gives the piece considerable versatility as a bedside or sofa side table, enabling the surface to be positioned over the user's lap. The piece remained in production with Herman Miller for only seven years from 1949, but in 2002 Vitra Design Museum re-released the table using models and drawings supplied by Nelson's archive in New York. Herman Miller also resumed the production of the tray table in 2000.

DAR (1948)
Charles Eames
(1907–78)
Ray Eames (1912–88)
Herman Miller
1950 to present
Vitra 1958 to present

Charles and Ray Eames's pro-phetic dining chair, DAR, or Dining Armchair Rod, was a revolutionary piece of design that altered ideas about furniture form and construction. Built entirely with industrial materials and processes, the moulded, reinforced polyester seat is supported by a metal-rod base. The success of the chair's construction, which allowed for full mass production, was the result of Charles's previous research into new materials. In 1948, he entered the Museum of Modern Art's 'International Competition for Low-Cost Furniture Design' with a second-prize-winning proposal for chairs made from fibreglass –

the promising new synthetic material set to replace moulded plywood in furniture production. Herman Miller produced a number of his competition designs, and the DAR, one of the initial produc-tion pieces, anticipated the in-novative partnership the Eameses were to have with the company over the next two decades. The DAR embodies Modernism's mass-production intent: the universal seat shell, interchange-able with a range of bases, allowed for a number of variations. It was a clear articulation of the couple's intention 'to get the most of the best to the greatest number of people for the least.'

TUBINO LAMP (1948)

Achille Castiglioni
(1918–2002)
Pier Giacomo
Castiglioni (1913–68)
Arredoluce
1949 to 1974
Flos 1974 to 1999
Habitat
1999 to c.2013

Achille and Pier Giacomo Castiglioni's Tubino Lamp, or 'little tube', is that rare piece of design: an aesthetically appealing product that exploits technological breakthrough and captures the spirit of an era. In the United States, General Electric had just developed a small, 6-watt fluorescent tube. On its arrival in Italy, the Castiglionis went to work creating a metaphor for this cost-effective utilitarian product. The result was a minimalist design that stripped away unnecessary decoration and material to illustrate the workings of illuminated light in a bold, flexible form. Using industrial materials such as metal tubing, enamelled metal and aluminium, the Milanese brothers simply took one of the new bulbs and set it next to the switch and the reactor, which was joined to the starter. An aluminium plate behind the lamp reduced glare and reflected the light. The exposed linear design, as the Castiglionis said, 'subordinated the fixture itself to the effects of light it produces.' Manufactured by Arredoluce, then Flos, and Habitat, the Tubino remains a great example of the Castiglionis' belief that design must restructure an object's form and production process.

PP 512 FOLDING CHAIR (1949)
Hans Wegner
(1914–2007)
Johannes Hansen
1949 to 1991
PP Møbler
1991 to present

Hans Wegner was instrumental in shaping twentieth-century Danish design with his exquisitely refined furniture, of which the PP 512 Folding Chair is a prime example. The son of a master cobbler and himself a cabinetmaker, Wegner was steeped in the handicraft traditions of his native Denmark. As a result his furniture was characterized by high-quality craftsmanship and by an instinctual and sensual response to his chosen materials – principally wood. The PP 512 Folding Chair, articulated in oak with a woven cane back and seat, is lower and wider than most other folding chairs. Yet despite being low slung and having no arm rails, it is noted for its comfort and how easy it is to get in and out of. The PP 512 comes with two little handles on the seat front and a bespoke wooden wall-hanging hook – a unique feature according to current manufacturer PP Møbler. Almost Shaker-like in its simplicity, the PP 512 was designed in 1949 for Johannes Hansen's Møbelsnedkeri, or cabinetmaker's workshop. The enduring popularity of the PP 512 Chair has ensured its uninterrupted production since 1949, both in its original oak form and in ash.

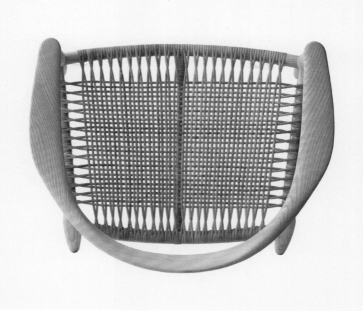

PP 501 THE CHAIR (1949)
Hans Wegner
(1914–2007)
Johannes Hansen
1949 to 1991
PP Møbler
1991 to present

Hans Wegner said that design is 'a continuous process of purification, and simplification'. His The Chair is the result of gradual refinement, rather than innovation. It can be seen as a distillation of his Y Chair CH 24 (1949), which in turn was inspired by chairs of the Ming dynasty. In early versions, the top rail (back) of the chair was covered with cane. This was not only a response to the woven cane seat, but also to hide the joints between the arms and the back. Wegner later used a W-shaped finger joint to join the parts, which requires great skill to produce. Because of this he decided to show off the joint, and the cane coverings were removed. This idea of displaying the joint was a turning point for Wegner, and he designed many chairs based on this idea, with the beautiful joint becoming a signature feature. The Chair has been produced in a number of versions, including one with a woven cane seat and a leather upholstered seat. Now produced by the Danish company PP Møbler, it remains a favourite of contemporary designers and architects.

FAZZOLETTO VASE (1949)

Fulvio Bianconi
(1915–96)
Paolo Venini
(1895–1959)
Venini
1949 to present

Fulvio Bianconi's Fazzoletto (Handkerchief) Vase is a variation of Piero Chiesa's 1935 Cartoccio Vase. Bianconi's vase differed in its asymmetrical tips, created by spinning molten glass and leaving gravity to form random peaks. What started as a globe changed into a fluttering freeform in space, as if a lace handkerchief were taken up by the wind. The vase is produced in three variations. The most common Lattimo model is a milky-coloured white glass, which has an opacity created by micro-crystals that reflect incoming light. The A Canne model derives its name from a thin, heated rod that allows the molten glass to be drawn out in extremely long pipes, whereby coloured glass is laid over an opaque base. For the Zanfirico model, two glassmakers attach metal rods to the ends of the molten mass and draw it out, rotate it and twist it to create a spiral shape. The Fazzoletto Vase quickly became one of the most popular of Venini's products and was sold internationally in two sizes: 35 cm (14 in) and 27.5 cm (11 in). It has been in production for decades and has become an icon of 1950s Italian glass making.

**Y CHAIR CH 24
(1949)**
Hans Wegner
(1914–2007)
Carl Hansen & Søn
1950 to present

Inspired by portraits of merchants seated in Chinese chairs, Danish furniture designer Hans Wegner made a series of articulate contributions to the dialogue between East and West. In 1943, Wegner designed the Chinese Chair, which used as its points of departure chairs of the Ming Dynasty, the Modernist quest for structural simplification and Scandinavian reverence for material integrity. The chair became the basis for many future pieces, at least nine of which Wegner designed for Fritz Hansen. The Y Chair CH 24, designed in 1949, differed significantly from the earlier pieces that used substantial rectangular rail and seat structure. In the Y Chair, round front and back rails, as well as rectangular side rails that impede racking, were used between round legs and a seat structure of round rails and woven paper cord. Back oak legs angle inward then gracefully make double curves to join the shaped arc of the back's top rail. Distinguishing this chair and providing its name is the distinctive Y-shaped, flat back splat. The total effect is a lightweight, elegant, durable and a refined piece of furniture, rooted in Eastern and Western tradition but conceived for contemporary manufacturing techniques.

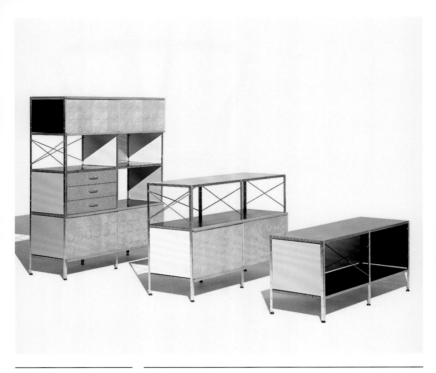

**EAMES STORAGE
UNIT (1950)**
Charles Eames
(1907–78)
Ray Eames (1912–88)
Herman Miller
1950 to 1955,
1998 to present
Vitra 2004 to present

The Eames Storage Unit was conceived as a kit of parts. First the upright supports, made from L-section steel bars painted black in five different lengths. Next horizontal shelves in lacquered plywood. Finally, vertical panels forming backs and sides in several materials including embossed plywood, perforated metal and Masonite in a range of finishes and colours. There were also sliding doors, drawers and wire X-frame braces. A huge variety of arrangements could be assembled from this collection of elements. By making discrete components interchangeable the Eameses were able to provide the potential

for bespoke cabinets from mass-produced parts. The unit's flexibility followed, on a more intimate scale, the principles of 'Case Study House No. 8' – the Eameses' own home built in 1949. ESU was produced by Herman Miller in 1950 but withdrawn in 1955, and then re-introduced in 1998. The promise of flexible function and construction turned out to be more alluring to designer and manufacturer than to the customer of the time. Yet ESU has been significant in its exploration of modularity, spawning many subsequent, though less richly idiosyncratic, storage facilities for both the office and the domestic market.

FIXPENCIL 2 (1950)
Caran d'Ache
Design Team
Caran d'Ache
1950 to present

In 1924, Caran d'Ache was a small pencil factory in Geneva, Switzerland. Today, the name is a byword for fine quality drawing and art materials. Its reputation is built on the back of product innovation, of which the Fixpencil design has proved the most influential. The Fixpencil 2, designed in 1950, is an updated version of the original of 1929. It benefits for subtle changes to its precursor, such as the slim, hexagonal, all-metal black shaft housing the lead, the push-button mechanism mounted on the top end of the pencil and a clip added to the shaft just below the push-button. When Caran d'Ache bought the patent for a spring-loaded mechanical clutch pencil from the Geneva-based designer Carlo Schmid in 1929, it established a benchmark against which all others would be measured. The updated Fixpencil 2 allowed for even greater control, due to its new lightweight shaft. Caran d'Ache has further developed the pencil to include lead diameters ranging from 0.5 to 3 mm (0.02 to 0.12 in), as well as launching an inexpensive plastic model. Fixpencil 2 remains a common sight in offices and homes, and is exported around the world.

MARGHERITA CHAIR (1950)
Franco Albini
(1905–77)
Vittorio Bonacina
1951 to present

The Margherita Chair is part of a group of designs by Franco Albini from the early 1950s that combines traditional techniques with modern beauty. The chair's form is resolutely of its period and relates to contemporary experiments by Eero Saarinen, Charles and Ray Eames and others. Whereas his peers may have experimented with plastics, fibreglass and advanced plywood mouldings to produce the bucket form resting on a pedestal base, Albini chose rattan and Indian cane – easily worked and readily available materials. In the years immediately after World War II traditional craft skills like basket making were more available to Italian designers than technological processes like moulding plastics. This was one reason why Albini chose cane for his designs. The cane structure of the Margherita Chair, like the wire furniture by Harry Bertoia, is dematerialized, its volume reduced by its transparency. It is almost as if Albini only designed the frame without the upholstery. Albini's architecture and furniture designs are regarded as fine examples of Rationalism, a particular strand of mid-century Italian Modernism. They often demonstrate a sensitive use of materials and a carefully thought-through approach to manufacture.

ARABESQUE TABLE (1950)
Carlo Mollino
(1905–73)
Apelli & Varesio
c.1950s to 1960
Zanotta
1998 to present

Turin-born designer and architect Carlo Mollino had a love for sensuous shapes that is reflected in his Arabesque Table. The table has an undulating form with an upper and lower glass surface supported by a cascading frame of moulded plywood, which is bent to form a magazine rack. It was designed for the living room of one of Mollino's commissioned interiors, Casa Oregno, and was also used in his Singer Store, both in Turin. The Arabesque Table has been described as a 'cocoon of lovers perched on four insect legs.' The shape of the glass top is believed to be taken from a Surrealist drawing of a woman's back by Leonor Fini, while the wooden frame makes reference to the sculpture of Jean Arp. Mollino embraced decoration and sensuality, and was inspired by Art Nouveau and the work of Antoni Gaudí, as well as by natural and human shapes. He produced pieces that were more sculptural than functional. Indeed, very few of his pieces made it into production, and were instead one-off designs or part of interior projects and bespoke commissions. The Arabesque is one of the few Mollino pieces by Zanotta available today.

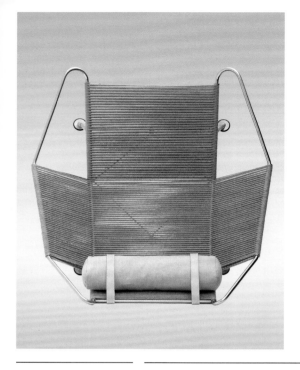

FLAG HALYARD
CHAIR (1950)
Hans Wegner
(1914–2007)
Getama 1950 to 1994
PP Møbler
2002 to present

The unlikely combination of rope, painted and chrome-plated steel, sheepskin and linen in Hans Wegner's Flag Halyard Chair are unprecedented in furniture manufacture. Wegner's motivation in using such contrasting materials was not to exploit their textural interplay but more simply to demonstrate his ability to design innovative, practical and comfortable furniture in any material. At the time Wegner created this design, he had been experimenting with chairs made from plywood shells supported on metal frames. The origin for replacing the plywood with a metal frame strung with rope

is not clear. But there is an apocryphal story that Wegner conceived this design whilst on the beach near Aarhus: he supposedly modelled the grid-like seat in a sand dune, presumably with some old rope that lay close to hand. (A 'halyard' is a line which hoists or covers a sail.) Since the chair is often used as an advertisement for Wegner's work, one assumes that it has always been produced on a large scale. Initially it was made by Getama in limited numbers, but was never a runaway commercial success. More recently, it has been put back into production by PP Møbler.

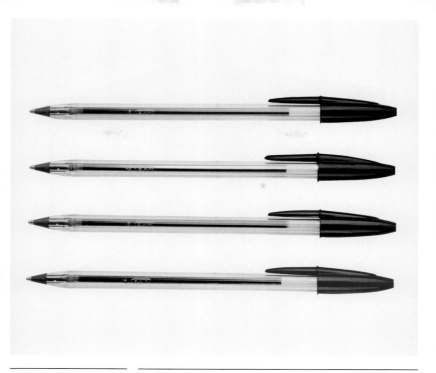

BIC® CRISTAL PEN (1950)
László Bíró
(1899–1985)
Décolletage
Plastique Design
Team
©Société Bic
1950 to present

The Bic® Cristal Pen is an iconic invention due to the genius of the ballpoint mechanism, but it is the inexpensive commodification of the pen by Bic® that has made this little scribbler one of the most indispensable and enduring products ever produced. László Bíró patented the pen in 1943. As a young journalist, he was frequently annoyed by the difficulties involved in using a fountain pen. He realized that a technique used in printing, by which a rotary cylinder ensures uniform application of ink, could be adapted for use in a pen. The design depended on precision ball bearings and special ink with the viscosity to allow smooth application without drying up. Bíró sold the patent rights to several manufacturers and governments who wanted the pen for use in pressurized cabins of military aircraft. It was French manufacturer Marcel Bich who developed an industrial process for the pens that lowered the unit cost dramatically. In 1950, Bich introduced his pens – called 'Bic', a shortened version of his name – into Europe. In recent years the pen cap has been redesigned to allow airflow through it, as a safety measure against choking if accidentally swallowed.

LTR TABLE (1950)
Charles Eames
(1907–78)
Ray Eames (1912–88)
Herman Miller
1950 to present
Vitra Design
Museum
2002 to present

The use of metal rod bases featured in much of the furniture designed by Charles and Ray Eames throughout the 1940s, and evolved into a signature style for the couple. The Eameses had developed a mass-production technique for welding wire rods in the late 1940s. The LTR small occasional table was conceived to suit this manufacturing process at a reasonable cost. The supporting structure for the plastic-laminated plywood tabletop reveals its construction with striking visual honesty. Two U-shaped metal rods are screwed to the underside of the tabletop to provide support, while thinner resistance-welded metal cross bracing provides additional stability. The edges of the table are bevelled at a twenty-degree angle to expose the top's layers of plywood, a detail in keeping with the Eameses' love of honest materials. 'The details are not details,' said Charles, 'they make the product.' The designers experimented with various surfaces such as gold leaf, silver leaf and sealed patterned papers. However, these were discarded on the grounds that they were impractical for mass production. Today, these light-weight yet durable tables are available with either an ash veneer or high-pressure laminate in black or white.

MARGRETHE BOWL (1950)
Sigvard Bernadotte
(1907–2002)
Acton Bjørn
(1910–1992)
Rosti Housewares
1950 to present

Bernadotte and Bjørn, founded in 1950 by Sigvard Bernadotte (at one time second in line to the Swedish throne) and the architect Acton Bjørn was the first industrial design consultancy in Scandinavia. The Margrethe Bowl was one of the company's first major success stories. The name 'Margrethe' poetically referred to the Danish princess, who had just been crowned. The bowls were at least partly designed by Jacob Jensen for a plastics manufacturing firm called Rosti. A design was produced making use of studies of function, hence the thin pouring lip on one side and the fuller side for the handgrip. Resistant thermoset

melamine – a material which can confront high temperatures – created the famous weight of the bowl. Margrethe was first offered to the public in 1954, in three sizes, and in white, pastel green, yellow, and blue. In 1968, the 'Tivoli colours' (olive, orange, red, and mauve), a version with a rubber ring on the base, and five bowl sizes were brought onto the market. Attempts at improving the design have failed abysmally. Over fifty years later, the Margrethe Bowls are still in production, and found in kitchens in all corners of the world.

ULMER HOCKER STOOL (1950)
Max Bill (1908–94)
Hans Gugelot
(1920–65)
Zanotta
1975 to present
Wohnbedarf Zurich
1993 to 2003
Vitra 2003 to 2009
wb form
2011 to present

Max Bill's Ulmer Hocker Stool of 1950 is a design committed to the values of pre-war Functionalism, having little affinity with its more organically conceived, avant-garde contemporaries. Constructed of ebonized wood in a simple tri-planar form and detailed only with one cylindrical, offset footrest, the stool is an articulation of geometric, architectural clarity. The context in which the stool was conceived underlines the tension of post-war German design. The Hochschule für Gestaltung – the design school at Ulm that the Swiss-born Bill co-founded in 1951 – was an important centre for design debate. Bill and his colleagues initially promoted a curriculum predicated upon a new Bauhaus model. However, by the end of the decade, Bill's philosophy was increasingly at odds with a younger generation of students and teachers, now committed to a curriculum emphasising theoretical ideologies. Bill's own work during his tenure at the school took on an extreme geometry; indeed, the severity of his designs attracted criticism that they lacked humanizing qualities. The stool continues to be produced by the Milan furniture manufacturer Zanotta, and it is now offered in varnished, layered birch or black lacquered MDF, and marketed under the name Sgabillo.

ICE CUBE TRAY
(1950)
Arthur J. Frei
(1900–71)
Inland Manufacturing
(General Motors)
1950 to 1960s
Various
1960s to present

During World War II, Inland Manufacturing Division of General Motors helped the US war effort by producing one of the most famous carbines. When the war finished, Inland resumed its original appliance accessories production, and Arthur J. Frei, an engineer at Inland since 1931, returned to his position. In 1950, Frei patented a freezing tray that was destined to become an indispensable fixture in modern households. The ice cube tray consists of a container pan, a partitioning grid and a hand lever that mechanically dislodges the ice cubes. The simplicity of this design has endured technical and material innovation and is still produced today. Although Frei's design became famous, ice cube trays were invented earlier than 1950; the first household refrigerator invented in 1914 featured an ice cube tray. Frei worked at Inland well into the 1960s and was the proud inventor of twenty-three patents for a variety of ice cube trays. The city of Dayton, Iowa, where Inland Manufacturing was based, has immortalized the ice cube tray by building a monument to it on its Inventor's River Walk, next to the Wright Flyer, pop top cans and the cash register.

WHISK (1950s)
Designer Unknown
Various
1950s to present

The whisk, as an example of good industrial design for home use, combines purity of form with economic efficiency. A series of stiff wire loops are joined at the narrow handle – usually made from stainless steel, bamboo or copper. The looping of the wires, so they cross and overlap at the base, forms a cage that maximizes the aeration of the liquid mixture and makes the whisk flexible enough that it can be pressed against the bowl sides, enabling the mixture to be thinned and separated easily. The thin cylindrical wires of the loops decrease the metal surface area and cause the liquid to flow and divide freely over the whisk. The equal weight distribution of the wires also facilitates easy stirring. Whisks are handcrafted, often using tensile-strength stainless steel wire. Each wire is soldered and sealed into the handle, making the whisk durable and preventing the mixture from entering the handle. Today, plastic versions are available for use with non-stick cookware. A combination of good performance with timeless design and cost-efficiency has ensured that the whisk remains an unchanged and much-used industrial household object.

LUISA CHAIR (1950)
Franco Albini
(1905–77)
Poggi 1950 to 2000
Cassina
2008 to present

The stark angularity of Franco Albini's Luisa Chair could lead a viewer to think that here was a minimalist who imbued his designs with the rigorous austerity of Modernism. Such thinking could not be farther from the truth. Albini's work did indeed help to herald in a style of furniture that combined the new forms of Modernism, but the beauty of his design ideas lay in their diversity and versatility. Albini designed with a range of materials, including steel wires and canvas, metal and glass, and rattan, as well as hardwoods for the Luisa. All these designs were underpinned by a sensitivity to the materials and an understanding of structure. But the key aspect of Albini's design was his enthusiastic marrying of Modernism with craft traditions. Nowhere is this more evident than in the Luisa, which displays a Spartan, Rationalist clarity combined with sensitivity to context. An elegant design whose formal, expressive lines are unimpeded by decoration, the Luisa's dramatic profile and ergonomic rigorousness demonstrate Albini's commitment to architectonics and his consistently unorthodox approach to construction and form. Produced by Poggi, the Luisa Chair won a coveted Compasso d'Oro prize in 1955.

TRAPÈZE TABLE
(1950)
Jean Prouvé
(1901–84)
Ateliers Jean Prouvé
1950
Tecta 1990 to 2000
Vitra 2002 to present

Sculptural simplicity and mass-production methods are hallmarks of Jean Prouvé's work. Both are well represented in the Trapèze Table, originally designed, like the Antony Chair, for a university campus in Antony, France. The table's name refers to the distinctive shape of its paired legs, constructed from lacquered black sheet steel and reminiscent of aircraft wings. Combined with the thick, obliquely canted edges of the black laminate tabletop, the legs emphasize the massiveness of the construction. It would be difficult to find another table in twentieth-century furniture design that summarizes industrial chic in the same way as the

Trapèze. Prouvé was a champion of affordable modern furniture and housing, and a pioneer of prefabrication. His furniture pieces reflect his architectural style, using clean, straightforward lines with an attention to techniques like electric welding and folding sheet metal. Although many of Prouvé's designs were created for French universities, their use has been adapted through the years, helping them to become enduring icons. Vitra's recent reissuing of the Trapèze Table, among other pieces, has meant that Prouvé's furniture has left the realm of the collector to return to one of mass production.

CARAFE SURCOUF (1950s)
La Rochère Design Team
Verrerie La Rochère
1950s to present

The process of aerating red wine has been well known for centuries. The bulbous form of the hand-blown Carafe Surcouf, with its elongated neck leading to a squat chamber, enables the maximum amount of air to reach the largest surface area of wine. This surprising contrast between straight neck and rounded body set the Carafe Surcouf apart from earlier decanters, and yet it was a product of pure mechanical function. The combined efficiency and modernity of the crystalline Carafe Surcouf made it the favourite decanter among both professional and amateur sommeliers. The technician

glassmakers at La Rochère decided not to create a cork, joking that the carafe was made to be emptied. The curious name for the decanter, which has an impressive capacity of 150 cl (2.6 pt) was borrowed from one of France's most distinguished vessels. At the beginning of World War II, the Surcouf was the world's largest submarine, and it featured a vast storage chamber. The comparisons of form between the French naval submarine and the decanter make for an interesting parallel. La Rochère still employs the hand-blown method of glass manufacture, which dates back to 1475.

BISLEY MULTIDRAWER CABINET (1951)
Freddy Brown
(1902–1977)
Bisley 1951 to present

One of the primary reasons for the success of the Bisley Multidrawer Cabinet is the simplicity of its design. An anonymous, almost monolithic block, it blends into any environment, making it ideal for both domestic and office use. Indeed, its seemingly uninspired appearance is the secret of its popularity. Freddy Brown was a sheet-metal worker who started a one-man car repair business in 1931. During World War II, he moved his business to Bisley in Surrey, England, and undertook various defence contracts, naming his company after its new location. In the years following the war, Bisley used its increased manufacturing capacity to produce office products. The solid and durable construction of its military products was transferred to items like the Multidrawer Cabinet which has remained one of the hallmarks of the brand. The cabinet is made of welded steel and can stand alone or support a desktop. It is available in a variety of configurations, with drawers mounted on ball-bearing slides to provide a smooth and efficient action. In 1963, Bisley ceased its car-repair activities and focused exclusively on the manufacture of steel office equipment. Today it is the largest manufacturer of office furniture in the UK.

WIRE CHAIR (1951)
Charles Eames
(1907–78)
Ray Eames (1912–88)
Herman Miller
1951 to present
Vitra 1958 to present

The influence of fine art is often considered secondary to the industrial processes and ideology of systems favoured by Charles and Ray Eames. However, in the Wire Chair, the piece's sculptural quality combines with its industrial process to achieve its landmark status. The artistic input of Ray Eames is married with Charles's engineering sensibilities to create a design of balanced values from both disciplines. The organic form offers comfort without the need for upholstery, although the chair easily accommodates seat or back pads. It is a design that may be translated via an interchangeable range of bases to suit a wide variety of applications. The most iconic of these is the 'Eiffel Tower' base, which creates a dramatic vision of fine cross-hatching of chrome or black steel. The chair used the new technology of resistance-welding. Although there is still some debate over whose design came first, Charles and Ray Eameses' chair or Harry Bertoia's mesh furniture for Knoll, the first American mechanical patent was awarded to the Eames design. The Wire Chair proved to be immediately successful and the international market for this now timeless design remains strong.

LADY ARMCHAIR
(1951)
Marco Zanuso
(1916–2001)
Arflex 1951 to 2015
Cassina
2015 to present

Marco Zanuso's Lady Armchair became an instant success when it was introduced in 1951. The chair's organic form, with its kidney-shaped armrests and its playful style, became an emblem of 1950s furniture. The armchair design featured a metal frame combined with injection-moulded polyurethane foam padding and polyester fibre with an adhesive velveteen. It employed a break-through method to join the fabric seat to the frame and an innovative reinforced elastic strap. In 1948, Pirelli opened a new division, Arflex, to design seating with foam-rubber upholstery and commissioned Zanuso to produce

its first models. His Antropus Chair came out in 1949, followed by the Lady Armchair, which won first prize at the 1951 Milan Triennale. Zanuso was able to use foam latex to sculpt forms and create visually interesting contours. Zanuso lauded the new material, 'One could revolutionize not only the system of upholstery, but also the structural manufacturing and formal potential.' Zanuso's relationship with Arflex reflects his dedication to analysing materials and techniques to maintain high quality in mass production. The Lady Armchair's embodiment of these ideals means it is still in production by Cassina today.

AKARI POD LAMP AND LIGHT SCULPTURES (1951)
Isamu Noguchi
(1904–88)
Ozeki & Co.
1952 to present
Vitra Design Museum
2001 to present

Isamu Noguchi's reinterpretation of the Japanese paper lantern is a Modernist design that has had tremendous impact in the West. Fashioned from paper handmade from the bark of the mulberry tree and a thin wooden structure, Noguchi's lamp retained the basic principles of traditional lantern manufacture, but without the customary painted decorations. The lamp was entitled 'Akari', which translates variously as 'light', 'sun' or 'moon.' From the first lamps produced in 1951, Noguchi went on to create a range of organic and geometric shapes. He designed over 100 variations of hanging, standing and floor lamps from the 1950s to the 1980s. In 1951, Noguchi visited Gifu, the Japanese manufacturing centre of traditional paper products. He was invited by the city's mayor to design a lamp for export that would help to revitalize the paper-craft industry. Sketching out his first ideas that same day, Noguchi created a fusion of sculpture with design. The Akari lights were a collaboration with the Gifu paper-lantern producers Ozeki & Co. Priced at only a few dollars (the first at around $7.50), the lamps were an inexpensive and adaptable form of Modern design that have spawned many imitators.

ANTELOPE CHAIR
(1951)
Ernest Race
(1913–64)
Race Furniture
1951 to present

With the exception of its painted plywood panel seat, the Antelope Chair is made up entirely of thin circular sections of painted steel rod, bent and welded into shape. Because of the relative uniformity of the section, the chair has the appearance of a line drawing in space. Ernest Race's design used thin, solid steel to draw a generous and organic shape and, through this linear device, produced a chair that appeared both airy and substantial. Its horn-like corners suggest the name 'Antelope.' The chair was designed for the outdoor terraces of London's Royal Festival Hall, which formed part of the Festival of Britain exhibition of 1951.

The chair was widely publicized throughout this event and came to symbolize forward thinking and optimism for design and manufacturing in Britain. Its dynamic legs ending in ball feet also reflected the popular 'atomic' imagery of molecular chemistry and nuclear physics, which were seen as progressive sciences. The chair was manufactured by Race Furniture, a company Race founded in 1946 in collaboration with engineer Noel Jordan. It was the Antelope's flamboyant image that captured the essential spirit of the period.

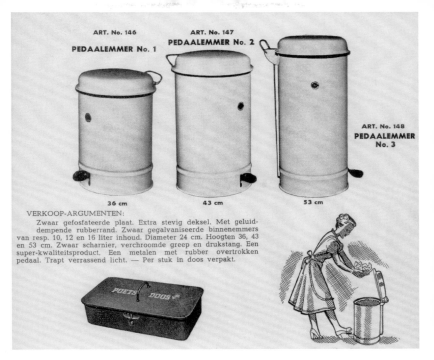

ART. No. 146
PEDAALEMMER No. 1

ART. No. 147
PEDAALEMMER No. 2

ART. No. 148
PEDAALEMMER No. 3

36 cm   43 cm   53 cm

VERKOOP-ARGUMENTEN:
    Zwaar gefosfateerde plaat. Extra stevig deksel. Met geluid-
dempende rubberrand. Zwaar gegalvaniseerde binnenemmers
van resp. 10, 12 en 16 liter inhoud. Diameter 24 cm. Hoogten 36, 43
en 53 cm. Zwaar scharnier, verchroomde greep en drukstang. Een
super-kwaliteitsproduct. Een metalen met rubber overtrokken
pedaal. Trapt verrassend licht. — Per stuk in doos verpakt.

POETS DOOS

BRABANTIA PEDAL BIN (1952)
Brabantia Design Team
Brabantia
1952 to present

It may be ubiquitous today, but the flip-top lid and pedal of the Brabantia Pedal Bin was once a novel idea. Brabantia was formed in Aalst, Netherlands, in 1919, and started out making milk sieves and watering cans. In 1930 it turned to the production of umbrella stands, and in 1947 to the first version of its wastepaper bin. The idea of developing a lid to contain odours and a pedal to prevent back strain soon provided the bedrock of Brabantia's business. As the bin incorporated metal in both sheet and wire form and needed to be corrosion-resistant, it was a far from simple process. Indeed, its difficulty is evidenced by the fact that the production process for the Brabantia Pedal Bin has been continually reworked and refined since 1952. The major changes to the design occurred in 1957 with the addition of a rim at the bottom of the bin to protect the floor and, a year later, the inclusion of a plastic inner bucket. Although today's model looks remarkably similar to the original version, it is no longer made by craftsmen in Aalst but by numerous factories around the world.

DIAMOND CHAIR
(1952)
Harry Bertoia
(1915–78)
Knoll 1952 to present

Harry Bertoia wanted to create furniture that allowed the user to sit on air. In his own words, 'If you look at these chairs, they are mainly made of air, like sculpture. Space passes through them.' The Diamond Chair accomplishes this with a seat made from steel wire floating on thin rod legs. In 1943 Bertoia accepted a position at Eames's studio and contributed to his furniture designs, particularly the Wire Chair. In 1950, after leaving Eames, Bertoia started to work full time on his sculpture, but was persuaded by his friends, Florence Knoll and her husband Hans, to create anything that he wished. The result was the 1952

Diamond Chair, one in a series of chairs and benches that Bertoia created for Knoll. It is a most improbable shape for a chair and at first sight might even seem uninviting. But once seated, the sitter is transported by Bertoia's dream of sitting on air. Using resistance-welding technology, Bertoia first bent the wires by hand and then placed them in the jig for welding. Bertoia's Diamond Chair stands as one of the finest examples of mid-century American design.

NAVITIMER (1952)
Breitling Design
Team
Breitling
1952 to present

The 1950s was an exciting period of technical advancement and growth for the aviation industry. Capitalizing fully on its well-deserved reputation among the industry's key players, the Swiss firm Breitling introduced its Navitimer chronograph in 1952. As a piece of professional equipment, the Navitimer's aesthetic is inevitably based on clarity and precision; its visual appeal lies in an air of sturdy reliability. However, what made the chronograph indispensable for pilots was its in-built 'navigation computer.' The Navitimer featured a slide rule, a working instrument that enabled the wearer to calculate all basic navigation readings such as climbing and distance rates, fuel consumption, average speed and distance conversions. In the pre-computer era, an instrument of this kind that was also a precision watch was a powerful tool. The chronograph most significantly featured a 24-hour configuration enabling space travellers to distinguish between midnight and noon, thus allowing them to monitor with less confusion the passing of time in the vacuum of outer space. The Navitimer's essentially unchanged form has imbued it with a cult status that connects it to the glory days of aviation history.

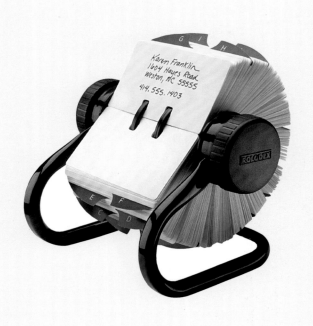

ROLODEX ROTARY CARD FILE (1952)
Arnhold Neustadter
(1910–96)
Rolodex
1952 to present

Arnhold Neustadter was, by all accounts, a fastidious and highly organized man. His numerous inventions from the 1930s on relate to the recording and organization of information, and all share the suffix '-dex.' The first of these was a spill-proof inkwell, dubbed Swivodex, followed by the Clipodex, the Punchodex and the Autodex. Neustadter's best-known invention is the Rolodex, a slotted-card filing system based around a rotating cylinder. Development started on this in the 1940s, but it was not until 1958 that it hit the mass market and became an almost instant success.

Its system of operation is entirely intuitive. The chrome-plated steel frame has an austere style that is echoed in the simplicity of the double-sided knob. Despite vast changes in the nature of clerical work since the 1950s, the Rolodex remains a fixture of millions of office desks worldwide and continues to sell several million units every year. In the digital era it is no surprise that the interface has been adapted for computers, as the company (now part of Rubbermaid) continues to develop the theme. Neustadter would doubtless approve of the company's development of the Electrodex.

KILTA (1952), TEEMA (1981)
Kaj Franck (1911–89)
Arabia 1952 to 1975,
1981 to 2002
iittala
2002 to present

Kaj Franck started work for the Finnish ceramics manufacturer Arabia in 1945 to redesign its production of utility ware. Franck believed that the traditional concept of fine tableware, one grand service with a multitude of different pieces, had long outlived its usefulness. The range that he produced, known as Kilta and launched in 1952, was a highly successful set of ceramics appropriate to the needs of the modern family. Most pieces of the Kilta range, which was made from inexpensive earthenware, were intended to be multifunctional and adaptable. The underlying geometry was developed from

three basic shapes – the circle, the square and the rectangle. All pieces were in a single colour – brown, black, white, yellow or green – and were fired once to help keep the cost down. The pieces were available individually, and a group could be assembled from a variety of colours over a period of time. In 1975 Kilta was taken out of production, which allowed Kaj Franck to make a series of improvements. The adapted range was reissued in a more resilient stoneware in 1981, under the new name 'Teema', meaning 'theme.' Teema has been part of the iittala collection since 2002.

SAUNA STOOL
(1952)
Antti Nurmesniemi
(1927–2003)
Liljamaan
Puusepäntehdas
1952
Various
1952 to present

Antti Nurmesniemi's low stool was designed for a specific task, to provide seating before and after visiting the sauna. The shape of the seat – made from layers of plywood bonded together, then carved – allows water to drain away easily, while providing firm support. The four slightly splayed teak legs make the stool steady and well balanced. This stool was designed at the beginning of Nurmesniemi's career, and was made for the Palace Hotel in Helsinki. The hotel was constructed for the Olympic Games of 1952, an event that acted as a catalyst for the revival of Finnish style, marking an era when young Finnish designers desired to develop a new, international language of design. Originally mass produced by G. Soderstrom, the stool is presently manufactured on a much smaller scale. The form has over the years been refined by Nurmesniemi to make manufacture simpler and more cost effective. Later stools have a rounder seat, rather than the more oval seat of the early stools. Functional, rugged and rustic, this unpretentious design is an invitation to sit down. Surprisingly comfortable, it has found many uses outside of its original function as a sauna stool.

ANT CHAIR (1952)
Arne Jacobsen
(1902–71)
Fritz Hansen
1952 to present

Seen from the front or the back, the necked profile of the Ant Chair's seat, cut and bent from a single sheet of plywood, is instantly recognizable. The Ant is probably Arne Jacobsen's most famous chair and is the piece that brought his work to the attention of an international audience. Although Jacobsen had designed several pieces of furniture before he came to the Ant, its form and his use of materials mark both a clear departure from his earlier work and a well-defined formal starting-point for the evolution of his later work. The Ant Chair was designed in 1952 for the canteen of the pharmaceutical company Novo. Jacobsen's main intention was to produce a chair that was light in weight and stackable. By using thin steel rods for the legs and moulded plywood for the seat, he followed the precedent set by Charles Eames's LCW Chair of 1945. But Jacobsen was also building on the experience of his manufacturer, Fritz Hansen, in its production of Peter Hvidt and Orla Mølgård-Nielsen's AX Chair of 1950. Whatever his sources, Jacobsen managed to leave the work of his predecessors far behind.

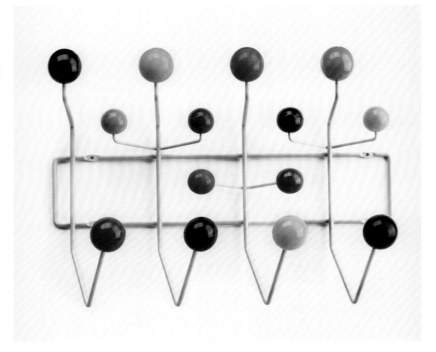

HANG-IT-ALL (1953)
Charles Eames
(1907–78)
Ray Eames (1912–88)
Tigrett Enterprises
Playhouse Division
1953 to 1961
Herman Miller
1953 to 1961,
1994 to present
Vitra Design
Museum
1997 to present

This hanging device, made from wooden balls and painted wires, was intended for children to organize anything from coats, scarves and gloves to toys and roller skates. The delightfully coloured balls – red, pink, blue, magenta, ocre, yellow, green, and violet – that appear to float freely in space, enhance the sense of playfulness appropriate for a child's environment. The Hang-It-All is incomplete until the child chooses and arranges the objects to hang on it. Like an empty frame or skeletal structure for a mobile, the piece cleverly encourages creativity and involvement. Throughout Charles and Ray

Eameses' remarkably productive careers, they maintained their desire to satisfy the consumer's needs and their interest in experimenting with new materials and types of production. This piece meets the need for order in a child's room, while its experimental quality is evident in its structure, which uses an inexpensive method of mass production that simultaneously, instead of individually, welded metal wires together. The original rack was manufactured by both the Tigrett Enterprises Playhouse Division and Herman Miller until 1961. It has been reintroduced by Herman Miller and Vitra Design Museum.

STANDARD LAMP (1953)
Serge Mouille
(1922–88)
L'Atelier de Serge
Mouille 1953 to 1962
Éditions Serge
Mouille
2000 to present

The Standard Lamp is made from black lacquered metal with a white lacquered interior and aluminium reflector. The breast-shaped shade is characteristic of Mouille's work; as well as providing a container for the electrical fitting and a shade to diffuse the light, its form also has organic and erotic connotations, in a manner inspired by Surrealism. Mouille trained as a silversmith in Paris before establishing his own studio. He was acquainted with many avant-garde architects and designers, including Jean Prouvé and Louis Sognot. Jacques Adnet, who was director of the decorative arts company Süe et Mare's Compagnie des

Arts Français, commissioned the Standard Lamp in 1953. Using spare metal structures and angled shades inspired by natural forms, Mouille's lamps fitted well within the language of organic Modernism. Although they were never produced in large quantities, the fixtures earned him an important place in the history of post-war French design. His early lamps, including the 1953 Standard Lamp, were reissued by the artist's widow, who created Éditions Serge Mouille in 2000.

COCOTTE MINUTE
(1953)
Frédéric Lescure (nd)
Groupe SEB
1953 to present

The Cocotte Minute is, according to its French manufacturer, a direct descendent of a cooker that dates back to the late seventeenth century, when inventor Denis Papin devised a pressurized container that facilitated the softening of bones and hides. Papin's contraption trapped steam inside the sealed container, forcing the pressure to build and raising the temperature at which water boils, thereby reducing the cooking time drastically. Three hundred years on, the domestic pressure-cooker effectively used the same engineering, although in a much safer and more convenient way, early explosions notwithstanding.

In Europe, one pressure cooker quickly superseded all others: the Cocotte Minute, developed by Frédéric Lescure and manufactured in 1953 by SEB. The Cocotte enabled a nation of cooks to whip up traditional recipes in a fraction of the time and with an intensity of flavour lost in the hours of oven cooking. Fifty years later a staggering 50 million Cocottes had been produced. There have been cosmetic restylings and improvements along the way. However, the essential components – including different settings, a recipe book, a heat diffuser and a range of sizes, engineering and base design – have remained the same.

SE 18 FOLDING CHAIR (1953)
Egon Eiermann
(1904–70)
Wilde & Spieth
1953 to present

Germany came late to the post-war market for inexpensive folding chairs, but this model was an international success. Egon Eiermann, one of Germany's foremost architects, developed the SE 18 Folding Chair for Wilde & Spieth in just three months. The SE 18's appealingly practical folding mechanism was a key factor in its success. The rear and front legs were fixed to each other with a swivel mechanism. Meanwhile, a strut underneath the seat ran down grooves in the rear legs, pulling them forward when the seat was folded. When it was unfolded, the strut and the upper end of the groove acted as a stop.

Launched in 1953, the smooth beechwood and moulded plywood SE 18 was an immediate hit, particularly in the domestic German market. Its robust build, low price and minimal storage space meant it was widely used in canteens, school halls and council chambers. Despite stiffer competition abroad, the SE18 also made inroads internationally. Eiermann and Wilde & Spieth's collaboration yielded numerous variations – thirty models in all – until the designer's death in 1970, and the business still produces nine of them.

ROTRING RAPIDOGRAPH
(1953)
Rotring Design Team
Rotring
1953 to present

In the current age of computer-aided design, photorealistic visualizations and virtual walk-throughs, it is hard to understand the impact a small, unassuming technical pen had on the design scene of the early 1950s. The Rotring Rapidograph was a godsend for architects, designers, illustrators and engineers because it freed them from the traditional technical pen, which would often clog or leave unsightly ink blots on the page. The new pen's simple innovation was to replace the piston-filling mechanism with a disposable ink cartridge, which maintained a constant pressure and ensured a steady flow of ink.

The pen was popular not only for its convenience and labour-saving qualities, but also for its good looks. The gently tapering, dark brown barrel, tipped with a shiny, needlepoint stainless-steel nib, was certainly a notch above the mass-produced, disposable ballpoint pens introduced around the same time. The colour-coded bands around the top of the barrel indicated the thickness of the nib and also added a dash of colour. The pen is still in production, although the days when a set of well-used Rotring Rapidographs sat at the side of virtually every drawing board have largely passed.

**PRIDE CUTLERY
(1953)**
David Mellor
(1930–2009)
Walker and Hall
1954 to c.1980
David Mellor
c.1980 to present

The beautifully attenuated and finely balanced forms of David Mellor's Pride Cutlery set the benchmark for post-war cutlery design in the UK. In Pride, Mellor developed a new, simplified language combining the meticulous attention to detail of the silversmithing tradition with the production methods of new industrial manufacturing technology. As a result, Pride emerged as a challenger to the Victorian and Regency cutlery that still dominated the high end of the cutlery market. Pride comprises a range of knives, forks, and spoons in silver plate. Originally the knife handles were bone and then xylonite, but are now being produced in a hard nylon resin in order to make them dishwasher-proof. Mellor has acknowledged the formal influence of eighteenth-century Georgian cutlery, but Pride is also unequivocally Modernist in its utilitarian approach. It is clear that the cutlery is explicitly designed to embrace the industrial manufacturing process. Even before the designer had graduated from the Royal College of Art, Walker and Hall proposed to manufacture his cutlery range. The range is now being manufactured in David Mellor's factory in the Peak District in the north of England, and remains one of the company's most popular lines.

ANTONY CHAIR
(1954)
Jean Prouvé
(1901–84)
Ateliers Jean Prouvé
1954 to 1956
Galerie Steph Simon
1954 to c.1965
Vitra 2002 to 2012

Prouvé took great pleasure in the engineering of his furniture and in the details of its construction. His designs were determined not by an attempt to achieve a particular look, but by the qualities and properties of the materials with which he was working. In the Antony Chair the materials used, plywood and steel, appear almost at odds in character and appearance. They have very different tasks to perform: one to provide a light, comfortable seat with just the right amount of give, and the other to offer the sturdiest possible support. The ingenious but honest way in which Prouvé combines these materials results in his peculiar look. In contrast to the smooth, chromed finishes so popular at the time, Antony's steel work is painted black with the marks of the welding and manufacturing processes clearly visible. The chair's wide, flat, tapering steel braces give it a sculptural quality reminiscent of the floating shapes in the mobiles of Alexander Calder, of whom Prouvé was a friend and admirer. Made for the Cité Universitaire of Antony, near Paris, in 1954, the Antony Chair was one of the last pieces of furniture Prouvé designed.

DOOR HANDLE
NO. 1020 (1953)
Johannes Potente
(1908–87)
Franz Schneider
Brakel 1953 to present

What makes a beautiful door handle? Johannes Potente's classic Door Handle No. 1020 for Franz Schneider Brakel just feels good in the hand. Potente worked for FSB for his entire career, from 1922 to 1972, and continued to design for the company after his retirement until his death in 1987. Trained as a toolmaker and engraver, Potente brought the precision of those professions to the design of door hardware. He was an 'anonymous' designer, sitting alone in his workshop carefully crafting door handles and concentrating on the substance of the handle, not on its style. No. 1020 was one of the first door handles to be cast in

aluminium, a material that was just becoming widely available in 1950. The unique qualities of aluminium, its lustre and light weight, add to the form that Potente developed. Although available in other materials, such as brass, bronze and steel, the aluminium version still seems to best express the form of the No. 1020. It is the designer's devotion to the product that singles out those of enduring beauty, and the door handle meets the criteria of a humble servant with resounding success.

STOOL X601 (1954)
Alvar Aalto
(1898–1976)
Artek 1954 to present

Alvar Aalto considered his L-shaped bent leg to be one of his most important contributions to furniture design. As with a number of his concepts, it was developed and refined over the years, often with contributions from Artek staff such as Maija Heikinheimo. The fan-leg Stool X601 was first created for an exhibition of Aalto's furniture held at NK, the Stockholm department store, in 1954. Each individual leg comprises five L-shaped sections that are glued together so that the top splays out in a fan shape. This is then connected to the edge of the stool seat by means of dowels. The fan-leg's main advantage over the simple L-shaped leg is aesthetic,

providing a much smoother and more sophisticated, organic transition between leg and top. Aalto referred to the L-shaped leg as the 'column's little sister', pointing out that it gave rise to a range of furniture analogous to the type of architecture originating from the use of the Doric column. Since he had developed several different types of leg – including the Y-leg produced in 1946 and the fan-leg – his furniture thus consisted of several different orders, each corresponding with a different leg type.

GA CHAIR (1954)
Hans Bellmann
(1911–1990)
horgenglarus
1954 to present

The design of the GA Chair, with its seat split in two, was an effort by Hans Bellmann to minimize the amount of material used. Bellmann was a designer in the best Swiss tradition of precision engineering, and throughout his career he sought to refine furniture to its most spare state. The chair that preceded the design of the GA was a similarly light-weight, plywood piece called the One-Point Chair. The seat of this chair was mounted on its frame by a single screw, hence the name. However, the success of this intelligent design was sullied by fellow Swiss designer Max Bill's claims that it was copied from one of his works. This, perhaps, explains the distinctive, split-seat look of the GA Chair, which to this day has never been imitated. Although Bellmann's legacy is not as passionately upheld as some of his contemporaries' (perhaps because he ended his career designing sanitation equipment), during the 1950s he was much in demand. It is the GA Chair, though, for which Bellmann is now best known, not only for its unusual split-seat form, but also for the unrivalled quality of its construction.

COFFEE TABLE
(1954)
Florence Knoll
(1917–2019)
Knoll 1954 to present

Florence Knoll's elegant glass and steel Coffee Table was designed as an unassuming component in a larger context of interior space. Its simple, high-quality construction in polished 1.6 cm (0.63 in) thick plate glass with a chrome-plated steel base offered an alternative to the heavy wood furnishings popular at the time. Knoll designed furnishings to complement the interiors of new, sleek, glass and steel skyscrapers, exemplifying her philosophy of the importance of unified design. This table, with its transparent top and minimal understructure, interpreted the play of light and the spatial qualities of these modern buildings. (The table was also available with tops in slate, marble and a range of veneered woods.) Knoll studied under Eliel Saarinen, and then at Cranbrook Academy, and the Architectural Association in London. Following World War II, she returned to the USA, studying and working with Mies van der Rohe, Walter Gropius and Marcel Breuer. This table is indicative of the strong principles of her design talents: quiet yet resolved, and flexible enough to work in many environments. Today, it remains not just popular but also relevant, and is still marketed in a range of sizes and configurations.

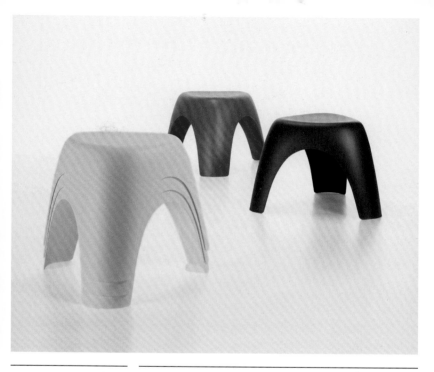

ELEPHANT STOOL
(1954)
Sori Yanagi
(1915–2011)
Kotobuki
1954 to 1977
Habitat 2000 to 2003
Vitra 2004 to present

When fibreglass became commercially available in Japan after World War II, Sori Yanagi used it for the first stool produced entirely in plastic. The stool was initially intended as a seat for the model makers in his atelier, and therefore needed to be light and stackable. A three-legged stool emerged with a shape that resembled the sturdiness of an elephant's leg, hence its name. Yanagi once said, 'I prefer gentle and rounded forms – they radiate human warmth.' The Elephant Stool, initially produced by Kotobuki in 1954, represents that new materials such as fibreglass-reinforced polyester resin were

being welcomed into domestic interiors. Yanagi was intrigued by the malleability of fibreglass, and the stool displays the soft contours that only this material would allow. This material was recently recognized as being environmentally damaging, and so Vitra and Yanagi worked together to create a new version in 2004, now made with injected-moulded polypropylene.
The stool is one of many in his vast body of work (which ranges from tableware to engineering structures) that was meticulously drawn and designed by hand before ever reaching the drafting table.

SOFA D70 (1954)
Osvaldo Borsani
(1911–85)
Tecno 1954 to present

Twins Osvaldo and Fulgenzio Borsani launched their company, Tecno, at the Milan Triennale in 1954. In the early 1950s industrial production was seen as a panacea for many of Italy's ills, and the first Tecno collection of highly engineered upholstered furniture captured this spirit. The Sofa D70 is both a product of industrial production and a clear expression of rational design thinking. The streamlined blades that make up the seat and back are at once practical elements and metaphors for a future based on mechanization. The back of the D70 could be lowered to make it into a sofa bed, or it could be folded to save space.

Housing shortages brought on by the war inspired the design of flexible furniture such as this. Osvaldo Borsani, chief designer and engineer of Tecno, introduced a variant sofa bed, model L77, in 1957. All the sofas and chairs in the range are constructed along a beam between the seat and back, and reveal the mechanisms for tilting the upholstered elements. In 1966 Osvaldo Borsani co-founded the influential design journal Ottagano and steered Tecno towards the leading position in contract and office furniture that it retains today.

SOFA 1206 (1954)
Florence Knoll
(1917–2019)
Knoll 1954 to present

Florence Knoll described her elegant sofas as 'fill-in-pieces that no one else wants to do.' As the design director of Knoll's Planning Unit, she commissioned some of the best of modern design. Her contribution to the mix was the background pieces or, as she says, 'meat and potatoes.' Sofa 1206 was created in response to one of those needs. Knoll defined the image of American corporate interiors in the 1950s with a style that used natural light, open spaces and informal groupings of furniture covered in elegant fabrics. The steel framework of the legs elevates the rectangular forms of the sofa, making it

appear to float above the carpet, and the modularity of the chair, settee and sofa series is reminiscent of Mies van der Rohe's Barcelona Chair. The thin, low arms act as a visual end to the piece rather than as true arms. The sofas were meant as perches, unlike the deep softness of most others then available, and act as a design bridge between crisp Modernism and the older, more traditional forms. Sofa 1206 succeeds at remaining in the background, letting other more flamboyant designs create a statement.

GARDEN CHAIR
(1954)
Willy Guhl
(1915–2000)
Eternit
1954 to present

The Garden Chair is made of a continuous ribbon of asbestos-free cement fibre-bond, with no added fixings or supports, moulded into a sinuous and elegant looped form. Using a single slab of cement the chair represents a brave and inventive use of an industrial material. Both light-weight and strong, the chair has a surprisingly tactile surface that is smooth and warm, yet incredibly hard wearing. The width of the chair is determined by the width of the existing slab, which is moulded into shape while the material is material is moist. This straightforward process ensured that the chair could be effectively and economically mass-produced. Originally called the Beach Chair, the Garden Chair was designed as a rocking chair for outdoor use. At the same time Guhl developed a table with two holes to hold bottles and glasses, which fit perfectly inside the Garden Chair for storage. He makes it clear that the chair was designed for outdoor use, 'People send me pictures of their chair, they paint flowers on them, they upholster them – it's their chair, let them do with it as they want, but I still wouldn't put it in my living room.'

ROCKING STOOL (1954)
Isamu Noguchi
(1904–88)
Knoll 1955 to 1960
Vitra Design Museum
2001 to 2009

The sculptor Isamu Noguchi did some of his best designs for Knoll. He blended his sculptural vocabulary with the functionality of furniture to a degree that is unique to American post-war design. When he designed the Rocking Stool, and matching Cyclone Low and Dining Tables, around 1954, Noguchi took traditional African stools as inspiration. But instead of using one piece of wood like the original stools, he combined wood for the stand and seat with five V-shaped metal wires. He used the metal wiring to build a very stable 'cyclone-like' construction. It was available in walnut and the

less common birch version. The combination of materials gave the stool a very modern look – perhaps too modern, since the stool was in production for just five years. Many of Noguchi's innovative designs were not understood by the American public. The tables, however, which were inspired by the same construction principle as the stool, have had more success and are still in production today. The stool was in production from 1955 to 1960, and re-introduced by Vitra Design Museum in 2001.

MAX AND MORITZ
SALT AND PEPPER
SHAKERS (1954–6)
Wilhelm Wagenfeld
(1900–90)
WMF 1956 to present

Max and Moritz Salt and Pepper
Shakers are discreet and visually
reticent, yet are perfectly proportioned. Made in glass with stamped
stainless-steel tops, they are held
together in a stainless-steel boat
in a satisfying play of forms. The
small-waisted vessels are a pleasure
to hold and make the contents
seem precious. Wilhelm Wagenfeld
must have been inspired by the
German cartoon characters Max
and Moritz, created by Wilhelm
Busch. From the mid-1950s to the
mid-1960s Wagenfeld worked with
one of the biggest metal manufacturers of cutlery, stamped metal
and glass, WMF (Württembergische
Metallwarenfabrik Geislingen). In

the Max and Moritz Salt and Pepper
Shakers he created an archetype
that became synonymous with the
company. Wagenfeld wanted to
convince by use, rather than by
visible design features. Therefore
these shakers have large, plug
openings instead of a screw top,
a feature first used in 1952. The
plugs were more economical
to produce and more convenient
to refill. Design for Wagenfeld
was not 'turning out wrappings',
but exploring the DNA of a thing
and its use in the hand. He was
interested in the idea of the
archetype-made-modern within
a timeless design, achieved with
these shakers.

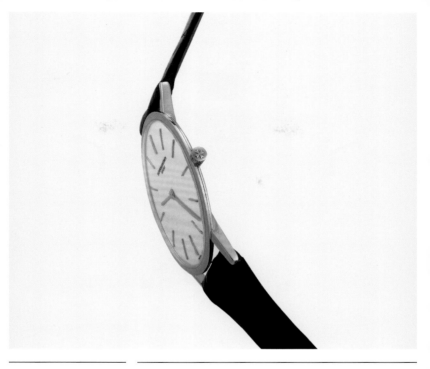

EXTRA FLAT WRISTWATCH (1955)
Vacheron Constantin
Design Department
Vacheron Constantin
1955 to present

Vacheron Constantin, based in Geneva, is the world's oldest watchmaker. Since its creation by Jean-Marc Vacheron in 1755, the company has set the benchmark for timepiece technology, pushing the boundaries of mechanical innovation while elevating the craft of watchmaking to a fine art. The Extra Flat Wristwatch of 1955 perfectly embodies this Vacheron Constantin philosophy and is a milestone in watch design. The dimensions of the movement are a principal constraint in watchmaking and the Extra Flat pushed the envelope to the limit to create a flat movement. At an astonishing 1.64 mm (.065 in), the movement is a technical tour de force: it includes a unique escapement and regulator innovation, which dispenses with the need for the shock protection and adjustment mechanisms that are normally required after cleaning and lubrication. The total thickness of the watch including the spherical glass case is 4.8 mm (0.19 in). Painstaking research, development, testing and honing produced the ultra thin movement, and the watch was initially more of a meticulously handcrafted work of art than a mass-market model. Yet the technological breakthrough of the Extra Flat continues to influence and inform watch design.

AUTOMATIC RICE COOKER (1955)
Yoshiharu Iwata
(1938–)
Toshiba
1955 to present

Yoshiharu Iwata's Automatic Rice Cooker for Toshiba was one of the first home electronic products to bring a recognizably Japanese style to an area of design mainly inspired by imported Western products, making it a milestone in Japanese industrial design. The most striking features of the rice cooker are its simple shape and pure white finish. Iwata, who went on to become general manager of Toshiba's design division, took his inspiration from the traditional Japanese rice bowl. Toshiba's rice cooker was not the first on the market, but similar products simply replaced the external heat source with an electric coil, and the rice

still had to be watched during cooking. Iwata's design offered a completely automated system with a timer switch that would cook rice perfectly. Overcoming the technical difficulties inherent in this technology took over five years from initial designs to products on shelves. The Automatic Rice Cooker was an instant success when it appeared in 1955, and by 1970, annual output had passed the 12 million mark. Itawa's design was credited with heralding a revolution in Japanese food culture and home lifestyles, helping to free people from the tyranny of time-consuming cooking.

CHAIR NO. 3107 (1955)
Arne Jacobsen
(1902–71)
Fritz Hansen
1955 to present

The hourglass form of Arne Jacobsen's Chair No. 3107, often known as the 'Series 7' chair, places it firmly in the era of the wasp-waisted New Look: the 1950s. Jacobsen was inspired to develop a light, stacking chair constructed from a moulded plywood seat supported on thin metal rod legs by the work of Charles Eames. The widely successful Ant Chair of 1952 was Jacobsen's first attempt in that direction, with Chair No. 3107 representing a further stage of development. It is a stronger, more durable and more stable modification of the three-legged Ant. The number of copies and illicit versions of Chair No. 3107 that continue to proliferate testify to the lasting popularity and success of this model. In Britain this chair gained widespread attention through a 1963 photograph by Lewis Morley of Christine Keeler, notorious for her involvement in the government scandal that became known as the Profumo Affair. The chair that Morley used as a prop was an unlicensed variant of Arne Jacobsen's designs, but the combination of Keeler's pose and Arne Jacobsen's Chair No. 3107 have become inextricably linked and now appear to be universally recognized.

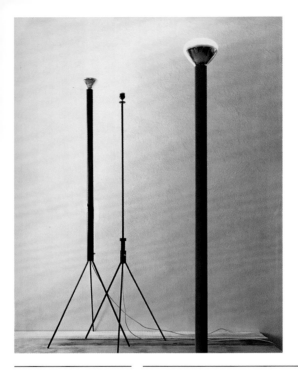

LUMINATOR LAMP
(1955)
Achille Castiglioni
(1918–2002)
Pier Giacomo
Castiglioni (1913–68)
Gilardi & Barzaghi
1955 to 1957
Arform 1957 to 1994
Flos 1994 to present

A conscious drive to rebuild the Italian economy after World War II led to Italian industry investing in low-tech objects, which could be exported easily. A series of products were developed that embraced this idea, while capitalizing on aesthetic appeal as a potent marketing force. The Luminator Lamp was one of these designs. The reduced design is based around a metal tube whose diameter is the width of the socket for the pressed-glass tungsten bulb with a built-in reflector at the top. Apart from its three-legged stand, the only other feature was the wire that came from the tube base. The success of the design

lies not only in its elegance but also in its structural stability. It was exported in large quantities and contributed to the economic revival of Italy. Despite its modern styling, the Luminator was not entirely without historical precedent: this style of indirect photographer's lighting was first suggested for domestic use by Pietro Chiesa with his Luminator of 1933. In a form of tribute, the Castiglionis adopted the same name for their own breakthrough approach to contemporary lighting design.

TULIP CHAIR (1955)
Eero Saarinen
(1910–61)
Knoll 1956 to present

The Tulip Chair's name is clearly derived from its resemblance to the flower, yet the creative impetus behind the design was not to copy a form from nature, but was the result of a variety of complex ideas and production considerations. This chair is part of a series called the Pedestal Group, whose members share this basic one-pillar support. This chair's stem-like pedestal was a result of Eero Saarinen's keen interest in combining the overall form with the actual structure of the chair and thus creating a better sense of unity. The Tulip has a reinforced, rilsan-coated aluminium swivel base and a seat

made of a moulded fibreglass shell, but because both have a similar white finish the chair appears to be made of one material. The base and shell are made in both black and white, with a removable foam cushion for seat or for both back and seat, with a zippered cover, fastened with Velcro. The chair is still available from its original manufacturer, Knoll. It was awarded the Museum of Modern Art design award and the Federal Award for Industrial Design, both in 1969, establishing its place in design history.

COCONUT CHAIR (1955)
George Nelson
(1908–86)
Herman Miller
1955 to present
Vitra 1988 to present

Manufacturer Herman Miller's advertisements to promote George Nelson's Coconut Chair made great play with the sculptural qualities of the design. Although its strong visual presence was clearly of great importance to Nelson and to Herman Miller (of which Nelson was design director from 1946 to 1965) the chair also fulfils the equally desirable aim of allowing sitters the freedom to occupy almost any position they choose on or 'in' the chair. The conventional arrangement of seat, back and armrests is replaced by a much more open composition of curves. In the open-plan spaces of the new homes of post-war America a chair was likely to occupy uncluttered, open space rather than be pushed against a wall. It must therefore have character and shape, and be attractive from all sides. The Coconut Chair becomes as much a piece of sculpture as an object of utility. If the chair appears to float on its 'wirey' supports, this is entirely deceptive. Made of sheet steel and upholstered in foam rubber with a fabric, leather or artificial leather cover, the shell is heavy and cumbersome. The most recent version, with a moulded plastic shell, is now much lighter.

AJ DOOR HANDLE
(1955–6)
Arne Jacobsen
(1902–71)
Carl F. Petersen
1956 to present

The curvaceous shape of Arne Jacobsen's famous door handle invites the user to grasp it. The gently arched lever of the handle fits snugly in the palm of the hand, while the thumb settles into the designated depression at the handle's base. Simply known as the AJ Door Handle, it was designed in 1955–6 for the SAS Royal Hotel in Copenhagen, where it can still be seen. Anticipating the trend for ergonomic design that was to follow years later, Jacobsen studied the shape of the hand and designed his door handle accordingly. Originally the handles were made in white bronze, a metal that did not discolour or need to be polished, but today they are available only in satin nickel and brass, and now in two sizes. Although mass produced, the handles are still finished by hand. At the time Jacobsen was architect for the entire SAS Royal Hotel, overseeing almost every aspect of its design, including the furniture, textiles and light fittings. Such attention to detail made the hotel one of the most outstanding achievements of twentieth-century architecture and design.

A56 CHAIR (1956)
Jean Pauchard (nd)
Tolix 1956 to present

Although the A56 Chair is one of the most successful and familiar chair designs of the twentieth century, its origins are far removed from the glittering world of designer glamour. In fact, the chair originated in a seemingly humble plumber's workshop in France. In 1933, the French industrialist Xavier Pauchard added a sheet-metal division, named Tolix, to his successful boiler-making work-shop. A year later, Tolix, based in Burgundy, France, released the Model A outdoor chair, part of a range of buckled, sheet-metal furniture fabricated according to Pauchard's designs. In 1956, his son Jean Pauchard added arms to the Model A to make the A56. Built around a tubular frame, with a central back splat and elegant, tapered splay legs, it combines functionality and decoration with a shiny, modern, jet-age style. The decorative piercing on the seat allows for drainage, while elegant grooves on the chair legs give stability when stacked. In addition to the basic steel finish, the Model A is available in twelve colours. Yet it is perhaps the chair's simplicity that makes it such a success – so successful that Tolix continues to produce the A56 to this day.

**JUNGHANS WALL
CLOCK (1956–7)**
Max Bill (1908–94)
Junghans
1956–7 to 1963,
1997 to present

Swiss designer Max Bill originally trained as a silversmith before studying under Walter Gropius at the Bauhaus school in Dessau. A painter, sculptor and architect, when he designed the Junghans Wall Clock he was the director of architecture at the Hochschule für Gestaltung in Ulm. The clock provides an excellent example of art and technology fused for mass production. As with all of Max Bill's work, it incorporated an obsession with precise engineering and proportions. Designed between 1956–7, with a mineral glass face and quartz movement housed in a slim aluminium casing, the style of the Junghans Wall Clock

has influenced clock designs ever since. Bill, influenced by Le Corbusier, employs the simple and direct principles of functionalist design, stripping the clock of any superfluous detail. His emphasis on lines over numbers preceded the minimalist style that would soon dominate the world of design. The clock has only minute and hour hands, with the minute hand moving very slightly, pulsing each second. Bill's skill as a silversmith combined with a meticulous attention to measurement and mathematical proportions ensure the clock displays clarity and precision, and contains all the essential elements for a great design.

BUTTERFLY STOOL (1956)
Sori Yanagi
(1915–2011)
Tendo Mokko
1956 to present
Vitra Design
Museum
2002 to present

Sori Yanagi's Butterfly Stool is, in many ways, simplicity itself. It is constructed of two identical plywood forms, connected under the seat by just two screws. A threaded brass rod acts as a stretcher and gives the stool stability. The name derives from the profile of the seat, suggesting a butterfly in flight, but the outline of the stool is also reminiscent of Japanese calligraphy and the shape of the gateways to Shinto shrines known as *Torii*. The Butterfly Stool was designed at a pivotal moment in Japanese history, as Japan was fast emerging as an industrial nation. Yanagi was not the first Japanese designer to design furniture that was essentially Western in form: Japanese interiors had been increasingly Westernised since the 1860s. Bent plywood was a technical innovation that had been developed by American and European designers and manufacturers, so the compound curves of the moulded plywood shells that make the stool can be seen as part of a global trend in mid-twentieth-century furniture design. The elegant, spare form of the stool may be superficially similar to contemporary, reductive Modernist design in the West, but it derives from a Japanese design sensibility.

LAMINO CHAIR
(1956)
Yngve Ekström
(1913–88)
Swedese Möbler
1956 to present

At first glance, Yngve Ekström's Lamino Chair is similar to armchairs created by other Scandinavian masters like Bruno Mathsson and Finn Juhl. Formed out of pressed laminate from a variety of woods, including teak, beech, cherry and oak, and lined most often in sheepskin upholstery, the Lamino possessed the pleasing form and utility that came to mark Scandinavian Modernism. But Ekström was shrewd as well as stylish, and designed the Lamino so as to ensure easy shipping. Customers bought the chair in two pieces, and screwed it together using a hexagonal key that was included in the packaging. Much

to Ekström's retrospective regret, the device was never patented, and a door was opened to a competitor named Ingvar Kamprad, who went on to create knockdown, screw-together IKEA furniture. Despite this oversight, Ekström and his brother Jerker built a healthy and iconic Modern design company dubbed Swedese around the Lamino Chair and its brethren, Laminett, Lamello and Melano. With more than 150,000 Lamino Chairs having taken up residence since its introduction in 1956, the chair continues to be a household name that has only increased in style and sentimental attachment.

5027 (1956), KARTIO (1993)
Kaj Franck (1911–89)
Nuutajärvi-Notsjö
1956 to 1988
iittala 1988 to present

The different pieces of utility glass – tumblers in two sizes, a bowl, two types of carafe, a vase and a candleholder – that comprise the 5027 range were designed by Kaj Franck in the 1950s for the Finnish company Nuutajärvi-Notsjö. It was only in 1993, that they were assembled into a single range and marketed under the name Kartio. Kaj Franck was well aware of the significance of colour in design, but the use of colour in his glassware has been something of a vexed issue, largely because of cost and the difficulty in achieving consistency from one batch to another. iittala currently produces the set in six colours, including clear, smoky-grey and four different shades of blue. Originally though, Nuutajärvi-Notsjö sold the set of six tumblers as a multicoloured harlequin set. It was one of its most influential and popular lines, primarily for this use of colour. Although the designs for the individual components of Kartio were produced over a period of time, they nevertheless form a sensible product grouping. Each piece is linked to the others by a simple but all-pervasive structural clarity and follows Franck's fundamental approach to design.

PK22 CHAIR (1956)
Poul Kjærholm
(1929–80)
Ejvind Kold
Christensen
1956 to 1982
Fritz Hansen
1982 to present

The PK22 Chair was designed when Poul Kjærholm was in his early twenties, and is one of the pieces that placed him among the great innovators of the Danish Modern movement. The lounge chair comprises a remarkably elegant, cantilevered seat frame encased in an envelope of leather or cane, and balanced on a polished stainless steel sprung base, which constitutes its legs. Two flat arcs of cut steel provide structural stability. Like many chairs from that period PK22 forgoes cushions and upholstery in favour of surfaces in tension. Kjærholm remains a favourite among rigorous Modernists for

his dedication to transparency in construction and use of readily comprehensible and profoundly considered materials. Through his masterful use of cantilevers and bent steel he refines the key furniture innovations of the first decades of the twentieth century. His furniture was among the finest examples of the International Style and PK22 is one of its early and most articulate expressions. The chair was initially issued by Ejvind Kold Christensen and in 1982 Fritz Hansen gained rights to reproduce the renowned 'Kjærholm Collection', of which the PK22 affirms its place as an elegant example of Danish Minimalism.

MARSHMALLOW SOFA (1956)
Irving Harper
(1917–2015)
George Nelson
Associates
Herman Miller
1956 to 1965,
1999 to present
Vitra 1988 to 1994,
2000 to present

When it first appeared in 1956 the bold outline, easy-to-clean surfaces and see-through structure of the Marshmallow Sofa could hardly have contrasted more sharply with the heavily uphol-stered, dust-gathering bulky sofas that dominated so many living rooms. Bright in colour, playful in shape and name, and somewhat resembling a wide-open waffle iron, the Marshmallow seemed already to be looking forward to the coming Pop era. Its round pads of colour are held together as if by a molecular structure. Irving Harper, staff designer from 1947 to 1963 at George Nelson Associates, has said that he designed the

Marshmallow Sofa over a single weekend. Like the Eameses, Harper liked to exploit the decorative possibilities of scientific and biomorphic imagery, and he was concerned with silhouettes and the lack of weights. The Marshmallow was marketed as suitable for lobbies and public buildings as well as for domestic use. The cushions could be interchanged for a new look or in order to equalize wear. Its unitary construction system also meant that it could be made available in a variety of sizes and customized colour combinations.

SUGAR POURER
(1956)
Theodor Jacob (nd)
Various
1956 to present

Long a part of the classic American diner made famous in the 1950s, the simple glass-and-metal sugar pourer has a surprising origin in central Germany. It was the brainchild of an inventor from Hanau named Theodor Jacob, who in 1956 patented a 'dispenser for granulated materials such as sugar', creating a model of simplicity and material modesty. Jacob's design comprised a glass container sealed with a screw-on metallic top and a metal tube that reached into the depths of the vessel. Bevelled at the bottom, the tube allowed for an exact portion to be dispensed each time the container was turned upside down. Bevelled oppositely at the top, the dispensing tube was covered with a small self-closing flap, providing assurance of the sugar's purity and non-contamination. In a cleverly concealed detail, Jacob added an additional moving sleeve that slid down the tube and over the lower bevel to allow restaurant management to regulate the dose of sugar even more precisely. In a final detail that in retrospect seems prophetic of the coming wave of commercialism, Jacob concluded his patent application with one additional note: 'The outer wall may also be used for advertising purposes.'

LOUNGE CHAIR (1956)

Charles Eames
(1907–78)
Herman Miller
1956 to present
Vitra 1958 to present

The Lounge Chair was originally designed as a one-off bespoke creation rather than a production piece. However, because of its overwhelming popularity Charles Eames set about adapting the design for production. In doing so he deployed the same meticulous moulding techniques that he had been exploring for nearly a decade. The prototype was made by Don Albison at the Eames Office, and the design was eased into production in 1956. The early designs were available in a choice of fabric, leather or naugahyde cushions with a rosewood ply base. It comprised three plywood shells, over which leather cushions embrace the structure. Charles Eames described the chair as having the 'warm, receptive look of a well-used first baseman's mitt'. The accompanying Ottoman, with one plywood shell, has a four-star aluminium swivel base. Rubber and steel shock mounts connect the chair's three shells and allow them to bend independently of one another. The leather cushions were originally filled with duck feathers, down and foam. Its welcoming form and stubborn elegance have assured its position amongst the most collected design pieces, remaining as popular today as it was when first produced.

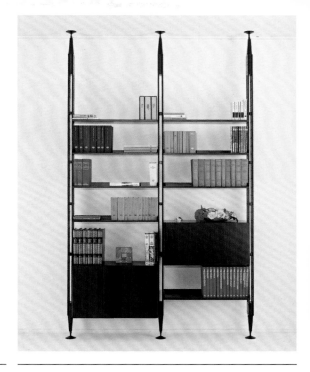

LB7 SHELVING UNIT (1957)

Franco Albini
(1905–77)
Poggi 1957 to 2000
Cassina
2008 to present

Extendable both in height and width, the modular LB7 Shelving Unit was the culmination of architect Franco Albini's experiments in flexible furniture. Since opening his architectural office in Milan in 1930, Albini concerned himself with the structure of furniture as well as buildings, developing a raw, industrial aesthetic that was exemplified by the LB7. Created for Poggi, the LB7 could be wedged into any room, with its feet pressed against both floor and ceiling, making maximum use of any space available. The shelves could be slotted in practically anywhere, allowing users to configure the unit to their own particular needs. With such an adaptable set up, very little space was wasted. Despite looking industrial, the LB7 unit was largely handmade, as Albini did not trust the quality of machine-made goods. The materials used to make the LB7 were walnut, rosewood and brass, seemingly luxurious materials today, but relatively inexpensive and readily available in 1957. Albini's practical attitude towards furniture design was at odds with many of his more style-obsessed contemporaries, yet while they have been largely forgotten, the pioneering work of Albini is still roundly admired and fetches a fortune at auction.

699
SUPERLEGGERA
CHAIR (1957)
Gio Ponti (1891–1979)
Cassina
1957 to present

Gio Ponti's Superleggera Chair, Model 699, is visually and literally lightweight. Constructed in ash, the spare frame enjoys an element of transparency. The 699 Superleggera is the culmination of a series of experiments by Ponti to realize a modern design based on the traditional lightweight wooden chair made in the fishing village of Chiavari. Ponti began to develop models based on the Chiavari chair as early as 1949, and Cassina produced at least three designs that show the chair's development. In 1955 Ponti returned to the project, aiming to create a smaller version. The Superleggera is superficially an unassuming chair, with minor mid-century overtones. On closer inspection it displays beautiful fine lines and carefully considered details. The triangular sections and tapering lines of the leg and back supports reduce weight both physically and visually. All the timbers are reduced to their minimum without compromising structure. The seat is finely woven cane, to avoid weighty upholstery. The Superleggera was shown at the Milan Triennale in 1957 and won the Compasso d'Oro prize. It is still produced by Cassina, testament to its enduring appeal and to Ponti's design legacy.

AJ CUTLERY (1957)
Arne Jacobsen
(1902–71)
Georg Jensen
1957 to present

The highly stylized and organic form of the AJ Cutlery, designed in 1957 by architect Arne Jacobsen, is a key example of functionalist design. Whilst being sculptural in form, it reveals Jacobsen's concept of design for ergonomic use and mass production. A stringent streamlined form is sustained through each piece, which consists of a unornamented strip of stainless steel. Originally consisting of twenty-one parts, the canteen included soup/bouillon spoons for right- or left-handed use. It was for his Scandinavian Airlines System (SAS) Royal Hotel project that Jacobsen designed the AJ Cutlery. The project produced

a number of other now famous designs, including the Swan and Egg chairs. All were devoid of ornament, but included strong silhouettes and a refined sculptural presence. The styling of the AJ Cutlery was far more exaggerated than that of its contemporaries: it was poorly received by the hotel visitors, and was soon replaced with cutlery that had been designed elsewhere. But the futuristic styling was clearly acknowledged when it was featured in Stanley Kubrick's science fiction classic *2001: A Space Odyssey*, and the cutlery is still produced by Georg Jensen today.

EGG CHAIR (1957)
Arne Jacobsen
(1921–71)
Fritz Hansen
1958 to present

Arne Jacobsen's Egg Chair, so-named because of its resemblance to a smoothly broken eggshell, is a modified, International Style version of the Georgian wing armchair. Along with Jacobsen's Swan Chair, the Egg was designed for the guest rooms and the lobby of the SAS Royal Hotel in Copenhagen. The chair owes an enormous debt to the Norwegian designer Henry Klein, who was a pioneer in furniture made from shaped plastic shells and whose own chair design from 1956, Model 1007, bears a clear resemblance to the Egg Chair. Jacobsen's design took a number of steps forward, particularly in making full use of

the sculptural possibilities Klein's moulding process allowed. The Egg fuses seat, back and armrests into a unified aesthetic whole, covered in either leather or fabric. The skilled hand tailoring that is required to fix the covering to the frame means that only six or seven chairs were produced per week: a production rate that still stands today. Since its first appearance, the Egg has developed an independent life as a prop and a symbol in films and advertisements. Nearly fifty years on from its conception, it still seems a chair made for the future.

HANGING CHAIR (EGG) (1957)
Nanna Ditzel
(1923–2005)
Jørgen Ditzel
(1931–61)
R. Wengler 1957
Bonacina Pierantonio
1957 to 2014
Sika Design
2012 to present

To Nanna Ditzel, chair design had the potential to be both practical and poetic. After meeting her first husband, Jørgen Ditzel, at school, they began working together, producing multipurpose furniture for small spaces. Experiments with wicker led to the Hanging Chair (sometimes known as the Egg Chair), which could be suspended from the ceiling. Ditzel maintained that for many years she had been attempting to create 'lightness, the feeling of floating' in her furniture design, and the Hanging Chair of 1957 came very close to realizing her ideal. It is important to recognize its distance from the dominant, rather sober ideas of

the day and to see how far away it was from the mainstream of contemporary Danish furniture design. With the Hanging Chair, not only did Ditzel tap into a free and easy spirit several years ahead of the rest of the world, but she also started to move the direction of Danish furniture design away from what she recognized as its overused and dogmatic Functionalism. Ditzel has been dubbed the 'First Lady of Danish Furniture Design', as a nod to her long-standing contribution to textile, jewellery and furniture design.

CUBO ASHTRAY
(1957)
Bruno Munari
(1907–98)
Danese
1957 to present

Pablo Picasso once called Bruno Munari – painter, writer, designer, graphic inventor, educator, philosopher – the new Leonardo. His playful, poetic, subversive and original approach to life and design is present in his posters, poems, lights and children's books. Munari's Cubo Ashtray is a deceptively simple and rational shiny melamine plastic box. Within it sits a discreet, removable, folded grey anodized aluminium-sheet insert. This resolves all the niggling functional issues of an ashtray – a place to rest or safely extinguish a cigarette, a lid to conceal ash and contain odours – with Munari's characteristically inventive and economic means. Designed in 1957, Cubo was one of the first products created by Danese and led to a life-long collaboration with Munari. The initial design for the Cubo Ashtray was three times the height that it is today. However, Munari opted for the shorter square shape. The first edition (1957–9) was a painted black anti-scratch steel model, with anodized aluminium in a natural colour, while the second edition, from 1960, saw the launch of coloured melamine models with an anodized aluminium ashtray in an opaque grey colour.

PRISMATIC TABLE (1957)
Isamu Noguchi
(1904–88)
Vitra Design Museum
2001 to present

Isamu Noguchi's career as an artist began as a studio assistant to the sculptor Constantin Brancusi in Paris in 1927. It was a defining experience for him and defined his interest in the use of natural materials and the development of simple, organic forms. Noguchi also embraced the work of Buckminster Fuller, whose ideas consolidated connections between organic structure and architecture. The Prismatic Table brings all these influences together and was designed as a result of Noguchi's experiments with sculptures of folded and bent aluminium that began in the late 1950s. It was originally designed as a prototype

between April and May 1957 for Alcoa and conceived as part of a programme that explored new uses for aluminium. It was designed in black, but was advertised as having multicoloured interchangeable elements. Its faceted design combines Noguchi's exploration of new materials and science and technology, and has been likened to the traditional Japanese art of origami. This table was Noguchi's last piece of furniture design. Its Modernist style is simple and appealing, and in 2001 it was put into production for the first time in black and white, attracting new devotees to Noguchi's work.

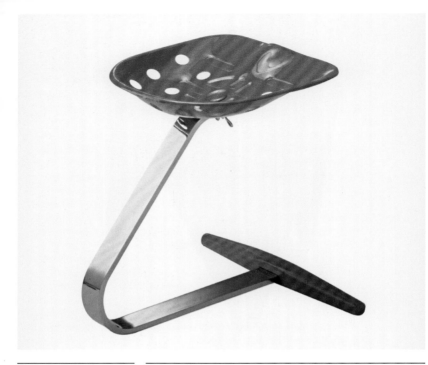

MEZZADRO CHAIR (1957)
Achille Castiglioni
(1918–2002)
Pier Giacomo
Castiglioni (1913–68)
Zanotta
1970 to present

At first sight, this is a strange and puzzling chair, which appears to sit outside of mainstream, rational, Modernist design culture, apparently favouring something more informal and artistic. In fact, it is an entirely rational piece but one in which the rationalization is constructed in parts. Achille Castiglioni asks first what is the most basic, comfortable seat form and concludes that it is the tractor seat. He searches for the optimal sprung suspension and produces the single cantilevered bar. Finally, he asks what is the most rudimentary stabilizer and finds it to be a log or length of wood. The assembled result produces a deliciously ambiguous tension between explicit formal discontinuity and implicit functional continuity. The first version of Mezzadro was exhibited in 1954 at the 10th Milan Triennale. In 1957, the current version was shown at an exhibition at the Villa Olmo in Como. However, this piece was so avant-garde that it was not until 1970 that it first went into production. Paradoxically both simple and complex, the Mezzadro Chair has high and predictive status, a latent catalyst eventually reshaping the design landscape of the latter half of the twentieth century.

COCKTAIL SHAKER (1957)
Luigi Massoni
(1930–2013)
Carlo Mazzeri (1927–)
Alessi
1957 to present

This groundbreaking product was first produced by Alessi in 1957 under the name Alfra (Alessi Fratelli), which was the name of the company from 1947 to 1967. The Cocktail Shaker was a huge production challenge because its extremely deep and narrow shape required not only innovation in the progressive technique of cold forming, but also an intermediate annealing cycle to prevent the material from cracking. In overcoming this, Alessi did much to establish its reputation for technical expertise and helped cement its move away from traditional production in nickel, brass and silver plate towards stainless steel. The shaker, available in 25 cl and 50 cl, was part of a complete bar set, which included an ice bucket, tongs and spirit measure. Their flawless, highly polished finish was fairly unusual at this time, and has become an enduring feature of Alessi products. The set, which became known as Programma 4, was exhibited at the Milan Triennale the same year. In common with the general Alessi policy of 'once introduced, never withdrawn,' Programma 4 is still in the catalogue forty-five years on, with the Cocktail Shaker selling up to 20,000 units every year.

G-TYPE SOY SAUCE BOTTLE (1958)
Masahiro Mori
(1927–2005)
Hakusan Porcelain
Company
1958 to present

If proof were needed that influential statements are not the preserve of grand-scale design, then the diminutive G-Type Soy Sauce Bottle would put forward a substantial argument. Designed in Japan in 1958 by Masahiro Mori for the Hakusan Porcelain Company, this unassuming ceramic bottle grew into a national tabletop icon on the back of a low price point, national distribution and the promise of a drip-free pouring experience. Standing only a few inches tall, the bottle's crisp outline has been kept free from handles or any other superfluous detail. In place of a handle, the bottle is picked up by pinching the high waist that sits just below the lid. Tilt it forward and a smooth flow of soy sauce quickly emerges from the right-angled spout. Apart from the lid, which is set into the bottle to expose an elegant rim, and a ceramic glaze that reflects light to a flattering effect, the design trades on its practicality alone. The bottle marched out into the marketplace to swiftly establish itself as a national design emblem. The G-Type continues to be sold in vast quantities throughout the world today.

SWAN CHAIR (1958)
Arne Jacobsen
(1902–71)
Fritz Hansen
1958 to present

Arne Jacobsen's Swan Chair, made from a moulded lightweight plastic shell supported on a cast aluminium base, was, like its companion the Egg Chair, designed for the SAS Royal Hotel in Copenhagen, and was so named for its distinctive profile. The sources that lie behind one of Jacobsen's most popular designs include his own work: for instance, the shape of the Swan's seat and back is related to one of the Series Seven chairs and also to some of Jacobsen's other preliminary designs for plywood furniture. The arms, too, have echoes in earlier designs. But, on the other hand, Jacobsen was also influenced by the work of his contemporaries, including the Norwegian designer Henry Klein on the moulding of plastic chair seats, and the internationally influential work of Charles Eames and Eero Saarinen on shell and fibreglass seating. In the Swan, Jacobsen deftly combined and improved on ideas from all of these sources, fusing them with such meticulous attention to detail that he succeeded in creating something so distinctive that it has come to define an era.

CONE CHAIR (1958)
Verner Panton
(1926–98)
Plus-linje 1958 to 1963
Polythema
1994 to 1995
Vitra 2002 to present

Verner Panton's interest lay in experimenting with plastics and other newly available man-made materials. His innovative geometric forms in vibrant colours became synonymous with the 1960s Pop Art era. The design of the Cone Chair represents a conscious decision by the designer to divorce himself from any preconceived notions of what a chair should look like. Here, a conical metal shell with a removable upholstered seat is placed point-down on a cross-shaped metal base. The chair was originally designed for Kom-igen (Come Again), his parent's restaurant on the island of Funen in Denmark. Panton was responsible

for the design of the interior, and all the elements – walls, tablecloths, waitresses' uniforms and the upholstery of the Cone Chairs – were red. Danish businessman Percy von Halling-Koch, owner of the furniture company Pluslinje, saw the chair at the opening of the restaurant and offered to put it into production immediately. Panton continued to add designs to the Cone range, including a barstool (1959), footstool (1959) and chairs made of fibreglass (1970), steel (1978) and plastic (1978). The range, now produced by Vitra, continues to inspire a new generation of consumers over fifty years after its creation.

DESK (1958)
Franco Albini
(1905–77)
Gavina 1958 to 1968
Knoll 1968 to present

Franco Albini worked in a number of fields, including architecture, product design, urban planning and interiors, in the neo-rationalist style established in Italy in the 1920s and 1930s, which sought to unite European Functionalism with Italy's classical heritage. Hallmarks of the architectural style included strict geometric forms and the use of state-of-the-art materials such as tubular steel – traits still clearly visible in Albini's 1958 minimalist desk. Albini was particularly preoccupied with the fine balance between space and solid forms, which the desk exemplifies. By using raw materials he quotes the tradition

of the artisanal, and simultaneously uses minimal forms. The 1.28 cm (0.5 in) polished plate glass rests on a frame of chrome-finished square steel tube. The 'floating' drawers, of ebonized oak wood or white lacquer, have an open rear section where magazines or small books can be placed. The desk was first produced by Gavina from 1958 but found a wider market through Knoll, which bought Gavina in 1968. The pared-down quality of the desk's design, with its complete absence of ornamentation, means it remains effortlessly modern today, and Knoll still produces it.

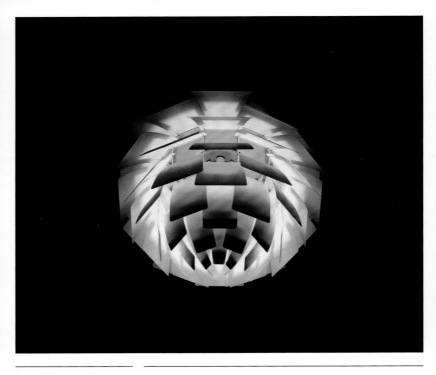

PH ARTICHOKE
LAMP (1958)
Poul Henningsen
(1894–1967)
Louis Poulsen Lighting
1958 to present

Poul Henningsen's PH Artichoke Lamp, with its spiky cascade of copper-toned louvred shades, is one of the twentieth century's most striking pieces of lighting. Manufactured by Louis Poulsen Lighting in Copenhagen, it is by far the grandest of architect Henningsen's many designs for light fittings and represents the culmination of several decades of work. Most of Henningsen's designs involve a series of concentric parabolic-section cowls – usually painted white on the reflective surface – that enclose the bulb. Henningsen calculated the shapes of the shades with great precision, producing a series of diagrams cleverly demonstrating the path of light rays through them and the subsequent even dispersion of light about a room. In the PH Artichoke Lamp he follows his basic theories, but the shades are opened up and broken into a dynamic series of separate overlapping flaps. These are made from copper, painted white on the underside, and help to emphasize the warmth and mellowness of the light that is emitted. They work in the same way as Henningsen's more usual light shades – evenly reflecting light about a space – but transform the lamp into a singularly impressive and dramatic sculptural artefact.

P4 CATILINA GRANDE CHAIR (1958)
Luigi Caccia Dominioni
(1913–2016)
Azucena
1958 to present

Luigi Caccia Dominioni's P4 Catilina Grande Chair is an important product of the period when Italian design first became influential on an international scale. Azucena, a company that Caccia Dominioni set up in Milan in 1947 with Ignazio Gardella and Corrado Corradi Dell'Acqua, was one of the many design-led furniture manufacturers that emerged in the 1940s. The Catilina's steel structure is typical of the impulse to experiment with both materials and form that had become especially marked by the late 1950s. The chair underlines the Italians' stylistic departure from the straight lines of

mainstream European Modernism. The curved back frame, in metallic grey powder-coated cast iron, supports the oval seat, comprised of black polyester lacquered wood, with either a leather or red mohair velvet cushion. The graceful arch of the frame was centred on the idea of bending an iron bar into a sweeping ribbon, which gently curves only by a few centimetres, creating a comfortable and sinuous back and arm rest. Caccia Dominioni would continue to design furniture and other products for Azucena, while the Catilina became an archetype of Italian design, and has been in production ever since.

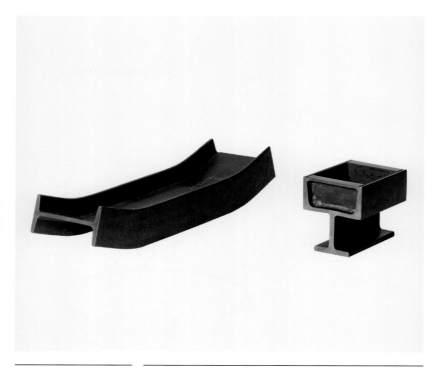

PUTRELLA DISH
(1958)
Enzo Mari (1932–)
Danese 1958,
2002 to present

By giving a chunk of raw iron I-beam a gentle upward curve on either side, Enzo Mari created a sophisticated, beautiful product out of a material commonly used as a building component. Mari, a designer always challenging the status quo, once described his approach to design thus, 'I take an industrial object, a pure, lovely object, I make a small change, I introduce a discordant element, that is design.' The Putrella Dish, made for Danese, could not be a better example of this attitude. Although often described as a fruit bowl, the Putrella has no prescribed function. By using iron, a material normally seen on a much larger

scale, Mari has captured this sense of vastness and set it on a tabletop. Originally conceived as one of numerous variations on the iron beam, the Putrella Dish proved the most durable design. Indeed, the Putrella's shape soon became something of a signature for the designer, who employed it in a later product, the Arran Tray for Alessi. Like all of the best radical designs it changes our approach to an everyday product such that we can never look at it in the same way again.

**EAMES
ALUMINIUM CHAIR
(1958)**
Charles Eames
(1907–78)
Ray Eames (1912–88)
Herman Miller
1958 to present
Vitra 1958 to present

This group of chairs is arguably one of the most outstanding ranges to be produced in the twentieth century. The Eames Aluminium Chair uses high-quality material specification combined with exceptional comfort derived from careful ergonomics and formal configuration. Each consists of a sheet of flexible, resilient material held under tension by cast aluminium bow-shaped stretchers between two cast aluminium side frames. The underside stretcher forms the link to the leg pedestal. The general principle is similar to the army camp bed or the trampoline. The specific genius of the chairs lies

in the sophistication of the side frame profile, formed in section like a symmetrical double T-beam (one 'T' on top of another), which controls the form and provides all of the facility for attaching membrane, stretchers and optional arms. Herman Miller first produced the original Eames Aluminium Group (sometimes called the Leisure or Indoor/Outdoor Group) in 1958. In 1969, a variant of the system was produced that added 50 mm (1.9 in) thick pads onto the basic membrane and was called the Soft Pad Group. Both ranges are still made today and are now produced by Vitra and Herman Miller.

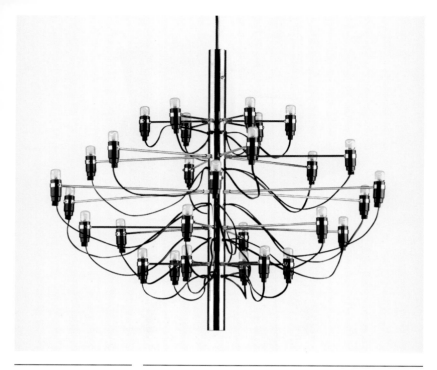

2097 CHANDELIER (1958)
Gino Sarfatti
(1912–84)
Arteluce 1958 to 1973
Flos 1974 to present

With the 2097 Chandelier for Arteluce, Gino Sarfatti has taken the traditional candelabra form and provided it with an innovative modern twist, not only in terms of novel design solution, but also in its technological inventiveness. Gino Sarfatti is one of the most important figures in Italian post-war lighting design, responsible for around 400 lamp designs for Arteluce, the company he founded in 1939 that was sold to Flos in 1974. Model 2097 is important in the Arteluce canon principally because it reinvents the chandelier within a Modern idiom. The hanging lamp is refined and rationalized, comprising only

a central structure of steel with brass arms, which results in a simple suspension fixture. The connecting flexes and bulbs are exposed and these raw, unadorned features are intrinsic to the beautiful symmetry and integrity of the piece. Model 2097 currently forms part of a series of re-editions by Flos. In many ways, 2097 marks the end of an era, and the new age of lighting design characterized by an obsession with the possibilities of new materials such as plastic, and ever more futuristic, space-age forms.

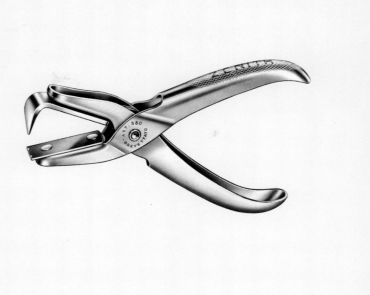

ZENITH 580 STAPLE REMOVER (1958)
Giorgio Balma
(1924–2017)
Balma, Capoduri & Co
1958 to present

If imitation is the sincerest form of flattery, the Zenith 580 Staple Remover is without doubt one of the most admired desktop designs of the past fifty years – so plentiful are the imitations. Designed by Giorgio Balma in 1958 in Voghera, Italy, the jaw-like grip of the staple remover leaves little doubt about the equipment's physical prowess, or the manufacturer's claim that it can remove any staple, big or small. Made from nickel-coated iron, it could almost be mistaken for a set of heavy-duty pliers. The handles, which are ergonomically engineered for comfort, are spring-loaded for added control. Manufacturer

Balma Capoduri & Company was founded in 1924, and the first independently branded Zenith line of products, comprising a tray and related accessories for copying letters, was rolled out at Milan's trade fair during the same year. The company has since become known for their office equipment, much lauded for its simple durability and timeless design. The stapler's individual components are separately tested before assembly before Zenith agrees to attach its famous life-time guarantee. The Zenith 580 Staple Remover is a simple statement of high-quality manufacturing and style.

TC 100 TABLEWARE (1959)

Hans 'Nick' Roericht (1932–)

Rosenthal
1959 to 2006
HoGaKa
2010 to present

Hans 'Nick' Roericht's TC 100 Tableware was designed for his diploma graduation project at the Hochschule für Gestaltung at Ulm, where he was a student under Tomás Maldonado. Roericht's design explicitly illustrates the design philosophy of the Ulm school, which openly encouraged 'system design' based on research into both use and manufacture. The success of this set lay not only in its Modern styling and ease of use, but also in its consideration of storage. The homogenized system is based on two modular forms: a constant angle was used for the sides of all bowls and plates, and a vertical interlocking arrangement for the cups, pots and jugs. The design allowed all the different pieces with the same diameter to be stacked, regardless of their type. Manufactured in chip-proof porcelain, this tableware is extremely tough and hard wearing. Since first being manufactured by Rosenthal in 1959, TC 100 has become an archetype and been widely imitated. It presents a model for how rational Modernist design ideals can be successfully implemented to produce an enduring, attractive and extremely practical set of tableware.

LAMBDA CHAIR (1959)
Marco Zanuso
(1916–2001)
Richard Sapper
(1932–2015)
Gavina/Knoll
1963 to present

Automobile construction methods are a recurring influence on Marco Zanuso's work and can be seen in particular in his Lambda Chair for Gavina (designed with Richard Sapper). But although the chair adopts methods of working sheet steel typically used in car manufacture, the inspiration to use this technique was purely architectural: Zanuso transferred a technique for creating vaults out of reinforced concrete to the design of the Lambda Chair. Preliminary sketches of the chair, originally to be made in sheet steel, show the influence of his studies on vaults. Eventually the Lambda prototype was cast out of polyvinyl, which tapped into new thermo-setting materials. Zanuso wanted to create a chair out of a single material, but did not know what shape the design would take. He says that the chair's ultimate appearance, which looks as though it was inspired by a plant, was probably 'a subconscious act'. Throughout his career, Zanuso consistently managed to create design that represented both innovation and comfort. As with most of Zanuso's designs, the research into the Lambda Chair was long and complex, but it has provided a blueprint for future plastic chairs that is still widely used today.

MONO-A CUTLERY (1959)
Peter Raacke (1928–)
Mono-
Metallwarenfabrik
Seibel 1959 to present

The most telling insight into what makes the Mono-A Cutlery set deserving of its status is that, in the forty-five years since it was first designed and manufactured in Germany, it remains free from significant alteration. Mono-A, the first design of what later became an extended series, was the perfect embodiment of late 1950s Modernism. Cut from standardized sheet metal, the crisp one-piece knives, forks and spoons made for a rather austere statement. Yet this was nonetheless attractive to a young post-war Germany busy embracing the democratic design ideal. Even when the strict utilitarian brief was

softened by the addition of teak and ebony handles, in the new Mono-T and Mono-E series the resultant tableware remained as moderate as the original. Peter Raacke, the cutlery's designer, was a young German gold- and silversmith who adhered closely to a refined purism that instilled in his tableware a classic appeal, impervious to the changing fashions of the early 1960s. And herein lies the essence of Mono's persistent commercial success. It remains as optimistic and modern a statement today as it did when it first appeared in 1959, and now stands as Germany's best-selling cutlery design.

PANTON CHAIR
(1959–60)
Verner Panton
(1926–98)
Herman Miller/
Vitra CH/D
1967 to 1979
Horn/WK-Verband
1983 to 1989
Vitra 1990 to present

The Panton Chair is deceptively simple – an organically flowing form that makes maximum use of plastic's infinite formal adaptability. The back of the chair flows into the seat, which in turn flows into an undercut base. The whole integrated shape creates a stacking, cantilevered chair, highly distinctive in its complex but autonomous unity. This was the first chair made of an unjointed continuous material for both serial and mass production. Panton first exhibited a prototype at the start of the 1960s. It took until 1963 to find visionary manufacturers, Vitra in Switzerland and Herman Miller in the United States. Eventually, the first viable

chairs emerged in 1967 as a limited edition of 100–150 pieces using cold-pressed fibreglass-reinforced polyester. Since its debut the chair has undergone several more manufacturing halts and changes to resolve structural fatigue and improve manufacture. Since 1990 Vitra has produced it in injection-moulded polypropylene. The original Panton Chair's seven bright colours and its informal flowing shape captured and epitomized the Pop Art culture of the period. As such the chair was much used in media and rapidly began to represent the 'anything is possible' technical and social spirit of the 1960s.

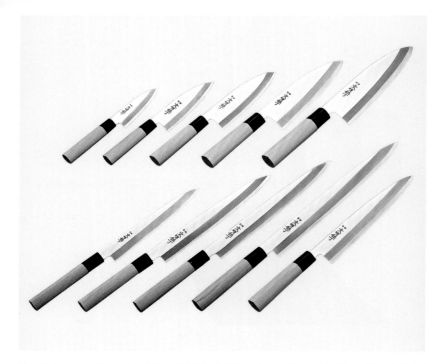

BUNMEI GINCHO
KNIFE (1960)
Designer Unknown
Yoshikin
1960 to present

An amalgamation of tradition
and modern technologies, this
beautiful knife, influenced by
samurai swords, was developed
for preparing Japanese cuisine.
The Bunmei Gincho ('the civilized
silver one') Knife was first produced
in 1960 by the Yoshida Kinzoku
Company, later shortened to
Yoshikin. Yoshikin was inspired
by medical scalpels to use
high-grade stainless steel
containing molybdenum, which
is highly corrosion-resistant and
easy to maintain. The Bunmei
Gincho Knives were the first
Japanese-style professional knives
to be made of stainless steel.
They were awarded a medal by

the Japanese Catering and Hygiene
Association in 1961, and were
later purchased by the Japanese
imperial household. In subsequent
years the knives were marketed
worldwide and the reputation
of the product continues to the
present day. The factory is located
in Tsubame, an area renowned for
the production of metalwork. With
its wood handle and plastic blade
junction, the Bunmei Gincho Knife
requires care. However, its affinity
to its use and elegance make
it the perfect knife with which to
prepare beautiful Japanese food.

SANLUCA CHAIR
(1960)
Achille Castiglioni
(1918–2002)
Pier Giacomo
Castiglioni (1913–68)
Gavina/Knoll
1960 to 1969
Bernini 1990 to present
Poltrona Frau
2004 to present

At first glance the Sanluca looks like an old-fashioned chair. Seen from the front it resembles a seventeenth-century Italian baroque chair, but it was also influenced by the futuristic sculpture of Umberto Boccioni. The use of hollow, modelled panes gave the chair a spacious and aerodynamic look. This witty paradox is characteristic of all Castiglioni designs. The concept of the Sanluca was revolutionary. Instead of building a frame, which was then upholstered, Achille and Pier Giacomo Castiglioni fixed pre-modelled and pre-upholstered panels to a stamped metal frame. This industrial technique was common in the manufacture of car seats, and the Castiglioni brothers hoped that their chair could be similarly mass produced. Unfortunately, this was not the case, due to its complicated construction. The chair consists of three parts: seat, back and sides made from pre-formed metal and covered with polyure-thane foam and legs made of rosewood. The original chair, produced by Gavina in 1960 and by Knoll International from 1960 to 1969, came in leather or cotton. In 1990, Bernini reissued the chair in natural, red or black leather with minor technical adjustments, supervised by Achille Castiglioni.

SPLÜGEN BRÄU
LAMP (1960)
Achille Castiglioni
(1918–2002)
Pier Giacomo
Castiglioni (1913–68)
Flos 1961 to present

In 1960, brothers Achille and Pier Giacomo Castiglioni were commissioned by Aldo Bassetti to design the interior of his Splügen Bräu beerhouse and restaurant, housed in a building designed by Luigi Caccia Dominioni in Milan.
The Castiglioni brothers designed several of the fittings for the project, including this pendant lamp, which hung gracefully above each table. The shade is made from thick, corrugated polished aluminium with a highly polished spun aluminium reflector. The ribbed body aids heat dispersal from the silver-domed bulb that lets off an indirect but concentrated light. The overhead

supplementary lighting reflected off the polished surface of the shade, helping to accentuate the presence of the hanging light and its eye-catching ripple effect. In 1961, leading Italian lighting manufacturer Flos put the lamp into production and it continues to enjoy commercial success today. In addition, the Castiglionis' designs for an ashtray, umbrella stand, high-backed bar stool, beerglass, and bottle opener for the Splügen Bräu have been manufactured over the years. The Castiglioni brothers' functional purist approach was always lifted with a playful twist and continues to inspire designers around the world.

CONOID CHAIR
(1960)
George Nakashima
(1905–90)
Nakashima Studios
1960 to present

In an era when bent plywood and metal were the materials of choice for most furniture designers, George Nakashima unashamedly celebrated wood in its most naked state. Although the Conoid Chair is more refined than many of his designs, the richness and texture of the woods used are still very much in evidence. Nakashima's intimate knowledge of joinery made for an impressively solid chair, with a cantilevered construction that was not as precarious as his critics claimed. The Conoid Chair was conceived on Nakashima's estate in New Hope, Pennsylvania. Just three years earlier he had completed the building of the

Conoid Studio, whose concrete-shell roof is said to have inspired the Conoid collection, which also included tables, benches and desks. Nakashima was born in America to Japanese parents, both of whom were descended from Samurai families. Equally influential on his furniture designs was the American Shaker style. While most American furniture designers were preoccupied with testing technological limits, Nakashima encouraged a more craft-based approach. Yet his style was entirely modern, as was his core belief in functionality. His work continues to be in demand today.

606 UNIVERSAL SHELVING SYSTEM (1960)
Dieter Rams (1932–)
Vitsœ
1960 to present

The reductionist outline of the 606 Universal Shelving System is based on geometric simplicity with minimum decoration. Its strength rests with this style, married with strong practical characteristics. The 606 is a wholly flexible shelving and storage system, composed of sheets of anodized aluminium, 3 mm (0.12 in) thick, which hang from an extruding wall-mounted aluminium track with 7 mm (0.04 in) aluminium pins. The system can be readily dismantled and easily accommodates the addition of more components from the range, including drawer sets, cabinets, hanging rails and shelves. The idea for the shelves

developed when Dieter Rams, employed by Braun from 1955–1995, suggested to Erwin Braun that he design an exhibition room for the company to display its products. The shelves were first produced by Vitsœ + Zapf and later by Vitsœ. The first versions of the 606 were in the same colour palette as such Braun products as the SK4, with off-white and beech lacquered doors and drawers. This understated approach was reflected in Rams's belief that the shelving system should be like a good English butler: 'there when you need them, and in the background when you don't.'

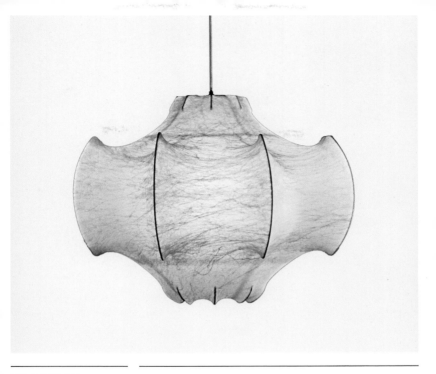

VISCONTEA COCOON LAMP (1960)
Achille Castiglioni (1918–2002)
Pier Giacomo Castiglioni (1913–68)
Eisenkeil/Flos
1960 to 1995, 2005 to present

George Nelson's experiments with metal-frame lamp structures inspired Achille Castiglioni to produce a series of decorative lamps for Flos in the 1960s. The Viscontea Cocoon Lamp is one of this series. While Flos had produced earlier designs by the Castiglionis, it was the Viscontea that made the company's name by using cocoon: a film of plastic polymers, or spun fibreglass produced in the United States. Italian importer Arturo Eisenkeil had researched possible new applications for this material and decided to collaborate with Dino Gavina and Cesare Cassina to create Flos, a company to produce lighting fixtures. The

company was originally established in Merano, Italy, and the first cocoon lights to be created were the Viscontea, Taraxacum and Gatto by the Castiglioni brothers. The polymer would spray cobweb-like filaments that created a permanent, but flexible, membrane that was waterproof and would resist corrosion, dust, oil, gas, and even citric acid, alcohol and bleach. Cocoon, used for any type of surface or material, could revert back to its original shape after bearing a heavy load. Flos eventually discontinued their production once their individual cocoon licence expired but resumed it in 2005.

OX CHAIR (1960)
Hans Wegner
(1914–2007)
AP-Stolen
1960 to c.1975
Erik Jørgensen
1985 to present

The large, tubular 'horns' and general bulk of this chair have provided it with its English name of Ox Chair. In Danish it is called the Pållestolen, which translates as Bolster or Pillow Chair. Both names give an idea of the comfortable freestanding mass of this large easy chair – one of Wegner's favourite designs. It is claimed that this design has no precedents, but the form is related to the English wing armchair, one of the 'timeless types' of furniture much studied and adapted by the followers of Kaare Klint. The Ox Chair looks very much like a chromed-steel and leather update of this traditional form. The chair

was intended to be situated towards the middle of a room, away from any wall, so it would be viewed as a sculpturally whole object. In its design Wegner was especially aware that the sitter should be able to adopt a number of different seating positions. Sitters are encouraged to slouch, sit asymmetrically and to swing their legs over the arms. The Ox Chair has a monumental quality that would dominate a room. A more slender version, without the horn-like protuberances, was produced as a companion piece.

SARPANEVA CAST IRON POT (1960)
Timo Sarpaneva
(1926–2006)
Rosenlew & Co.
1960 to 1977
iittala
2003 to present

A black cast-iron cooking pot lined with white enamel, the Sarpaneva Cast Iron Pot is both modern yet familiar, its shape taken in part from the simple forms of Finnish folk traditions. These historic roots are emphasized further by the pot's detachable wooden handle to facilitate lifting the pan off the stove and carrying it to the table. Timo Sarpaneva was true to the tenets of Scandinavian Modernism, where the human being rather than the machine was placed on a pedestal, and believed in good design sold at reasonable prices. In this pot, which was made using traditional cast-iron techniques, Sarpaneva anticipated

a more relaxed, modern way of eating and opened the way for oven-to-table ware. He preferred to work in ways that revealed the high quality of his country's craft tradition, believing that, 'If you are not familiar with the traditions you cannot renew them.' Sarpaneva saw tactile pleasure and natural forms as important parts of design. The Sarpaneva Cast Iron Pot was originally manufactured by Rosenlew & Co. It was so beloved that it was reproduced on a Finnish postage stamp, and was reintroduced by iittala in 2003.

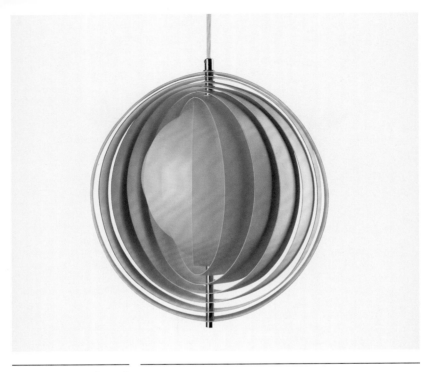

MOON LAMP (1960)
Verner Panton
(1926–98)
Louis Poulsen
1960 to c.1970
Vitra Design
Museum
2003 to 2009
Verpan
2010 to present

An early light by Danish designer Verner Panton, the Moon Lamp is a complex, abstract hanging form made of ten metal rings of diminishing sizes, fitted onto mobile bearings so that each ring can be rotated to adjust the quality of light. The first versions were produced in white lacquered aluminium, and later in plastic. The lamp can be packed flat for transportation. Verner Panton produced some of the most innovative furniture and lighting of the post-war period, exploiting the properties of new materials such as acrylic, foam, plastic and glass fibre-reinforced polyester. His work is closely connected to

the Op and Pop Art movements of the late 1950s and 1960s. He trained as an architect, and was taught by the influential lighting designer, Poul Henningsen, who introduced him to the idea of product design as a radical (as well as commercial) practice. Henningsen's PH series of lamps (produced by Louis Poulsen from 1924) uses a similar shuttering system of overlapping leaves. The Moon Lamp was included in a retrospective of the designer's career by the Vitra Design Museum in 2000, which put it back into production in 2003.

MIXING BOWLS (1960)
Sori Yanagi
(1915–2011)
Uehan-Shoji
1960 to 1978
NAS Trading
Company
1978 to 1994
Sato-Shoji
1994 to present

When Sori Yanagi designed this set of five mixing bowls, he started with models rather than with drawings, saying, 'When you make an object that is to be used by hand, it should be made by hand.' Numerous experimental models determined the size and shape of each bowl. The smallest bowl, designed for making dressings or sauces, is 13 cm (5.1 in) in diameter, and the largest bowl at 27 cm (10.6 in) is useful for washing vegetables or as a wine cooler. The bottoms of all the bowls are flat and extra thick, making them heavier than conventional ones. Made of stainless steel, the surface has a matt

brushed finish. The edges are carefully rolled over so they do not catch washing up tools or debris. Originally, the bowls were designed for the Uehan-Shoji Company, but since 1994 they have been made by Sato-Shoji. In 1999 Yanagi designed strainers to fit each bowl using punched stainless steel sheets. His rediscovery by a younger generation in recent years has seen these bowls and strainers become one of the bestselling ranges of kitchenware in Japan, appreciated for their functionality and their beauty.

RATTAN CHAIR (1961)
Isamu Kenmochi (1912–71)
Yamakawa Rattan
1961 to c.1985
YMK Niigata
2011 to present

The intricate criss-crossing of rattan stems and the circular, cocooning shape lend Isamu Kenmochi's lounge chair the appearance of a nest. Called variously the Rattan Chair, the Lounge Chair or the 38 Chair, it was designed for the bar of the New Japan Hotel in Tokyo, as part of Kenmochi's brief to update the Yamakawa Rattan Company's range of products. The Rattan contrasts an unconventional shape with traditional methods of production. The construction of rattan furniture is a wonderfully simple procedure that starts with the harvesting of good-quality rattan, a solid timber vine.

The rattan is first steamed until it becomes pliable. It is then fitted to a jig, to form the required shape, and left to cool. Although Kenmochi was a staunch supporter of traditional construction techniques, he was also an avid researcher into cutting-edge production methods – particularly those of aircraft construction. The billowing, airy appearance of the Rattan Chair, a true break from convention, has made it an enduring design that is still produced by the same company today, albeit with slight variations. Indeed, it proved so successful that Kenmochi subsequently added a sofa and stool to the Rattan range.

EJ CORONA CHAIR
(1961)
Poul Volther
(1923–2001)
Eric Jørgensen
1961 to present

The EJ Corona Chair, designed in 1961 by Danish architect Poul Volther, is visually and structurally symbolic of tensions within the Scandinavian furniture industry in the early 1960s. Poised on the cusp of a dramatic decade of design, the chair nonetheless responded to ideological and manufacturing tenets of the previous decade. Its structure is defined by four graduated and curving elliptical shapes that seem to hover in space. The neoprene-upholstered plywood forms were initially manufactured in leather and later in fabric. They are supported by a chromium-plated steel frame and pivoting base.

The frame of the original model was constructed in solid oak and produced in very small numbers by Danish furniture manufacturer Erik Jørgensen. By 1962, plywood had replaced the oak to afford larger-scale production. The influence of Pop Art and design was certainly felt amongst Scandinavian designers in the 1960s, but a truthful use of materials, as realized in the EJ Corona Chair, continued to convince Scandinavian designers that quality production was the ideal. The extremely comfortable chair remains one of Erik Jørgensen's most popular products.

MAYA CUTLERY
(1961)
Tias Eckhoff
(1926–2016)
Norsk Staalpress/
Norstaal 1961 to 2007
Stelton
2007 to present

Tias Eckhoff helped to move Norwegian design out of the shadow of its neighbours during the 1950s. Eckhoff's designs, including ceramics, glassware and tableware, have an enduring quality and many have remained in production for several decades. Simplicity is a key aspect of his work, inspired, according to the designer, by a farmyard upbringing where he observed how big problems were dealt with through simple remedies. Eckhoff tempers a rational and scientific approach with a strong artistic sensibility that ensures his designs are beautiful as well as practical. His Maya Cutlery was the first product

of a relationship with Norsk Staalpress (now Norstaal) that would yield a number of flatware sets. Maya is created in brushed stainless steel and made from pressing stainless steel plates. The relatively generous spoons and knife blades contrast with short handles in a sculptural way that was distinctively Scandinavian. There are thirty-five steps involved in production, with the extremely difficult process of grinding and polishing done by hand. The twenty-piece set, Norstaal's biggest seller, was modified in 2000 with the addition of a slightly longer soup spoon, dinner knife and fork and were resized by Eckhoff himself.

MARQUINA 1961
CRUETS (1961)
Rafael Marquina
(1921–2013)
Various 1961 to 1971
Mobles 114
1971 to present

Several generations of holiday-makers travelling to the Costa Brava, north of Barcelona, will recognize Rafael Marquina's brilliant oil and vinegar cruets, which have been celebrated all over Catalonia for more than forty years. The glass cruets are among the true gems of Modernist design. The elegant simplicity of the Marquina 1961 Cruets set belies the sophistication of its design. A removable spout sits like a stopper in the flat-bottomed, conical glass. It is held in place by the friction of the ground surface of the glass. A little groove is cast into the side of the stopper to allow air to flow into the cruet as the liquid flows out. If it did nothing more than that, it would be worthy of acclaim. But the flared neck of the glass acts as a funnel to catch drips, which re-enter the bottle through the air groove – a brilliant solution to a perennial problem. Marquina is somewhat of a design poly-math, crossing with ease into the worlds of architecture and fine art. And while his international legacy may be tied to these cruets, he is revered in his native Catalonia as a visionary Modernist.

MOULTON BICYCLE (1962)
Alex Moulton
(1920–2012)
Alex Moulton
Bicycles 1962 to 1975,
1983 to present

The Moulton was the world's first small-wheeled production bicycle with suspension. Alex Moulton worked with Alec Issigonis as the suspension designer on several ground-breaking vehicles, including the Mini and the Austin 1100. It was working on the Mini, with its winning combination of small wheels and suspension, which inspired the first Moulton Bicycle. The advantages of small wheels (16 as an alternative to 27 inch tyres) are their inherent strength and their reduced size, which allows more space for load carrying. The foreseeable disadvantages of increased rolling resistance and hardness of ride are solved by high-pressure tyres and suspensions. Moreover, the lower aerodynamic drag of small wheels means they will go faster with less effort. Moulton developed the first serious bicycle to break with the seventy years of proven success of the diamond-frame into a product. His design was bought by Raleigh in 1967, but was taken out of production in 1974. He went on to develop a second generation of bicycles using the small-wheel-suspension concept, which have been in production since 1983. These are manufactured by his own company, Alex Moulton Bicycles, as well as under licence by specialist manufacturer, Pashley.

MAX BILL
WRISTWATCH
(1962)
Max Bill (1908–94)
Junghans 1962 to
1964, 1997 to present

Swiss artist Max Bill was one of the Modern Movement's true Renaissance men, and his progressive Modernist credentials are perfectly encapsulated in the simple, practical wristwatches he designed for German precision watchmakers Junghans. The Max Bill Wristwatch marked the beginning of the trend to commission well-known product designers and architects to design watches – a discipline once the sole preserve of a company's in-house watch-maker. Bill was an architect, painter and sculptor as well as a stage, graphic and industrial designer. The clarity and precision of his wristwatch collection make

it very much a product of the Ulm school ethos, which he co-founded in 1951. The watch designs – white and black faces with a diameter of 34.2 mm (1.34 in) – are character-ized by a simple no-fuss digit configuration inside a polished stainless steel case featuring a seventeen-jewel Swiss hand-winding movement mechanism. The pared-down design of the watch recalls the earlier minimal-ist Wall Clock range that Bill designed for Junghans in 1956–7. Junghans and fellow German manufacturers Braun saw in Bill and the Ulm school an opportunity to associate their names with leading-edge designs.

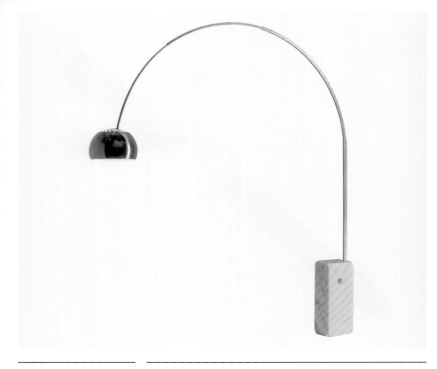

ARCO FLOOR LAMP (1962)
Achille Castiglioni
(1918–2002)
Pier Giacomo
Castiglioni (1913–68)
Flos 1962 to present

Inspired by everyday products, the Arco Floor Lamp was developed as a freestanding interior version of a standard street lamp. Arco comprises an arching arm fixed to a rectangular base of white Carrara marble. The telescopic arm supports the light at a distance of over 2 m (6.6 ft) from the base, allowing for a dining table and chairs to be positioned comfortably under the shade. The arm, made of satin-finished stainless steel with a Zapon-varnished aluminium reflector, weighs over 45 kg (100 lb), but the designers incorporated a hole into the marble base to allow a broom handle to be inserted, enabling two people to lift it. Arco was produced during the Castiglioni brothers' most prolific period of lighting design, from the late 1950s to the early 1960s. Together with Flos, the producers of Arco, they redefined the nature and purpose of interior lighting, affording it a sculptural as well as a functional role. The Arco Floor Lamp has become one of the most admired design objects of the post-war period and is a regular prop in various media, perhaps most famously in the James Bond film *Diamonds Are Forever*.

TANDEM SLING CHAIR (1962)
Charles Eames
(1907–78)
Ray Eames (1912–88)
Herman Miller
1962 to present
Vitra 1962 to present

Public seating is not the most glamorous of design commissions, but it is one of the most challenging. It has to be comfortable, sturdy, easy to maintain and attractive without being overwhelming. The Tandem Sling Chair fulfils all the criteria, the sleek black and aluminium design remaining smart more than fifty years after it was launched at Washington's Dulles International Airport. Its designers, husband-and-wife team Charles and Ray Eames, turned their talents to aluminium after World War II when the aluminium industry was looking for new outlets for production. Thus began their Aluminium Group series, which included the Tandem Sling Chair that was light and comfortable and resistant to corrosion. They developed an aluminium-frame chair on which the seating – foam pads sealed between two layers of vinyl for a durable finish – is suspended like a sling. The practicalities of the chair are numerous – the seats are wide and padded with an open seat-to-back angle to provide optimum comfort, and the support-beam design leaves plenty of space under the seats for luggage. The aluminium frame is joint-free for maximum strength and there are no stitch lines in the seat portion where dust can gather.

TMM FLOOR LAMP (1962)
Miguel Milá (1931–)
Gres 1962
Santa & Cole
1988 to present

In 1950s Spain, a design industry, whether modern or traditional, hardly existed. Despite this, Miguel Milá created a design of lasting relevance and modernity. Unlike many icons of design, the TMM Floor Lamp was praised from its very inception and has since become an icon. In 1956, Milá's maternal aunt commissioned a light from him. The resulting lamp, named TN, was a precursor of the TMM Lamp. The TMM, short for Tramo Móvil Madera, was designed in 1962 as part of a competition to design an interior using low-cost furniture. The self-assembled, all wood structure supported an easily adjustable

light with simply integrated cord light switch. While the do-it-yourself packaging was not new in world design at that time, it was still novel in Spain. The timelessness of the TMM resides in its modesty of form and use of natural, warm materials, which together possess a serenity. It is a signature piece reflecting Milá's insistence that he is 'a pre-industrial designer' who willingly embraces the history and skills of traditional craftsmen, and insists on a rigour that sees no discord between the modern and the sensual.

POLYPROPYLENE STACKING CHAIR (1962)
Robin Day
(1915–2010)
Hille Seating
1963 to present

The familiar form of Robin Day's Polypropylene Stacking Chair belies its significance in the history of furniture design. The simple shape of the single-piece shell, with deep-turned edge and finely textured surface affixed to a stacking base, remains the most democratic seating design of the twentieth century. Robin Day became aware of polypropylene in 1960, and Hille supported his quest to realize the potential of the material. Although the material was low cost, the tooling was extremely expensive and refinement towards production was a slow process of fine-tuning the shape, wall-thickness and

fixing bosses. The development of the Polypropylene Stacking Chair was pioneering; with no precedents in the field of manufacturing, the process was arduous. Available in a host of colours and a variety of base options, the chair was an immediate success. The design sealed Hille's status as the most progressive furniture manufacturer in Britain and a true force within international markets. Despite the fact the Polypropylene Stacking Chair was quickly copied, in excess of 14 million licensed chairs have been sold in twenty-three countries.

SLEEK MAYONNAISE SPOON (1962)
Achille Castiglioni
(1918–2002)
Pier Giacomo
Castiglioni (1913–68)
Alessi 1996 to present

The Sleek Mayonnaise Spoon was designed in 1962 as a promotional item for Kraft and bore the company's logo on the handle. It was produced specifically to retrieve the last remnants of food from jars of mayonnaise, peanut butter and jam – all items produced by Kraft. The spoon features a narrow, curved tip, with one side of the bowl curved while the other is straight, allowing it to slide along the side of the container. A thumb rest on the handle makes it easier to grip. The design incorporated the use of Polymethylmetacrylate (PMMA), a flexible, hardwearing and hygienic plastic, to allow maximum movement. The spoon's designers, the prolific Castiglioni brothers, played an important role in Italian design. They were allied to the ideals of Neo-Modernism, and their designs exhibit a strong awareness of form, production and the user. The use of plastic and bright colours are characteristic of Italian domestic homeware design and the 1960s Pop sensibility. Alessi has had the Sleek Mayonnaise Spoon in production since 1996 in a wide range of bright primary colours. Sleek is the perfect domestic spoon: fun, practical and guaranteed to brighten up any kitchen.

FORMOSA
PERPETUAL
CALENDAR (1962)
Enzo Mari (1932–)
Danese
1963 to present

Enzo Mari produced many beautiful designs – from children's toys to office furniture and accessories – during his collaboration with manufacturer Danese. The Formosa Perpetual Calendar is one of the most popular. An aluminium calendar with mobile lithographic PVC pages, its design is minimal, graphic and modern. Date, month, and day of the week are changed by switching the individual placards hanging on the metal back plate. The calendar's legibility, due to the clear typeface (the ubiquitous Helvetica) and grid formation, means it is still a relevant object for the office today. It is available in either a red or

a black version and has been sold all over the world and translated into many languages. Mari's statement, 'Real design is about who produces rather than who buys', explains his attitude towards the product as the meeting between the designer/artisan and the manufacturer. Only in this way, he believes, can designers create products that maintain their cultural, social and economic purpose. Mari believes that mass production should compromise neither beauty of form nor functionality, and these theories have developed into an applied philosophy of 'rational design'.

RING-PULL CAN END (1962)
Ernie Fraze (1913–89)
Dayton Reliable Tool
& Manufacturing
Company
1962 to present
Stolle Machinery
(Alcoa)
1965 to present

The Ring-Pull for aluminium drinks cans was the holy grail of the American beverage industry. Widespread popularity of cans was thwarted by the fact that consumers needed to carry can-openers with them to get at the drink. The necessity for a self-opening can was evident, but the field was littered with unsuccessful prototypes. After a picnic where he had been reduced to using his car bumper to open a can, toolmaker Ernie Fraze of Muncie, Indiana, set out to develop the pull-tab opener. He created a see-saw mechanism that used leverage to rip the can open along a pre-scored line.

The rivet that held the lever to the can was attached by cold-welding and used only the material of the can itself. The idea was sold to Alcoa, and in 1962 the first 100,000 orders were placed by the Pittsburgh Brewing Company. Fraze's invention continued to be refined by scores of individuals and companies. In 1965, the tab opening was replaced by the ring, and in 1975 the non-removable tab was developed by Daniel F Cudzik. The tab-opening drinks can epitomizes accessibility and convenience, and the application of tremendous creativity to a mundane problem.

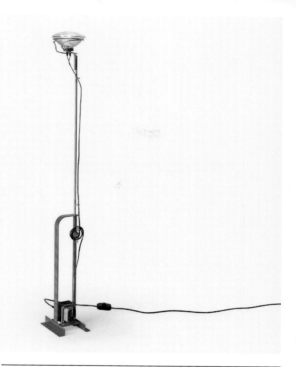

TOIO LAMP (1962)
Achille Castiglioni
(1918–2002)
Pier Giacomo
Castiglioni
(1913–68)
Flos 1962 to present

The extendable Toio Lamp was produced by the Castiglioni brothers in the early 1960s as part of a series of 'ready-made' products. Borrowing a concept associated with Dadaism, the Castiglionis used found objects as the basis for industrial products. The Toio Lamp is constructed almost entirely from ready-made components: a 300-watt car reflector bulb, attached to a metal stem that is weighted by the transformer at the base pedestal. The electrical wire is pinned to the stem by fishing-rod screws. Products such as this one and the Mezzadro and Sella stools, both from 1957, celebrate the ingenuity of the mundane or everyday object, with the minimum of intervention. The Castiglioni brothers developed an industrial style that was at once humorous and thought-provoking. Their work had its roots in the Italian Rationalist movement, which was predicated on a functionalist approach to design. Achille Castiglioni also championed an approach to design that demonstrated a strong awareness of the user. Products had to appeal on an emotional level, and be as satisfying to use as to look at. The Toio Lamp is featured in major museum collections, including the Victoria and Albert Museum in London.

SPAGHETTI CHAIR
(1962)
Giandomenico
Belotti (1922–2004)
Pluri 1970
Alias 1979 to present

Giandomenico Belotti, Carlo Forcolini and Enrico Baleri founded the furniture manufacturer Alias in Bergamo, Italy, in 1979. The company's first product was Belotti's Spaghetti Chair, made from strips of coloured PVC that are stretched taut around a slender tubular-steel frame to form the seat and back. The designer had originally conceived the chair in 1962 under the name Odessa. When first exhibited in New York, it assumed its new name, inspired by the pasta-like strips. The chair was an instant bestseller. The simple, structural shapes employed by Belotti provide a clean-lined and

uncomplicated framework for the unusual yet highly practical rubber-string seat. The graphic and light appearance does not distract from the all-important issue of comfort. The PVC flexes according to the weight and shape of the user, able to accommodate virtually anyone who sits on it. One could draw parallels with the rope seat constructions of Poul Kjærholm and Hans Wegner, redefined by Belotti in a newer, more durable material. Today, the chair is available in a large variety of colour options.

LEISURE OUTDOOR FURNITURE COLLECTION (1962–6)
Richard Schultz (1926–)
Knoll 1966 to 1987, 2012 to present
Richard Schultz Design 1992 to 2012

Unhappy with the quality of most outdoor furniture, Florence Knoll Bassett asked Richard Schultz to design some outdoor furniture that looked new and would not fall apart after exposure to the elements. Schultz experimented with corrosion-resistant aluminium for the frames and Teflon for the seating. After intense research and development, he introduced the Leisure Collection and it was an immediate success. The line consisted of eight different pieces, including tables and seating, but it was the Contour Chaise Lounge and the Adjustable Chaise Lounge that were the signature designs that revolutionized the outdoor market. They were so airy as to be almost invisible in the garden. Sculpturally minimal and elegant, the Adjustable Chaise had a cast and extruded aluminium frame with a polyester-powder-coated finish, cast-aluminium wheels with rubber tyres and Teflon mesh upholstery. Quickly recognized as an iconic design, its status was solidified when the Museum of Modern Art in New York purchased it for its permanent collection. The line was updated with new woven vinyl-coated polyester-mesh upholstery and reintroduced as the 1966 Collection by Richard Schultz Design before being re-released by Knoll in 2012.

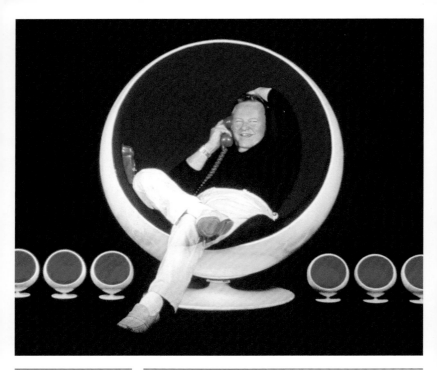

BALL CHAIR (1963)
Eero Aarnio (1932–)
Asko 1963 to 1985
Adelta 1991 to 2016
Eero Aarnio Originals
2016 to present

Pioneering plastics designer Eero Aarnio sought to design a chair that would generate a private space. The result was the Ball Chair (called the Globe Chair in the US). Produced in moulded fibreglass on a painted aluminium base, with reinforced polyester seating, it was presented at the Cologne Furniture Fair in 1966. The fibreglass sphere is perched on a swivelling central leg, creating the illusion that the sphere is floating while enabling it to rotate 360°. The upholstered inside, fitted with a red telephone, creates a cocoon. The design reflected the dynamic social style of the 1960s, and the Ball Chair became a metaphor of its time,

featuring in films and on magazine covers. It pays tribute to Eero Saarinen's Tulip Chair, which was the first to introduce a one-legged pedestal base. In a way, the Ball Chair was a contemporary version of the traditional club chair, but Aarnio's treatment of the object as a kind of mini-architecture makes this chair very contemporary. In 2016, the rights to all of Aarnio's designs were transferred to Eero Aarnio Originals, and the Ball Chair is still available, with fifteen interior colour options in fabric by Kvadrat.

USM MODULAR FURNITURE (1963)
Paul Schärer
(1933–2011)
Fritz Haller
(1924–2012)
USM U Schärer
Söhne 1965 to present

The highly resolved USM Modular Furniture range is based on three simple components: the sphere, connecting tubes and steel panels. From these basic elements an infinite range of configurations may be realized and a host of storage needs satisfied. The spheres act as joints to link a skeletal framework constructed to the user's specification and panels enclose storage areas where required. The ingenuity of the system relies on Fritz Haller's ability to rationalize the design to this minimal component count without sacrificing functionality. Paul Schärer commissioned Haller in 1961 to design a new factory for

USM. Schärer was so impressed with Haller's architecture that he commissioned the architect to design a range of modular furniture for the offices. Thus the Haller system was born. Schärer and Haller soon realized they had a viable commercial product. USM Modular Furniture was launched in 1965 and transformed USM from metal manufacturers into makers of high-quality office furniture. The system has changed little over the last fifty years. Its timeless qualities and spare decoration provide use for both the home and the office. It generates a $100 million turnover in Western Europe alone.

ZAISU (1963)
Kenji Fujimori
(1919–93)
Tendo Mokko
1963 to present

In the traditional Japanese home, people sit directly on the *tatami* floors. In response to a desire for something to lean back on while sitting, and to add an element of formality, the *zaisu* ('*za*' meaning to sit on the floor, and '*isu*' is chair) was invented. This design by Kenji Fujimori in 1963 has become recognized as the definitive *zaisu* – able to be stacked and inexpensively mass produced. Although minimal in form, it is very comfortable to sit on, with the back shaped to support the spine. The hole in the bottom of the seat prevents the chair from slipping and also reduces the chair's weight.

This chair, of exceptionally high quality, is produced by Tendo Mokko, a pioneer of moulded plywood products. Fujimori's Zaisu was designed for the guestrooms of the Morioka Ground Hotel. It remains very popular, particularly for Japanese-style hotels and, recently, for Japanese restaurants outside of Japan. It is now made in three different types of plywood – keyaki, maple and oak. In the 1950s Fujimori studied product design in Finland. His fusion of Scandinavian and Japanese thinking into a single object has resulted in an innovative seating solution.

BARBOY (1963)
Verner Panton
(1926–98)
Sommer 1963 to 1967
Bisterfeld & Weiss
1967 to 1971
Vitra Design Museum
2001 to 2009
Verpan
2011 to present

The early 1960s saw many new materials and technologies become available, and it was a boom period for Verner Panton and his curvaceous, colourful furniture. The Barboy was designed during this period for the German company Sommer and manufactured until 1967 under the trade name 'Declina'. Like most of Panton's work, it reduces an object to an externally minimal form. Untypically though, it is made using a traditional technology from earlier in the century: formed plywood. The cylindrical components – housing bottles, glasses, or corkscrews – rotate around a pivot. The Barboy was finished with a very high-gloss lacquer, available in red and violet, two of Panton's favourite colours, as well as black and white. Of the few more geometric pieces Panton designed, the Barboy remains the purest. It is perhaps this purity of form that has ensured the Barboy's survival. Production was taken over by another German company, Bisterfeld & Weiss, from 1967 until 1971. Finally, after thirty years out of production, it was reissued by the Vitra Design Museum. The black or white options available on the reissued version probably help it to sit happily apart from Panton's fantastical full-colour environments.

NESSO TABLE LAMP (1963)
Giancarlo Mattioli (1933–)
Gruppo Architetti Urbanistici Città Nuova
Artemide 1965 to 1987, 1999 to present

Winning a design competition does not always lead to success, but it did in the case of the Nesso Table Lamp, designed by Giancarlo Mattioli and Gruppo Architetti Urbanistici Città Nuova. A competition formed by the manufacturer Artemide and the cutting-edge magazine *Domus* in 1965 resulted in the introduction of the lamp. Artemide was a leader in plastic furniture and lamps in the 1960s, which led to its involvement with revolutionary design group, Memphis. The Nesso form uses the translucent quality of plastic to its best advantage, creating a shape that glows from within, mimicking the glow of phosphorous. It embodies Italian style of the 1960s in its use of colour; bright orange and white were prevalent in all things plastic. Artemide has recently introduced a smaller version of the lamp, named Nessino, which is manufactured in many transparent colours, including red, blue, orange, grey, and yellow. The transparency enhances the design, revealing the internal structure and the light sources. The Nesso endures as an icon of 1960s Italian design, outliving many of its contemporaries because of its clarity of purpose, and by the way it simply declares itself a lamp.

SUPERELLIPSE
TABLE (1964)
Piet Hein (1905–96)
Bruno Mathsson
(1907–88)
Bruno Mathsson
International
1964 to present
Fritz Hansen
1968 to present

At first glance, the Superellipse Table might appear a simple, straightforward design. On closer scrutiny, its incredible complexity becomes apparent. The table's shape, somewhere between a rectangle and an oval, is the outcome of lengthy mathematical research. In 1959, Piet Hein, a Danish poet, philosopher and mathematician, was asked to design a town plaza in Stockholm to help ease the flow of traffic. A circle or oval would not prove space efficient and a rectangle would produce too many corners for cars to turn. Hein produced an entirely new shape, which he termed the Superellipse. Bruno Mathsson,

a pioneering designer and crafts-man from Sweden, saw the potential in the Superellipse and began working with Hein to translate it into a table. Its space efficiency proved useful as a table in cramped city apartments. Below the tabletop a self-clamping leg made of metal rods is both rock solid and easily detachable for transportation. The Superellipse was produced by Karl Mathsson's small family firm, Mathsson International, which is still producing it today. Four years after its design, Fritz Hansen began producing a similar table, attributed to Piet Hein with contributions by Bruno Mathsson and Arne Jacobsen.

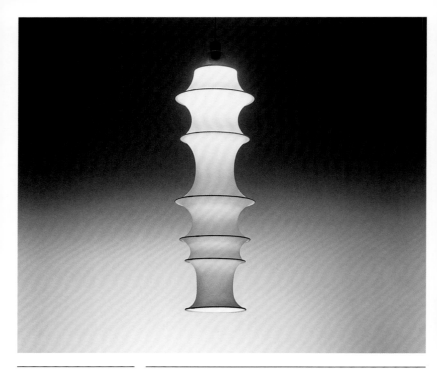

FALKLAND LAMP
(1964)
Bruno Munari
(1907–98)
Danese
1964 to present

It is difficult to imagine that this long lamp comes in such a small box. Once unpacked and hung from the ceiling, the Falkland Lamp extends to its full 165 cm (66 in) length. Designed by the Italian artist and designer Bruno Munari, it has been manufactured by Danese since 1964. The shade is made from a stocking-like, white elastic knitwear tube, attached to a stainless steel cone. Within the tube six aluminium rings of three different sizes are attached. When hung from the ceiling, the weight of the carefully positioned rings stretches the material of the tube into a scalloped sculptural form. There is also a freestanding version, Falkland Terra, in which the sleeve is suspended from a long rod within, which is attached to the base. The Falkland Lamp is thought to have been inspired by the growing interest in space travel, but Munari's works were also often inspired by nature. The shape of the Falkland Lamp is reminiscent of bamboo. Munari described this relationship as 'industrial naturalism', ie. the imitation of nature using technology and man-made materials. From this philosophy a flexible, lightweight, foldable and beautiful lamp was created.

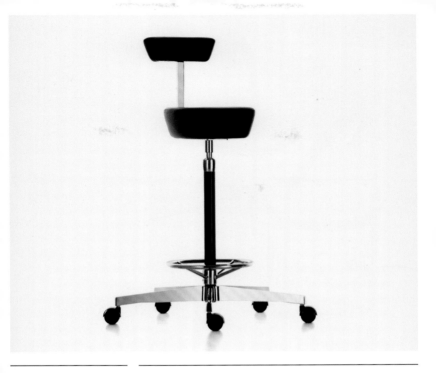

PERCH STOOL
(1964)
George Nelson
(1908–86)
Bob Propst
(1922–2000)
Herman Miller
1964 to 2006
Vitra 1998 to 2019

This tall, narrow stool was a part of the 1964 Action Office that George Nelson designed with Bob Propst. The Perch Stool was so called because the designers wanted workers to have a place to perch while doing stand-up work. In keeping with the ergonomic belief that movement is healthy, the Perch's design encourages the user to change work positions regularly throughout the day. The Perch has a small, foam-padded, height-adjustable seat. A separate padded backrest may also be used as an armrest. The ring-shaped tubular steel footrest helps the sitter stay perched in a comfortable position. The

Nelson-Propst collaboration was instrumental in the creation of new office furniture that could cater to changes in office planning. Whilst still in production by Herman Miller, Vitra also started producing the Perch in 1998 due to the increasing demand for furniture suitable for flexible working environments being adopted by employers in a bid to cater for a mobile workforce. The Perch Stool, which provides both standing and sitting positions, and which can also be employed by those standing in informal and dynamic conference scenarios, continues to respond to the evolving needs of the workplace.

CESTA LANTERN (1964)
Miguel Milá (1931–)
DAE 1980s to 1995
Santa & Cole
1996 to present

Designed by the Barcelona-born architect turned industrial and interior designer Miguel Milá, the Cesta Lantern is a landmark piece in modern Spanish design. Although the lantern is instantly recognizable to the generation of 1970s households that grew up with it, the uninitiated would be forgiven for questioning exactly which continent the design hails from. The delicate cherry wood frame, incorporating a tall, domed handle, suggests Chinese or Japanese precedents, while the ambient glow of the oval glass dome seems possibly Mediterranean. Milá's inspiration came, in fact, from

the traditional lanterns that were hung outside coastal homes as a signal to returning fishermen. Yet he created a lamp that feels more at home on the contemporary terraces, salons and balconies of Spain's more discerning residences. The frame and the attached sweeping handle use heat-curved cherry wood to elegant effect, and all mechanical components are made from wood and concealed from view. In 1996, the design was upgraded by replacing the Manila cane frame with cherry wood, upgrading the plastic shade to an opal crystal globe and by adding a dimmer.

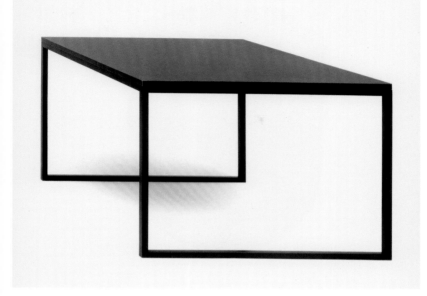

TAVOLO 64 (1964)
A. G. Fronzoni
(1923–2002)
Pedano 1972 to 1974
Galli 1975 to 1978
Cappellini
1997 to present

Minimalism has become a fashionable word, used rather loosely to describe objects that have been pared down to the bare essentials through a combination of simple forms, materials and colour (or lack of it). A G Fronzoni's Tavolo 64 encapsulates the true meaning of the word, as the designer's reductionist approach gave rise to an object that consists only of the essential elements needed to function. Developing the concept mathematically, Fronzoni captured the necessary dimensions for efficiency using a square tubular-steel base with a wooden top of the same thickness. The geometric design

is produced in black or white. Fronzoni believed that the pure, graphic and unobtrusive form, derived from his dislike of waste and excessive decoration, would place more emphasis on the objects and environment surrounding it. A bed, chair, armchair and shelving unit also accompanied Fronzoni's table design of 1964. The collection reminds subsequent designers of the overriding importance of remembering practicality before becoming too concerned with technical and material innovations, ergonomic subtleties and emotionally driven styling touches.

MAX 1 TABLEWARE (1964)

Massimo Vignelli
(1931–2014)
Giovenzana 1964
Heller 1971 to present

Max 1 Tableware was designed by Massimo Vignelli in 1964 and received the coveted Compasso d'Oro at the Milan Triennale. The modular service was originally produced by the Italian company Giovenzana before being mass produced by the newly formed American company Heller. Originally marketed as Max 1 Tableware, in 1972 further items were added to the service marketed as Max 2. The Max 1 set consisted of a rectangular base tray, six sets of large plates, small plates and small bowls, two more small bowls with lids, and a large bowl with lid. The service was expanded from 1970 with the addition of a sugar bowl, creamer and the cup and saucer. The cup was soon replaced with a mug, called the Maxmug, which became a bestseller. The final pieces added to the line included a series of trays designed in 1978. Vignelli's dinnerware has been in continuous production by Heller since 1971. The stacking system had the function of being space saving, but the design also showed the potential for plastics to look good in the home and be used for an integrated alphabet of shapes.

MODEL 40/4 CHAIR (1964)
David Rowland
(1924–2010)
General Fireproofing
Company
1964 to present
Howe 1976 to present

This chair is one of the most elegant and efficient stacking chairs ever produced – a triumph of structural engineering and visual refinement. It consists simply of two side frames made from 10 mm (0.39 in) round steel rods. The separate seat and back are made of contoured panels in pressed steel. This basic description, however, does not convey the sophisticated realization of the ingenuity with which Rowland puts these parts together. The exceptionally thin profile together with carefully devised nesting geometry means that these chairs stack together with no gaps between them.

Forty stacked chairs take up only 4 feet in vertical height, giving rise to the chair's pragmatic name: 40/4. Rowland ingeniously added flat flanges to the back leg elements, which not only provided necessary rigidity but also enabled the chairs to be locked together in rows. A plastic foot detail is also used to connect the chairs together in line. Locking chairs in line turns a linked group into a lattice beam. Four link-locked chairs can be picked up together. Unsurprisingly, the chair has been much copied, but none of the copies have yet outranked the original – and definitive – model.

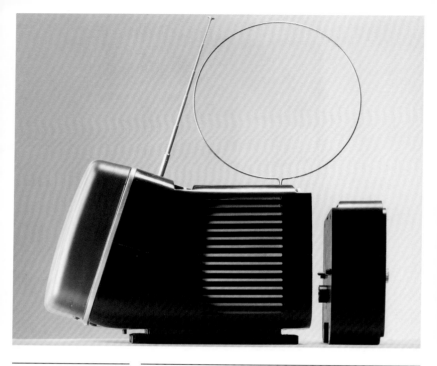

ALGOL PORTABLE TELEVISION (1964)
Marco Zanuso
(1916–2001)
Richard Sapper
(1932–2015)
Brionvega
1964 to present

The Algol, which was the first truly portable television (the original model could be powered by battery), was designed keeping its materials, production and its user very much in mind. Marco Zanuso and Richard Sapper gave industrial design a new sense of freedom and responsibility that was different from that of other rationalists of the time. The Algol, a descendent of Brionvega's Doney 14 television (1962), which had also been designed by the pair, is filled with character and intimacy; Zanuso compared the model to a small dog that watched in on its landlady. The designers placed the controls and antenna at the junction of the tilted curve and the main body of the set, which gives the television a simple organic unity and allows the controls to be found easily in the dark. The plastic of the casing was carefully considered to make cleaning easy, and its metal handle, which sits flush when not in use, feels reassuringly sturdy when the television is carried. The internal components are also arranged rationally to allow for easy maintenance and compactness – design ideas that heralded the onslaught of component miniaturization.

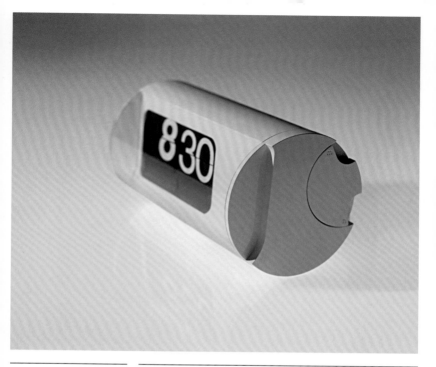

CIFRA 3 CLOCK (1965)
Gino Valle
(1923–2003)
Solari di Udine
1966 to present

Solari was a successful manufacturer of measuring devices and information systems when it asked architect Gino Valle to design a table clock. The company's technology was a precursor of digital displays that used revolving, silk-screened flap numerals and text for automated transport terminal displays. The original Cifra 3 Clock was mains-powered and consisted of a simple round tube of coloured plastic, with the opaque half containing the mechanism and the transparent half displaying the time. The most striking element of the design is the system for setting time. On the left side of the tube, a disc is clicked up or down to change the minutes and hours. Valle could have used the more conventional approach of buttons, but the satisfaction of rotating the disc control with only one hand contributes a lot to the design. The later battery version added a second tube to the back, and its liberating factor of portability appealed to a new generation. Valle said that he did not enjoy designing products – his interest had waned considerably by the mid-1970s – and it is a pity. It is clear his contribution added to the dialogue of product design had significant potential.

TS 502 RADIO
(1965)
Marco Zanuso
(1916–2001)
Richard Sapper
(1932–2015)
Brionvega
1965 to present

The Brionvega TS 502 Radio's distinctive plastic clamshell symbolized the synthetic pop aesthetic of the 1960s. Designed by Marco Zanuso and Richard Sapper, it took advantage of the advent of battery-powered transistors by creating a light-weight, portable FM radio that appealed to a young market. The use of ABS plastic dramatically differed from its traditional wooden-veneered competitors. The bold exterior was saturated in strong vibrant colours such as bright red and orange, as well as minimalist white and black. Like that of a James Bond gadget, its technology was hidden away, only becoming apparent when the user opened up the sleek plastic form to reveal the analogue dials and controls on one side and the integral speaker on the other. Zanuso and Sapper collaborated on a succession of iconic televisions and radios for Brionvega. The company emerged during Italy's post-war boom and established themselves at the forefront of consumer electronic design by employing leading designers to create their radical product range. Recently reissued with up-to-date technology and a return to its original interface panel, the Brionvega TS 502 continues to appeal today.

SUPER ERECTA SHELVING SYSTEM (1965)
Slingsby Design Team
Slingsby Metro
1965 to present

The Super Erecta Shelving System was developed in 1965 by Slingsby in Bradford, Great Britain, and the Metro Corporation of the United States. It is simple, requires no tools to put together and is endlessly flexible. The modular system means consumers can purchase a starter pack of four posts and as many shelves as required and can then buy more materials as needed. New units are then connected to the existing unit with an ingenious S-hook. The simplicity of the system is the secret to its enduring commercial life and also why it inspired product designers looking to produce cheap, self-assembly furniture for the new house owners of the property boom in the 1980s. As developers began to adapt industrial spaces into apartments during the 1980s and 1990s the industrial language of products like the Super Erecta Shelving began to filter into domestic design. The importance of the legacy of the Super Erecta System was acknowledged by its inclusion in an exhibition at the Victoria and Albert Museum, London, in 1997, entitled 'Flexible Furniture', further marking its move from a highly successful commercial product to an acknowledged ingenious design.

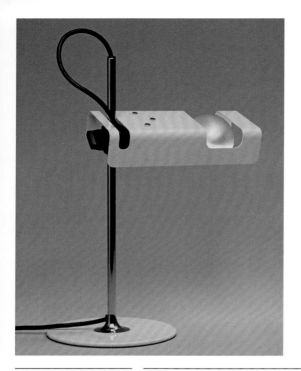

SPIDER LAMP (1965)
Joe Colombo
(1930–71)
Oluce 1965 to 1990s,
2003 to present

Of all the careers affiliated with the pioneering 1960s, Joe Colombo's body of work puts forward one of the most memorable representations, of which the Spider Lamp is considered a landmark. Colombo's design philosophy was unflinchingly modern and, as showcased here, he embraced new materials and technologies. The rectangular light fixture is designed to incorporate a new lighting innovation of the time, the distinctive onion-shaped Cornalux bulb by Philips. Silver coating was applied to the underside of the unit, and a neat rectangular cutout in the casing exposed the bulb to view. Made from a stamped-plate design, painted in a range of colours including white, black, orange and brown, the light box clamps to a tubular chrome stand by means of an adjustable melamine joint. The lamp can travel the full length of the stand from the top where the flex joins, down to the circular metal base that provides an anchor for the slim stand. Colombo designed the lamp as part of the Spider Group series, which featured table, floor, wall and ceiling models. Joe Colombo's death in 1971, aged only forty-one, cut short a career full of promise.

SEDIA UNIVERSALE (1965)
Joe Colombo
(1930–71)
Kartell 1967 to 2012

Colombo's designs have become inextricably linked with the political and social context of Italy in the 1960s and 1970s and its emerging Pop culture. His work can be characterized by its innovative use of new materials and a modular, flexible approach to furniture. His early training as a painter resonated in his work as a designer, and throughout his career he drew heavily on the organic forms of post-war Expressionism. Colombo's furniture designs attracted the interest of Giulio Castelli of furniture manufacturer Kartell. The 1965 Sedia Universale (Universal Chair) was the first

chair design to be moulded entirely from one material. Colombo originally designed it to be manufactured in aluminium, but his interest in experimenting with new materials led to a prototype moulded in thermoplastic. He designed the chair with interchangeable legs. It could function as a standard dining chair, with the option of shorter legs for more casual use or for use as a child's chair, or a longer base element for use as a high chair or bar stool. Colombo's furniture offered a fresh new appearance, colourful and flexible, which perfectly suited the spirit of the 1960s.

PK24 CHAISE LONGUE (1965)
Poul Kjærholm
(1929–80)
Ejvind Kold
Christensen
1965 to 1981
Fritz Hansen
1981 to present

Despite his long career as a furniture designer, Poul Kjærholm's output was relatively small, in part because he struggled to find a manufacturer to meet his exacting standards. Eventually, on the recommendation of Hans Wegner, he teamed up with Ejvind Kold Christensen. The result of that collaboration was a small collection of sleek furniture in the International Style, with the PK24 Chaise Longue as its centrepiece. Most of Kjærholm's seating, belying his training as a cabinet-maker, is made from thin strips of chrome-plated steel upholstered with visually and texturally contrasting materials like leather

or, in the case of the PK24, woven cane. Kjærholm divided the PK24 into a separate, very stable base, supporting a long reclining seat that can be tipped on its runners in adjustment. The most dramatic element of the PK24 is the unfolding sweep of the seat, which is cleverly attached to the U-shaped base by means of an adjustable strap. The PK24's perfection lifts it beyond the role of the chair into the realm of sculpture, crowned with an upholstered headrest. It still functions as seating, but the irregularities of the human form might destroy such an immaculate vision.

THRIFT CUTLERY (1965) /CAFÉ CUTLERY (1982)
David Mellor
(1930–2009)
Walker and Hall
1966 to c.1970
David Mellor
1982 to present

David Mellor was a designer whose name is synonymous with British cutlery design. The cutlery service of 1965 was developed by Mellor as the Thrift service (reissued as Café). Following his 1963 commission to design a new range of silver for use in British embassies, Mellor was asked to produce new tableware for use in government canteens, hospitals and prisons, and by British Rail. For many traditionalists the radical element in the design of Thrift was that Mellor cut down the traditional eleven-piece setting to a five-piece set. The successful juxtaposition of manufacture and design became

an inherent feature of Mellor's work, perhaps most importantly through his shaping of the knife, fork and spoon. The monolithic knife from the Thrift range is a flash of startling modernity. The round bowls of the spoons, the short four-pronged fork and the smooth form of the handles all contribute to Thrift's success as a modern standard worthy of national distribution. Encouraged by the spirit of the age, Mellor was concerned with the possibilities of design for production in stainless steel, a material that was durable and allowed for mass production of one-piece designs such as Thrift.

DSC SERIES CHAIRS (1965)
Giancarlo Piretti
(1940–)
Castelli/Haworth
1965 to present

Since 1963 Giancarlo Piretti had been thinking about a chair suitable for both domestic and public spaces that would infringe upon the materials and technologies of the established canon. He began focusing his attention on pressure die-casting aluminium, which was then mostly used in the production of motors. Although Piretti's pioneering ideas did not fit in with Castelli's main production of wooden office furniture, Castelli let him experiment. The result was the 106 Chair, with its seat and backrest as shells of pre-shaped plywood held together by two press-moulded aluminium clamps, fixed using only four screws.

Presented in 1965 at the Salone del Mobile, the unconventional 106 was an immediate success and soon spawned a family of chairs: the DSC Series. Thus the 106 generated the Axis 3000 and Axis 4000 collective seating ranges: all stackable, interconnecting, fitted with different accessories, and even supplied with their own transport trolley. Today the chairs are widely used in a variety of offices and public spaces – a tribute to their versatility. A great achievement for its ambitious creator, the DSC Series established Piretti's trademark synthesis between technological experimentation, practicality and elegance.

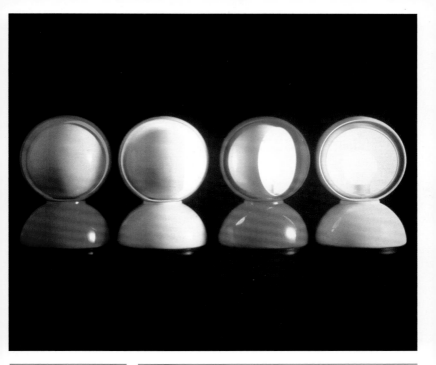

ECLISSE LAMP
(1965)
Vico Magistretti
(1920–2006)
Artemide
1967 to present

The Eclisse (eclipse) is a bedside lamp made of an enamelled metal casing that houses two overlapping, half-spherical shells held on a pivot so they can be turned to regulate the light. Vico Magistretti experimented with spherical and organic forms in both lighting and furniture. In 1964 he sketched designs for a pod-like lamp attached to a bedhead; this grew into the Eclisse the following year. In 1968 he revised the idea to create the Telegono Lamp, which is made of plastic. The Eclisse Lamp exemplifies Magistretti's technical and visual preoccupations in the 1960s. His design method involved making a study of use

and submitting sketches rather than technical drawings to manufacturers. Technicians would then develop the means by which his idea could be realized. Magistretti claimed that, in the case of the Eclisse, the nature of the mechanism was not important as long as it facilitated the basic idea of the light, i.e. that it be adjustable from a small blade to a full beam. The Eclisse Lamp won the Compasso d'Oro in 1967 and is featured in many museum collections. It has remained as a bestseller for Artemide since it was first produced.

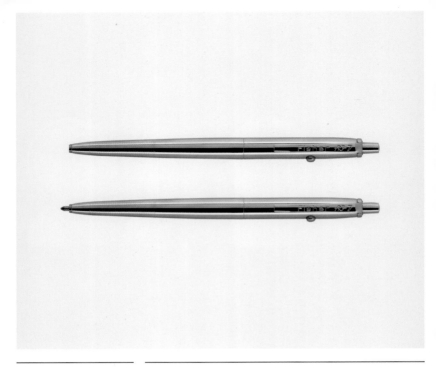

AG-7 SPACE PEN
(1965)
Paul C. Fisher
(1913–2006)
Fisher Space Pen Co.
1965 to present

Paul C. Fisher's 1965 AG-7 Space Pen could write in any position and in virtually any environment. The cartridge was pressurized with nitrogen, negating the need for gravity to assist ink flow. Further, Fisher used thixotropic ink, a semi-solid ink that liquefied only against the shearing action of the rolling ball. The control of the supply of ink was something of a revolution, as all other ballpoints either bled or dried up. The durable AG-7 not only had an infinite shelf life, but also was dependable in diverse environmental conditions. It could write under water and upside down. Its finely tapered shaft with a circular milled grip was not dissimilar to other pens on the market, but its shape created a futuristic vision. Fisher's company went on to exploit the pen's visual possibilities with a host of casing designs. The pen design came at an opportune time. In October 1968 the AG-7 Space Pen was used on the Apollo 7 mission, replacing the pencils used on earlier missions. The topicality of space travel raised the profile of the Space Pen, while the extreme conditions in space provided ready proof of the pen's performance.

UMBRELLA STAND
(1965)
Gino Colombini
(1915–)
Kartell
1966 to present

A ubiquitous design, Gino Colombini's 1965 Umbrella Stand combines functionality with technical innovation. The stand is made out of ABS plastic and available in striking colours such as cobalt blue, yellow, red, smoke grey and silver, and sometimes sold with a mounted ashtray. Originally intended for everyday domestic use, the stand is among the first designs to exploit the potential of injection-moulded plastics as a material for high-volume mass production. The stand combines low-cost manu-facturing with principles of structure, material and unity of design. A disciple of Franco Albini,

Colombini was the head of Kartell's technical department from 1953 to 1960, and produced diverse ranges of small, plastic household goods. His enduring reputation in design was ensured by his timely use of plastics at a time when they were gaining favourable acceptance by large audiences. Colombini's work belongs to a second phase of Italian design, where designers projected their optimistic visions of a new society towards smaller, everyday objects and accessories. Colombini's designs were given the recognition they deserved, and he received the prestigious Italian Compasso d'Oro award four times between 1955 and 1960.

PLATNER CHAIR AND OTTOMAN
(1966)
Warren Platner
(1919–2006)
Knoll 1966 to present

Warren Platner's Chair and Ottoman were a technical tour de force not only in their innovative steel-wire construction, but also in the optical conundrum that their structure created, effectively making these pieces the furniture equivalent of Op Art paintings. Platner arrived at the design by welding a series of curved, vertical steel rods to a circular frame, creating a 'moiré' effect, much like a Bridget Riley canvas. The modern mantra of combining elegant design with technological innovation was central to Platner's approach and one which he had honed working with legendary designers Raymond Loewy,

Eero Saarinen and I. M. Pei. The Platner Chair and Ottoman, with their shiny nickel finish and red moulded-latex seat cushions on rubber platforms, were rooted in luxurious functionality. Indeed, when asked to describe their inspiration, Platner refered to the decorative period style of Louis XV. The nine-piece Platner collection, which included a side chair and a lounge chair with complementary stool, received the American Institute of Architects International Award in 1966. It continues to be a popular draw in the Knoll catalogue, as much for its comfort as for its dazzling Op Art effects.

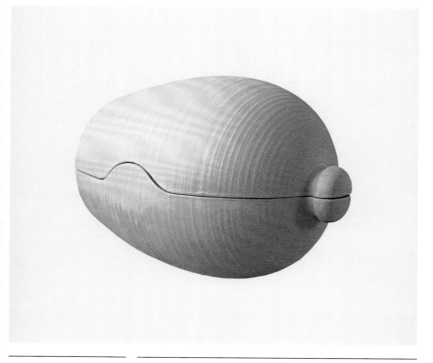

CHICKEN BRICK (1966)
Designer Unknown
Habitat, Weston
Mill Pottery
1966 to present

The terracotta Chicken Brick is a clear example of good design at its most unpretentious and sincere. Instantly recognizable for its distinctive and somewhat quirky, comical, bulbous form, the Chicken Brick is simple and honest, with no excess features or ornament. Cooking in wet terracotta clay pots is an ancient tradition that dates back to the Etruscans, and this type of oven existed in continental Europe for centuries before Terence Conran put it into his Habitat shops in 1966. However, it was because of its sales through Habitat that the Chicken Brick became so popular in the United Kingdom. The Chicken Brick creates an enclosed environment for baking in any oven. The terracotta heats evenly and allows for uniform cooking of the food, while the sealed environment maximizes the flavours without any drying out. The brick itself imparts a unique flavour. In the 1960s, the Chicken Brick's appeal was both practical and exotic. Today, it still appeals to our health-conscious generation as no basting or fat is required. Although at first glance this rotund little object may seem slightly absurd, it is a practical, functional and successful design.

BULB LAMP (1966)
Ingo Maurer
(1932–2019)
Ingo Maurer
1966 to present

The Bulb Lamp is the ultimate Pop Art lighting product: a bulb within a bulb, the casing an exaggerated replica of an everyday product. The inner bulb is chromed to reflect and diffuse the light, and is set within a crystal glass casing with a chromium-plated neck. Bulb is the first of a series of bulb-featured objects produced by Ingo Maurer. 'The bulb is my inspiration,' he has said. 'I have always been fascinated by the light bulb because it is the perfect meeting of industry and poetry.' In 1966 he created three bulb products: Bulb, Bulb Clear and Giant Bulb. He made a number of early versions that were sold through word of mouth,

but it swiftly grew into a viable business. Trained as a graphic designer, Maurer worked as a commercial artist in the 1960s before producing the Bulb Lamp as an experiment in translating Pop Art ideas into product design. He founded his studio, Design M, now known as Ingo Maurer, in Munich in 1963, and by the 1980s the company had grown from design studio to full-scale manufacturer. Ingo Maurer still produces the Bulb Lamp today.

LAMY 2000 FOUNTAIN PEN
(1966)
Gerd Alfred Müller
(1932–1991)
Lamy 1966 to present

When it was introduced in 1966, the Lamy 2000 marked a defining moment in the evolution of the fountain pen. Its precision technology and sleek, Bauhaus-inspired modern design set it apart from its competitors. The pen was designed by Gerd Alfred Müller, who had made a name for himself with the Sixtant electric shaver design for Braun (1962). With the Lamy 2000, Müller approached the design in the no-fuss tradition of the German Modernist. Yet the pen is much more than a minimalist piece of precision engineering; it is also a gem-like luxury item. The Makralon and stainless steel brush-finished instrument boasts a platinum coat and 14 ct gold nib. The Lamy 2000's spring-mounted clip is made from solid stainless steel, and its innovative spring allows the clip to hold the pen in place. Müller's fountain pen set a benchmark in terms of its clean lines and modern monochromatic palette, as well as its advanced ergonomics and improved reliability and durability. Lamy had been a modestly sized firm, but with the success of the Lamy 2000 the company repositioned itself into one of the foremost design-led manufacturers of writing instruments in the world.

TIMOR CALENDAR
(1967)
Enzo Mari (1932–)
Danese
1967 to present

The Timor is one of a series of perpetual calendars that Enzo Mari designed for Danese in the 1960s. Its shape was inspired by the train information signals that Mari remembered from his childhood in the 1940s. The precision of Timor's graphics is evident in Mari's other plastic products for Danese, such as the Colleoni Pencil Holder, Hawaii Egg Cups, Borneo Ashtray and Tongareva Salad Bowl. Mari's choice of ABS plastic as the primary material was due to its durability and ease of assembly as well its low cost, given the complexity and number of parts involved. Mari felt these factors were more important than

issues of taste, although the smooth, glossy surface and precision of the moulded ABS undoubtedly adds to the timeless appeal of the product. Timor's name has no particular significance, other than that, at the time, all Danese products were named after islands. When asked about the practicalities of the calendar, Mari admits he does not use one himself, saying, 'I don't want to have to remember to change the date every single day!' Despite this, the calendar is a beautiful object that is still in production today.

TONGUE CHAIR (1967)
Pierre Paulin
(1927–2009)
Artifort
1967 to present

In the late 1950s the Dutch furniture manufacturer Artifort made an important decision. By engaging Kho Liang Ie, a visionary designer and connoisseur in art and design, as an aesthetic adviser, the company radically modernized its collection. The Tongue Chair by Pierre Paulin is indicative of Artifort's revolutionary approach to design during this era. Paulin trained as a sculptor, but his interest in furniture design grew during the early 1950s when he was working for Thonet. The Tongue, a stackable, ultra hip, almost mattress-like piece of lounge furniture, gave new meaning to the concept of sitting, suggesting that the sitters might drape themselves over its curves rather than sit upright. The new shape was made possible by borrowing production techniques from the car industry. A metal frame was covered with webbing, rubberized canvas and a thick, comfortable layer of foam. Traditional upholstery was radically simplified by using a piece of elastic fabric in a range of bright colours with a zipper over the frame. The Tongue Chair was quite radical for its time in terms of its shape, yet its comforting form which embraces the body has proved its success throughout the years.

CYLINDA-LINE
(1967)
Arne Jacobsen
(1902–71)
Stelton
1967 to present

Cylinda-Line originated as a number of rough sketches on a napkin by designer Arne Jacobsen. Launched as a range of eighteen stainless-steel homeware pieces, all the individual items present a successful negotiation of Jacobsen's dual commitment to organic form and to the clean lines of Modernism. From the original sketches Cylinda-Line was developed over a three-year period. Since the technology did not yet exist to create Jacobsen's pure cylindrical forms in stainless steel, it was necessary to develop new machines and welding techniques. These gave a rigorous precision to the seamless

cylindrical forms, and the extremely high machine tolerances yielded sleek, brushed surfaces. The collection was put on the market in 1967 and immediately attracted considerable international attention for its striking black nylon handles of rectangular outlines and interior arcs, which both contrast and offset the cylindrical body. Jacobsen's Cylinda-Line represents the broadest and most commercially successful application of formalist principles for the domestic consumer, and the range was a triumph for neo-Functionalism as a mass-market product.

PASTIL CHAIR
(1967)
Eero Aarnio (1932–)
Asko 1967 to 1980
Adelta 1991 to 2016
Eero Aarnio Originals
2016 to present

The Finnish designer Eero Aarnio rose to glory in 1966 with the unveiling of the capsule-like Ball Chair. His next big hit was the Pastil Chair of 1967, which won the American Industrial Design Award in 1968. This candy-coloured seating object, also referred to as the Gyro Chair, was the 1960s answer to the rocking chair. Aarnio had essentially designed a new type of furniture that is comfortable, yet playful and suitable for use both indoors or out. Its shape was taken from the sweet, or 'pastil'. Aarnio's prototype for the Pastil was made from polystyrene, so that he could work out the measurement and its potential

as a rocking chair. The oil crisis of 1973 halted production of many of his polyester designs. In the 1990s, a revival of interest in the design of the 1960s brought several pieces back into production by Adelta, manufactured in moulded fibreglass-reinforced polyester. Eero Aarnio Originals now create these pieces in a variety of colours, allowing the consumer to choose between lime green, yellow, orange, tomato red, blue, pink and the more restrained black and white.

BLOW CHAIR (1967)
Gionatan De Pas
(1932–91)
Donato D'Urbino
(1935–)
Paolo Lomazzi (1936–)
Carla Scolari (1930–)
Zanotta
1967 to c.2013

An enduring visual statement of the 1960s, the Blow Chair was the first inflatable design to be successfully mass-produced. Its comic, bulbous shape was inspired by Bibendum, Michelin's nineteenth-century publicity character, while its technology was pure twentieth century. Its PVC cylinders, for instance, are kept together by high-frequency welding. The chair was the first collaboration produced by DDL Studio, started by Gionatan De Pas, Donato D'Urbino and Paolo Lomazzi in 1966 in Milan. DDL's aim was to design simple and inexpensive objects for a fresh, alternative, youthful style of living. The company also experimented

with materials, looking to pneumatic architecture installations for inspiration. The studio approached practical furnishing with designs permeated with irony and lightness, characteristics that are reflected in the Blow Chair. The chair, which can be easily inflated at home, is a milestone in furniture design. It was created for both indoor and outdoor use. The Blow's lifespan was expected to be short and even came with a repair kit, and its cheap price reflected this. When it first came out, it generated a huge amount of publicity for Zanotta. In the 1980s the company revived it as a design classic.

SACCO CHAIR (1968)
Piero Gatti (1940–)
Cesare Paolini (1937–83)
Franco Teodoro (1939–2005)
Zanotta
1968 to present

Italian manufacturer Zanotta jumped on the 'Pop furniture' bandwagon with the production of the Sacco Chair, the first commercially produced beanbag seat designed by Piero Gatti, Cesare Paolino and Franco Teodoro. The designers originally proposed a fluid-filled transparent envelope, but the excessive weight and complications of filling it eventually led to the ingenious choice of using millions of tiny semi-expanded polystyrene beads. Soon, the beanbag became the seat of choice of the fashionable jet set. However, due to the difficulties of patenting a sack of polystyrene balls and the ease of manufacturing, it was not long before the market was flooded with cheap Sacco reproductions. Its advertising campaign for the beanbag established a sense of lifestyle that matched what the chair represented – something fun, comfortable, cool and of its period. Hence, what began as a high-quality designer piece of furniture quickly developed into a low-cost, mass-produced space filler. Although today beanbags are largely deemed unfashionable, the Sacco Chair survives as a symbol because of its pioneering design and as a representation of the 1960s mood of optimism.

CLAM ASHTRAY
(1968)
Alan Fletcher
(1931–2006)
Mebel 1972,
1992 to present
Design Objectives
1973 to 1976

Launched in 1971, the melamine Clam Ashtray was a familiar sight in the trendy homes of the era. The Clam, measuring 14 cm (5.5 in) in diameter, was designed by British graphic designer Alan Fletcher, who first pictured a shape which resembled Dutch Edam cheese. Each Clam consists of two halves, made from a single mould; when closed, they contrast perfectly to form a graphic sculptural object. The machine cutting was so precise that even without a hinge the two halves slotted tightly together. When opened and turned on their backs, the separate clams become instant ashtrays, with the snaking serrated edge providing a natural resting place for a burning cigarillo. Italian manufacturer Mebel was enthusiastically promoting the virtues of melamine and used it to create a wide range of household goods. Design Objectives, based in Devon, United Kingdom, made fifty editions of a pressed brass and chrome version. The Clam Ashtray's simple form, so effectively executed, has been found in all corners of the world – from banks in Buenos Aires, to bars in Bangkok – not only being used as an ashtray, but also to hold paperclips, pins, stamps, buttons, keys, or spare change.

PYRAMID FURNITURE (1968)
Shiro Kuramata
(1934–91)
Ishimaru 1968
Cappellini
1998 to present

Shiro Kuramata remains one of the most innovative designers of the mid to late twentieth century. His work varied in both style and use, but all his designs were products of his approach to materials. The Pyramid Furniture is a transparent acrylic set of drawers with seventeen graduated drawers in contrasting black. His preoccupation with shape is an enduring theme in his work. His obsession with the square, for example, was explored in a series of designs for drawers executed between 1967 and 1970. The Pyramid Furniture was the most dramatic of his designs from this period, with its architectural form and stacked drawers decreasing in size. The traditional feet have been replaced by castors, cleverly incorporating both movement and versatility. The Pyramid Furniture reflects the confidence and creativity of design that grew out of post-war Japan. With its unconventional form, it clearly illustrates the designer's passion for the unusual, the sensual and the ephemeral. Kuramata reconsidered the relationships between form and function and in doing so created new designs that in turn imposed his own surrealist, minimalist ideas onto everyday objects.

LIVING TOWER
(1968)
Verner Panton
(1926–98)
Herman Miller
1969 to 1970
Fritz Hansen
1970 to 1975
Stega 1997
Vitra 1999 to present

Verner Panton designed modern furniture with personality, and nowhere is this more pronounced than in his Living Tower, or 'Pantower', which was shown as part of the 1970 Cologne Furniture Fair. A novel, almost impertinent design, it embodies the spirit of the 1960s. It almost defies definition, as it falls between being a seating unit, storage area or a work of art. The frame is made of birch plywood, padded with foam and covered in Kvadrat wool upholstery. Today it is available in three colours: orange, red and dark blue. Panton was born in 1926 in Gamtofte, Denmark, and studied at the Royal Danish

Academy of Fine Arts. He worked at Arne Jacobsen's architectural office from 1950–52, and in 1955 he set up his own design office. In 1958 he caused an uproar at the Fredericia Furniture Fair with his novel chair designs, hanging them from the ceiling of his stand like the works of art they indubitably were. The success of the Living Tower lives on as an example of a work of art, combining the features of a chair into a sculptural form.

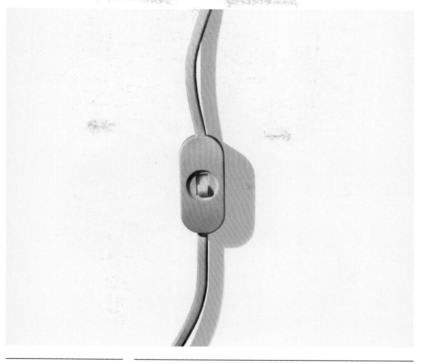

VLM SWITCH
INTERRUTTORE
ROMPITRATTA
(1968)
Achille Castiglioni
(1918–2002)
Pier Giacomo
Castiglioni (1913–68)
VLM/Relco
1968 to present

The VLM Switch, or Interruttore Rompitratta was not the first switch designed by the Castiglionis, nor even their first in-line switch. Yet Achille Castiglioni insisted that it was the single design of which he was most proud. In 1967, VLM had just opened a modern plant for producing accessories for lights and approached the Castiglioni studio seeking a newly designed switch. The brothers designed a simple, anonymous switch that has sold well in excess of 15 million. Its softly curved underside allows it to sit comfortably in the palm of the hand. If grappling in the dark, the sharper edges of the top casing identify the correct orientation with only the slightest touch. The switch itself rests neatly within a middle indentation and slides securely on or off with an audible click – the sound of a hidden half-bearing snapping into place, held taut by a cleverly concealed spring placed between it and a metal strip used either to complete or break the electric current. Thousands of people across thirty countries use this switch daily without any awareness of the design or the designers, a testament to the absolute triumph of this product.

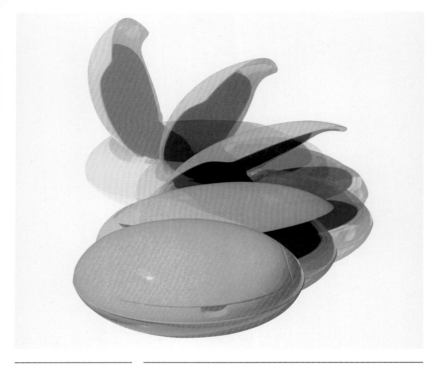

GARDEN EGG CHAIR (1968)
Peter Ghyczy (1940–)
Reuter 1968 to 1973
VEB Schwarzheide
DDR 1973 to 1980
Ghyczy
2001 to present

If the purpose of garden furniture is to bring something of a domestic interior to an outside space, then Peter Ghyczy's Garden Egg Chair is perhaps the perfect design. Housed in an egg-like shell made of fibreglass-reinforced polyester, the flip-top chair back folds down to create a waterproof seal so that it can be left outside. In complete contrast to this hard, impervious exterior, the interior has a soft, plush, fabric-lined detachable seat. In this way the Egg fuses classic ideas of comfort with modern materials and methods of fabrication. While Ghyczy remains silent about the inspiration behind his design, the fusion of natural form and contemporary craftsmanship may suggest some connections with the Art Deco movement, while the overall style is instantly recognizable as pure 1960s Pop. Ghyczy left Hungary after the Revolution of 1956 and moved to West Germany, where he studied architecture before joining Reuter, a company that produced plastic products. The Garden Egg Chair was reissued by the designer's own firm, Ghyczy, in 2001. While the design remains the same, the new model is made of recyclable plastic and incorporates an optional swivel base.

TAM TAM STOOL (1968)
Henry Massonnet
(1922–2005)
STAMP
1968 to present

Also known as the Diabolo Stool, because of its shape, the Tam Tam Stool was born out of the new production possibilities presented by the 1960s plastics boom. Henry Massonnet's company, STAMP, produced plastic iceboxes for fishermen, but in 1968 Massonnet decided to harness the potential of his injection-moulded production process and apply it to the manufacture of tough, portable and economic stools. The Tam Tam came in a variety of colours and split into two identical pieces so that it might be more easily transported or stowed away. It was a huge success and more

than 12 million were sold. However, following the oil crisis of 1973 and its consequent effect on the plastics industry, production of the Tam Tam slowed down. Sacha Cohen, the founder and development manager of Branex Design, contacted Massonnet and the stool was put back into production by STAMP using the original colours, mould and materials. The stool continues to be produced in the same factory, but now comes in thirteen colours and a variety of patterns. Branex Design, with the exclusive world rights, is the distributor of the Tam Tam, ensuring its worldwide commercial success since 2002.

BOLLE VASES (1968)
Tapio Wirkkala
(1915–85)
Venini 1968 to present

Tapio Wirkkala's multicoloured free-blown Bolle Vases were designed for the Italian company Venini, who commissioned him during the mid-1960s to create new glass pieces using traditional methods. These vases are remarkable for the subtle sense of static equilibrium Wirkkala achieved by appearing to balance coloured bands of different thicknesses within both the encased volume and its carefully delineated profile. The Bolle Vases were a departure for Wirkkala, who made use of incalmo, the sixteenth-century glass-making technique and speciality of the Murano-based glass industry, in which two flaming masses of glass vessels, usually of different colours, are grafted on to one another to create one piece. During his time working with Venini, Wirkkala set out to exploit local expertise, using a range of colours and a thinness of glass unavailable to him in Finland. His Finnish work was often driven by a desire to evoke feelings about his homeland, hence the feeling of weightiness and apparent coldness. His output for Venini, on the other hand, was abstract, usually far more thinly blown, and much more colourful. The Bolle Vases have been, almost since their inception, one of the company's most popular lines.

**MARCUSO DINING
TABLE (1969)**
Marco Zanuso
(1916–2001)
Zanotta
1971 to present

The Marcuso Dining Table's sleek lines, glass top and stainless-steel legs make it a cult classic. Its position within Italian design history is unusual, however, for the complex technological research that made its production possible. The design of glass and metal tables had illustrious precedents. Yet the joining of the two materials had never been truly resolved. It was while observing a vent window of a car that Marco Zanuso was inspired to create a glass and stainless-steel table devoid of any heavy structure. After two years of research, he and Zanotta invented and patented a special gluing method that invisibly held the materials together. The result is a glass surface that appears barely placed on the stainless-steel legs. In reality it is very firmly stuck, as the legs are screwed onto stainless-steel discs fixed to the glass top. The technological achievement of the Marcuso Dining Table was a first for the 1960s, and it became an immediate commercial success. It has often been compared to a modern glass and steel building, with its construction voluntarily exposed. These qualities have ensured it is still in production by Zanotta today.

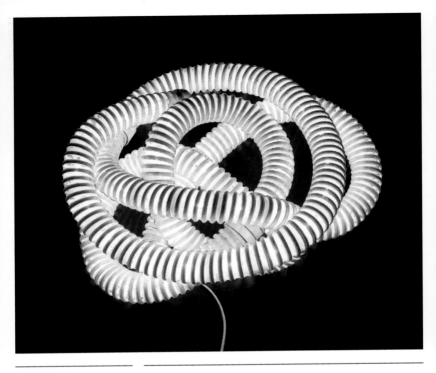

BOALUM LAMP (1969)

Livio Castiglioni
(1911–79)
Gianfranco Frattini
(1926–2004)
Artemide 1970 to
1983, 1999 to present

The Boalum Lamp is an experiment in both its form and its technology. The light is flexible and can be arranged in different configurations to create strikingly sculptural effects. It is made from industrial translucent PVC tubing lined with metal rings, with each section housing four low-watt bulbs. PVC, a soft and pliable plastic skin developed in the 1930s and originally used for cable and wire insulation, was one of the iconic materials of the 1960s, especially in its use for inflatable furniture. In the Boalum Lamp each unit can be plugged into another, creating what *Domus* magazine described in 1969 as, 'an endless snake of

light'. The lamp can be coiled or left straight, hung on the wall, or draped on furniture or the floor. Boalum was the ideal lighting product to complement the era's soft, inflatable, pliable and fluid furniture. Livio Castiglioni was the eldest of three brothers, all of whom led influential careers in post-war Italian design. He designed the Boalum Lamp with Gianfranco Frattini for Artemide, who first produced the lamp from 1970 to 1983 and reissued it with some adaptations in 1999.

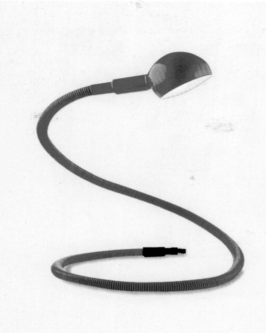

HEBI LAMP (1969)
Isao Hosoe
(1942–2015)
Valenti
1974 to present

This small task light is comprised of a flexible metal tube covered in PVC, with an enamelled aluminium shade. The Hebi, which means 'snake' in Japanese, has a fully adjustable arm and rotating shade to provide localized lighting. The metal tube can be twisted to lie flat so that the lamp can stand on a table. The lamp also comes in a shorter version, which can be inserted into a clamp. The Hebi is a sophisticated example of design combined with engineering. Hosoe found the simple, flexible tube, which cost a mere fifty cents for fifty metres, in a store in Milan. He collaborated with Valenti to create a lamp that could support itself

by folding the tube to form a base. Hosoe was born in Japan in 1942, where he trained in aerospace engineering. He moved to Italy in 1967 and worked as a product designer. The Hebi is still in production since it was first introduced by Valenti, an industrial lighting company that became associated with innovative products in the 1960s. The Hebi Lamp was one of Valenti's most successful products of the period, capturing the futuristic and quirky spirit of the 1960s.

UTEN.SILO (1969)
Dorothee Becker
(1938–)
Ingo Maurer
1969 to 1980
Vitra Design Museum
2002 to present

Uten.Silo encapsulates the spirit of adventure and experimentation in 1960s plastics design. Moulded in a single piece of ABS, it represents all that plastic is capable of. With its bright, shiny colours of black, white, orange and red and its smooth, molten surface, it could not have been made out of any other material. Dorothee Becker first had the idea for a wooden toy with geometrically shaped notches and matching elements. But Becker abandoned the idea when her own children showed no interest in it. The inspiration behind the final design of Uten.Silo owed much to a hang-up toilet bag she remembered from her childhood. Uten.Silo was originally called 'Wall-All' and was first put into production by Ingo Maurer, (formerly known as Design M), the company founded by Becker's husband, the designer Ingo Maurer. Following its initial overwhelming success, production of Uten.Silo was halted in 1974 as plastics fell out of favour following the oil crisis. A smaller version, Uten.Silo II, was manufactured in 1970 by Ingo Maurer, but that too was discontinued in 1980. In 2002, Vitra Design Museum reissued Uten.Silo and the smaller model, as well as a version in chromed plastic.

TUBE CHAIR (1969)
Joe Colombo
(1930–71)
Flexform 1970 to 1979
Vitra Design Museum
2006 to 2016
Cappellini
2016 to present

Joe Colombo's Tube Chair is an enduring example of the Italian designer's pioneering Pop explorations. Four plastic tubes of varying sizes covered in polyurethane foam and upholstered with vinyl came concentrically nested in a drawstring bag; once unpacked, the buyer was able to combine them in any sequence via tubular steel and rubber connecting joints. From task chair to chaise longue to a full-on couch (when two sets were joined), Colombo's machine for living was decidedly different from those proposed by earlier designers. Rather than follow accepted definitions of what a chair – or any design object – was,

Colombo created products that were embedded with recombinant possibility out of materials that were strange and unfamiliar to the majority of Italians. The Tube Chair fell into a category of design that Colombo termed 'structural seriality', or single objects that could multitask in a number of ways. Colombo's natural aversion to rectilinear lines was turned into a design aesthetic when he began experimenting with production processes using plastics in his family's electrical conductor factory in 1958, and again when he started collaborating with adventuresome Italian manufacturers like Flexform, which produced the Tube in the 1970s.

CYLINDRICAL STORAGE (1969)
Anna Castelli Ferrieri
(1918–2006)
Kartell 1969 to present

The apparently simple and utilitarian form of Anna Castelli Ferrieri's storage units proved highly influential at the time of their design. The bright and integrally coloured units exploited the progressive technology of injection-moulded ABS plastic, while the clean lines and functional design offered a low-cost storage solution. The materials, simplicity and modularity of the design allowed for enormous flexibility. Any quantity of units could be stacked, providing a wide range of opportunities for use, whether in the bathroom, bedroom, kitchen or living areas. Add-on features such as castors

or doors increased the appeal. Ferrieri trained in architecture and worked alongside Franco Albini before establishing her own architectural office. In the mid-1960s she turned her attention to product and furniture design and was appointed design director at Kartell – a company she helped become an international leader in design-led plastic products. The highly successful Cylindrical Storage units are still produced by Kartell, continuing to compete in price within a crowded marketplace, while the design proves to be timeless.

TAC TABLEWARE (1969)
Walter Gropius (1883–1969)
Rosenthal
1969 to present

Walter Gropius was one of the great enforcers of principles in twentieth-century architecture and industrial design. Through the founding of the Bauhaus in 1919, Gropius implemented a new schooling approach in which craftsmen, artists and business-men would coexist under the same roof. He emigrated to the United States in 1937 and founded The Architects Collaborative (TAC) in 1945, where he created notable architecture such as the Harvard Graduate Center (1948–1950). After the war, German ceramics firm Rosenthal actively sought an intelligent policy towards inter-national design. They commissioned Beate Kuhn's organic and sculp-tural ceramics in the 1950s, and took on American Raymond Loewy for a coffee service in 1954. Gropius's TAC Tableware for Rosenthal merged Kuhn's and Loewy's design tendencies with its own distinct bulbous form characterized by its emphasis on the curve. The hemispherical elevation of the teapot was reminiscent of the elementary shapes adopted in the Bauhaus, while the streamlining of the handle made references to the styling of that period. The tableware appeared in Rosenthal's Studio-Line collection in 1969 and has remained in production ever since.

MONACO WRISTWATCH (1969)
TAG Heuer Design Team
TAG Heuer 1969 to 1978, 1998 to present

One icon helped to create another when Steve McQueen took the wheel of his Porsche in the 1971 movie *Le Mans*, conspicuously wearing the new Heuer Monaco Wristwatch. Today it is still referred to by collectors as the 'Steve McQueen'. But the Monaco was far more than a celebrity trinket. It was one of the first chronograph watches with an automatic movement, for which Heuer teamed up with fellow Swiss companies Breitling, Buren and Dubois Depraz to develop the micro-rotor 'Chronomatic' movement. Aside from its highly distinctive blue face and orange hands, the Monaco had the added

distinction of being the first chronograph with a square waterproof case. The watch was taken off the market in 1978, but returned twenty years later in a slightly different form, with its crown winder located at 3 o'clock, instead of at 9 o'clock. TAG Heuer (so named since the 1985 merger with the TAG group) has also rung the changes since then, most ambitiously in 2003 with the Monaco 69, which combined analogue and digital chronograph faces in the same double-sided case. The watch's chunkiness did not stop the company releasing two ladies' versions in 2004.

UP SERIES
ARMCHAIRS (1969)
Gaetano Pesce
(1939–)
B&B Italia 1969 to
1973, 2000 to present

Designer Gaetano Pesce established his reputation as one of the most unconventional designers of the Italian design scene of the 1960s with his UP Series of anthropomorphic armchairs for the company then called C&B Italia. Premiered at the 1969 Milan Furniture Show, the series was made up of a set of seven chairs. The organic shapes lent the design a simple but comfortable appeal, but the real innovation was found in the packaging. The chairs were moulded out of polyurethane foam, compressed under a vacuum until they were flat and then packaged in PVC envelopes.

The expanded polyurethane took on volume when the envelopes were opened and the materials came into contact with air. This inventive and technologically advanced use of materials allowed Pesce to engage the purchaser as an active participant in the product's creation. At the time Pesce described his UP Series as 'transformation' furniture, intended to turn the act of purchasing into a 'happening'. The UP Series also included the UP 7, a giant foot, like a fragment of a colossal statue. But it is the UP 5, reissued by B&B Italia in 2000, that has enjoyed a successful revival.

SELENE CHAIR
(1969)
Vico Magistretti
(1920–2006)
Artemide
1969 to 1972
Heller
2002 (now ceased)

Vico Magistretti was not the first designer to attempt a single-moulded plastic chair, but the Selene Chair is one of the most elegant expressions of this particular design paradigm. It succeeds mostly because it exploits rather than resists the material from which it is made and the technology used to make it. Magistretti was already a highly experienced architect and designer of furniture, lighting and other products by the 1960s when he began experimenting with plastics. The decade preceding this design saw huge advances in plastics technology and many new synthetic materials became viable for mass production. The Selene Chair is made of injection-moulded polyester reinforced with fibreglass. The manufacturer was Artemide, a technologically advanced company who proposed the material to Magistretti. The chair's most striking feature is the innovative S shape of the legs. They are effectively thin planes of plastic without a solid core. The shape gives the legs structural solidity while reducing the weight of the chair. The form also means the legs can be moulded integrally with the seat and back. As if this were not advantageous enough, the Selene Chair is also stackable.

IN ATTESA WASTE-PAPER BIN (1970)
Enzo Mari (1932–)
Heller 1971
Danese
1971 to present

The In Attesa, meaning 'waiting' in Italian, is a waste-paper bin of beguilingly simple design. It appears to be a simple cylinder, gently canted towards the user; closer inspection reveals a more complex form that integrates subtle and ingenious details. The bin is not in fact a pure cylinder. It tapers gradually outwards towards its top to free it from its moulding tool and to allow stacking. Inside the bottom of the bin are three concentric rings creating the impression of a target. The bull's-eye hides the blemish made by the plastic injection point on the reverse. The rings appear circular but, because the base cuts through the tube of the body at an angle, they are all in fact ellipses, dimensioned to trick the eye. In 1971 the bin was released simultaneously by the Italian company, Danese, and the US company, Heller. It is one of many products Mari has designed for Danese since 1957. In 1977 a straight-sided version named Koro was produced, and in 2001 Danese (now the sole manufacturer) released Scomparto In Attesa, a semicircular compartment that sits inside the bin to allow waste to be separated.

PLIA FOLDING CHAIR (1970)
Giancarlo Piretti (1940–)
Castelli/Haworth
1970 to present

Since it first went into production in 1970, over 4 million examples of Giancarlo Piretti's Plia Folding Chair have been sold by Bologna-based furniture manufacturer Castelli. This modern translation of the traditional wooden folding chair – consisting of a polished aluminium frame and a transparent, moulded perspex seat and back – was revolutionary in post-war furniture design. Its key feature is a three-metal disc hinge component. The backrest and front support, as well as the seat and rear support, are constructed within two rectangular frames and one U-shaped hoop. Together with the clearly visible hinge mechanism,

the Plia's folding form is reduced to a single compact unit thickness of five centimetres. Piretti produced both domestic and contract furniture as Castelli's in-house designer. His design ethos for the company – functional, inexpensive, space saving and geared to large-scale production – was embodied in the Plia Chair. With its rounded edges and corners, and intended for both indoor and outdoor use, it quickly became popular for its lightness and flexibility. Stackable when folded either out or flat, sleek, functional and structurally elegant, the Plia Chair continues to hold its own.

KEY RING (1970s)
Designer Unknown
Various
1970s to present

The humble double-circuit metal key ring is a modern marvel, a tiny masterpiece of engineering and utility that nearly all of us carry and few appreciate. The underlying concept of the key ring is hundreds of years old, but its present refined state is the product of modern precision manufacturing and metallurgy. It was only introduced in the early 1970s, replacing the older bead-chain. Its essential design consists of a tight spiral of steel, which coils over on itself to complete two circuits. Its almost limitless flexibility has led to a whole industry of promotional, souvenir and advertising key chains, all designed for the simple metal loop, and most often coming with one attached. It is not an exaggeration to say that this prosaic little ring holds a good deal of our lives – access to homes, workplaces and vehicles – together. And in honour of that small but important role, we reward the little ring with unlimited customization, going so far as to imprint our personalities on it. It is one of the most intimate design objects we can ever own, and one of the cheapest and least regarded.

FURNITURE IN
IRREGULAR FORMS
(1970)
Shiro Kuramata
(1934–91)
Fujiko 1970 to 1971
Aoshima Shoten
1972 to 1998
Cappellini
1986 to present

Shiro Kuramata invented a new design vocabulary: the sensation of floating lines and release from gravity, transparency and the construction of light. His furniture pieces are realized in a process of meticulous craftsmanship and a painstaking attention to detail. Furniture in Irregular Forms designed in 1970, consists of chests of eighteen slightly different drawers moving on four simple rollers. Two versions were produced: Side 1 (pictured) with its wave-like running curve along both sides, and Side 2 which had straight, vertical sides but curved in and out along its front plane. The minimalist structure and

reduced means of the chest of drawers create a strong impression, making it highly recognizable. Even today, it embodies an extraordinary combination of a minimalist functional sculpture with lightness of form. The pieces stem from Kuramata's experimentation with drawers during the late 1960s. When Cappellini reissued the design in 1986, there was a renewed interest in Kuramata due to his postmodernist approach, during a period when he was already revered for his conceptual approach to furniture and interior design.

OPTIC CLOCK
(1970)
Joe Colombo
(1930–71)
Ritz-Italora 1970s
Alessi
1988 to present

Committed to imagining the environment of the future, Italian architect and designer Joe Colombo defined the Pop era interior. The Optic Clock, designed in 1970, is one of his enduring classics. As stylized as Colombo's aesthetic was, it was always driven by practicality. In this instance the clock's casing, which is made of red or white ABS plastic, projects out over the clock face like the rim of a camera lens to prevent light reflections. The casing also projects at the back so that it can be tilted upwards, while there is a hole in the top to hang the clock on a wall. The graphic treatment of the numbers plays on the clock's inherent roundness, but the traditional hierarchy is inverted so that the minutes and seconds are numbered rather than the hours. In this way, the fat hour hand with its circular eye, frames the dots so that people can tell the time at a glance, while the slender minute and second hands make the precise time much easier to read. The Optic Clock was produced in the same year as the first digital watch, and it aimed at the same precision as the digital clocks that would start to replace the analogue variety in the coming decade.

BOBY® TROLLEY (1970)
Joe Colombo
(1930–1971)
Bieffeplast
1970 to 1999
B-Line
2000 to present

The Boby® Trolley typifies Joe Colombo's approach to designing multifunctional solutions for the home and office. It was designed to satisfy the storage requirements of a draughtsman, although it demonstrated a multifunctional purpose within both the home and the office. It is a modular design of injection-moulded ABS plastic, available in a host of colours. Set within the trolley are revolving drawer units, drop-in trays and open storage. Its flexibility of use is enhanced by the addition of three castors. Colombo's design is softened through a finely balanced mix of radii: the appealing curves of what is essentially a box are

sensitively designed. The design could have been realized economically only in plastic and its impact on the cultural use of that material is significant. The Boby® Trolley endures as an accessible piece of design that encapsulates the Colombo philosophy of use of materials and technology. B-line continues to supply a demand for the design, despite technological and user changes within the contemporary design studio. The storage capabilities and flexibility of the Boby® Trolley outweigh the reality of the conceptual, paper-free design office.

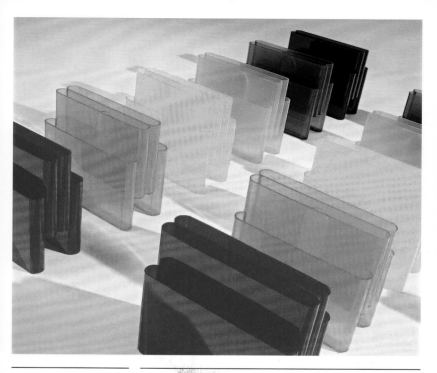

MAGAZINE RACK
(1970)
Giotto Stoppino
(1926–2011)
Kartell 1971 to present

The Magazine Rack was an important piece within Italy's exciting early-1970s climate of design and production. Architect and designer Giotto Stoppino first developed the idea for it in 1970. Made of plastic in a variety of colours, its essential construction was of two pocket elements bridged by another, smaller element that functioned as a handle. Its synthetic, moulded and usefully flexible form, which can be stacked easily, fits the design and production mandate of its Milan-based firm, Kartell, to produce durable yet interesting objects that exploited new technologies and the ideologies

of Pop design. Domestic objects such as the Magazine Rack were the result of new plastics such as polypropylene, which allowed for a limitless range of cast forms and colours. It is a manufactured object representative of Italy's reputation as a centre of design innovation and experimentation at the turn of the decade. It now is most recognizable in its adapted form, a semi-transparent and coloured four-pocket version, introduced in 1994 as a unique variation on the original design. This reinterpretation is still produced by Kartell. A silver, semi-transparent finish was introduced to the line in 2000.

BALL PENTEL R50 PEN (1970)
Pentel Design Team
Pentel 1970 to present

The distinctive green-barrelled Ball Pentel R50 is one of the most successful pens in the world, with over 5 million produced each year. Launched in 1970, the pen introduced the world to rollerball technology and a disposable pen that could match the refined writing finish of a traditional fountain pen. Unlike ballpoint pens, which use a viscous oil-based ink, rollerballs use a thinner, water-based ink that both allows them to write more smoothly and dry more quickly, and gives that fountain-pen-like finish. The ink is held in a fibre cylinder, which, while wet to the touch, does not leak or spill ink. The cylinder is

pressed down onto a fibre 'spike' that transfers the ink by capillary action to a hard alloy tip. Crucially, this ink storage and transfer method, developed in Japan where Pentel originates, does not rely on gravity, allowing the pen to continue functioning regardless of the angle at which it is held. Unlike ballpoint pens, the body of the Ball Pentel borrows the traditional outer shape and feel of a fountain pen – albeit formed out of plastic – while delivering the splatter-free ease of use that had led to the success of the ballpoint pen.

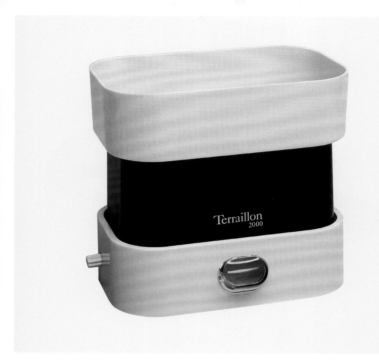

KITCHEN SCALE BA2000 (1970)
Marco Zanuso
(1916–2001)
Terraillon
1970 to present

Kitchen scales have historically involved two elements: the display and the receptacle for food, which tended to be kept distinct. Marco Zanuso was the first to approach a scale as a holistic product. His Kitchen Scale BA2000 encloses its mechanistic system, and is made into a simple-to-use domestic tool. When designing products to be manufactured, Zanuso, a noted architect, did not alter his process. In architecture he reconfigured space to achieve a desired flow; in products he reconfigured their components to achieve a desired use. For this scale the architectural logic is quite beautiful: the lid can be used either with food on top of it, or reversed and used as a container for liquids or grains. For the display the wheel is hidden and appears less mechanical. With the clever use of magnification and angle, the display is visible when the countertop is lower than eye-level. The Kitchen Scale BA2000 is a superior example of converting complexity into simplicity, and at a modest price. Its continued and unbroken production is testament to this, even with the influx of modern digital pressure pads on the market.

SPIRALE ASHTRAY
(1971)
Achille Castiglioni
(1918–2002)
Bacci 1971 to c.1973
Alessi
1986 to present

The simple yet elegant design of the Spirale Ashtray belies its ingenuity. Such an apparently effortless solution is the mark of an archetype, and is typical of Achille Castiglioni's approach to design, where familiar objects are subtly improved and redefined by a careful attention to practical detail and an appreciation of everyday human behaviour. A lifelong smoker himself, Castiglioni designed the Spirale Ashtray in response to the dilemma of the absent-minded smoker who leaves cigarettes smouldering in the ashtray. A spring coil holds the cigarette over the bowl and prevents

it from falling as it burns down. The spring is removable, making a messy cleaning task easy. Originally made by the Italian company, Bacci, in 1971, the ashtray was produced in both white and black marble, and in silver plate. The ashtray was transferred to Alessi in 1986, where it was made in 18/10 stainless steel. Alessi now produces the ashtray in polished steel mirror in two diameters: 12 cm (4.7 in) and 16 cm (6.3 in). Amongst the collections of design aficionados, this ashtray is one of those rare pieces whose proportion and uncomplicated combination of elements speak to all.

KV1 MIXER TAP (1971)

Arne Jacobsen
(1902–71)
Vola 1972 to present

Water taps and bathroom fittings remained untouched by the vision of the designer until surprisingly late in the twentieth century. The KV1 Mixer Tap, part of a series of fittings in a range called Vola, is probably the world's first commercially successful designer tap. Most of the design work was carried out by Teit Weylandt, working under Arne Jacobsen. However, the basic idea, including the underlying mechanism, had already been worked through by engineer and industrialist Verner Overgaard, the owner of the company IP Lund (now called Vola). On the basis of Overgaard's preparatory work, Jacobsen quickly recognized the potential for the visual rationalization of the unit. By restricting the vocabulary of forms used in the design to a range of cylinders and by cleverly combining the lever controlling the force of water with the rotating knob that governs its temperature, Weylandt produced an object that seemed an improbable simplification of and improvement on existing models. Like many of the designs from Arne Jacobsen's office, it seems to have been created for a time that has yet to come.

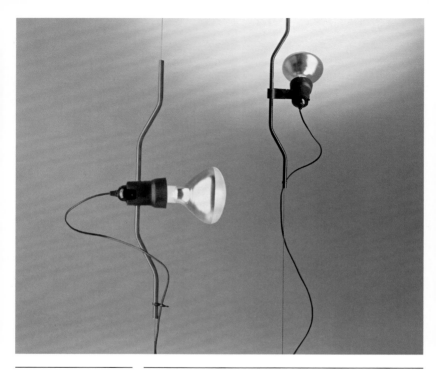

PARENTESI LAMP
(1971)
Achille Castiglioni
(1918–2002)
Pio Manzù (1939–69)
Flos 1971 to present

Achille Castiglioni acknowledged Pio Manzù as the originator of the Parentesi Lamp. Manzù imagined a fixed vertical rod with a cylindrical box that would slide up and down it, with a slit for the light and the chosen position held in place with a screw. When Manzù died prematurely in 1969, Castiglioni continued to develop the idea, replacing the rod with metal cable that is hung from the ceiling and kept taut by a rubber-coated iron weight. A chromed or enamelled stainless-steel tube, shaped like a bracket (on which the product name was based), slides up and down the cable and supports a rotating rubber joint,

to which is fixed the lamp-holder with electric lead and 150-watt spotlight bulb. The shape of the steel tube creates enough friction with the taut wire to prevent the spotlight from moving, but it can be slid up or down effortlessly by hand. The light fixture and bulb are able to swivel 360 degrees on the vertical and horizontal axes. Most of the components used in the lamp are widely manufactured items, packaged and sold like a kit to be easily assembled by the customer.

TIZIO LAMP (1971)
Richard Sapper
(1932–2015)
Artemide
1972 to present

The Tizio Lamp has become emblematic of both extreme functionalism in design and an aspirational designer lifestyle. Although developed as a work lamp, it has achieved popularity in domestic interiors, as much at home in today's loft apartments as in a 1970s studio. In 1970, Ernesto Gismondi, co-founder of the lighting company Artemide, suggested that Richard Sapper design a work lamp. The result was a lamp that combined new technology (halogen light) with a carefully engineered and flexible structure. The Tizio Lamp uses a system of counterweights to hold the bearing arm in position,

so that the lamp can be adjusted with the touch of a finger. The bearing arm can rotate through 360 degrees on its heavy base, and the small reflector turned to face in any direction. The lamp is made of metal with a strong but lightweight fibreglass-reinforced nylon coating. The joints are not screwed together, but fixed with a form of snap fastening, so that if the lamp falls, the joints snap apart rather than break. In totality (it is made of over 100 components), it is a remarkable combination of engineering and ingenuity in a spare and elegant form.

PROGRAMMA 8 TABLEWARE (1971)
Eija Helander (1944–)
Franco Sargiani (1940–)
Alessi 1971 to 1992, 2005 to present

Programma 8 Tableware represents an important phase in the history of Alessi production. In the early 1970s Alberto Alessi invited his architect friend, Franco Sargiani, and the Finnish graphic designer, Eija Helander, to work on the design of a new range of stainless-steel tableware that began with a brief for an oil jug. The initial project expanded into a revolutionary series of adaptable and flexible forms. The result was Programma 8, a large-scale assortment of trays and containers based on a modular system of squares and rectangles. The tableware was radical for a number of reasons: it used steel in its own

right and not as a substitute for more expensive materials, its shape was unlike any other and it acknowledged that younger professional consumers were living in homes where space was at a premium. Programma 8 offered practicality, not only in its idea of allowing several items to co-exist simultaneously, but also because the collection was stackable. The modular set was reissued by Alessi in 2005, and now includes ceramic containers with polypropylene covers, along with the original containers for oil, vinegar, salt and pepper, as well as various trays and cutting boards.

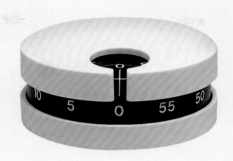

MINITIMER KITCHEN TIMER
(1971)
Richard Sapper
(1932–2015)
Ritz-Italora/Terraillon
1971 (now ceased)

The circular Minitimer Kitchen Timer is characteristic of product designer Richard Sapper's intelligent fusion of technology and style. The design is understated and pragmatic; the mechanism revolves inside the outer casing so that the remaining time is visible from above and the side in the small circular window. The 7 cm (2.75 in) diameter, discreetly small timer, is produced in black, white or red, and is loosely reminiscent of scientific or car instruments. The success of the design has been recognized since its initial production. Ritz-Italora, based near Milan, is the original manufacturer, and the French company, Terraillon, has produced it under licence since its debut in 1971. Sapper's creative approach to engineering is apparent in his most familiar designs. While he became a specialist in electronic products, such as radios, televisions and lighting, he became known for his designs for the casing of such products. This may explain the success of the timer, as its casing cleverly sandwiches the middle section. The Minitimer is an elegant and discreet object with a lengthy and dedicated following, and is part of the permanent collections at the Museum of Modern Art and the Pompidou Centre.

OMSTAK CHAIR
(1971)
Rodney Kinsman
(1943–)
Kinsman Associates/
OMK Design
1971 to present

Overtly expressing the high-tech style of the 1970s, British designer Rodney Kinsman's Omstak Chair is one of the most elegant evocations of the decade's furniture manufacturing mandate to produce high-quality, low-cost objects of beauty and practicality on a large scale, utilizing industrial materials and systems of production. Available in a number of coloured paint finishes, the chair is composed of an epoxy-coated, stamped sheet-steel seat and back, attached to a tubular steel frame. Its design allows it to be stacked and clipped in rows, thus making it a popular choice both with cost- and fashion-conscious buyers as well as with institutions. A graduate of London's Central School of Art and Crafts, Kinsman recognized early in his career that only low-cost and multipurpose products would capture a market in times of economic uncertainty. As younger consumers were an important demographic within his projected buyer profile, the chair needed to satisfy economic, as well as stylistic demands. To that end, his consultancy practice, OMK Design, utilized industrial materials and inexpensive methods of production. Intended for use both indoors and out, Kinsman's Omstak remains in production to this day.

CUBOLUCE LAMP (1972)

Franco Bettonica
(1927–99)
Mario Melocchi
(1931–2013)
Cini&Nils
1972 to present

The Cuboluce Lamp is literally a box of light lit with a single 40-watt bulb housed in an ABS plastic (acrylonitrile-butadi-ene-styrene) container. The action of opening the lid switches on the light, while the angle of the lid determines the brightness. Highly characteristic of Italian product design of the early 1970s, the Cuboluce shows a sophisticated use of high-quality plastics and a desire to create a smooth and minimalist housing for electrical components. The light can be used as a bedside or table light, and its discreet and inviting form makes it an object of fascination even when switched off. Designed by Franco Bettonica and Mario Melocchi (as Studio Opi), the Cuboluce is one of a range of products based on cuboid and cylindrical forms created for the Milanese company Cini&Nils. Others include an ashtray, magazine rack, ice bucket and flower vase, all made of melamine or ABS plastic – a tough, rigid material that it is commonly used in the auto-motive industry and for cased products such as computers. The Cuboluce and other Cini&Nils products are now part of the permanent design collection of the Museum of Modern Art in New York.

WIGGLE CHAIR
(1972)
Frank Gehry (1929–)
Jack Brogan
1972 to 1973
Chiru 1982
Vitra 1992 to present

The molten curves of the Wiggle Chair display not only Frank Gehry's expressive use of form but also his humour in reworking historical references – in this case Gerrit Reitveld's Zig-Zag Chair of 1934. Gehry's chair is made of cardboard, built up in thick layers to achieve a strong, solid appearance. The rich tactile surface belies the paucity of the paper it is made of. Gehry liked it because it, 'looked like corduroy, it felt like corduroy, it was seductive'. The Wiggle Chair was conceived in 1972 as part of a seventeen-piece set of furniture called Easy Edges, manufactured by Jack Brogan. The set was conceived as mass-market, low-cost furniture selling for as little as $15. Although it became an immediate success, Gehry withdrew the series after only three months, concerned that he would become known simply as a popular furniture designer, when his ambition lay in architecture. The series was briefly reissued by Chiru in 1982, then four pieces were put into production by Vitra in 1992. Vitra is a fitting home for Easy Edges as Gehry is the architect of the Vitra Design Museum in Germany, which houses an international collection of classic chairs.

TRIPP TRAPP CHILD'S CHAIR (1972)
Peter Opsvik (1939–)
Stokke
1972 to present

The Tripp Trapp Child's Chair was the first chair developed specifically with the needs of children in mind. Deceptively simple in design, it gives support while allowing the child freedom of movement. The Tripp Trapp was designed in 1972 by the Norwegian designer, Peter Opsvik, after seeing his two-year-old son sitting uncomfortably at the table with his feet dangling and his arms unable to reach up to the table top. Opsvik created a chair that allows children from the age of two to sit at the family table in comfort and at the same height as adults. As the child grows, the seat and the footrest can be adjusted in height as well as depth, enabling children of all ages to sit in the correct posture at the right height with their feet well supported. Peter Opsvik is one of Norway's best-known designers, celebrated for his work in ergonomic and sustainable design. The Tripp Trapp is made of cultivated beech and can be bought either untreated or varnished and in a number of different colours. Over 10 million chairs have been sold worldwide since its launch in 1972.

KURVE FLATWARE
(1972)
Tapio Wirkkala
(1915–85)
Rosenthal
1990 to 2014

The Kurve cutlery range is among the defining designs to come out of the long and prolific association between Finnish-born designer Tapio Wirkkala and Rosenthal, the established-yet-experimental homeware design company based in Germany. The matt-finish stainless-steel Kurve Flatware cutlery range, which was produced posthumously by Rosenthal in 1990, draws on Finland's Arctic landscape and traditions, and particularly the domestic designs of the region's indigenous Sami people. The pared-down ergonomics of the Kurve forms recall the simple cutlery of the Sami. Wirkkala shared their ancient

craft sensibility, always carving his cutlery patterns and prototypes from wood in the early stages, and would only authorize production when he was satisfied with the 'grip' of the wooden model. Wirkkala believed passionately in the idea of the creator as artisan and that the intrinsic quality of the materials should dictate the design, very much in the Scandinavian humanist tradition. Yet a sculptural beauty and poetry permeate the sensual curves of the Kurve range. From 1957 on Rosenthal gave free rein to Wirkkala's design vision, a collaboration that yielded a full collection of elegant homeware.

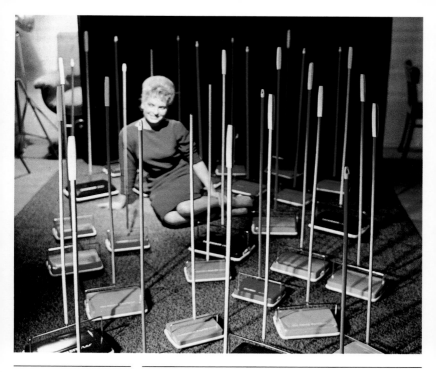

ROTARO CARPET SWEEPER (1973)
Leifheit Design Team
Leifheit
1973 to present

The modern carpet sweeper is essentially a mechanical version of the dustpan and brush, something halfway between bristles on a stick and the modern vacuum cleaner. Although the first carpet sweeper was patented in 1811, and mass-produced versions were developed in the USA during the second half of the nineteenth century, it was in Günter Leifheit and Hans-Erich Slany's productions that the device achieved its most celebrated and perfect form. Leifheit designed a slim version that incorporated a retractable handle, thus allowing it to be pushed under large items of furniture, as well as a top-removing dustpan. The 1973 Rotaro merges the clean lines and strong geometry of German Modernism of the 1930s, with a touch of the more recent American modern style. The sweeper runs on six wheels that drive three rotating brushes, which displace dirt and debris that are then swept up by a central brush roller. The brushes are height adjustable, with four settings, in order to accommodate various types of flooring. The Rotaro is composed of a sheet-metal housing, a wooden axle and strong natural pig bristles, making it one of the most enduring sweepers on the market.

SOMMELIERS
RANGE
GLASSWARE (1973)
Claus Josef Riedel
(1925–2004)
Riedel Glas
1973 to present

The 240-year-old Riedel brand has been a family glass-making business for eleven generations, creating hand-blown and now machine-made products. Professor Claus Josef Riedel, the ninth generation of glassmakers, was the first to realize that the shape of the glass influences the flavours and features of different wines. By replacing traditional coloured and cut glass with a thinly blown, long-stemmed, simple shape, he transformed stemware into the first functional wine glass, reducing the glass to its essential form: bowl, stem and base. This crucial change began with the Sommeliers range of ten different shapes, introduced in 1973 and developed with the help of the Association of Italian Sommeliers (ASI). Georg Riedel, Claus's son, developed the Sommeliers series further. Almost yearly new glasses were added, not only for wine but also for champagne, fortified wines and spirits. Today the Sommeliers collection consists of no less than forty different glasses. When the series started, the glasses stood out for their unusual dimensions and perfect balance. Today, even machine-produced glasses imitate the size and shapes of this range, but the refinement of a Riedel Sommeliers glass can never be matched.

TOGO SOFA (1973)
Michel Ducaroy
(1925–2009)
Ligne Roset
1973 to present

The early 1970s were a time of possibility for furniture designers, with new materials regularly coming on-stream and opening up fresh creative possibilities. Michel Ducaroy, head of design with French company Ligne Roset, responded with what today is still seen as a breathtakingly bold, if somewhat 'period', departure: the world's first all-foam sofa. The Togo three-seater sofa is made entirely of Dacron, a polyester fibre, and has no frame. Covered in loose upholstery, the foam is quilted into a form that suggests all manner of associations, from a bent stovepipe to a tube of toothpaste or a large caterpillar. Ducaroy played to the material's squishy qualities by creating an almost shell-like mass that positively sucked the leg-weary owner into its welcoming folds. Togo proved so popular at the Paris Furniture Fair of 1973 that Ducaroy and Ligne Roset were soon working on creating a range of complementary pieces, including 'fireside' chairs and a corner seat. A flexible, mattress-style sofa bed followed in 1976 and an attempt, in 1981, to marry all-foam construction to a less unified form than the Togo. But it is the Togo which is considered contemporary today.

SCIANGAI COAT STAND (1973)
Gionatan De Pas
(1932–91)
Donato D'Urbino
(1935–)
Paolo Lomazzi
(1936–)
Zanotta
1973 to present

The Sciangai Coat Stand consists of eight beechwood rods screwed together at the centre. Despite its elegant finish, the Sciangai is little more than a compact bundle of sticks. Yet, when released, these sticks fold out in a spiral to create one of the most striking coat stands around. In choosing to call their stand 'Sciangai', the designers have created a pun: Sciangai is the Italian name for the game of Pick up Sticks, where one stick is removed from a pile without disturbing the others. This sense of fun is carried through in the design, which expands from a diameter of 41 cm (16.5 in)

to one of 65 cm (26 in). It is available varnished, in black, or in bleached or wengé-stained oak. Created by the architects Gionatan De Pas, Donato D'Urbino and Paolo Lomazzi, the Sciangai is portable furniture reduced to its most primitive form. Its collapsible nature follows the design group's pioneering development of temporary architecture and inflatable furniture, most famously the Blow Chair of 1967, as well as its interest in flex-ible, adaptable mobile living. In 1979, at the Milan Triennale, the Sciangai won a prestigious Compasso d'Oro award.

SALT AND PEPPER RASPS (1973)
Johnny Sørensen
(1944–)
Rud Thygesen
(1932–2019)
Rosendahl
1973 to present

Rud Thygesen and Johnny Sørensen are known for their furniture design using laminated wood that is the embodiment of the high-quality Danish design tradition. Both designers attended the The Royal Danish Academy of Fine Arts, graduating in 1966. Their design output reflects a dedication to craftsmanship and quality of materials, while also displaying ingenuity and invention. The pair considers materials and technology as key parameters in the design process. The Salt and Pepper Rasps illustrate their characteristic sophistication and inventiveness. The rasps are made from aluminium and are easier to use than traditional wooden mills. The clever design has a patented mechanism that enables the user to hold the mill in one hand, and use the thumb press to activate the grinding mechanism that releases freshly ground seasoning. The two slender cylindrical rasps sit in a purpose-designed holder. The success of the design is in its beauty and innovation, in keeping with the Danish design tradition. The work of Thygesen and Sørensen enjoys an international reputation, and many of their designs can be found in collections throughout the world, including the Museum of Modern Art.

PONY CHAIR (1973)
Eero Aarnio (1932–)
Asko 1973 to 1980
Adelta 2000 to 2016
Eero Aarnio Originals
2016 to present

These small, colourful, abstract ponies may look as though they are intended for small children, but Eero Aarnio conceived them as playful seating for adults. The user could either 'ride' the horse by facing the front, or sit sideways on it. The padded, fabric-covered stools with tubular frames make clear reference to Pop sensibility, playing with established expectations of what adult furniture should be and how we should decorate our homes. In doing so Aarnio transforms the much-beloved children's hobbyhorse into something for adults. During the late 1960s many Scandinavian designers experimented with

plastic, fibreglass and other synthetic materials. These new materials allowed for new forms and new solutions to seating. Led by Aarnio and Verner Panton, these designers investigated the boundaries of what furniture could be. Both Panton and Aarnio emphasized geometric shapes that were then transformed into usable pieces of furniture. The Pony is simply a child's chair all grown up, in terms of scale at least. The Pony chair is currently available from Eero Aarnio Originals, and the upholstered stretch fabric of white, black, orange, pink and green still provides adults with an object of imagination and joy.

SERVOMUTO TABLE (1974)
Achille Castiglioni
(1918–2002)
Zanotta
1975 to present

The Italian word *servomuto* translates as 'dumb waiter', a most suitable name for Achille Castiglioni's table design from 1974. Made from a base of polypropylene, a steel rod and a table top in layered plastic laminate or hard polyurethane, this lightweight side table facilitates absolute utility while remaining elegant in its visual simplicity. The use of few component parts in manufacture makes this an affordable proposition for many commercial and domestic environments. The extending steel rod acts as the supporting stem of the table and the waist-height knob on the top invites the user to effortlessly move the table around at a whim. The Servomuto was the third design, after an ashtray and an umbrella stand, by Castiglioni in his I Servi series of accessory products using the same base and rod components. They were originally produced by the Italian lighting company Flos, but in 1970 the furniture manufacturer Zanotta took on the designs and invited Castiglioni to add more to the series. This design, available in black, white or dual colour finishes, has subsequently been joined by another six items, and is still produced by Zanotta today.

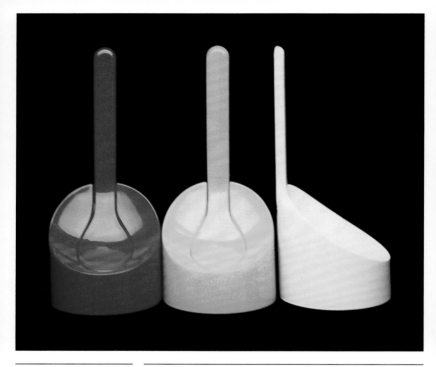

CUCCIOLO TOILET BRUSH (1974)
Makio Hasuike
(1938–)
Gedy 1974 to present

The sculptural form of the Cucciolo Toilet Brush belies its purpose as a simple tool designed to perform one of the most unpleasant household tasks. Awarded the Compasso d'Oro prize in 1979 and put on display in the Museum of Modern Art, the humble toilet brush has been transformed by Makio Hasuike into an object of beauty. When Hasuike was approached by Gedy, he started by considering aspects of hygiene. The most hygienic object he could think of was a plate, so he began to think of a brush-holder with no hidden areas. Hasuike was aware that the bathroom had evolved into a room that was on show to guests, so he wanted to allow the owner a sense of pride in the object. Not only should it be functional, economical and durable, it should also be a joy to use and something to be looked at and admired. The resulting design was a simple form with a shallow cavity to collect the drops of water from the brush. The Cucciolo was such a success that for years it was the signature design of Gedy, and it continues to be the company's bestseller.

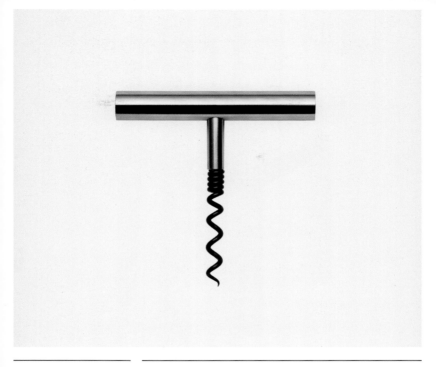

CORKSCREW (1974)
Peter Holmblad
(1934–)
Stelton
1974 to present

Peter Holmblad was originally employed as a salesman by Stelton, then just a small company making stainless-steel items for domestic use. However, he clearly had an understanding of the significance of design and had one major advantage in this respect: he was Arne Jacobsen's foster son. By the 1970s he had become the owner of the firm and achieved some fame as the person who had badgered the initially unenthusiastic Jacobsen into designing his well-known Cylinda-Line series. Jacobsen's set of homeware was produced in brushed stainless-steel and won for Stelton a good degree of international recognition.

Although Holmblad wanted Jacobsen to extend the range of products (he was hoping for a cocktail shaker), Jacobsen was not interested in alcohol and could not be persuaded. After Jacobsen's death, Holmblad developed the range by introducing small kitchen tools. His straightforward modernization of the corkscrew was originally made in nickel-plated steel. The screw is now produced in steel, but is Teflon-plated and meshes seamlessly with the rest of Stelton's products. Along with the corkscrew, Holmblad's series consists of a bottle opener, cocktail measure, cheese/bar knife, and cheese slicer.

4875 CHAIR (1974)
Carlo Bartoli (1931–)
Kartell 1974 to 2011

The cartoon-like quality, soft curves and compact proportions of Carlo Bartoli's 4875 Chair owe much to its two famous predecessors at Kartell: Marco Zanuso and Richard Sapper's Stacking Child's Chair of 1960 and Joe Colombo's Model 4867 Chair of 1965. However, unlike both earlier chairs, which were moulded in ABS, the 4875 was made from polypropylene, a more versatile, harder-wearing plastic that was much less expensive. Bartoli began his design for the 4875 by examining the structures of Colombo's and Zanuso and Sapper's chairs. He used the same single body, incorporating the seat and backrest in one moulding. Four cylindrical legs were then moulded separately. Propitiously, during the two years that it took to develop the design, polypropylene was invented. Kartell took advantage of this and decided to manufacture the 4875 in the new material, with the addition of small ribbings under the seat to reinforce the leg joints. By the 1970s, plastics had fallen out of fashion, so the 4875 Chair never achieved the same status of its predecessors at Kartell. Nevertheless, the chair became an immediate bestseller and in 1979 it was selected for the Compasso d'Oro award.

CHAMBORD COFFEE PRESS (1974)
Carsten Jørgensen
(1948–)
Bodum
1982 to present

Working on the principles of the French press, the Chambord Coffee Press made it possible for anyone to make a good cup of coffee in the home. Its ease of use has made it instantly and enduringly popular. The shape and construction of this coffee maker allows for the simplest method of brewing coffee. The French press was actually invented by the Italian Attilio Calimani in 1933. However, since then Bodum has become synonymous with the brewing process, and variations on the Chambord are found in most European homes. This coffee plunger is the cafetière designed by Carsten Jørgensen for Bodum in 1982. The combination of the heat-resistant Pyrex glass beaker, chrome frame and black, durable bakelite plastic knob and handle have made it renowned worldwide for its timeless design. It is as popular today as when it was first launched. The uncomplicated and modest design is accompanied by practicality: the Chambord can be completely dismantled, allowing ease of cleaning and replacement of any parts. With the Chambord, Bodum aimed to develop a new design language for coffee makers, incorporating beauty, simplicity and excellent materials into everyday life.

VERTEBRA CHAIR
(1974–5)
Emilio Ambasz
(1943–)
Giancarlo Piretti
(1940–)
KI 1976 (now ceased)
Castelli/Haworth
1976 (now ceased)

The Vertebra Chair was the first office chair to respond automatically to the user's movement, using a system of springs and counterbalances to support everyday work. The name Vertebra was chosen to express the intimate relationship between the user's back and the movement of the chair. It is considered one of the first office chairs to embody the study of how people work and how designers can support that work. The design included automatic seat and back movements that responded to the user's motions and thus eliminated the need for manual adjustment. The term 'lumbar support' was established

with the introduction of the Vertebra, as chairs previously prescribed the user's position but did not necessarily support them. The chair's mechanisms were mostly under the seat-pan, or the two 4 cm (1.6 in) thick tubes supporting the chair's back. Vertebra also introduced a new visual vocabulary to furniture design, with its cast-aluminium base and flexible tubular-steel frame. It won several design awards and has had only very slight alterations over the years. The work of Ambasz and Piretti introduced a new dialogue about furniture that continues, just as their Vertebra Chair does, forty years later.

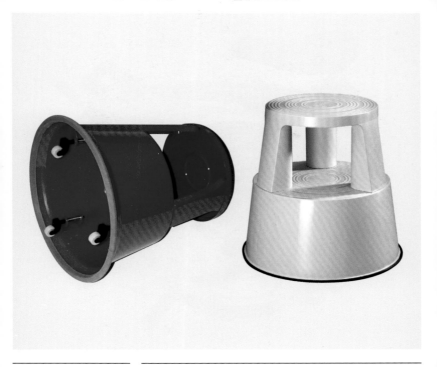

KICKSTOOL (1975)
Wedo Design Team
Wedo
1976 to present

Stools must do two contradictory things: first, they must provide a secure base to stand on and second, they should be mobile. Wedo (Werner Dorsch) solved this problem with the Kickstool. It has three castors mounted on its base, allowing it to roll freely. This means that it can be pushed across the floor by foot, leaving the arms free for carrying books or files. These castors would make the stool dangerously unstable to stand on if it were not for the really innovative part of the design. Once weight is placed on top of the stool – for instance, by standing on it – the entire stool sinks a centimetre, locking the castors and bringing the broad circular rim of the base into contact with the floor. This makes it extremely stable, with a broad footprint and a low centre of gravity. This stability is assisted further by the stool's circular plan, so it does not have to be aligned after being repositioned. The design is extraordinarily simple, but its sheer superiority to other, more traditional solutions has made the Kickstool an emblem of the librarian's and archivist's trades.

**BROMPTON
FOLDING BICYCLE
(1975)**
Andrew Ritchie
(1958–)
Brompton
1976 to present

The success of the Brompton
Folding Bicycle, a fantastic parcel
of small wheels and hinged steel
tubes, has grown out of several
factors: frustrating urban traffic
conditions, high instances
of bicycle theft and an interest
in cycling as a healthy means
of transport. This level of interest
has prevented the Brompton from
being just a specialist product,
and it has become an increasingly
common sight among suited
commuters as well as young
people more often seen on BMXs.
The Brompton is manufactured
not just in the UK, but in London,
which is some feat in itself.
Andrew Ritchie, on finding

no willing manufacturer to take on
his invention, started manufacturing the Brompton himself and has
committed his factory to constantly refining its manufacturing,
design and engineering. To fold
and unfold the bike requires a
couple of big wing-nut type fixings
to secure the two hinges, while
the rear triangle and wheel simply
swing underneath the frame. It is
lightweight – between 10 and 12
kg (22 to 26.5 lb) – and a very
reasonable ride. The Brompton
may not be the bike to go round
the world on, but is definitely the
one to choose for getting around
almost any city.

TRATTO PEN
(1975–6)
Design Group Italia
Fila 1976 to present

Since its creation, the Tratto Pen has helped form the curves, corners and scribbles of countless writings and drawings. Manufactured by Fila, the pen was designed by the Milan-based company, Design Group Italia. With the Tratto Pen, the company started a line of writing instruments that would reshape the traditional pen into a modern, innovative and sleek design object. Design Group Italia launched the Tratto Pen fineliner, 1975–6, whose lithe form and exquisite mark-making ability ensured it was an instant triumph, and in 1978, with the addition of a clip, the Tratto Clip fineliner was introduced. Both the original and the clip fineliner were highly praised, winning the Compasso d'Oro in 1979. The Tratto's success continued with the introduction of the Tratto Symbol synthetic point pen (1990), the Fila Tratto Matic ballpoint pen (1994) and the Tratto Laser needlepoint pen (1993). These pens continued the legacy of their predecessors with an organic and pure form, and the introduction of new nibs ensured Tratto's popularity in the writing world. The Tratto Pen has proven itself instrumental in creative expression; the pen's success lies in the hands of countless thoughts yet to be transcribed.

SUOMI TABLE SERVICE (1976)
Timo Sarpaneva
(1926–2006)
Rosenthal
1976 to present

In the mid-1950s Philip Rosenthal began commissioning well-known designers to produce ranges of high-quality Modern domestic porcelain for the American market. The award-winning Suomi Table Service, designed by Timo Sarpaneva, is one of Rosenthal's more popular lines and has remained in production since its introduction in 1976. Sarpaneva was by training a sculptor, and, although he is best known for his work in glass, the Suomi range has a quality reminiscent of his passion for creating beautiful shapes. Originally produced in an undecorated white porcelain, the service has a rounded-square form echoing the shape of a water-smoothed pebble. Suomi (Finnish for Finland) is also produced with a range of discreet surface decorations of faint indentations. The patterned variants have titles like Rangoon, Anthrazit, Pure Nature and Visuelle Poésie, but it is not clear whether Sarpaneva, whose own sculptural work is abstract and often monumental, was consulted over the decoration. The Pompidou Centre permanent collection of contemporary design in Paris accepted the Suomi range in 1992, simply reiterating the success of this project.

NUVOLA ROSSA BOOKCASE (1977)
Vico Magistretti
(1920–2006)
Cassina
1977 to present

In 1946, for one his earliest pieces of furniture, Vico Magistretti designed a bookcase that resembled a stepladder propped against a wall. Nearly thirty years later Magistretti was again inspired by ladders in his Nuvola Rossa Bookcase, with its collapsible frame and six removable shelves. Drawing on a tradition of anonymous design, he created a new, now reworked object that was both immediately useful and of continuing relevance. The shelves, with their equated distances, function as a wall or a room divider, creating a new environment on each side. Magistretti's unwavering approach stands in sharp contrast to that of many of his contemporaries. When Cassina launched Nuvola Rossa in 1977, a new, highly stylized, self-expressionism had begun to take hold in Italian design, casting aside mass production. In the midst of wave upon wave of ideology and style, Magistretti designed a simple but elegant, modest but clever, highly saleable, mass-produced bookcase. Cassina continues to produce Nuvola Rossa in lacquered beechwood and walnut. Although it does not yet qualify under Magistretti's rule that a good design lasts fifty or even a hundred years, it is surely close enough.

VACUUM JUG
(1977)
Erik Magnussen
(1940–)
Stelton
1977 to present

Erik Magnussen's insulated Vacuum Jug for Stelton reflects its designer's instinctive feeling for form coupled with his strict, almost austere approach to function. The jug was the first product Magnussen designed for Stelton after he succeeded Arne Jacobsen as the company's chief designer. It was intended to complement Jacobsen's famous Cylinda-Line of 1967. Magnussen developed a design that utilized an existing glass bottle liner (thus immediately reducing production costs) and introduced a unique, T-shaped lid with a rocking stopper mechanism that opened and closed automatically when the jug was tilted, allowing it to be operated easily with one hand. Originally the jug was made in stainless steel to match the other products in the Cylinda-Line, with the lid made from POM plastic. From 1979 the body of the jug was also produced in shiny, scratch-resistant ABS plastic and available in several colours (today in fifteen colours). The use of plastics turned an otherwise expensive item into an affordable one. The jug – which was awarded the Danish Design Centre's ID Prize in 1977 – became an instant success and continues to be one of the company's best-selling products.

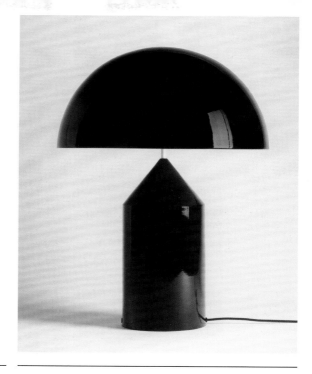

ATOLLO LAMP
233/D (1977)
Vico Magistretti
(1920–2006)
Oluce
1977 to present

The Atollo Lamp is one of Vico Magistretti's most famous lamps and was winner of the Compasso d'Oro award in 1979. It is a table lamp made of painted aluminium; its simple geometrical composition transforms an accessible domestic object into an abstract sculpture. The lamp is composed of two distinct elements: a cylindrical support and a spherical top. The top is connected to the lamp's base by an element so slim that, when the lamp is turned on, the unit appears to be suspended in mid-air. The many lamps that Magistretti has designed are a combination of abstract geometries and light effects.

Details such as joints, wires and plugs are always concealed; what prevails in these objects is a great formal simplicity and balanced composition. The Atollo's concept was realized by Magistretti in a series of sketches, but it took time for Oluce, the oldest Italian lighting design company still active today, to put such a technically complex idea into production. For many years Magistretti was an art director and chief designer for Oluce, where he conferred his unmistakable stamp and where the Atollo was one of its most successful products.

CAB CHAIR (1977)
Mario Bellini (1935–)
Cassina
1977 to present

Mario Bellini – architect, industrial designer, furniture designer, journalist and lecturer – is one of the most notable figures in today's international design community. His Cab Chair, produced in Milan by Cassina since 1977, endures as a symbol of late twentieth-century Italian innovation and craftsmanship. An enamelled tubular steel frame is encased by a form-fitting leather cover, closed by four zips that run along the inside legs and under the seat. Reinforced only by a plastic plate within the seat, the effect is taut, luxurious and uniform. Whereas tubular steel furniture up to that point relied on contrasting materials for visual impact, Bellini here combines the two elements, metal and covering, to create an enveloped, elegant structure. By 1982 the chair had become synonymous with high-quality Italian design; the Cab family now consists of eight different pieces including a lounge chair and bed. All are available in thirteen different colours. In Bellini's early career he acted as chief design consultant for Olivetti (from 1963) and it has been suggested that the leather skin of the Cab Chair is a reference to traditional typewriter casings.

9090 ESPRESSO COFFEE MAKER (1977–9)
Richard Sapper
(1932–2015)
Alessi 1979 to present

Designed by Richard Sapper, a pioneer of Postmodern industrial product design ideology, the 9090 Espresso Coffee Maker was awarded the Compasso d'Oro at the 1979 Milan Triennale. The stainless-steel columnar coffee pot was praised not only for its sleek lines and 'exceptional' success in reinventing the espresso coffee maker, but also for its innovative design. The wide base gives the coffee maker both sturdiness and stability, but also the ability to boil the water evenly and quickly to avoid scorching the coffee. Sapper's design included a non-drip spout and a widely heralded innovative

click system that opened and closed the pot to allow water and coffee to be added. Designed between 1977 and 1979, the 9090 exemplified Alessi's intuition that the kitchen would be a good arena for new strategic initiatives. With the Bialetti Moka cafetière dominating the market in Italy, the Alessi strategy was to commission a state-of-the-art design that would retail for a much higher price than any in their existing range. Sapper's solution was a revolutionary coffee maker with no traditional neck or spout, futuristic in shape and with pared-down decoration.

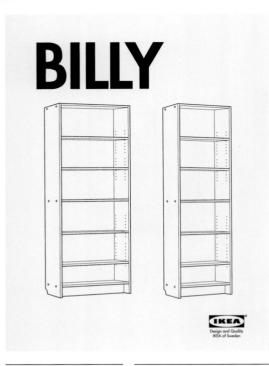

BILLY

BILLY SHELF (1978)
IKEA
IKEA 1978 to present

The Billy Shelf is a design phenomenon. This simple, flexible, self-assembly storage system is one of the most popular design products in the world. Since it was launched by IKEA in 1978 it has sold more than 60 million pieces. Of course, IKEA is also a phenomenon in its own right. IKEA established the idea of fully integrating home furnishing by developing modular, interlinking systems as opposed to individual, one-off products. The Billy system is the key exemplar of IKEA's raison d'être. Billy has evolved from simple, adjustable shelving units to a whole series of bookcase and storage combinations featuring corner units, glass doors, CD towers and TV benches. It is made of particle board, which is cheap to mass produce and easy to assemble. These components are veneered in a selection of materials ranging from birch and beech, to white, dark and grey metallic finishes. IKEA has always sold bookcases, but Billy is optimized in terms of flexibility and material consumption. The IKEA mantra of functional, low-cost design has seduced a global audience and the clean lines, high versatility and low cost of its best-selling Billy system have greatly contributed to this Scandinavian seduction.

FRISBI LAMP (1978)
Achille Castiglioni
(1918–2002)
Flos 1978 to present

Achille Castiglioni is quite rightly considered one of the greatest designers of the last century. His Frisbi Lamp represents his trademark wit and lightness of touch, but is also recognized as an icon of design. Its popularity and apparent simplicity have caused it to appear regularly enough for it to seem commonplace. This is despite its unusual solution to the problem of deflecting glare from a hanging light. Castiglioni's approach to lighting design often started with an in-depth appraisal of a particular bulb. This lamp followed on from earlier research completed with his brother, Pier Giacomo, and was designed to provide both soft, reflected light and direct light. This was achieved by means of a suspended white translucent metacrylate disc with a large central hole. This hole directs light onto a tabletop, while the opal plastic disc holds, diffuses and reflects the remainder of the light. A small spun and polished metal bowl houses the incandescent bulb. This bowl is fixed to the stem, from which three tiny steel wires are suspended. These in turn support the opal plastic disc, which appears to float magically in space when seen from a distance.

5070 CONDIMENT SET (1978)
Ettore Sottsass
(1917–2007)
Alessi
1978 to present

The 5070 Condiment Set designed by Ettore Sottsass for Alessi is characteristic of the company's ethos to create objects that make the commonplace special. Synonymous with Postmodernist design of the 1980s, Sottsass was one of Italy's most expressive and successful designers. He began his design association with Alessi in 1972, and the 5070 Condiment Set is one of his early works for the company. Sottsass's design defined what was expected of a successful condiment set. The containers are sophisticated crystal glass cylinders, each topped with a polished stainless-steel dome, and stand neatly on their holder. The high quality of the materials evokes a sense of style while being practical (the glass reveals the contents). The set remains truly utilitarian, essential as a table centrepiece and an item of daily use; designed in the late 1970s it was ahead of its time and gave an insight into the design style that would become dominant through the 1980s. The proof of the enduring success of the set is its ubiquity; found widely in Italian restaurants, bars and homes, the 5070 Condiment Set created an industrial and domestic standard for the table since its launch.

GACELA CHAIR
(1978)
Joan Casas i Ortínez
(1942–2013)
Indecasa
1978 (now ceased)

No chair is more representative of modern café culture than the Gacela Chair, designed by Joan Casas i Ortínez. Constructed out of an anodized aluminium tube, the Gacela's simple, clean lines make it a versatile design fit for indoor or outdoor spaces. A graphic designer, industrial designer and lecturer, Casas i Ortínez started working with Spanish manufacturer Indecasa in 1964. His Clásica collection of stacking chairs, of which Gacela is part, is today hailed as a classic of European café furniture. The Clásica collection is the result of more than twenty-five years of Indecasa history. Gacela was designed with either aluminium or wooden slats and cast aluminium joints for additional strength. The aluminium slats were also available painted in powdered polyester or could be given a personal touch with adhesive labels suitable for external use. Gacela's lightness, durability and stackability made it a bestseller. The chair is the perfect example of Casas i Ortínez's statement that, 'Design for me means creating products for industry, for sale, that are functional and please thousands of people and that over the years will acquire classic status, becoming part of our surroundings.'

MAGLITE (1979)
Anthony Maglica
(1930–)
Mag Instrument
1979 to present

The design of the Maglite suggests a strong consideration of its purpose, being free of superfluous decoration – practically a tool for lighting. The casing, precisely made by machine, employs high-quality rubber seals and high-resolution optics, and there is even a spare bulb housed within the body of the torch. The Maglite was introduced in the USA in 1979. It was intended to be an improvement on existing torches available to the police, firefighters and engineers: a portable lighting source in lightweight, anodized aluminium that would be reliable and robust. Invented and produced by Anthony Maglica, the reliable and durable

Maglite was positively received by its target market. With a commitment to product innovation and refinement, Maglica quickly developed a family of torches based on the key features of the original design. The differing sizes and weights exploited new markets and found a receptive consumer within the domestic market. By 1982, Mag Instrument employed 850 people and the Maglite range was distributed worldwide. The original form and ideals of the Maglite remain unchanged, whether the torch is miniaturized to be carried on a key ring or uses the trademarked Rechargeable Flashlight System.

BOSTON SHAKER
(1979)
Ettore Sottsass
(1917–2007)
Alessi
1979 to present

The Boston Shaker, part of the Boston Cocktail Set, represents Ettore Sottsass's deeply rooted belief that his products should be instruments to enhance the experience of the user, rather than being purely functional. The set, which takes its name from a traditional American Boston cocktail shaker, comprises a wine cooler, stand, ice bucket, ice tongs, shaker, strainer and stirrer. The design comes from an in-depth investigation into professional tools for bars and for wines, which was carried out in the late 1970s by Sottsass, along with Alberto Gozzi of the Scuola Alberghiera, Italy's famous

training school for the hotel trade. The shaker itself is composed of polished stainless steel and thick glass, adding a sense of decadence to the business of shaking, stirring, muddling and mixing. Sottsass, born in 1917, studied at the Turin Politecnico before setting up his studio in Milan in 1960. In 1972, he began designing for Alessi. He had a strong desire to get away from the perfect form, to rediscover fun and create surprise and improvisation between the user and the environment, whether in large-scale architectural schemes or small-scale tableware and cutlery.

BALANS VARIABLE STOOL (1979)
Peter Opsvik (1939–)
Stokke 1979 to 2006
Varier
2006 to present

The Balans range was a new type of office seating, designed following revolutionary ergonomic principles. First developed in Norway in the 1970s by the Balans group, which included Hans Christian Mengshoel, Oddvin Rykkens, Peter Opsvik and Svein Gusrud, and introduced at the Copenhagen Furniture Fair of 1979, the Balans line now encompasses twenty-five different models covering a wide range of seating types. The Balans Variable Stool is perhaps the best known and most recognizable of the range. It was one of the first models, designed by Opsvik, and overturned accepted principles about how a chair is used and

what it should look like. It is only in the last thirty years or so that people have been required to sit at an office desk for hours on end, often with detrimental effects on the lower back and spine. The Balans Variable Stool shifts the angle of the seat and introduces knee supports and rockers. These improve the posture of the back by shifting the user's weight forwards and changing the angle between the hips and legs, allowing the knees to support the body and the back muscles to soften and relieve tension.

POST-IT® NOTES (1980)
Spencer Silver
(1941–)
Art Fry (1931–)
3M 1980 to present

Originally thought of as a hymn bookmark, Post-it® Notes have acquired mythical status in innovation history. This is echoed by the numerous creation stories attributed to it. It is, however, a story of two scientist-inventors, their persistence and the innovation culture of the company they worked for. It took some five years of internal company use for the versatile 3M Company to release the now unmistakable, unbelievably useful, not-so-sticky, canary-yellow notes in 1980. In 1968, Dr Spencer Silver was working on improving tape adhesives. He formulated an adhesive that was strong enough to stick on to surfaces, but left no residue after removal. The fitting application, the idea of using scrap-paper bookmarks, was discovered by Art Fry, then a new-product development researcher. The idea was slow to gain acceptance, but in 1980 the Post-it® took off and made its way, in viral-like acceptance, into offices and homes alike. The wide range of applications and the cultural significance the Post-it® has propagated since its introduction is a testament not only to the clarity and brilliance of the invention and its design but also to the power of simple tools that respond to human behaviour.

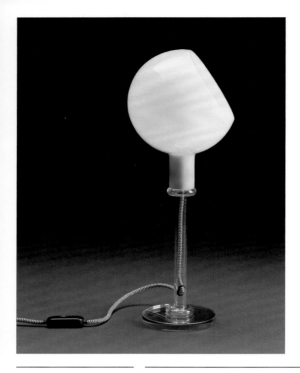

PAROLA LAMP (1980)
Gae Aulenti
(1927–2012)
FontanaArte
1980 to present

The Parola Lamp is a halogen standard lamp, comprising a glass shade on a glass stem and base. It is also available in wall-mounted and table versions. It was designed by Gae Aulenti in conjunction with Piero Castiglioni for the Milanese glass manufacturer FontanaArte. Aulenti is an architect best known for her museum buildings, exhibition installations and interiors. In 1979 Aulenti was appointed artistic director for FontanaArte, a post she held until 1996. The Parola Lamp, one of the first products produced under her directorship, is made from three elements, each demonstrating a different glass process. The shade is a palely coloured glass sphere with a slice removed, imitating a partial eclipse, made from blown opaline glass. The stem, through which the electrical cable is visible, is of clear glass, and the bevelled base is made from ground natural crystal. The 'eyeball' shade harks back to a form popular in the 1960s, one Aulenti herself had used for an earlier design. Aulenti said, 'I never thought of lamps in terms of technical lighting or like a machine for making light, but like forms in a harmonious relationship with the context for which they are created.'

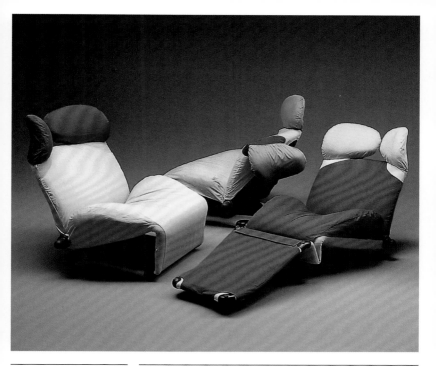

WINK CHAIR (1980)
Toshiyuki Kita
(1942–)
Cassina
1980 to present

The Wink Chair was the first item that brought Japanese designer Toshiyuki Kita international recognition. Wink, which sits lower than the average lounge chair, reflected both the more relaxed attitude of a younger generation as well as traditional Japanese sitting habits. Design-wise it is an achievement in comfortable, flexible and adaptable seating thanks to side knobs at the base, which allow the chair to be transformed from an upright to a lounger. The two-part headrest can move backwards or forwards into a 'winking' position for more support. Its panda-like, folding 'ears' and the pop colours of its

zips led to its nickname 'Mickey Mouse', yet these features are not solely stylistic: the zips were added so the upholstery could be removed and washed. A designer with roots in both European and Japanese culture, Kita never associated himself with a particular school or movement. He instead chooses to develop a wholly individual style full of wit and technological competence, which is well summarized in his Wink Chair. In 1981, the chair was selected for the permanent collection in the Museum of Modern Art.

TAVOLO CON RUOTE (1980)
Gae Aulenti
(1927–2012)
FontanaArte
1980 to present

There are virtually no design elements to the Tavolo con ruote, yet it speaks eloquently of advanced design sensibilities in the late 1970s and early 1980s. Gae Aulenti's coffee table, manufactured by the Italian firm FontanaArte comprises four outsized rubber-tyred wheels that raise a sheet of glass only a few centimetres above the floor. It is minimal yet expresses durability: the wheels would normally be found on industrial machinery rather than in the living room. There is also a degree of humour in the juxtaposition of these heavy-duty components with a mere sheet of glass, and the inappropriateness of their appearance in the home. Yet Aulenti has not turned to craft traditions and the marks of hand production to achieve this, as other designers might. The design should be regarded in the context of the High-Tech movement in architecture that celebrated industrial components and found perfect expression in the Pompidou Centre in Paris, completed in 1977. In 1980, the year she designed this table, Aulenti was also working on projects at the Pompidou Centre. She is one of very few female Italian designers of her generation to have enjoyed international recognition.

ACETOLIERE OIL AND VINEGAR CRUETS (1980)
Achille Castiglioni
(1918–2002)
Rossi & Arcanti
1980 to 1984
Alessi 1984 to 2013

Best known for their wry re-appropriation of industrial components to create instantly recognizable products, Achille and Pier Giacomo Castiglioni were also masters of observing and solving the minute, mundane problems presented by everyday objects. And so it was that when Achille was asked by manufacturer Cleto Munari to contribute oil and vinegar cruets for a collection of silverware for everyday use, he began by undertaking rigorous analysis. The result, christened Acetoliere, and produced initially in limited numbers by Rossi & Arcanti (in silver plate and crystal) and later by Alessi, is unmatched

in its functionality. Acetoliere's improvements upon a standard oil and vinegar cruet are manifold. The oil dispenser is larger than the vinegar because it is usual for more oil to be used. The hinged lids, their flat surface broken up with a shape reminiscent of a cat's head, are counterbalanced with weights that allude to saxophone keys and rock gently open as pouring begins. Each vessel is balanced like a pendulum and will not tip without positive movement. There is no protruding spout; instead, a lip that is bent inwards catches the drips.

LA CONICA
COFFEE MAKER
(1980–3)
Aldo Rossi (1931–97)
Alessi
1984 to present

La Conica was the result of a project between Alessi and Alessandro Mendini in 1983. Mendini and ten other architects, Aldo Rossi amongst them, were invited to reinterpret domestic objects. Rossi approached the design of household products as architecture in miniature, which is clearly reflected in his design for the La Conica coffee maker. He was fascinated by the geometric simplification of basic architectural forms, with the cone being a recurrent theme. In response to the brief, Rossi embarked on a programme of rigorous research into the making and serving of coffee, a subject that he saw as

perfectly symbolizing the dialectic relationship between architectural townscapes and the 'household landscape' into which his miniature monument would fit. The coffee maker was to become something of a motif in Rossi's architectural drawings, appearing as buildings in the urban panorama. The other designs resulting from the Alessi project were produced in silver, with only ninety-nine copies manufactured for each design. But La Conica, the first product of the Officina Alessi brand, has now become symbolic of 1980s design, with far more than ninety-nine copies being produced and sold.

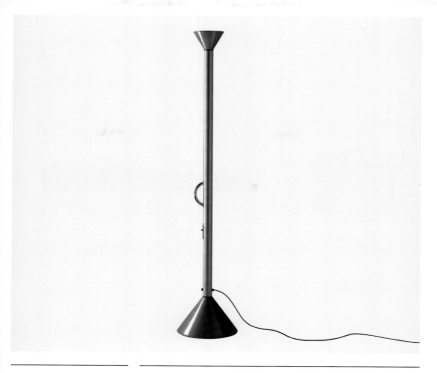

CALLIMACO LAMP (1981)
Ettore Sottsass
(1917–2007)
Artemide
1982 to present

Ettore Sottsass was, by the 1970s, a leading figure among Italy's design vanguard, successfully establishing a new design language. In 1981 he joined forces with like-minded designers to form the Memphis Group. Works from Memphis's first collection came to exemplify the Postmodern spirit. Among the most articulate was the Sottsass-designed Callimaco Lamp, a 500-watt halogen floor lamp with an integral dimmer. The intense white light, which emanated from the small red cone at the top of the 1.8 m (6 ft) bright yellow and green aluminium base, enlivened the object, which otherwise was mute about its purpose. Callimaco defies the convention of standing a lamp next to a seat to illuminate reading. At 500 watts, the light it produces is too bright to be observed directly and the use of halogen lights in a domestic setting was a relatively new phenomena. With a handle attached to the central tube, it makes visual references to a megaphone. Yet Callimaco confounds expectations by conveying not sound, but light, intensely radiating from its mouthpiece-like canopy. In the context of a myriad Postmodern flights of fantasy, Callimaco is a provocation and an authoritative standard bearer of Memphis.

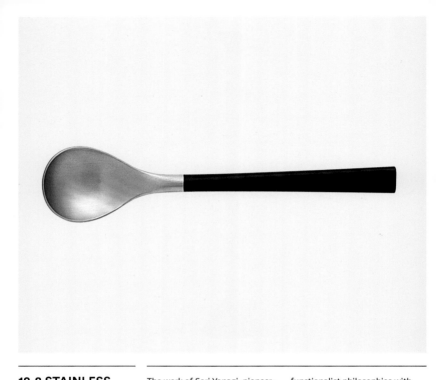

18-8 STAINLESS STEEL FLATWARE (1982)
Sori Yanagi
(1915–2011)
Sato-Shoji
Corporation
1982 to present

The work of Sori Yanagi, pioneering industrial designer, represents a perfect marriage of form, function and aesthetic. Inspired by natural forms, his 18-8 Stainless Steel Flatware is produced by Sato-Shoji and seeks to bring practicality, style and a pleasing tactile quality to any dining table. Each setting consists of five elegant and durable pieces of flatware plus four serving utensils. The characteristic organic shapes reflect the designer's preference for 'gentle and rounded forms that radiate human warmth'. Yanagi believes the designer's role is not to repackage old ideas but to take them forward. In his work, he has always sought to blend functionalist philosophies with traditional Japanese design. Yanagi began his career in the architectural office of Junzo Sakakura, where he first met Charlotte Perriand, and became her assistant from 1940 to 1942. In 1952 he opened his own office in Tokyo, and soon after became a founding member of the Japan Industrial Designers' Association. As modernization and Westernization overwhelmed post-war Japan, Yanagi promoted design that did not compromise the traditional Japanese environment. As a prime example of this, the 18-8 flatware set has been in continuous production since its first manufacture.

COSTES CHAIR
(1982)
Philippe Starck
(1949–)
Driade
1985 to present

The quirky yet sleekly sophisticated Costes Chair epitomizes
the 1980s Neomodern aesthetic.
Veneered in a rather austere
mahogany, with an upholstered
leather seat, its design pays
homage to Art Deco as well as
to traditional gentlemen's clubs.
The chair was originally designed
as part of the interior scheme
for the Café Costes in Paris, but is
now mass-produced by the Italian
manufacturer Driade. Philippe
Starck first came to prominence
in 1981, when he was one of eight
designers selected to furnish
President François Mitterrand's
private apartments. On the
strength of this he was

commissioned to design the
interiors for the Café Costes.
Starck produced a luxuriously
avant-garde interior that was
dominated by an axial, theatrical
staircase. The three-legged chair
was designed, apparently, so that
the waiters wouldn't trip over the
legs, and the three-legged motif
would soon become something
of a Starck signature. Starck
went on to become one of the
most famous designers of the
late twentieth century, and in the
process, and no doubt due to his
showmanship and ability to
command the attention of the
world's press, helped to establish
the cult of the celebrity designer.

GLOBAL KNIFE
(1982)
Komin Yamada (1947–)
Yoshikin
1983 to present

Global Knives created a sensation when launched onto the world's culinary stage in 1982 as an alternative to traditional European-style cutlery. Japanese industrial designer Komin Yamada was commissioned to develop a superior, radical knife made with the best materials and employing the most modern design concepts. The result was the avant-garde Global Knife. Yamada had access to a large budget for his exploratory and innovative design, allowing him to create a chef's knife that appealed equally to the professional and domestic market. Made from an extremely high-grade stainless steel (molybdenum/vanadium), the

Global Knife has a remarkably sharp blade that is resistant to rust, stains and corrosion, owing to being ice-tempered and hardened. With close reference to tradition, as with the Samurai sword, the Global Knife is carefully weighted to ensure perfect balance in use. There is no unnecessary material included and the thick, round handle is inviting to hold. Further evidence of Yamada's genius, the two-millimetre diameter 'black dot' design on the handle means that the 'too smooth' or 'too cold' impression is avoided, resulting in a decorative signature design that doubles with the practical effect of securing a firm, warm grip.

PHILIPS COMPACT DISC (1982)
Philips/Sony
Design Team
Philips/Sony
1982 to present

Requests from the sports broadcasting industry for instant replays in the early 1960s set manufacturers on the road to today's compact disc technology. In 1978, Sony teamed up with Philips to develop a standard, universal format to hold audio, and in 1982 a prototype compact disc (CD) emerged. With a diameter of just 11.5 cm (4.5 in), each CD comprises a thin, highly reflective metallic layer pierced by a series of pits of varying lengths on the readable side of the disc. A thin layer of acrylic and a thicker layer of durable polycarbonate protect these pits. Each pit appears to the laser that reads the disc as a slightly raised bump of a certain length, corresponding to a predefined value linked to a rapidly changing series of digital signals that are translated into images, sounds or data. The prototype was adjusted in size to accommodate the whole of Beethoven's Ninth Symphony, with the final commercial version offering 77 minutes of music, significantly longer than a double-sided LP. Further technological advances have since produced CDs that can store increasingly large amounts of data that are easily recordable, error-free and reproducible.

**FIRST CHAIR
(1982–83)**
Michele De Lucchi
(1951–)
Memphis
1983 to present

When Memphis opened its controversial show in Milan in 1981, its new visual style and philosophy of furniture, accessories and fashion was met with enthusiasm. The event was seen as an innovative confrontation with the classical Modernism and the dreary engineered product design of the time. In this Postmodern context Michele De Lucchi created his First Chair, a design that appealed because of its shape and figurative details. It was rather uncomfortable to sit on, and seemed more to resemble a skinny sculpture than a practical chair. Its attraction could be found in its design

elements and materials. The shape's resemblance to a sitting figure is obvious, and its sense of lightness, mobility and fun provoked an emotional response. The chair was originally made in small series in metal and lacquered wood. As with many of the products created by the Memphis group, the First Chair represents a brief period in design trends, but Memphis has kept this chair in production to the present day. A graduate of architecture, De Lucchi moved into radical architecture with Memphis, then began designing products for Artemide, Kartell and Olivetti before opening his firm, aMDL.

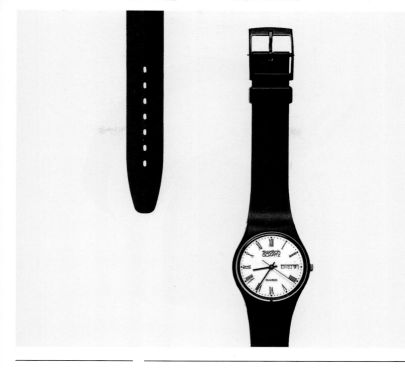

SWATCH 1ST COLLECTION WRISTWATCHES (1983)
Swatch Lab
ETA 1983

With the introduction of a wide range of new timepiece technologies in the 1970s, analogue mechanical watches suddenly appeared obsolete, with previously revered Swiss products among the worst hit. In March 1983, the Swatch Group introduced Swatch – a collection of twelve watch models. Designed by Ernst Thonke, Jacques Müller and Elmar Mock, the first Swatch was an accurate quartz analogue product with only fifty-one parts, instead of the up to 150 parts that are found in conventional watches, allowing automated assembly and a truly affordable retail price. GB001, the first

Swatch, had a black plastic wrist band and housing for its glow-in-the-dark, white face and strikingly legible, sans serif numbers in an analogue configuration with an optional day/date window. It set standards such as silent movement, ultrasonic welding, injection moulding and waterproof, damage-resistant housings. Those standards have since been applied to countless different customised Swatch designs by the likes of Matteo Thun, Alessandro Mendini, Keith Haring, Yoko Ono, Vivienne Westwood and Annie Leibovitz. To date, more than 250 million watches have been sold.

9091 KETTLE (1983)
Richard Sapper
(1932–2015)
Alessi 1983 to 2013

The two-litre stainless steel 9091 Kettle from 1983 – gleaming, elegant and substantial – can be considered the first true designer kettle. It was created by Richard Sapper, who was inspired by the barges and steamships blowing their foghorns as they sailed up and down the Rhine. The kettle's large dimensions 19 cm (7.5 in) tall by 16.5 cm (6.5 in) wide, its sleek, shiny dome and its high price tag put it right at the centre of the ideal home. There is a certain hauteur to the upright dome, a geometric purity that distinguished it from the cosy, homely traditional shapes of earlier kitchenware. The kettle's sandwiched copper base ensures good heat transmission for use on any stove. A polyamide handle is set back on the kettle to avoid steam hitting the hand, and a sprung mechanism operated by a trigger on the handle opens the spout for pouring or filling. But what really sets the kettle apart is its whistle. Its pipes, pitched in E and B, are specially made by craftsmen in the Black Forest. Sapper always said it was important to 'bring a bit of pleasure and fun to people.'

CAN FAMILY WASTE BIN (1984)
Hansjerg Maier-Aichen (1940–)
Authentics
1984 to 2018

The Can Family Waste Bin is one of the best examples of simple, pared-down elegance in design and combines quality with its use of inexpensive plastic and multipurpose application for the kitchen, bathroom and all living areas. Such simplicity was new and almost shocking, but by the end of the century the style was to become almost ubiquitous and copies became commonplace. The Can is one of the signature products in the German company Authentics' Basics range. Available in six sizes, it was designed by Hansjerg Maier-Aichen, who had worked with Authentics since 1968 and who took over the reins of the company in 1975. Maier-Aichen redirected the company's position in 1996, concentrating its efforts in the design and manufacture of plastics to produce inexpensive but high-quality household products for everyday use. Making the most of the inherent qualities and production techniques of plastics, the new Authentics range introduced designs that could not be achieved in other materials and, thanks to a subtle colour language of translucent hues, set a much-copied trend in motion.

PASTA SET
COOKWARE (1985)
Massimo Morozzi
(1941–2014)
Alessi 1985 to present

Massimo Morozzi launched his
career as one of the founding
members of the radical design
group Archizoom in Florence in
1966, along with Andrea Branzi,
Paolo Deganello and Gilberto
Coretti. When the group dissolved,
Morozzi continued with his design
research before returning his
attention to furniture and objects
in the 1980s. In 1985, he presented
the Pasta Set project to Alberto
Alessi, owner of the renowned
Italian housewares brand Alessi.
With it Morozzi introduced a clever
innovation into the overcrowded
market of kitchen utensils, which
rapidly inspired endless imitations. The Pasta Set incorporates

a metal colander with plastic
handles inside the pan, so that
the user could simply lift the pasta
out of the boiling water without
the need to drain it in a separate
colander in the sink. As the water
heats the metal colander during
the cooking process, the pasta
remains hot when removed from
the water. The lid has a hollow
plastic knob for the steam
to escape. The Pasta Set won the
Gold Medal at the Ljubljana Bio 11
in 1986 and was later joined
by Morozzi's Vapour Set in 1990,
a similar design for steam cooking.

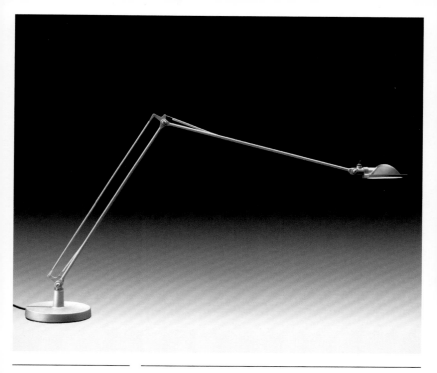

BERENICE LAMP (1985)
Alberto Meda (1945–)
Paolo Rizzatto (1941–)
LucePlan
1985 to present

The Berenice Lamp is one of the signature hi-tech products of Milan-based lighting company LucePlan. The table lamp, which uses low-voltage halogen, has a slim and elegant form and a fluid action. The use of a transformer enables the electricity to be conducted through the structure without the need for wires on the armature. The lamp is assembled from forty-two components using thirteen different materials, including metals, glass and plastics. The metal armature is made from stainless steel and die-cast aluminium elements, with reinforced nylon joints that can stand up to friction when the position of the lamp is adjusted. The head of the lamp is made from Rynite™, an injection-moulded thermoplastic polyester resin, often used for the manufacture of tough miniature components, such as those used in rifles. The coloured glass reflector (in blue, green or red) is made from borosilicate glass, again chosen for its heat resistance, durability and also because it can be manufactured using strong colours. In 1987 the Berenice received a special mention at the Compasso d'Oro awards, and in 1994 designers Alberto Meda and Paolo Rizzatto were awarded the European Design Prize for their work.

9093 WHISTLING KETTLE (1985)
Michael Graves
(1934–2015)
Alessi
1985 to present

The 9093 Whistling Kettle designed by American Michael Graves is one of the most commercially successful mass-produced products to come out of the Postmodern design movement of the 1980s. Commissioned by Alessi as a hob kettle specifically aimed at the American mass market, Graves's design followed Richard Sapper's earlier 9091 Kettle (1983), also produced by Alessi. With the simple clean form, minimal decoration and restrained use of materials, the kettle is fundamentally an example of straightforward Modernist design. However, the twist of the addition of the bird and the use of bold colour in the handle breach the bounds of Modernism. The red moulded plastic bird whimsically suggests a source for the kettle's whistle. When launched in 1985, the kettle became an instant success, appealing to the top end of the consumer market with its combination of mischievous and radical design, and with high sales figures it earned its label as a Postmodern design classic. The kettle is still in production and is now available with a matt finish as well as the original polished surface, and with differing colours for the handle and bird.

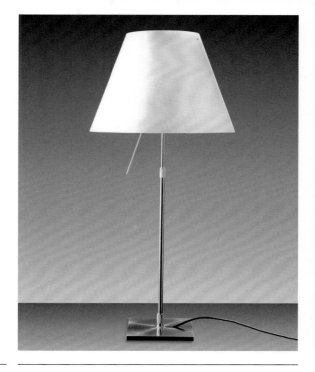

COSTANZA LAMP (1986)
Paolo Rizzatto (1941–)
LucePlan
1986 to present

Initially designed as a floor lamp in 1986, and then subsequently released in table and hanging versions (both 1986), the Costanza Lamp is the minimum distillation of what such an object should be: base, shaft and shade. And it is in this elegant simplicity and lack of superfluous ornament that much of this lamp's timeless appeal lies. Yet perhaps a better reason for the Costanza's classic status lies in the way in which Paolo Rizzatto's design incorporates qualities of both flexibility and modernity within its apparently timeless and strictly traditional appearance. The Costanza, in the floor and table versions, is supported on a telescopic aluminium shaft, which allows the user to adjust the height of the lamp to suit its particular setting. Made of silk-screened polycarbonate, the lamp's shade is light, rigid, easily washable and just as easily replaceable. Its switch is rather longer than is strictly necessary, designed to attract attention and as a counterpoint to the lamp's slender stand. The Costanza seems to have been designed to make its owner aware of the fact that an object that lacks ornament is often the most ornamental object of all.

TOLEDO CHAIR
(1986–88)
Jorge Pensi (1946–)
Amat/Knoll
1988 to present

Spain did not figure largely in the development of twentieth-century design history. One exception was Grupo Berenguer – comprising Jorge Pensi, Alberto Liévore, Noberto Chaves and Oriol Piebernat – who came together in Barcelona in 1977 and set about defining a modern, refined and functional style. Pensi eventually founded his own design studio in 1984. His design for the Toledo Chair was originally intended for outdoor use at Spanish street cafés, but its subsequent popularity brought sales success across the world. The designer opted for a slender-lined, polished and anodized cast aluminium structure, lending the chair a slick and refined appearance coupled with comfort. The slits in the seat and backrest, which are apparently inspired by Japanese Samurai armour, allow rain to drain through the corrosion-resistant chair. The Toledo Chair is light and stackable, essential criteria for outdoor café culture. As a logical accompaniment, Pensi also designed a café table and introduced fabric, leather or polyurethane seat and back upholstery options for the chair. The phenomenal success of the award-winning Toledo Chair, produced by Amat, marked the start of a prosperous career for Jorge Pensi, who has become one of Spain's leading design consultants.

OFFICIAL SWISS RAILWAY WRISTWATCH (1986)
Hans Hilfiker
(1901–93)
Mondaine Team
Mondaine Watch
1986 to present

The Swiss have turned time keeping into an art form and the Official Swiss Railway Wristwatch is perhaps the most recognizable Swiss-branded timepiece. Its uncomplicated circular face provides a clean backdrop to the simple block-shaped hour markers and the handsomely proportioned minute and hour hands. In contrast to the monochrome background, a bright red second hand replicates the stationmaster's handheld red departure signal. Lettering on the face includes SBB CFF FFS (acronyms for the Swiss Federal Railway in German, French and Italian) and the words 'Swiss Made' just below the 6.

The Official Swiss Railway Wristwatch was introduced in 1986 by Mondaine, the Swiss luxury goods group, as an inspired replica of the classic Swiss Railway Station Clock designed in the 1940s by Swiss industrial designer Hans Hilfiker. Shrewdly capital-izing on the clock's status, Mondaine produced their success-ful wristwatch version, which continues to be sold in many countries. Although available in different shapes and sizes, it is the original circular-faced version that is most revered. Undoubtedly, it is likely to remain as one of the most successful monikers of Swiss branding.

KO-KO CHAIR (1986)
Shiro Kuramata
(1934–91)
Ishimaru 1985
IDÉE 1987 to 1995
Cappellini
1986 to present

The Ko-Ko Chair, constructed from black-stained ash and chromed metal, reflects its designer's fascination with contemporary Western culture. Shiro Kuramata was one of a number of artists who sought to synthesize Japanese tradition with groundbreaking new technologies and Western influence. He used modern industrial materials such as acrylic, glass, aluminium and steel mesh to create functional yet often poetic and humorous pieces. He desired to eliminate gravity in his constructions, creating lightweight pieces that appear to float in space. Kuramata's designs are dependent on a minimalist aesthetic and concept of proportion that derive from traditional Japanese architecture and methods of storage. He received a traditional training in woodcraft, opening his design office in Tokyo in 1964. He gained prominence in the 1970s and 1980s for his many furniture designs and commercial interiors. In the early 1980s Kuramata became involved with the Milan-based group, Memphis. The Ko-Ko Chair falls into the lines of Postmodernism, as encouraged by Memphis: its abstracted form refers to an object to be sat upon, with the slight gesture of a backrest hinted at by the steel band.

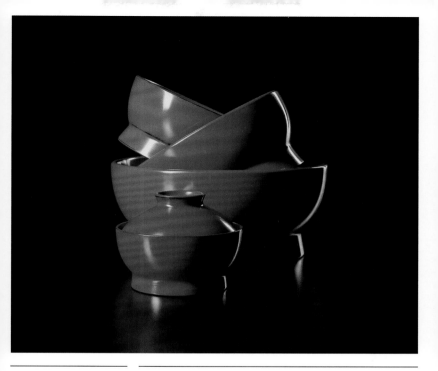

WAJIMA CEREMONY LACQUERWARE
(1986)
Toshiyuki Kita
(1942–)
Ohmukai-Kosyudo
1986 to present

Toshiyuki Kita has made a career out of introducing contemporary design into traditional Japanese crafts. Over the past four decades, Kita has taken his designs to craftspeople in isolated villages in Japan, employing their nearly obsolete skills in the manufacture of commercially viable products for an international audience. Reinterpreting traditional *urushi* (lacquer) forms, the innovative 1986 Wajima Ceremony Lacquerware includes a fruit bowl, soup dishes and rice boxes. It was designed for traditional lacquer manufacturer Ohmukai-Kosyudo and employs an ancient lacquer technique in the traditional colour palette of red and black. While the forms of the Wajima pieces may look thoroughly Japanese to a Western eye, Kita – who has moved between both Milan and Osaka since 1969 – has in fact pushed the boundaries of Japanese design to create something quite startling to the native viewer. Whereas traditional Japanese lacquerware is quite diminutive, Kita's pieces have an extended scale and a graphic, functional form. Kita makes a virtue of the strong colour combinations and sculptural forms of traditional lacquerware by exaggerating them, bringing them to a size of decorative objects to be admired.

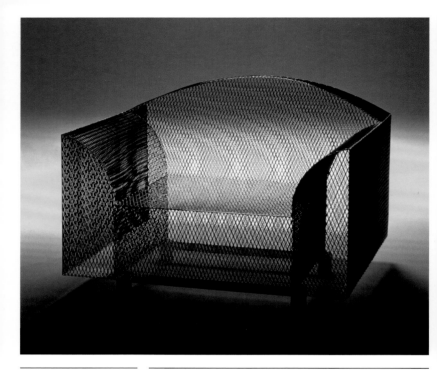

HOW HIGH THE MOON ARMCHAIR (1986)
Shiro Kuramata
(1934–91)
Terada Tekkojo 1986
IDÉE 1987 to 1995
Vitra 1987 to 2009

The generous size and classical outline of the How High the Moon Armchair seem to contradict its use of unaccommodating industrial steel mesh. Yet the chair offers great comfort beyond immediate expectations and the design remains important as an example of provocative and intellectual thinking. The skeletal structure of fine steel mesh is a legacy of Shiro Kuramata's strong Modernist background. Mesh had appeared in Kuramata's work before this, but in a more planar, two-dimensional way. With the design of How High the Moon, Kuramata defined the key structural elements of seat, back, arms and base. The curved planes balance harmoniously with the flat, and play against the inherent rigidity of the material. Although the steel raw material is low-cost, the design requires fine, labour-intensive welding of pattern-cut and pressed sheet metal, plated with copper or nickel, that create an expensive seating design. Kuramata would not substitute the production technique of hundreds of individual welds for any other solution that would compromise the transparency and fine lines of planes meeting each other. Kuramata's approach to acrylic, glass and steel was highly influential for a generation of designers.

TOLOMEO LAMP
(1986)
Michele De Lucchi
(1951–)
Giancarlo Fassina
(1935–2019)
Artemide
1987 to present

Michele De Lucchi and Giancarlo Fassina presented a prototype of the Tolomeo Lamp to Artemide's product developers. The garish and provocative style associated with the Memphis Group (that De Lucchi co-established in 1981) had been stripped away in favour of an approach that explored notions of tension and movement. Tapping into Artemide's inherent desire to drive innovation, De Lucchi had proposed a light that could adjust and hold still at any angle, using a cantilevered structure and a system of spring balancing. The diffuser, which could be fully rotated, was matt anodized aluminium, while the joints were polished aluminium. The lamp is available in three versions, with interchangeable supports for the table and the floor, and with a clamp for a desk. Tolomeo displayed more flexibility than its predecessor, Tizio, designed by Richard Sapper for Artemide, and was quickly proclaimed a perfect union of form with function. It won a Compasso d'Oro award in 1989 and attained significant sales for Artemide. The original version has now been developed as a table, floor, wall or ceiling lamp. Available in polished and anodized aluminium, the light is still selling strongly across the world today.

S CHAIR (1987)
Tom Dixon (1959–)
Cappellini
1991 to present

There is something anthropomorphic about the S Chair. Perhaps it is the cinched waist, curvaceous hips and suggestion of a spine and ribs. Or perhaps the chair is more resonant of a serpent than of a human form. Either way, the S Chair's appeal is fundamentally organic, arising from its sinuous, ribbon-like form and the use of natural rush upholstery. The outline is created from a welded bent-metal rod, around which the rush is woven. The S Chair bears comparison with two older designs: the wooden Zig–Zag Chair (1932–33) by Gerrit Rietveld and the plastic Panton Chair (1959–60) by Verner Panton. The undulations of the S Chair seem more freehand than either of these designs, but the ribbon-like form and cantilevered seat suggest comparisons. The chair marks a transition in Tom Dixon's career. His earlier works were generally one-offs or limited-edition metal objects, often created from recycled metal. He initially made S Chairs in his own London workshop but quickly licensed the design to Cappellini. The company continues to produce it and has experimented with velvet, leather and other upholstery. The original, however, remains the most sensual.

I FELTRI CHAIR
(1987)
Gaetano Pesce
(1939–)
Cassina
1987 to present

The I Feltri Chair, made of thick wool felt, resembles a modern-day shaman's throne. While the base is soaked in polyester resin, the top is soft and malleable, enfolding the sitter like a regal cloak. Gaetano Pesce's work is characterized by his innovative use of materials, his obsession with exploring and developing new production techniques, and his insistence on producing objects that provoke controversy and challenge complacency. I Feltri premiered at the 1987 Salone del Mobile as part of Pesce's 'Unequal Suite' presented by Cassina. The pieces of this suite – a wardrobe, table, modular sofa and armchair –

were entirely different from each other in style and aesthetic. What they did share was an unskilled, 'disobedient', handmade appearance, intended as an antithesis to the high style, high production values predominant at the time. Pesce had intended that by using low-tech, inexpensive manufacturing processes, the chair could be mass-produced in developing countries from old rugs. Cassina, however, was not interested in such high ideals. 'I remember them telling me that they were obliged to take care of their own workers,' Pesce recalls. Today, the chairs are exquisitely crafted out of thick felt and priced accordingly.

MILANO CHAIR
(1987)
Aldo Rossi (1931–97)
Molteni & C
1987 to present

The Milano Chair is an example of the happy coexistence of tradition and innovation. It was conceived to be made of hard wood, with versions in cherry wood or walnut, and its slatted backrest and seat are surprisingly comfortable, making the most of the flexibility of the slatted wood. Aldo Rossi was primarily concerned with architecture and urban living. Yet his product designs naturally convey his theories, and the Milano Chair, with its references to traditional design, reflects his belief that architecture cannot dissociate itself from its city's heritage. The sweeping lines of the chair's backrest look somehow at odds with the principles embodied in Rossi's imposing structures and innumerable drawings. Rossi probably felt more freedom designing industrially designed objects, as these imply a use that needs to adapt to different settings and are not rigidly inserted into an urban environment. A series of drawings illustrates how the chair might be used in different situations: in an informal meeting around a table, with a dog on the floor or in a studio setting. The Milano Chair continues to stand as a strong emblem of Rossi's important body of work.

GHOST CHAIR
(1987)
Cini Boeri (1924–)
Tomu Katayanagi
(1950–)
Fiam Italia
1987 to present

Although a seriously weighty piece of furniture, Cini Boeri and Tomu Katayanagi's Ghost Chair looks as light as air. Made from one slab of solid glass, this is a daring piece of design produced by the truly innovative Fiam Italia, founded by Vittorio Livi. Cini Boeri, a Milanese architect and designer, had been developing a number of ideas for Fiam when one of the senior designers, Tomu Katayanagi, suggested a glass armchair. It was not until she saw the 'magical paper maquettes' proposed by Katayanagi that she became open to the idea. With Livi's assistance, the technical problems were resolved and the chair has since

become a firm icon of avant-garde furniture design. The Ghost Chair is capable of bearing a load of up to 150 kg (330 lb), even though the curved floating crystal glass is a mere 12 mm (0.5 in) thick. Fiam still produces the chair today, warming large sheets of glass in tunnel furnaces before bending them into shape. Numerous designers, including Philippe Starck, Vico Magistretti and Ron Arad, have designed for Fiam since, but few have matched the startling, almost surreal, impact achieved by Boeri and Katayanagi with their Ghost Chair.

TARAXACUM '88 CHANDELIER (1988)
Achille Castiglioni
(1918–2002)
Flos 1988 to present

Although the design bears the same name as a previous 1960 light, Taraxacum '88 is a completely different design. Achille Castiglioni designed it for the Milan lighting fair, Euroluce, and it was immediately adopted by the Triennale Museum to illuminate some of its galleries. Taraxacum '88 (its name is Latin for 'dandelion') is made of twenty die-cast polished-aluminium equilateral triangles, each accommodating three, six or ten bulbs. A number of these triangles are hinged together to form an icosahedron, a twenty-sided form, the Platonic shape closest to a sphere. It is produced in two sizes, with a total of 60 or 120 Globolux light bulbs. Castiglioni conceived Taraxacum '88 as a light that could replace the classic multi-flame chandelier, with its emphasis on decoration. Taraxacum manages both to be a modern chandelier with a simple, coherent design, and to provide the same lighting scope provided by many flames. Following Castiglioni's own classification of his work, Taraxacum '88 could be seen to belong to the 'redesigned objects' category, meaning a traditional object that the designer has perfected or updated according to current needs and technological developments.

CHAIR AC1 (1988)
Antonio Citterio
(1950–)
Vitra 1990 to 2006

Designed by Antonio Citterio and introduced in 1990, Vitra's Chair AC1 is notable for its lack of levers. At the time of its launch, the office industry had become obsessed with height adjustability, producing chairs that were full of gadgets and tended to look rather cumbersome. In this environment Citterio's pared-down product came as a refreshingly elegant change. The adaptable material Delrin is used for the backrest shell, with CFC-free foam polyurethane upholstery. The chair has no concealed mechanism, making it look very clean and light. Instead, the flexible back connects, via the armrests, to two points on the seat. This allows the position of the seat's surface to change with the angle of the back, meaning the two elements are completely synchronized. The length and height of the seat, lumbar support and the counter-pressure of the backrest can be adjusted depending on the height and weight of the user. The AC1 comes in an array of different fabric finishes, and the five-legged, star-shaped base in plastic as well as polished or chrome-plated aluminium. Citterio also designed a sister model, the bulkier AC2, for the more executive end of the market.

ARÁ LAMP (1988)
Philippe Starck
(1949–)
Flos 1988 to 2016

The Ará Lamp is one of many lighting designs by the irrepressible Philippe Starck. Although the design maintains the characteristics of many lamps, with its circular foot/base, upright, tapering stem and adjustable hood to protect and direct the light source, the light is switched on and off by adjusting the head up and down. The lamp uses highly reflective chrome steel that evokes glamour, wealth and an intelligent understanding of contemporary design. The balance between the three components of base, column and shade is weighted towards the symbolic value of the shade. Its organic, flame shape is a form

Starck has used throughout his work, from small-scale door handles and toothbrushes, to furniture and the massive sculptural 'flame' on top of the 1990 Asahi Building in Tokyo. It is this distinctive vocabulary that assists the Ará towards the achievement of classic status, while at the same time calling attention to itself as a Starck-designed object. Philippe Starck displays the characteristics of one of a handful of super-designers who have managed to influence a generation of designers and manufacturers and who have had a powerful impact on domestic and interior landscapes.

KIVI VOTIVE CANDLE HOLDER (1988)
Heikki Orvola (1943–)
iittala 1988 to present

The Kivi Votive Candle Holder is an object so simple it barely seems to have been designed. It is made from chunky, lead-free crystal and comes in thirteen colours: including clear, yellow, red, green, turquoise, grey and pink. These may have been inspired by the colour cubes of Leo Moser and Moser Glassworks, the famous Bohemian glassmakers who use nine shimmering colours in some of their stemware. Yet glassmaking is very much part of the Finnish tradition and has been ongoing for the last 300 years. In this design, the glass enriches the light produced by the candle, adding to the ambience of the

room. The holder can be used on its own or in a cluster and is competitively priced. Since its launch Kivi has established itself as a quiet, contemporary classic by adhering to iittala's values of durability, quality, modernity and a feeling of joy. Heikki Orvola went on to win Finland's most important design award when he picked up the Kaj Franck prize in 1998, and works in a range of materials including ceramics, cast iron and textiles, as well as making avant-garde sculptures, tableware and dinnerware.

PLY-CHAIR OPEN BACK (1988)
Jasper Morrison
(1959–)
Vitra 1989 to 2009
Vitra Design Musem
2009 to present

Jasper Morrison's Ply-Chair Open Back is not only a classic design but also offers an insight into Morrison's utilitarian design approach. The overtly spare, strict formulation of the chair's front legs and seat suggests pure functionalism, balanced against the gentle curve of the back legs and back rail to support the sitter. Concave crossbars provide a cushioning effect beneath the thin plywood skin of the seat. The construction and fixing devices are exposed, revealing the composition and simplicity of the design. The Ply-Chair was conceived for an exhibition, 'Design Werkstadt', in Berlin in 1988. Morrison designed and constructed the chair with limited equipment, in a material he considered relevant and as a reaction to the stylistic exuberance of the period. With sparse facilities to hand (sheet plywood, a jigsaw and some 'ship's curves'), the design evolved from two-dimensional cut shapes to a three-dimensional seating design. Rolf Fehlbaum of Vitra recognized the enduring qualities of the design and went on to produce the Ply-Chair with an open back and a second version with the back filled in. Morrison's utilitarianism belies extravagance and short-term fashions and proves his designs are of lasting quality.

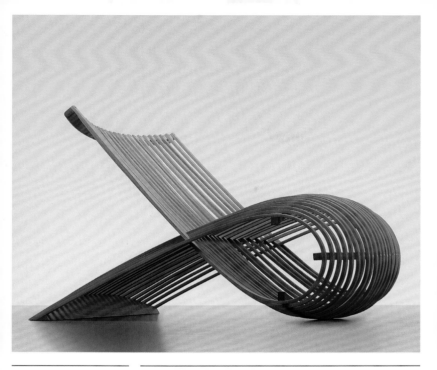

WOOD CHAIR (1988)
Marc Newson (1962–)
Cappellini
1992 to present

The Wood Chair was designed by the Australian designer Marc Newson for an exhibition in Sydney of chairs made from Australian wood. Intent on stretching a wooden structure into a sequence of curves in order to emphasize the natural beauty of the material, Newson set about finding a manufacturer capable of producing the chair. Every company he approached told him that his design was impossible to make until he tracked down a manufacturer in Tasmania who agreed to produce the chair in a supple local pine. In the early 1990s, Newson began working with Italian furniture

manufacturer Cappellini, who offered to make reproductions of his early designs, including the Wood Chair. Newson has said, 'I have always tried to create beautiful objects with challenging technologies.' The Wood Chair is an early example of this design philosophy, taking the inherent qualities of the material, in this case Tasmanian pine, and stretching it to expose its natural beauty and design possibilities. Newson's approach to design is not simply to tinker with existing typologies, but to take a long, lateral look at them and imagine how the perfect version might be.

MISS BLANCHE CHAIR (1988)
Shiro Kuramata
(1934–91)
Ishimaru 1988

The Miss Blanche Chair is believed to have been inspired by a floral dress worn by Vivien Leigh in the film *A Streetcar Named Desire*. The cheap artificial red roses floating in acrylic are meant to represent the frailty and vanity of Blanche DuBois and also make ironic reference to the faded charms of chintz upholstery. The arms and back of the chair are gently curved, suggesting a feminine elegance, however, the angularity of the piece and the manner in which the aluminium legs are inserted into the underside of the seat introduce an uncomfortable tension that acts as a counterpoint to any notions of feminine sweetness. One of Japan's most important designers, Shiro Kuramata loved the idea of combining seemingly non-negotiable concepts. Miss Blanche represents the culmination of a period in Kuramata's career that explored transparency. Kuramata particularly loved working with acrylic, which he saw as an ambiguous material, cold as glass, yet warm as wood. During the final stages of Miss Blanche's production he reportedly telephoned the factory every thirty minutes to make sure the floating effect of the artificial flowers was achieved.

SILVER CHAIR
(1989)
Vico Magistretti
(1920–2006)
De Padova
1989 to present

With numerous awards and titles, Vico Magistretti has been recognized as one of the pioneers of post-war Italian design. After thirty years of designing furniture, Magistretti designed the Silver Chair in 1989 for De Padova, where it continues to be produced. The chair illustrates one of the most consistent and significant themes of Magistretti's work in that it balances idiosyncratic originality with reference to the traditional. The Silver Chair is a reinterpretation of what he considered to be an archetypal bentwood chair, similar to Chair 811 attributed to either Marcel Breuer, Josef Hoffmann or Josef Frank, and featured in a Thonet catalogue from 1925. The original was made of solid steam-bent beech with rattan, cane or perforated plywood, while Magistretti's is made from polished welded aluminium tube and sheet material, with a polypropylene seat and back. It is available with or without arms, castors and a pedestal base. In an interview published by De Padova in 2003, the Silver Chair is explained by Magistretti as 'a homage to Thonet, who had produced a similar chair... I've always loved Thonet chairs, even if these are no longer made of wood and straw.'

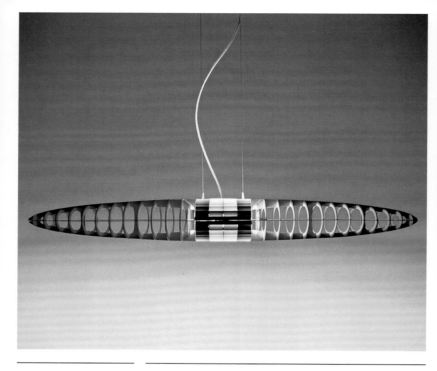

TITANIA LAMP
(1989)
Alberto Meda (1945–)
Paolo Rizzatto (1941–)
LucePlan
1989 to present

The beauty of the Titania Lamp is that it appears almost transparent from the front but solid if seen sideways, giving a new experience each time it is seen from a different angle. The lightness of the outer shell allows it to be hung from virtually any part of the ceiling, and a lead counterweight allows the height to be adjusted with the minimum amount of fuss. Designed by Paolo Rizzatto and Alberto Meda, from a distance the lamp appears rather complex and fragile, yet in fact it is elegant and easy to use. The striking, elliptical outer casing, made from lamellar aluminium, holds a number of blades made of silk-screened polycarbonate, which come in five different colours. By slotting a different coloured shade into the outer shell, the colour of the light changes. The interchangeable blades simultaneously reflect the central light source and dissipate heat from the bulb. Titania managed to be both contemporary and decorative, while at the same time being highly engineered and vaguely organic – not completely surprising, as Meda's background was in engineering. A floor model with an aluminium stand was introduced in 1995, but it is this suspension lamp that attracted the most attention.

PAPER COLLECTOR (1989)
Willi Glaeser (1940–)
TMP 1989 to present

The magazine or newspaper rack is an object found as often in the home as in the office. Launched in 1989, Willi Glaeser's version gives a contemporary twist to this ubiquitous design object. Swiss designer Glaeser is known for his pared-down work using chrome-plated steel wire to create objects with a high level of practicality, solid in form yet elusive. Glaeser had the ingenious idea of rethinking the use of the rack as just a holder for ephemeral printed material and combining it with a waste bin. Engaging with modern concerns for sustainability and recycling, Glaeser's rack holds newspapers, magazines and waste paper neatly and in an ordered manner, allowing them to be easily collected and recycled. The Paper Collector is available in two sizes, one to hold standard broadsheet publications folded in half, and another to cater for folded tabloid newspapers, magazines and waste paper. The clean and straightforward form of this modern, functionalist design has no added decoration or features. A thoughtful example of precision-crafted design, the rack secured its position as a prime example of high design and eco-awareness that developed in the late 1980s.

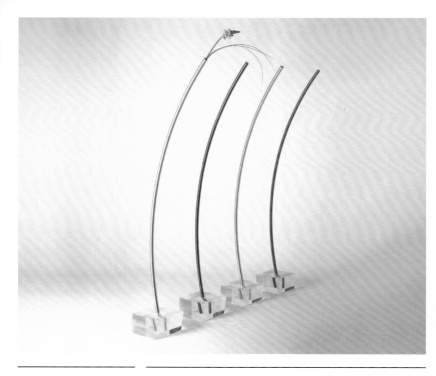

EPHEMERA FLOWER VASE (1989)
Shiro Kuramata
(1934–91)
Ishimaru 1989
Spiral 1989 to 2019

Taking the Japanese tradition of flower arrangement and fusing it with Western modes of design, Shiro Kuramata developed a fresh way of looking at the flower and its vase. Kuramata first produced the Ephemera Flower Vase for a solo exhibition at the Yves Gastou Gallery in Paris in 1989. Each long-necked vase resembles a wilting flower, or a human head bent in prayer, referencing themes of solitude and the transient nature of organic and human life, which is reinforced by the vase's name. Constructed from acrylic and aluminium with a stained alumite finish, and holding a single flower each, Kuramata's stem-like vases receive and transform natural and artificial light, making them appear transparent and less dense. Kuramata's fascination with acrylic was based on its ability to capture, enclose and permeate light within an object. By inventing a new design language concerning the ephemeral, and playing with gravity, Kuramata imposed surreal and minimalist ideals on familiar objects. In Europe, Kuramata's work has had a profound effect on the progress of design to the extent that the French Ministry of Culture awarded him the title of 'Chevalier de l'Ordre des Arts et des Lettres'.

CROSS CHECK CHAIR (1989–92)
Frank Gehry (1929–)
Knoll 1992 to present

The best designs are sometimes those that arise from the simplest ideas. In this instance the aim was to exploit the structural and flexible properties of laminated maple strips. The Cross Check Chair was designed by the Canadian-born architect Frank Gehry, best known for radical organic buildings such as the Disney Concert Hall in Los Angeles and the Guggenheim Museum in Bilbao. The inspiration for the chair was the woven structure of apple crates that Gehry remembered from childhood. In 1989 furniture manufacturer Knoll established a workshop in Santa Monica, California, close to Gehry's own studio, and for the next three years the architect experimented with laminated wooden structures. The frame is constructed of 5 cm (2 in) wide hard white maple veneers and extremely thin strips, which are laminated to 15.24 to 23 cm (6 to 9 inch) ply thickness with high-bonding urea glue. Thermoset assembly glue provides structural rigidity, minimizing the need for metal connecters, while allowing movement and flexibility in the backs of the chairs. The chair previewed at New York's Museum of Modern Art in 1992 and has won Gehry and Knoll numerous design awards.

Nach Allerorten Sommer
ist uns das Reisen zumute. So lange, bis wir die Landkarte nicht mehr in ihre Falten
legen, die Türen abschliessen und nicht merken, dass wir uns beim Aufstehen um
eine Stunde getäuscht haben.

ELLICE BOOKMARK (1990)
Marco Ferreri (1958–)
Danese
1990 to present

Marco Ferreri's Ellice reimagines the humble bookmark as a jewel-like yet fundamentally functional work of art. To address the perennial problem of page marking, Ferreri experimented with chemically photo-cut, ultra-thin steel plate and eventually arrived at Ellice. The bookmark is a slender blade of stainless steel – a material that was chosen for its tough, lightweight, flexible properties and its ability to be processed industrially. A small spherical brass insert on the upper part of the blade has the prosaic function of holding the bookmark steady between the pages and provides a decorative effect.

To add to this aura of luxury and exclusivity the Ellice comes wrapped in an origami-inspired pleated sheet of instructions inside a magnetic rubber sheath. But the Ellice is not a trinket to be coddled and cosseted; it is a lightweight, washable, endlessly usable bookmark that doubles as a handy letter opener. It is also a fine example of the commitment to the spirit of experimentation in its design objects and objectives by the Italian company Danese. Ellice continues to be one of its bestsellers, and also continues to be treasured by all its owners.

JUICY SALIF CITRUS SQUEEZER (1990)
Philippe Starck
(1949–)
Alessi
1990 to present

Conceived by the French designer Philippe Starck, this cast aluminium lemon juicer was created for the Italian manufacturer Alessi. The Juicy Salif has achieved the seemingly impossible task of making a citrus squeezer controversial. Widely derided as being hopelessly difficult to both use and store, it has also become a piece that is a mainstay for any museum collection. For those who consider design from a principally aesthetic viewpoint, the Juicy Salif is a jewel-like and much-loved reference point within the world of practical, utilitarian and often visually monotonous kitchen utensils.

Starck challenges the norm that a squeezer must comprise three elements: the squeezer, sieve and container. The Juicy Salif hones down the form to a single, elegant shape. It is this simplification that fuels his critics and makes the squeezer the ultimate symbol of extravagant hedonistic consumerism. But love it or hate it, the Juicy Salif undoubtedly exemplifies a shift in late twentieth-century product design. It is this product, more than any other freely available and affordable item, that defines the move from the consumer's priority being one of need to one of want.

LAMY SWIFT PEN
(1990)
Wolfgang Fabian
(1943–)
Lamy
1990 to present

Since its launch in 1990, the Lamy Swift Pen has demonstrated itself commercially accountable to its manufacturer. The first capless rollerball to incorporate a retracting safety feature, this design provides ammunition for the Modernist argument that innovation and traditional core values can coexist. The Swift's satin-effect nickel-palladium-coated shaft exemplifies German design understatement. Designer Wolfgang Fabian, working as a freelance for Lamy, came up with the retractable clip as a way of indicating whether the pen was safe to place in a pocket. A push of the tip simultaneously exposes the rollerball nib and retracts the clip. This design innovation responded to the recently refined Lamy M66 refill cartridge; while it offered a smooth and capacious flow of ink, there was clearly potential for leaks. With Fabian's practical as well as elegant solution, the Swift user can confidently carry the retracted pen in a shirt pocket. Lamy first forged its reputation in 1966 with the launch of the Bauhaus-styled Lamy 2000 fountain pen designed by Gerd A Müller. The Lamy Swift embodies the Bauhaus philosophy and it enforces the notion that modern design can add value to a time-tested tool without undermining its integrity.

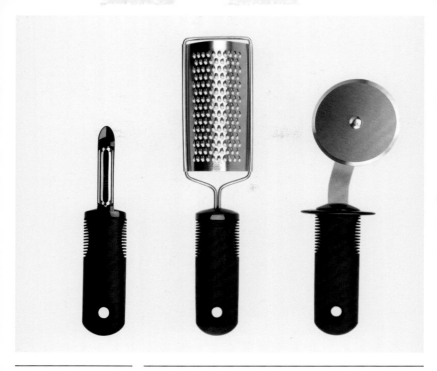

GOOD GRIPS
KITCHEN TOOLS
(1990)
OXO Design Team
OXO International
1990 to present

'Why do ordinary kitchen tools hurt your hands?' This question prompted Sam Farber's development of a series of easy-to-use kitchen tools, Good Grips. His wife, Betsey, suffered from arthritis and had difficulty in using conventional kitchen tools. Farber, a Harvard graduate entrepreneur, established OXO to create products that can be easily used by people of all types of abilities, sizes or ages. He approached the New York-based industrial design company, Smart Design, to develop a range of products, and the company produced a range of affordable, comfortable, high-quality and good-looking tools. As its name

implies, the key to Good Grips Kitchenware lies in its handle. It is made from Santoprene, a polypropylene plastic/rubber that is soft and flexible and prevents slippage. With its patented flexible fins, inspired by bicycle handlebars, the handle fits comfortably into the hand of any user. Good Grips tools have won many major design prizes and, while they are part of the design collection of the Museum of Modern Art, they have also been recognized by the Arthritis Foundation. The products that fulfilled a design brief originally intended for a minor demographic now meet the demands of a wider public.

LA CUPOLA COFFEE MAKER
(1990)
Aldo Rossi (1931–97)
Alessi
1990 to present

The La Cupola Coffee Maker is deceptively simple, composed of Rossi's standard components: cones, cubes, spheres and pyramids. Comprised of two aluminium cylinders topped by a dome, it is an iconic piece that was successful both in achieving Rossi's aim of making something where 'use and decoration are one', and in making something for true mass production. Commissioned by Alessi to design a coffee maker, Rossi researched the theme of brewing and serving coffee. Rossi sought something so 'laconic' that it would become private and domestic in perpetuity. In manufacturing

terms La Cupola was simply a new interpretation of the classical aluminium coffee maker. It is made of cast aluminium, like the classic Moka Express original, and is then hand polished. The boiler has a thick-flanged aluminium base to guarantee even heat distribution and to protect the body from the flame or heat source. It is finished with a polyamide handle attached to the body and a polyamide knob, in pale blue or black, to top off the cupola. An architect who has been claimed by both Modernists and Postmodernists as one of their own, Rossi has produced work of lasting significance.

THREE SOFA DE LUXE (1991)
Jasper Morrison
(1959–)
Cappellini
1992 to present

Most of Jasper Morrison's projects reveal a great interest in sculpture in terms of a strong sense of volume, mass, proportion and space perception. Unlike that of many industrial designers, his work shows a preoccupation with basic polarizations such as light and heavy, open and closed, and positive and negative spaces. The Three Sofa de Luxe is such a piece. Its soft physical presence within a geometric block of foam and textile creates a negative form reminiscent of a lying silhouette of a stylized human figure. This furniture 'floats' on four short, thin metal legs. The effect suggests a small, intimate landscape,

creating an instantly recognizable and memorable product. The design's 'cut-out' image dominates the piece, and yet seems to perform no practical purpose. The turn of the twenty-first century saw a revived interest in the sofa, and a large group of designers created all kinds of more or less spectacular 'sofa landscapes', which ignored for the most part economic and social considerations in favour of creating more bombastic and monumental pieces. In this context, Jasper Morrison's simple Three Sofa de Luxe was re-evaluated and confirmed as a successful design.

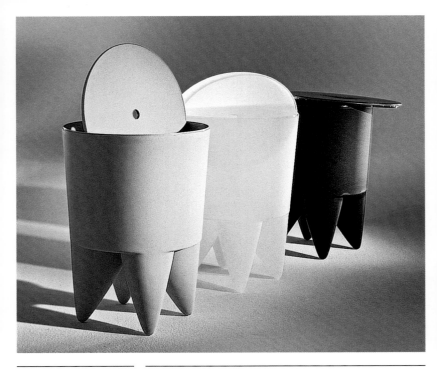

BUBU STOOL (1991)
Philippe Starck
(1949–)
XO 1991 to present

It may look a little straightforward and a lot like a cartoon cow's udder, but the Bubu Stool is actually an extremely versatile design. Produced using injection-moulded polypropylene, it is light and easily transportable, can be used either indoors or outdoors and comes in a variety of opaque and translucent colours. Although notionally a stool, the Bubu is also a table and a storage container. The seat lifts up to reveal a space that can be used for everything from cooling drinks to housing plants. Starck describes the shape of his product as an upside-down crown, encouraging, as he does with many of his designs, a sculptural

reading of the object that opens up its comic and cartoonish possibilities. Metaphors aside, it is the Bubu's relatively low cost and multifunctional nature that have made it a popular success. Indeed, it is perhaps the perfect example of Starck at his best: practical, stylish, inexpensive and a little weird. Originally sold by France's 3 Suisses mail-order company, it has been manufactured by XO since 1991 and sells in quantities of around 40,000 per year.

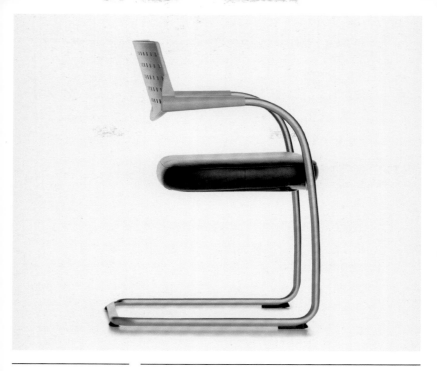

VISAVIS CHAIR (1992)

Antonio Citterio
(1950–)
Glen Oliver Löw
(1959–)
Vitra 1992 to present

Perhaps the secret to the success of the Visavis Chair is its timelessness. Based on simple geometries and well-used materials, every element is clearly formed and easily comprehended. The cantilevered metal frame clearly refers to chairs by Marcel Breuer and others of the 1920s, while the moulded plastic seat back brings the chair up to date. The pierced square motif in the back recalls Viennese Secessionist design. The chair is the work of the Italian architect and designer Antonio Citterio with the German designer Glen Oliver Löw, who have designed many successful chairs for Vitra since 1990. The

manufacturer launched an updated design, the Visavis 2, in 2005 offering numerous variations of material and finish. Although the Visavis Chair was designed as a conference chair, it is equally suited to the home. Vitra has since introduced Visasoft, a fully upholstered variant of the chair and the Visaroll, with four legs on castors. The family of chairs has been a Vitra bestseller. Unlike more eccentric designs, Visavis chair's success may actually rely on its neutrality and its ability to harmonize with any interior.

LUCELLINO LAMP (1992)
Ingo Maurer
(1932–2019)
Ingo Maurer
1992 to present

Trained as a typographer and graphic designer, German designer Ingo Maurer has developed lighting design as his specialization. A recurrent theme in his work is a fascination for the bare light bulb, which he often combines with lightweight materials like paper and feathers. In doing so, Maurer underlines the illusive, immaterial nature of his objects. This is especially true for the Lucellino Lamp, which derives its name from the Italian words *luce* ('light') and *uccellino* ('little bird'). A special incandescent light bulb is coupled with small hand-crafted wings, made of goose feathers. Copper wire supports the wings

and a red electric cord completes the design. The lamp is available in wall sconce and table lamp versions. Functional as it may be, it strikes primarily as a piece of art, which appeals beyond practicality. Not surprisingly, Maurer is often considered an outsider in the smooth design world. Yet the reputation of his designs has scattered them throughout the world, where the designer works for many international companies. Apart from working on tiny pieces, Maurer also has larger commissions, such as the 40-metre-long light sculpture made for the Lester B Pearson International Airport in Toronto.

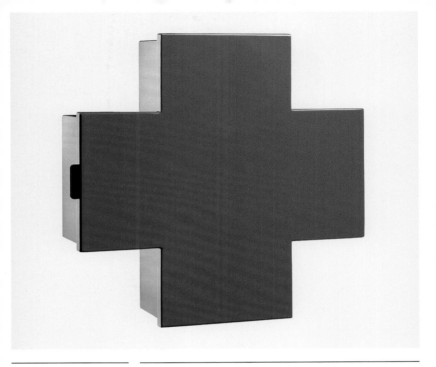

RED CROSS CABINET (1992)
Thomas Eriksson
(1959–)
Cappellini
1992 to present

The cross-shaped cabinet designed by Thomas Eriksson is a first-aid box that combines multiple languages. First, the red colour and symbol of the cross refer to the international Red Cross help organization. The Red Cross Cabinet also speaks of the natural language of function; the simple box is well suited to contain all necessary items for first aid. Like the other works of the Swedish designer/architect, which comprise furniture, lighting and architecture design, the box advocates the usage of internationally well-known images. Like they did a century ago, the Swedes continue to establish a firm relation between the use of natural materials like pale-coloured pine, linear forms and simple shapes, and last, but certainly not least, rationality. The combination leads to the non-standardized grace, elegance and beauty of plain Swedish design. What is interesting about Thomas Eriksson's work is the way he mixes the Swedish approach to design with globally familiar symbols. His designs can be found not only in Swedish-based companies like Scandinavian Airlines (SAS), IKEA and Hästens, but also in the collections of international companies and museums like Cappellini and the Museum of Modern Art in New York.

ASHTRAY (1992)
Aart Roelandt
(1954–)
Stelton 1992 to 2004

In reimagining the traditional open ashtray form as a closed container, Aart Roelandt's Ashtray for Stelton is, in effect, an ashtray for non-smokers, as the sight and smell of cigarettes disappear under the lid. The design for the satin-polished stainless-steel ashtray was arrived at by serendipity, according to Roelandt, a graduate of the Academy of Industrial Design in Eindhoven, Netherlands. While experimenting with a system of boxes with self-closing swivel-top lids, Roelandt was struck by how the box would be ideal as an ashtray as it closed automatically and could therefore 'enclose the nasty odours and the sight of cremated cigarettes', according to the non-smoking designer. The ashtray removes the need to extinguish a cigarette, because once the laser-cut lid is closed the oxygen inside is either used or replaced by smoke, which in turn extinguishes the cigarette. The ashtray is constructed by forging sheets of stainless steel into tubes and milling the cylinder-shaped container. Finally, the laser-cut lid is incorporated and both pieces are hand polished. As a result of its impeccable design credentials the multifunctional ashtray is currently being sold in more than seventy countries.

BRERA LAMP (1992)
Achille Castiglioni
(1918–2002)
Flos 1992 to 2015

The Brera Lamp demonstrates Achille Castiglioni's long experience with Functionalism, modernity and design fashions – an experience that allowed him to create a very modest and simple suspended lamp in opaline glass. A thin thread of stainless-steel wire hangs from the ceiling, suspending a milky-white glass oval. The quality of light corresponds to the accuracy of the glass shape. When it is switched off it resembles a Constantin Brancusi sculpture, but a fine, glimmering translucent body of light appears when it is switched on. The Brera Lamp demonstrates an outstanding beauty and is an exciting industrial product using the most advanced technology. Castiglioni's design looks rather technical, comprising a steel wire and a glass ball, and is reduced to the minimum. The glass quality and shape are somehow reminiscent of classical kitchen lamps of the 1950s, and the hanging wire was typically used in the 1970s and 1980s for highly industrial lighting fixtures. For all that, this light object has a surprisingly basic elegance that is characteristic of most of Castiglioni's designs. It is definitely one of the elements that allow us to easily identify his products.

CHAIR NO. 2/.03
(1992)

Maarten van Severen
(1956–2005)
Maarten van Severen
Meubelen
1992 to 1999
Top Mouton
1999 to c.2012
Vitra 1999 to present

The work of Maarten van Severen rewards careful contemplation. A closer look reveals painstaking attention to detail, materials and forms. In Chair No. 2 the designer has striven to conceal every joint, so the chair is comprised only of planes intersecting lines. The plane of the seat and back tapers almost imperceptibly, and the front legs are not vertical, but subtly raked. Van Severen began making furniture in Belgium in the late 1980s. He is not concerned with ornament or decoration, and favours self-coloured and natural materials like beech plywood, aluminium, steel and, latterly, acrylic. These have an innate purity and elegance that complement his staid, geometric forms. Chair No. 2 is from a series of designs exploring reductive ideas. Early versions in aluminium and pale beech plywood were made by van Severen himself, but production was subsequently adopted by Belgian manufacturer Top Mouton. The Swiss furniture giant Vitra has also translated the design (under the name .03) into polyurethane foam, in eight mostly muted shades of grey, green and red. Whereas van Severen's originals are resolutely anti-industrial, Vitra's stackable versions embrace industrial production and include springs embedded in the chair back for comfort.

MOMENTO WRISTWATCH (1993)
Aldo Rossi (1931–97)
Alessi 1993 to 2000, 2004 to 2017

Aldo Rossi's Momento Wristwatch was the first watch to be manufactured by the Italian design company Alessi. Momento, like all Rossi's designs, is highly original and shaped around a bare geometrical form – in this case the circle. The watch is composed of a double steel case, within which an inner case encloses the movement and dial. The inner case can be removed and reinserted easily, making it possible to use it as both a wristwatch and pocket watch. Rossi, one of the most influential architects of the post-war era, immeasurably enriched the world of design with his imaginative ideas and sense of fun, which

Alessi recognized as mirroring its own approach to domestic design. Momento is astonishing in its simplicity and confirms Rossi as a leading exponent of Neo-Rationalism. The watch's changeable elements for different usage offer an alternative to the technological and functional emphasis of Modernism and also reveal Rossi's reductionalist approach to design. Rossi will always be remembered as one of the great masters of accessible, practical and fun design that became synonymous with Alessi, and for creating products that epitomized European Postmodernism of the late 1980s.

ELLEN'S BRACKETS
(1993)
Ali Tayar (1959–2016)
Parallel Design
Partnership
1993 to 2016

When writer Ellen Levy enlisted architect and designer Ali Tayar to create a Modernist Manhattan loft space, little did she know that one of its elements would turn out to be an award-winning mass-seller. The cool elegance of the aluminium shelving bracket that took her name became a hit with discerning individuals and designers alike. Tayar took inspiration from his mentor, Jean Prouvé, a mid-century pioneer in prefabrication. When a search for an appropriate shelving system to accompany the loft's prefabricated elements drew a blank, Tayar realized he would need something bespoke, and so began the process that ultimately produced the brackets. It was not until the brackets were installed that the idea of manufacturing them took root. In 1993, Tayar founded Parallel Design Partnership and began modifying the bracket for mass production. The prototype was in milled aluminium and, to be viable, the brackets would need to be extruded aluminium. Working with engineer Attila Rona, Tayar made incremental alterations that eventually yielded the production design. The brackets were an immediate success. A horizontal version with a different track and simplified bracket was later launched.

LALEGGERA
(1993–6)
Riccardo Blumer
(1959–)
Alias 1996 to present

Laleggera is an unusually lightweight stacking chair, constructed of a heartwood frame to which two thin layers of veneer are applied, with the hollow between them injected with polyurethane resin. While the heartwood frame alone provides sufficient strength to carry the weight of a person, the polyurethane prevents the chair from caving in, a technique borrowed from the construction of the wings of gliders. The chair's frame, of maple or ash heartwood, can be veneered with maple, oak or walnut, or is finished with a stain in a wide range of colours. The Italian architect and designer, Riccardo Blumer, has made a career out of exploring the qualities of lightness. The Laleggera Chair owes much to its elegant predecessor, Gio Ponti's ultralight Superleggera Chair of 1957, and is named in homage to its progenitor. While the Superleggera weighs 1,750 g (61.25 oz) the Laleggera is a little heavier, but still a featherweight at 2,390 g (83.65 oz). The Laleggera Chair won the Compasso d'Oro prize in 1998, much to the surprise of Alias, who had not envisaged a level of demand that would require setting up a special production plant.

85 LAMPS CHANDELIER (1993)
Rody Graumans
(1968–)
Droog
1993 to present

85 Lamps Chandelier is Rody Graumans's only contribution to Droog Design and among the company's first pieces. The chandelier formed part of Graumans' final exam at the Utrecht Art Academy. Droog Design, founded in 1993 as an international platform for young, unconventional Dutch designers, has now become synonymous with contemporary Dutch design. Graumans' chandelier is one of the few objects in the Droog collection that is a real, sellable consumer product. The design is as simple as can be. It comprises eighty-five 15-watt bulbs, black plastic sockets and equal lengths of black electric wire, which are gathered together by as many plastic connectors as necessary. The multitude of bulbs defines the elegant profile and provides a witty echo of a Louis XVI chandelier. With this design Graumans introduced a sense of fun into Dutch design, which has for decades been dominated by a Calvinistic, sober aesthetic approach. The simplicity of the chandelier is comparable to the Modernist lighting by the De Stijl architect, Gerrit Rietveld. Rietveld uses lighting components in a very well considered, constructive way, whereas the young and open-minded Graumans just lets things happen. The result is sublime.

MOBIL (1993)
Antonio Citterio
(1950–)
Glen Oliver Löw
(1959–)
Kartell
1994 to present

The Mobil Storage System is one of several significant designs produced by Antonio Citterio and Glen Oliver Löw since they began collaborating in 1987. The name 'Mobil' underlines the product's essential character as a unit that is light and easy to move and serves many functions. A tubular steel frame supports containers and drawers of semi-transparent plastic that can be positioned vertically or horizontally in two- or three-level columns, with or without handles and wheels. The system's metacrylate plastic has a satin-like effect and comes in sixteen colour schemes, including orange, smoke grey and lime

green. The flexibility of the units and the possibility of customization have made Mobil a commercial success. In 1994, the design won the prestigious Compasso d'Oro, and Mobil can be found in the permanent design collection at the Museum of Modern Art. Mobil fits Kartell's policy of striving for constant, creative experimentation with low-cost plastic materials. Mobil's multifunctional use is a hallmark of Antonio Citterio's furniture and product design output. A proponent of rational design, Citterio specializes in products that are flexible enough to adapt to the changing needs of the office or home.

MAMMUT CHILD CHAIR (1993)
Morten Kjelstrup
(1959–)
Allan Østgaard
(1959–)
IKEA 1993 to present

Scandinavian designers Alvar Aalto, Hans Wegner and Nanna Ditzel designed suites for children, but with the exception of school furniture, sales of the various models were quite limited. IKEA's Mammut range was to change that. The usual approach to designing furniture for children does not take into account the fact that a child's body is different in its proportions from an adult one, nor the different functional requirements of children's furniture. Morten Kjelstrup, an architect, and Allan Østgaard, a fashion designer, were wise to these factors, which partly helps to explain the robust proportions

of the Mammut Child Chair and the sturdy plastic from which it is made. Instead of following an adult's aesthetic preferences, Kjelstrup and Østgaard took their lead from cartoons on children's TV. The deliberately gawky and brightly coloured forms that are the result are immensely popular with children. Crucially though, the choice of IKEA as manufacturer has kept the Mammut cheap enough to appeal to the average adult's pocket. The Mammut Child Chair was originally produced in 1993. In 1994, the chair was given the prestigious award of 'Furniture of the Year' in Sweden, establishing its success and popularity.

BOOK WORM BOOKCASE (1993)
Ron Arad (1951–)
Kartell
1994 to present

The notion of a bookshelf made up of anything other than horizontal planes was inconceivable. At least, that was before Ron Arad dreamt up the idea of a flexible, snaking alternative. The now-famous London-based designer had been creating one-off workshop designs made from salvaged materials. The Book Worm Bookcase was one of them, born out of Arad's ongoing experiments with sheet steel. Kartell took on the design in 1994, and a year later the company created a colourful mass-market alternative using an extruded flexible thermoplastic polymer without jeopardizing the design's toughness, stability and functionality. Kartell was soon supplying Book Worm in a variety of colours as well as three different lengths. The configuration of the shape is entirely up to the purchaser, giving a mass-produced item a certain sculptural individualism. Each bookend is fixed to the wall and can tolerate a load of around 10 kg (22 lbs) on each support. Introduced by a company that has never shied away from the new, Book Worm has rapidly established its place as a recognizable icon of its time. The product redefined shelving and successfully reinforced the reputations of both Arad and Kartell as innovators.

LC95A, LOW CHAIR ALUMINIUM
(1993–5)
Maarten van Severen
(1956–2005)
Maarten van Severen
Meubelen
1996 to 1999
TM, division Top
Mouton
1999 to c.2012

The LC95A is a chaise longue made of a single sheet of aluminium that curves in on itself. The strength and suppleness of the aluminium allows a flexibility that affords the sitter great comfort, while the thinness of the sheet gives the chair a gravity-defying elegance. The design of the LC95A (LCA stands for Low Chair Aluminium) arose almost by chance. By taking a leftover piece of aluminium and folding it over itself, the form of a low chair became apparent. Maarten van Severen transformed this simple device into a chair by using a long thin sheet of aluminium, only 5 mm (0.2 in) thick, and connecting the two ends with a special rubber, achieving the correct tension and bend. The LC95A, like many of van Severen's designs, remained a one-off until Kartell approached him to produce a plastic version of the chair. Using a transparent acrylic plastic called Metacryl, and a much thicker plate of 10 mm (0.4 in), the chair was successfully translated into the more commercial LCP, and became available in bright colours such as yellow, orange, sky blue or clear.

AERON CHAIR
(1994)
Donald T Chadwick
(1936–)
William Stumpf
(1936–2006)
Herman Miller
1994 to present

Combining pioneering ergonomics, new materials and distinctive looks, the Aeron rethought the office chair. The chair's biomorphic design, without upholstery or padding, creates a radical new design approach constructed from advanced materials including die-cast glass-reinforced polyester and recycled aluminium. The chair's distinctive black Pellicle webbing seat structure is durable and supportive and allows air to circulate around the body. Designers Don Chadwick and William Stumpf extensively researched what an office chair ought to be with ergonomists and orthopaedic specialists, and created a user-centered chair. Featuring a sophisticated suspension system, the chair distributes the user's weight evenly over the seat and back, conforming to individual body shapes, and minimizing pressure on the spine and muscles. The design is available in three sizes, like a personalized tool. A logical series of knobs and levers allowed users to adjust numerous aspects, facilitating a customized, perfect posture. The Aeron has sold millions since it was introduced in 1994. Designed for disassembly and recycling, the chair reflects a growing concern for environmental issues.

SOFT URN VASE
(1994)
Hella Jongerius
(1963–)
JongeriusLab
1994 to present

The Soft Urn Vase is part of the early Droog Design collection, featuring conceptual products by young Dutch designers. The product, which comes in many colours, deals with the relationship between old and new, and between craft and industrial production. Hella Jongerius appropriated the archetypal form of the hand-moulded antique clay urn to inject it with a new structure. A close look not only reveals the opposing quality of the fabric – soft, strong, thin rubber instead of hard, fragile, thick ceramics – but also the seams and marks of an industrial casting process. The seemingly

unique piece proves to be a serial product. The visible marks of fabrication, deliberate faults in the manufacturing process and accidental residues are an essential part of the vase. Instead of polishing away all the unevenness of the surface as the industry has been doing for years, thereby equating beauty with smoothness and perfection, imperfection has become part of the charm and content of Jongerius's products. The imperfections of the skin become new ornaments and the material of Soft Urn suits its purpose even better than ceramics: the rubber will never break.

BIGFRAME CHAIR (1994)

Alberto Meda
(1945–)
Alias 1994 to present

Italian designer Alberto Meda's attention to technical aspects and quality of materials signifies a remarkable design approach, in which objects are viewed initially from the inside, as if the design had the task of, in Meda's words, 'liberating the intelligence contained in things… because each object and the material from which it is made inherently contains its own cultural and technological background.' The Bigframe Chair is typical of Meda's ideology in its use of state-of-the-art materials in ways that are stunning as well as structurally sound. The chair follows on from his 1987 sculptural Light Light Chair, which used a honeycomb core and a matrix of carbon fibre to achieve strength and lightness. The Bigframe uses tubular polished aluminium for the frame and polyester mesh for the seat and back, which provides an element of extreme comfort that is not usually achieved in non-upholstered seat design. With the Bigframe, Meda accomplished a combination of ergonomic sophistication with a visual coherence that demonstrates his engineering background. It clearly illustrates Meda's fascination with the apparent paradox of uncomplicated designs that are technically advanced yet organic in nature.

BOTTLE WINE RACK (1994)
Jasper Morrison
(1959–)
Magis
1994 to present

Wine consumption and connoisseurship have become worldwide preoccupations since the 1970s, and with them came a growth in the development of wine accessories and related products. In 1994, Jasper Morrison was commissioned by the Italian manufacturer Magis to design a wine rack. Morrison's ready-to-assemble solution is simply called Bottle. It has interlocking tabs that function as feet or stabilizing devices and allow the user to create a storage system that can sit on a shelf or table or be stacked into a wall-sized structure. Each modular piece consists of two injection-moulded polypropylene units with openings for six bottles and curved elliptical supports that both cradle individual bottles and provide the structural integrity required for the system to become a stacked wall. The clear or blue pieces are joined by anodized aluminium tubes. In many ways this, like most of Morrison's work, is an exercise in limits: colour, materials, form and organizational possibilities come together to create an elegantly controlled aesthetic impact. Still available from Magis, Bottle is a fine example of the stylistic vocabulary and simplicity that was the goal of many designers at the end of the twentieth century.

GIROTONDO HOUSEWARE (1994)
Stefano Giovannoni
(1954–)
Guido Venturini
(1957–)
Alessi
1994 to present

Girotondo, the Italian name for the children's nursery rhyme 'ring a ring o'roses', is a group of objects decorated with a perforated man motif resembling the paper-chain shapes children cut out with scissors. The first in the line of 61 products was a simple stainless-steel tray introduced in 1994. Much to Alessi's surprise it became an instant bestseller, and the little men soon invaded other products, appearing on everything from chopping boards to napkin holders, photo frames, key rings, bookmarks, candles and jewellery. The playful, cartoon-like quality of the Girotondo line marked a seismic shift in the Alessi product range,

and in product design in the 1990s generally. Two young Florentine architects, Stefano Giovannoni and Guido Venturini, who went by the *nomme de guerre* King-Kong, were introduced to Alberto Alessi by Alessandro Mendini. The freshness of their quirky, playful designs acted as a catalyst to Alessi's new line of thinking and to Alessi's 'Family Follows Fiction' workshop, which was responsible for the more colourful, humorous and mostly plastic output that characterized the company's products in the 1990s. Although the King-Kong partnership has now split up, both designers have since designed products independently for Alessi.

KAPPA KNIVES
(1994)
Karl-Peter Born
(1955–)
Güde 1994 to present

The Kappa collection comprises three sizes of chef's knife designed to perform all general kitchen duties. The knives' smooth surfaces and classic form make them essential items of kitchen equipment for the professional or keen amateur. The Kappa range has been produced in Solingen, Germany, by the firm of Güde since 1994. The knives are handmade in small numbers and their blade and handle are formed from a single piece of high carbon-chromium-vanadium stainless steel. First they are hot-drop forged before being ice-hardened, then hand-ground and polished. Traditional in form, the design is the result of many decades of refinement. There are twenty-five different items in the Kappa collection, within the three sizes, and each is designed for a specific purpose. Some of the knives have wavy serrations on the edge of the blade, an innovation developed by Franz Güde to maintain a sharp edge for longer. The knives are prized by professional chefs for their extremely sharp blades, beautiful balance and reassuring heaviness not found in knives with hollow or wooden handles. The Güde company's concentration on quality and craftsmanship has resulted in the retention of a valuable tradition and a superb knife.

MONO TABLES (1995)
Konstantin Grcic
(1965–)
SCP 1995 to 2003,
2015 to present
MUJI 2003 to 2015

When Konstantin Grcic designed the Mono Tables, he was in the process of examining Enzo Mari's Frate and Cugino tables. This was part of a larger reflection by Grcic on the vicissitudes of batch production, materials and finishes. He was not pursuing solutions for definitive forms, but rather seeking a process that married batch production with simplicity of materials and construction, to deliver high quality products economically. While his earlier works for SCP were predominantly of wood and relied on more obviously archetypal forms, the Mono Tables were different. They were an intentional move

towards metal and a purposeful family of products. They offered a vague outline of use, but their forms were not prescriptive. The result is a series of four intentionally utilitarian surfaces born from varied folds of matt grey, powder-coated sheet metal. Each top joins its solitary column along a folded matching plane to allow a simple, welded connection. Each column stands bolted to single-footed attention. Grcic's penchant for casual mobility works for both the users and the designer's own use of the tables, as they can be arranged in numerous ways or stored in various locations.

X-SHAPED RUBBER BAND (1995)
Läufer Design Team
Läufer
1995 to present

It would seem impossible to improve upon something as simple, inexpensive and brutally functional as a rubber band. Bands made of vulcanized rubber and designed to fasten bundles of stationary were patented in 1845 by Perry and Company of London, and they have changed little ever since. But the X-Shaped Rubber Band, produced by Läufer, proves that design is often at its best when deployed to rethink everyday objects. The product is a standard, extra-wide rubber band with two strips cut out of its centre and two narrow bridges of rubber between the gaps. Stretched and spread into an X-shape, it performs a function that would normally require two rubber bands. But although its various colours and variation on a seemingly fixed product make the X-Shaped Rubber Band seem incredibly new, part of its beauty lies in the way in which it performs essentially the same function as the traditional piece of string with which parcels are fastened. Indeed, because the rubber band is essentially H-shaped, when stretched into an X-shape it is distorted in exactly the same way as a single piece of string is when used to fasten a rectangular box.

MEDA CHAIR (1996)
Alberto Meda
(1945–)
Vitra 1996 to present

This was planned to be a match made in heaven – one of the world's greatest designers working with one of the most creative manufacturers, Vitra. The collaboration did not disappoint. The Meda Chair, designed by Alberto Meda in 1996, has the refined looks one would expect, is simple to use and is extremely comfortable. It has an uncluttered appearance, keeping mechanisms and levers to a minimum. Two pivots at the side allow the back to drop, which, at the same time, changes the shape of the seat. The process is controlled by a pair of springs that are located between the back of the chair and the bridge. The height can be adjusted by pressing a button below the right armrest, and the lever on the other side fixes its position. There are several versions of the chair, the Meda, Meda 2 and Meda 2 XL (which all have a five-star, die-cast polished aluminium base) as well as a conference version that completes the range. Beautiful without being obviously engineered or conspicuously high tech, the Meda is neither aggressive nor overtly male and remains one of the great office chairs.

WASHING-UP BOWL (1996)
Ole Jensen (1958–)
Normann
Copenhagen
2002 to present

The rubber Washing-Up Bowl by Ole Jensen was designed to protect fragile glasses and porcelain from the hard surface of the stainless-steel sink. The flexibility of the rubber allowed it to contain objects of any shape and size, and today the bowl may be found being used as a footbath, ice bucket, wine cooler and even for cleaning the tables at the Museum of Modern Art in New York. Jensen set about making a prototype for the bowl on a potter's wheel, achieving a handcrafted character in both its production method and style. The manufactured bowl was flexible and durable, and accompanied by a washing-up brush made of Chinese pig bristles and wood. It was first exhibited in 1996, then lay in the designer's workshop for a few years. Normann Copenhagen decided to start producing it in 2002, and now uses santoprene, an artificial rubber. It also produces the hog-and-wood bristle brush, a touch that carries a sense of traditional Danish domestic ware to the forty or so countries where it is distributed. Although among the most expensive of washing-up bowls, Jensen is pleased with its multipurpose profile, each bowl embedded with its user's character.

GINEVRA DECANTER (1996)
Ettore Sottsass
(1917–2007)
Alessi 1996 to 2001,
2003 to 2009

The simple, seductive form of the Ginevra crystal decanter creates an object of great beauty, with its shape reflecting the luxury of the art of drinking. But it is also remarkable in that it is the final piece in the tableware range designed by Ettore Sottsass for Alessi, a range that spans four decades and represents many of the designer's often radical and always influential ideas. The Ginevra Decanter and the accompanying glass range were originally introduced by Alessi in 1996, then redesigned and reintroduced in 2003. The elegantly attenuated decanter, shaped like a beautiful unadulterated bottle, was the missing link in the 'beautiful table' design philosophy of the designer. Sottsass always pursued the conceptual route in his designs, and the idea of the 'beautiful table' is not simply an aesthetic consideration; it is more about the ritual act of sharing, the notion of showing respect and care for the occasion of eating. Ettore Sottsass maintained that a 'beautiful table', where everything is clean and neat, and all the tableware is carefully laid in its proper place, invokes a feeling of engagement, participation, even communion, with the Ginevra Decanter a suitably sociable late guest.

ACQUATINTA
PENDANT LAMP
(1996)
Michele De Lucchi
(1951–)
Alberto Nason
(1972–)
Produzione Privata
1996 to present

With the establishment of Produzione Privata in 1990, Michele De Lucchi added yet another strand to his already varied oeuvre. It seems a paradox that the same person who designed the First Chair and who lists among his clients multinationals such as Deutsche Bank and Olivetti would come up with the idea of creating a line of designs to be produced solely by traditional craftsmanship. The Acquatinta Pendant Lamp is the purest example of Produzione Privata's glass workshop. De Lucchi was not interested in revitalizing older craft traditions to give them a more contemporary image. Experimenting with new

techniques, using, in his words, 'hands and mind', he created a unique piece each time. Designed in collaboration with Alberto Nason, the Acquatinta is revolutionary not as the reworking of a traditional shape, but for the irony of featuring a transparent lamp-shade. Over time, many different versions have been realized, including sand-blasted, opaque, etched and mirrored finishes. Acquatinta, along with its wood moulds, is today part of the permanent design collection at the Pompidou Centre in Paris, testimony to the fact that a timeless piece can be made with minimal means.

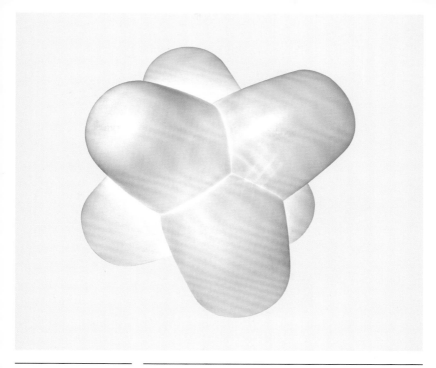

JACK LIGHT (1996)
Tom Dixon (1959–)
Eurolounge
1996 to 2002
Tom Dixon
2002 to 2018

Avant-garde designer Tom Dixon is a craftsman who focuses on new applications of traditional and modern materials and forms. He created the company Eurolounge in the 1990s to make design more affordable. The first object Eurolounge produced was the Jack Light, so-called for its resemblance to the children's toy. The object, available in red, blue and white, grew out of Dixon's desire both to make lamps in an industrial way and to make lighting multifunctional. The Jack Light, which gives off a soft glow, can be stacked into a high pile and, as it stands on the floor, can be used as a stool or support a tabletop. All these possibilities are the result of intense research into plastic manufacturing techniques. Dixon discovered that by using a rotary moulding technique a range of products could be created more cheaply without losing quality. The Jack Light would define Dixon's career, earning him the Millennium mark in the UK. Dixon works with many high-end Italian furniture, lighting and glass companies such as Cappellini and Moroso, he has received an OBE for services to the British design community and founded his eponymous brand in 2002.

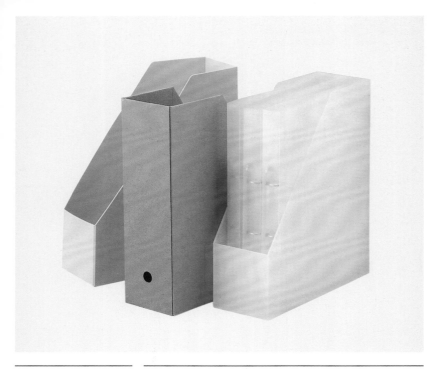

**POLYPROPYLENE
ANGLE FILE (1996)**
MUJI Design Team
MUJI
1996 to present

MUJI has always been associated with simple, basic products and pure design. The Polypropylene Angle File is a straightforward, functional product, practically a 'non-design' item without sophisticated details, made from translucent polypropylene. Today, it is a major piece within the larger office range of containers and boxes produced by MUJI. Like all the products in the line, the box is minimalist in shape, light and translucent in material and modest in the best sense. With this object MUJI represents its philosophy of a manufacturer of archetypes. In every way, the box is an everyday product; its

construction is suited to industrial production methods, making it easy to produce in high volume, and thus inexpensive to buy. When MUJI started this product line in 1996, the use of polypropylene was at its peak, and the translucent, matt-finish surfaces had conquered the world. MUJI was not interested in inventing something new but instead used this elegant and light material to develop a range of practical basics with the aim of satisfying a wide group of consumers. The file box does not have the appeal of the avant-garde, but charms us by its utilitarian nature.

KNOTTED CHAIR
(1996)
Marcel Wanders
(1963–)
Droog Design
Cappellini
1996 to present

The Knotted Chair is a design that provokes a complex range of reactions. It can confuse one into misunderstanding the material and technique of production, and users are often wary about the chair's ability to support their bulk. The lightness of the design in both transparency and weight will always bring a sense of awe. The finely knotted outline of the small four-legged chair is made from rope twisted round a carbon core. The carefully handcrafted form is then impregnated with resin and hung within a frame to harden; its final shape relies on gravity. The Knotted Chair is a highly individualistic design

that marries an inventive use of craft with both modern materials and strong ideals: 'a hammock with legs, frozen in space'. Marcel Wanders became a prominent force as part of the highly influential Dutch collective Droog Design. He continues to communicate similar messages through his own collection and designs for Moooi, Cappellini and a host of international producers inspired by his individualistic approach, saying, 'I want to give my designs visual, auditory and kinaesthetic information in order to be interesting to a wide group'.

BLOCK LAMP
(1996)
Harri Koskinen
(1970–)
Design House
Stockholm
1998 to present

Harri Koskinen is now design director for iittala, but one of his most famous designs was created while he was still a student at the University of Art and Design in Helsinki. The Block Lamp was the result of a technical exercise in which Koskinen explored the difficulties of casting an object in glass. In the finished piece the encased light bulb appears to be suspended in air. Two sections of hand-cast glass surround a bulb shape created by sandblasting, leaving a matt surface. Light is provided by the 25-watt bulb, which emits a soft, diffused light. Many see the lamp as a continuation of the Finnish

glasswork tradition established by Timo Sarpaneva and Tapio Wirkkala, who created works that carried the properties of ice. But for Koskinen, the lamp is not intended to represent a block of ice. It stands only for itself, or a block of glass. Koskinen received immediate recognition for this piece, which was put into production by Design House Stockholm in 1998. The Block Lamp follows in the Finnish design tradition, reflecting the natural environment, and is both an object of function and art.

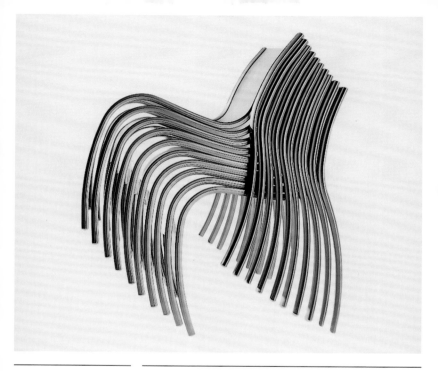

FANTASTIC PLASTIC ELASTIC CHAIR (1997)
Ron Arad (1951–)
Kartell
1997 to 2018

The Fantastic Plastic Elastic Chair is a lightweight stacking chair with a revolutionary production technique. Designed by Ron Arad for Kartell, the FPE is about making a chair on an industrial scale, simplifying the manufacturing by removing any excess material and processes, and creating a soft, sinuous and sensuous solution. The translucent lightweight chair is available in white and grey as well as vibrant red, yellow and blue, and lives comfortably indoors or outside. Two double-barrelled aluminium extrusions are cut to a staggered length, and an injection-moulded translucent polypropylene sheet is slotted into the extrusions. The metal and plastic are then bent together in a single piece, the unique process automatically bonding the plastic membrane that makes up the seat and back in place without any adhesives. The FPE's almost flat aluminium extrusions and injection-moulded sheet reduce the amount of material required while dramatically lowering the cost of the tooling required. This minimalist approach is reflected in a pared down structure that remains flexible until the weight of the occupant sitting locks the seat, creating a stiff and rigid structure from the most minimal use of materials.

CABLE TURTLE
(1997)
Jan Hoekstra (1964–)
FLEX/the
INNOVATIONLAB
Cleverline
1997 to present

The Cable Turtle is an award-winning design that tackles complex cable management of the ever-increasing multitude of electronic products we now use. Created by Dutch designer Jan Hoekstra, the product is a round shell with a polypropylene joint at its centre. The shell opens and the excess cable can be wound around the joint like a yo-yo. After gathering up the required length of cable, the user simply closes the flexible elastomer shell and aligns the ends of the cable with the lip-like openings on either side, enabling the cable to exit neatly from the pliable, doughnut-like form. The design is available

in two sizes: the small version holds about 1.8 m of electrical cable, while the giant variant can hold up to 5 m long. The device is designed to safely handle a load of up to 1,000W. The Cable Turtle's tactile form has a beguiling, playful quality that rejects traditional conservative office design. Manufactured from recycled plastic and available in eleven eye-catching colours, the simple and intuitive object has been recognized as a contemporary design classic, most notably winning Germany's Good Design Award.

DISH DOCTOR DRAINER (1997)
Marc Newson
(1962–)
Magis
1998 to present

Marc Newson's Dish Doctor Drainer for Magis is characteristic of his design vision. Acknowledged internationally for his funky, futuristic, but technically rigorous approach, Newson has designed products ranging from a concept car and a doorstop to this dish drainer. With its integral reservoir to collect water drips, the plastic Dish Doctor is ideal for use with small sinks and those without drainers. It is constructed in two pieces to allow the collected water to be easily poured away. The drainer, with its bright colour and quirky form, has more of the look of a toy or game than an unassuming piece of kitchenware. The height and position of the flexible pegs that hold the crockery in place are precisely designed to support any size of crockery. The two integrated cutlery drainers save on space and keep the cutlery apart. The Dish Doctor is a radical rethink of the design of a humble domestic object – a unique and fun product that is a desirable object in its own right. As one of the outstanding industrial design innovators of his time, Newson is a maverick who has revamped design as the new commodity fetish.

BOMBO STOOL (1997)

Stefano Giovannoni
(1954–)
Magis
1997 to present

Of all typologies of furniture, chairs have the unique ability to symbolize a culture's defining elements. Introduced in 1997, on the cusp of a new millennium, Milan-based designer Stefano Giovannoni's Bombo Stool has quickly become an icon of that pivotal era. At a point when all eyes were looking to the future, hearts were nostalgic for what was about to become the past. The Bombo Stool owes some of its success to its combination of retro styling with contemporary technology. It established its reputation in trendy public bars, restaurants and salons, where its adjustable height and range of fifteen colours gave it versatility. The stool's curvaceous form mimics the shape of a standard wine glass. Its bowl-like seat is balanced on a tapering stem, and opens out into a wide round base. The allure of the Bombo Stool lies in its combination of the Art Deco detailing of its injection-moulded ABS plastic and chromed steel trim, and the contemporary technology of its German gas-lift mechanism. The Bombo Stool has spawned a family of furnishings including the Bombo Chair, the Bombo Table and Al Bombo, a polished aluminium version of the original.

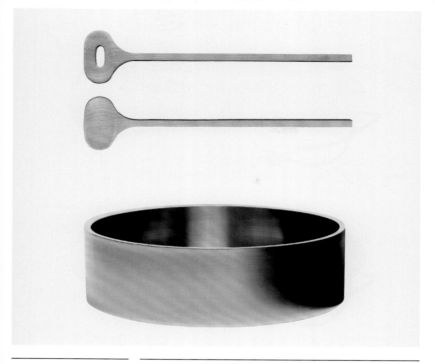

BOWLS AND SALAD CUTLERY (1997)
Carina Seth Andersson (1965–)
Hackman/iittala
1997 to 2006 (cutlery),
1997 to 2010 (bowls)

Scandinavian design has long been concerned with balancing chilly landscapes with warm, human-centred objects – whether cheery textiles, good lighting or comfortable, body-hugging furniture. Stockholm-based designer Carina Seth Andersson has continued this tradition in a set of serving bowls and utensils created for Finnish housewares company Hackman. Rather than resort to the expected idioms of 'classic' Scandinavian design, however, she presents something a little harder and much cooler. In order to accommodate both hot and cold food, Seth Andersson designed her bowls out of two layers of stainless steel; the pocket of air that rests between the layers keeps salads cool and pasta hot while enabling comfortable handling no matter what the temperature of the contents. The matt-brushed surface gives the bowls a distinctly sleek silhouette. The set also features two sinuous blonde birch serving tools with oblong heads – one gently scooped out, the other incorporating a lozenge-shaped slat. The birch utensils converse with the stainless-steel bowls in a dialogue of opposites: metal/wood, cold/warm, thick/thin.

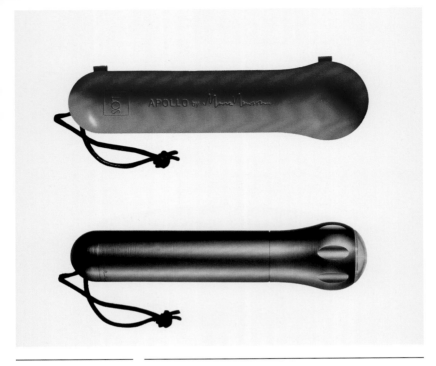

APOLLO TORCH
(1997)
Marc Newson
(1962–)
Flos 2000 to 2012

Precision manufacturing and dynamic curved forms come together in the highly distinctive work of Marc Newson. This combination is visible even in the relatively mundane context of a flashlight. Newson's Apollo Torch was created for the celebrated Italian manufacturer Flos, associated since its foundation in 1962 with innovators such as the Castiglioni brothers. It was another Flos alumnus, Philippe Starck, who recommended Newson to the company in the early 1990s. Flos launched an edition of Newson's Helice Lamp in 1993, and it decided to produce the Apollo Torch seven years later. Newson's Italian

experience marked a fascinating coming together of his self-made talent with the European tradition of design and manufacture that he had admired. The Apollo's sleek form, presented in milled aluminium, is an exercise in cool futurism that acknowledges the designer's love of space-age iconography, made more obvious still by its name. Its lines were made even cleaner by a head-rotating on-off mechanism, doing away with the need for the push button found on the Maglite, the Apollo's apparent inspiration. Like its predecessor, this futuristic variation on the theme also features a spare bulb in its base.

TOM VAC CHAIR (1997)
Ron Arad (1951–)
Vitra 1999 to present

In 1997, *Domus* magazine invited Ron Arad to create an eye-catching sculpture for a prestigious site in central Milan for the annual Furniture Fair. Arad made a tower of sixty-seven stacked chairs, each with a single curl of material to create a continuous seat and back. The chair is detailed with ripples that both articulate the surface and strengthen it. The Tom Vac Chair has proved to be one of Arad's most adaptable designs, perhaps because of the simplicity of the form. Unlike most chairs it has been successfully rendered in different materials. The chairs in the *Domus* tower were made of vacuum-formed aluminium,

which is one source of their name. The other is the photographer friend of Arad's, Tom Vack. Vitra has produced the chair with a variety of leg configurations. One version, with wooden rockers, was a deliberate homage to the Eameses' DAR rocking armchair from 1950. The version with stainless-steel legs can be stacked. There was even a version produced in clear acrylic, as well as a limited edition in carbon fibre, which transformed the character of the chair yet again.

GARBINO WASTEPAPER BIN (1997)
Karim Rashid (1960–)
Umbra
1997 to present

With its articulated, sinuous silhouette in a myriad of softly translucent pastels, and its low price tag, the Garbino Wastepaper Bin has sold more than two million since its launch by Umbra in 1997. The Garbino champions its designer's self-proclaimed sense of sensual minimalism and his adrenalin-laden vision for the democratization of design. In the shadow of this success, however, remains a tale of achievement in the face of the economic realities of producing low-margin, high-volume household utilitarian goods. Garbino's design allows an uninterrupted flow of resin during the injection process, uniform cooling and a simplified, symmetrical high-yield mould with markedly low wastage. The uniformly tapered sides allow easy stacking of large quantities, reducing costs of transport and retail stocking, while the shallow curve of the interior base discourages sticking during stacking and allows Umbra to avoid the expense of a lining tissue for each bin during shipment. Scratches from daily use are hard to see on the translucent matt exterior, and the edgeless concave base permits easy cleaning. The swooping rim, cut-out handle and curved profile have allowed the design to be patented and attempted counterfeits successfully prosecuted.

WAIT CHAIR (1997)
Matthew Hilton
(1957–)
Authentics
1999 to present

This fully recyclable plastic chair by British talent Matthew Hilton marked a turning point in his career, moving from high-value, low-volume furniture into the realm of affordable mass production. The chair is made from a single piece of injection-moulded polypropylene, incorporating strengthening ribs in the seat and back to give a stability that belies the naturally flexible light material. Engineering such a design took Hilton two years, with his work split between his own low-tech design approach and the sophisticated equipment made available by his manufacturer. Although it was launched in 1999 into a market already saturated with cheap plastic chairs, the stackable Wait Chair quickly achieved classic status. Hilton and Authentics cleverly attained a price point that was more expensive than standard, crudely designed alternatives but much cheaper than other all-plastic 'designer' chairs. The chair sidestepped the former through classic good design and avoided the status of the latter by deliberately dispensing with a fashionable avant-garde appearance. The result is an unobtrusive, good-looking, comfortable and affordable chair that is stackable, suitable for use indoors or out and available in various colours.

DAHLSTRÖM 98 COOKWARE (1998)
Björn Dahlström
(1957–)
Hackman/iittala
1998 to present

Dahlström 98, now produced by iittala under the name Tools, was designed by Swedish-born Björn Dahlström as a commission from Finnish manufacturer Hackman who wanted to develop an innovative range of cookware that was both beautiful and durable. Part of Dahlström's brief was to use a manufacturing technique developed by Hackman wherein a thick aluminium sheet is wedged between two thinner stainless-steel sheets, which are drawn together and shaped in a press. The sturdiness of steel combined with aluminium creates a high-performance material noted for even heat distribution. Dahlström was to produce professional-quality oven-to-tableware pots that would also appeal to the domestic market. The simple form of the casserole pot, for example, and its understated, matt, brushed-steel finish allow the food to be shown to its best advantage. Where a shiny, mirror surface shouts machine-made, the matt finish of the Dahlström 98 cookware has a more tactile, domestic feel. For the thick, hollow handles, Dahlström borrowed a technique typically used for producing cutlery. This elegant range surpasses the expectations of the original brief, and is realized as a beautiful object.

FORTEBRACCIO LAMP (1998)
Alberto Meda
(1945–)
Paolo Rizzatto
(1941–)
LucePlan
1998 to present

When it first appeared in 1998, the Fortebraccio Lamp was instantly considered a tour de force in lighting design, as it is one of the most versatile and flexible interior lighting systems ever produced. Designed by Alberto Meda and Paolo Rizzatto, the Fortebraccio was conceived as a practical tool. Its design idea was to make the light independent from the electric wiring, so the heads, arms and attachments are all designed for separate assembly, whereas the electrical parts are prewired to the heads. This made it possible to substitute different light sources on the same arms. As a result, a variety of different lamps can be easily composed: the two-armed table or floor lamp, the single-arm lamp, the spot with one head, or the floor lamp. The model is named after the charismatic Norman knight William of Altavilla, known as Fortebraccio, who was renowned for his big nose. And like the knight, one of the main features of the Fortebraccio is its 'nose' or handle, which directs the light into different positions. The Fortebraccio forms a perfect role model for the LucePlan manifesto dedicated to the 'constant search for simplicity as the solution to complexity'.

CITTERIO 98 CUTLERY (1998)
Antonio Citterio
(1950–)
Glen Oliver Löw
(1959–)
iittala
1998 to present

From the cook's knife to the teaspoon, every item in iittala's Citterio 98 range of flatware displays the same perfectly balanced proportions. With broad bases and slim central sections, the pieces are both heavyweight in performance and lightweight in looks. Designed by Antonio Citterio, with Glen Oliver Löw, the range has been a bestseller for iittala since it was introduced. Indeed, such has been the popularity of Citterio 98 that it rapidly became a symbol for 1990s design. Citterio 98 is an update of an enduring archetype: thin steel French café cutlery with wooden or plastic panels to lend weight to the handle. The duo observed the practical benefits of a heavy handle (it equals greater ease of use) but translated it into a product that is made solely from steel. To accentuate the softness of their design, Citterio and Löw used matt-brushed steel. Citterio and Löw have expanded the collection and the range now includes far more than the original, simple table setting. Although Antonio Citterio has designed everything from showrooms to entire kitchen units, it is this range of cutlery that has stamped his name on the history of modern design.

GLO-BALL LAMP (1998)
Jasper Morrison (1959–)
Flos 1998 to present

In the hundred or so years since the earliest opal pendant lights were turned on, designers should have exhausted this archetype, but with his Glo-Ball series, Jasper Morrison revisits the hanging glass globe in an exciting interpretation. Launched in 1998, the series has had tremendous commercial success. To produce the characteristic soft glow of the Glo-Ball, a clear glass core is dipped into a molten white opal glass, in a process known as flashing, and then hand-blown into the striking, slightly flattened oval shape. A diffuse, uniform glow radiates from what appears to be an entirely flat surface, which refuses even the slightest reflection when seen from afar; a mirage achieved by exposing the thin outer casing of opaline glass to acid to create a highly matt surface. The Glo-Ball avoids the industrially perfect sphere in favour of something oddly more natural, and the mechanisms that support each light disappear into its core unnoticed. The series mirrors the core of what Jasper Morrison has long been known for – an appreciation for the past, a pursuit of honesty in form and an ability to uncover elegance previously hidden by an unnoticed edge.

OPTIC GLASS
(1998)
Arnout Visser (1962–)
Droog
2004 to present

Optic Glass began life when designer Arnout Visser was asked by Droog Design to respond to its brief, 'The Inevitable Ornament'. Visser's response was to look for ornamental possibilities embedded in the materiality of objects, rather than in applied decoration. When examining camera lenses he discovered that the largest were filled with liquid. This sparked the notion that if a drinking vessel could be shaped similarly, perhaps the drink could provide a magnifying effect. Starting with specially made, tall, smooth-sided tumblers in heat-resistant borosilicate glass – replaced in production with a stubbier, off-the-shelf borosilicate glass – Visser heated the tumblers and concentrated blasts of air at the glass to morph the surface into a series of concave and convex areas. The resulting glass is an uncommon mix of industrial design and craft. Once it is filled, light reflects and refracts through its undulating skin. Optic Glass has a couple of serendipitous features Visser had not predicted. The bumps allow the glasses to stack without jamming and also create a comfortable supporting grip. Visser has since contributed many products to the Droog collection and has become known for his simple and elegant glass designs.

YPSILON CHAIR (1998)
Mario Bellini (1935–)
Vitra 1998 to 2009

The Ypsilon Chair is a sign of its times, combining the most advanced materials with a radical rethinking of office life. It was designed for business high-flyers and has a hard-edged appearance – and price tag – to match. The Ypsilon, which Mario Bellini designed with his son Claudio (1963–), is so-named for the Y-shaped structure of the chair's back. The chair's chief feature is the adjustability of the back and headrest to an almost fully reclined posture, while still holding the head and shoulders in a position where a computer screen can be viewed. The chair frames the sitter like an exo-skeleton:

it is simultaneously anthropomorphic and robot-like. A special gel in the lumbar region 'remembers' the form of the shape of the sitter's back. The taut, translucent chair back was inspired in part by the wooden beaded mats used by cab drivers to ensure ventilation. Vitra chairman Rolf Fehlbaum likens it to Marcel Breuer's famous 1926 illustration of the chairs of the future, where people will sit on nothing but air. Numerous critics have agreed and the chair has won prestigious prizes, including Best Product Design 2002 in Germany's Red Dot Design Award.

MAY DAY LAMP (1998)
Konstantin Grcic
(1965–)
Flos 2000 to present

May Day, International Workers' Day, refers to the annual celebration of working class strength. The lamp of the same name by German designer Konstantin Grcic has the appeal of a plain security or utility lamp – a working lamp – but on closer look it reveals more attention to detail than might be expected of a purely utilitarian lamp. Grcic has said that a formal signature is not what design should be about. Nevertheless his stripped-down, functional designs are definitely recognizable. May Day Lamp was not designed for a fixed position. The design of the handle suggests there are various ways of using the object: it can be suspended from a hook, held in the hand or put on a flat surface, where it will produce diffused light. The original line offered a choice of four different colours for the handle: orange, blue, black and green. The outer material is injection-moulded tapered opaline polypropylene diffuser. The light itself takes two different types of bulbs, and there is a push button switch on the handle. Once you start looking attentively at Grcic's seemingly plain designs, the clever elegance incorporated in all of them becomes apparent.

AIR-CHAIR (1999)
Jasper Morrison
(1959–)
Magis
2000 to present

Through designing several smaller, equally successful plastic products for the Italian company, Magis, Jasper Morrison was introduced to gas-assisted injection moulding technology and used it in the design of the Air-Chair. The gas assistance means that the molten plastic is forced under pressure to the extremes of the mould, leaving voids in the thicker parts of the moulding. In this design this means that the 'frame' of the chair is effectively a series of tubes, therefore using little of the glass-reinforced polypropylene and reducing its weight. It also means that a fully formed and finished, almost seamless chair can be produced in a matter of minutes. The efficiency of production means that the original Air-Chair retailed for less than £50 – unusually inexpensive for a piece of well-designed, beautifully made Italian 'designer' furniture. It is a genuinely successful, simple, everyday chair; the type of design that Jasper Morrison is so good at. The inevitable and immediate success of this indoor/outdoor, domestic/contract chair, which comes in a number of light colours, has led to the design of a whole family of other 'Air-' products: a dining table, low table, TV/video table and a folding chair.

**WALL MOUNTED
CD PLAYER (1999)**
Naoto Fukasawa
(1956–)
MUJI
2001 to present

MUJI, one of the most progressive companies in recent times, appears not to play by the same rules as typical manufacturers. The reasons are numerous, but the important factor is that it is not a manufacturer at all, but a retailer. MUJI and its key visionary, Masaaki Kanai, noticed the experiments that Naoto Fukasawa and IDEO Japan were making and encouraged Fukasawa to take his simple, wall-mounted CD player to production. It is a complex product because it treads a fine line between artistic humour and authentic innovation. The MUJI CD player centres on a Sony

Walkman CD module and has been reduced to minimal controls. Its on/off switch is a pull-cord, a highly original yet perfectly acceptable form of interaction for a wall-mounted object. A more recent redeisgn added an FM radio, remote control and backlit LCD display. Fukasawa now helps to oversee MUJI's product catalogue and continues to produce designs that are tangential to what the market might expect. His criteria are rooted so deeply in the human condition that his products feel as though we have already lived with them previously.

RANDOM LIGHT
(1999–2002)
Bertjan Pot (1975–)
Moooi
2002 to present

The Random Light demonstrates one of the mandates of good design – simple in appearance, complex in execution – but took three years to develop. Random by name and random by nature, the light 'just happened' according to its creator, Bertjan Pot. All the materials in the design – resin, fibreglass and balloons – were lying around in Pot's workspace. The light is a piece of classic craft design created with high-tech materials: epoxy and fibreglass, chromed steel and plastic. The fibreglass, soaked in resin, is coiled around the balloon, and the balloon is then removed through a hole in which the light

bulb is later placed. Marcel Wanders introduced the light to the well-respected Dutch manufacturer Moooi, who then brought out around 2,000 in the first two years of its production. The play of light is especially effective due to the light being produced in three sizes: 50 cm, 80 cm, and 105 cm (20 in, 32 in and 42 in), which can be hung at different heights. Pot first came to the notice of design aficionados as part of the duo Monkey Boys, which he founded in 1999 with Daniel White, but since 2003 has worked independently. The design was updated in 2019 with the launch of Random II.

LOW PAD CHAIR
(1999)
Jasper Morrison
(1959–)
Cappellini
1999 to present

The Low Pad Chair combines elegance and simplicity with cutting-edge production techniques. Its minimal styling and sinuous line give it a sense of weightlessness that owes much to the look of mid-century Modern design, while its moulded padding, gently rising from the seat and back to give comfort and support, gives it a sophisticated contemporary twist. Jasper Morrison openly acknowledges Poul Kjærholm's PK22 chair (1956) as the inspiration for the Low Pad. The initial idea was to develop a comfortable low chair with as little volume and the same reduction of materials as Kjærholm's classic. Morrison is known for his interest in new material technologies, and Cappellini was more than happy to encourage his experiments, helping him to source a company making car seats that had the skills and expertise to press leather. Morrison experimented with various shapes for the back of the chair, and finally settled on a plywood panel, with multi-density polyurethane foam moulded to the required profile, cut to shape, with leather or upholstery stitched over. The manufacturer's skills with upholstery were suited to Morrison's design, creating a balance between the shape and the finish.

RELATIONS GLASSES (1999)
Konstantin Grcic
(1965–)
iittala 1999 to 2005

The last decade of the twentieth century showed hardly any true innovation in the production of glass tableware. Yet in 1999, the Finnish producer iittala invited the Munich-based designer Konstantin Grcic to create a new range of glassware. Their collaboration led to an instant commercial and artistic success. The Relations Glasses are elegantly proportioned, tapered tumblers. In this design it is not only the outline of the glasses that is important, but also the precise definition of the thickness of the glass. The Relations set consists of three different tumblers, a carafe, a large tray and a low dish.

It comes in two colours, brilliant white and smoky-grey. Grcic was interested in using a machine for pressed glass, and chose to rework the archetypal cone-shaped glass, adding a step on the inside wall. The glass could now be cleverly stacked, while keeping the outer wall flush by creating a thicker inner wall. Because the glasses are produced using a double-sectioned mould, the range can be produced in large quantities. Grcic is a designer who is able to reduce his designs to their utmost essence, advocating purity and elegance.

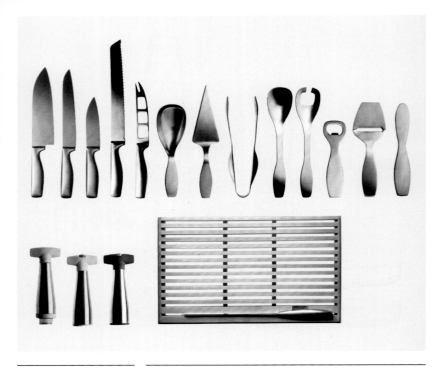

CITTERIO COLLECTIVE TOOLS 2000 (2000)
Antonio Citterio
(1950–)
Glen Oliver Löw
(1959–)
iittala
2000 to present

For over twenty years the work of Antonio Citterio has contributed to redefining and reshaping design. The Citterio Collective Tools 2000 illustrate his classic combination of practicality with luxury. Designed for iittala, the 2000 collection was preceded by the Citterio 98 Collection, designed in collaboration with Glen Oliver Löw, and formed a complementary set of cooking and culinary utensils for the earlier flatware range. The 2000 set of tableware and utensils consists of serving spoon, a cake server, serving tongs, a bottle opener and more. This set stands apart from others for several reasons, most

immediately the individual form used in the design. Manufactured in matt-brushed 18/10 stainless steel, all the pieces share the same generous proportions and a design that fits easily into the hand. The hollow handle construction has a perfect balanced weight, illustrating Citterio's dedication to harmony in form, material and function. Still widely available today, the Citterio Tools Collective 2000 is a familiar mainstay in the permanent design collections of many American and European museums, including the Museum of Modern Art in New York and the Architecture and Design Museum in Chicago.

LEM BAR STOOL (2000)
Shin Azumi (1965–)
Tomoko Azumi
(1966–)
lapalma
2000 to present

The manufacturer lapalma provided a modest brief for a simple, adjustable bar stool that soon developed under the intense observations of ergonomics that Shin Azumi brings to his industrial design projects. With the LEM Bar Stool, Azumi set out to grasp the particular requirements of a bar stool that set it apart from its cousin, the chair. He soon concluded that comfort and ease of use depended most importantly on the relationship between the seat and footrest. With a single, continuous loop of matt-chromed metal that first enclosed a plywood seat before dropping downward to form the footrest,

the LEM uniquely linked seat with footrest. This elegant and simple relationship depended, however, upon a far less simple engineering challenge. The slim rectangular tubes had to be bent into a loop with compound curves without producing visible wrinkles. Azumi's solution relied upon a new technology that had only recently been developed by a manufacturer of luxury automobiles. Together the seat and footrest are mounted on a rotating and adjustable gas-sprung column. The plywood seat and more industrial frame and base merge into the highly comfortable LEM.

STRAP (2000)
NL Architects
Droog
2004 to present

NL Architects were asked by Droog Design to create a system of displaying products for the Paris store of Mandarina Duck. Influenced by bicycles equipped with a strap at the rear to hold down articles, the Dutch designers decided to reinvent this rubber binder, which led to 'Strap'. The designers found the straps were manufactured by a variety of companies, and they finally found one who would provide just the rubber binder without the metal attachment that connects to the bicycle frame. Never before had the humble rubber band been adopted to be used on a wall. NL Architects's design features a double strap made of a soft, stretchable type of latex, flexible enough for displaying different types of objects. The Strap, as a product, is essentially reinvented by fixing it on to a wall with two small screws. Strap is available in nine colours, originally coordinated for the Mandarina Duck store by Droog Design. It is made using a press-casting technique, in which the fluid latex material is pressed between two steel moulds. The fascination of this product is the combination of a materialized vision and the investment of little material.

SPRING CHAIR (2000)
Ronan Bouroullec
(1971–)
Erwan Bouroullec
(1976–)
Cappellini
2000 to present

Since the mid-1990s a generation of young, influential French designers has emerged, with the brothers Ronan and Erwan Bouroullec among the most successful. Their best-known work to date has been with Cappellini in Italy, and the Spring Chair, which was nominated for a prestigious Compasso d'Oro award in 2001, was the first chair they designed for the company. The Spring Chair is not a particularly innovative form, but is nevertheless an elegant and refined design. The chair is constructed from a series of thin, moulded pads that connect to create a delicate lounge chair, supported on fine metal glides.

The headrest is adjustable, and the footrest is set on a spring that responds to the movement of the sitter's legs. The chair is composed of a shell of wood and polyurethane, with high-resilience foam, wool and stainless steel. There are four versions: the armchair, the armchair and footrest, the armchair and head-rest, and finally the armchair, footrest and headrest. Erwan describes the brothers' style as 'deliberately very simple with an element of humour'. The same spirit pervades work by some of their contemporaries and is characteristic of design of their generation.

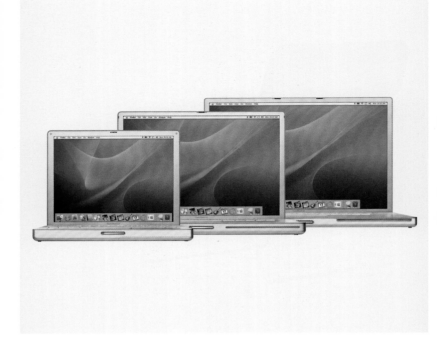

POWERBOOK G4 COMPUTER (2001)
Jonathan Ive (1967–)
Apple Design Team
Apple 2001 to 2006

Of all the products he has designed, Jonathan Ive regards the sleek, silver PowerBook laptop computer with its super-slick detailing, friendly radiuses and metallic keyboard, as the one (along with the iPod) that he is most proud of. Originally made of titanium, but later replaced by a more scratch-resistant aluminium alloy, the casing leaves no doubt that this is a serious product for a serious user. Sophisticated in an understated manner, compared to previous Apple products, the PowerBook plays safe with a chromophobic and minimalist aesthetic. The PowerBook has over ten years of innovative Apple laptop designs to draw upon, including the original grey machine of the early 1990s, the PowerBook Duo and the G3, with its softer 'feminine' form with a clamshell lid. The aluminium G4 plays it safe, with a cold 'masculine' style of rational technology and refined detailing. Originally only available in 12- and 17-inch versions, a 15-inch model followed within a year. With a mix of refined traditionalism and obsessive attention to detail, the PowerBook radiates confidence to and from its owner, signifying their shared maturity.

IPOD MP3 PLAYER (2001)
Jonathan Ive (1967–)
Apple Design Team
Apple
2001 to present

The iPod MP3 Player, along with Apple's iTunes software, represented joined-up thinking from an ever-wiser company. The iPod revolutionized the way people downloaded and listened to music. The original edition had a storage capacity of up to 1,000 songs with later generations increasing this to 40,000. The touch wheel made scrolling through an entire music collection quick and easy, while the 'shuffle' mode allowed for the ultimate personal jukebox experience. Its evolution primarily concentrated on size reduction, increasing memory, additional modes, such as recording of voice notes, and

eventually replacing the wheel with a touch screen. Aligning itself alongside the iMac G4, eMac and iBook computers, the minimalist purity of the iPod reflected the material and spiritual angst that accompanies relentless technological advancement. A hesitant transference from one era to another is effectively softened by the retro reassuring 'colour' aesthetic of 1960s Futurism. Perhaps then, it is not such a surprise that the iPod's appearance, 'colour' and flush radial interface were almost identical to another seminal portable music device: Dieter Rams's 1958 T3 pocket radio designed for Braun.

SEGWAY HUMAN TRANSPORTER (2001)
Segway Design Team
Segway
2002 to present

The Segway Human Transporter was the first electric-powered transport machine to balance itself and was designed to carry one individual at a time. Dean Kamen (1951–), president of DEKA Research and Development in the United States and founder of Segway LLC, had earlier designed the iBOT, a wheelchair that can climb stairs. The Segway HT stemmed from the balancing technology Kamen had developed for this earlier product. Now avaiabe in a number of models, including an all-terrain version, the scooters have no brakes and a maximum speed of 20 kph (12.5 mph). The rider, or driver, controls the direction and can stop the movement by turning a mechanism on the handlebar or by shifting his or her weight. The scooter consists of an in-built computer, five gyroscopes and a disc mounted on a base that allows the axis to turn freely in numerous directions while retaining its orientation. While its high cost prevented it from being a truly successful product for personal use, it has enjoyed a measure of success commercially: used by warehouse workers and, notably, tour groups. Despite its limited applications it has undeniably become a part of the zeitgeist.

OIL LAMP (2001)
Erik Magnussen
(1940–2014)
Stelton
2001 to present

Erik Magnussen's stainless-steel and borosilicate-glass Oil Lamp for Stelton is a contemporary table lamp that not only embodies the Danish design ethos of elegantly crafted forms, but also offers an energy-efficient solution to suit the new eco-aware culture. The small but perfectly formed lamp can be adapted for both indoor and outdoor use and even emergency lighting. When the lamp is filled it can burn for approximately forty hours. The durable fibreglass wick has almost eternal life and the lamp itself is easy to fill and clean. The Oil Lamp is a worthy addition to Magnussen's Stelton range, which includes the now iconic vacuum jug created in 1977. Indeed, Magnussen's Stelton collection essentially picks up the legacy of his predecessor, Arne Jacobsen, both in terms of offering a softer, humanistic take on Modernism and in understanding the symbiotic relationship between design and the industrial process. The rational yet sensual forms of Jacobsen's Cylinda-Line stainless-steel hollowware range for Stelton, 1967, are similarly present in Magnussen's Oil Lamp. The lamp makes perfect sense in terms of its minimal use of energy and low-maintenance design manifesto. It is an exemplar of stylish sustainability.

ONE-TWO LAMP
(2001)
James Irvine
(1958–2013)
Artemide
2001 to 2013

The One-Two Lamp seems at first glance to be a classic uplighter, shedding a stream of soft light upwards into any space. Constructed in grey-painted aluminium, the light has a slender stem topped with a curvaceous mushroom shade. The design has been honed down to a minimal, organic form. However, in typical Irvine fashion, this sparsely elegant design has a twist. Inset on the underside of the lamp's shade is a single halogen light, which can function as a traditional reading light. The floor-standing One-Two Lamp therefore serves as both an up- and a downlighter. This double emission allows for the possibility

of using a focused light source without reverting to the harshness of a bright overhead light.
The One-Two continues in a long tradition of Italian innovation in functional, chic and quirky design. Designer James Irvine studied at Kingston University and the Royal College of Art, both in London. In 1984 he settled in Milan where he ran his own studio. Irvine was one of a school of UK designers, including Jasper Morrison and Michael Young, known for combining innovative use of products with a sophisticated minimalist aesthetic.

JOYN OFFICE SYSTEM (2001)

Ronan Bouroullec
(1971–)
Erwan Bouroullec
(1976–)
Vitra 2002 to present

When the young French designers Ronan and Erwan Bouroullec started to design a new office system for Vitra in January 2001, they focused on the idea of a big table. It was to be a spacious workspace, with generous proportions; something with larger dimensions than a solitary desk, which can only belong to one person at a time. The idea of a table with flexible workspace for more than one person came from very homely origins: memories of the large family table. Joyn is an innovative furniture system where parts of a large tabletop can be fixed on to a central supporting beam, which rests on two trestles. This works with an ingenious 'click' system that requires no screws. Power and telecommunications run within a high-capacity central channel that acts like a raised floor. Wiring can be simply laid into the channel, linking all desktop office utilities. Joyn can be used in many ways, from individual work to teamwork and conferences. Additional and adjustable elements, like screens and blotters, called 'micro-architecture', can create areas for seclusion and specialized tasks. As nothing is fixed, work areas simply contract and expand to meet immediate needs.

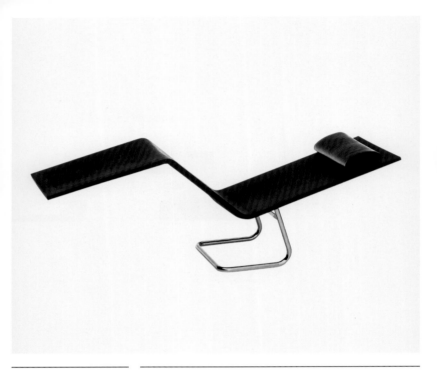

MVS CHAISE (2002)
Maarten van Severen
(1956–2005)
Vitra 2002 to 2019

Maarten van Severen first sketched the early version of his chaise longue CHL95 in 1994, when he was still producing each piece in his own workshop. With CHL98, developed in collaboration with Vitra and launched as the MVS Chaise in 2002, van Severen created an entirely new chaise longue. While the shape draws heavily on CHL95, its composition and finish are fresh. The surface material of polyurethane suspended by steel trim introduces flexibility and colour. Polyurethane was a revelation for van Severen. Finding a material that did not require an artificial cover or superficially applied colour allowed for an authenticity in the use of materials. In profile, the striking originality of MVS Chaise materializes. Gone is the reliance on the presumptively obvious need for four legs. In their place floats a chair on a single leg. With only the slightest shift in weight, the occupant pivots from reclining to fully resting. The uneasy anticipation of precarious balance proves entirely unfounded; the comfort is remarkable and carefree. Van Severen's uncompromising poetry of form sets him apart, and the MVS Chaise, which marries industry, unadorned materiality and sculptural beauty, embodies his unique language.

KYOTOP KNIVES (2002)

Kyocera Corporation
Design Team
Kyocera Corporation
2002 to present

The visual impact of KYOTOP Knives is stunning. With their black blades and wooden handles, they embody an uncompromising juxtaposition of traditional Japanese Minimalism with high-tech innovation. As high-quality kitchen items, KYOTOP belong to a heritage firmly rooted in invention and innovation. Founded in 1959, the Kyocera Corporation specialized in investigating the potential of zirconia ceramics. The blade of the KYOTOP knife is made from the same ceramic material as the other Kyocera knives, but its blade is pressed under high pressure in a carbon mould, which stains the blade its characteristic black colour. The ceramic blade does not rust and holds its sharpness longer than its steel counterpart. The zirconia ceramic blades are reputed to be almost as hard as diamonds and, although in reality they are susceptible to chips, the overall high performance and the lightness of the knife seem to outweigh this. The knives, from the outset, were models of style and achievement, and continue to ensure Kyocera's position at the forefront of the professional and domestic market. The range is now also available in white ceramic, which has aided the transition into the domestic kitchen.

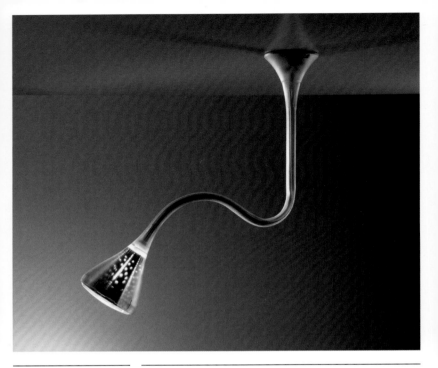

PIPE SUSPENSION LAMP (2002)
Herzog & de Meuron
Artemide
2002 to present

Most ceiling lights both hang and shine straight down. But the Pipe Suspension Lamp rejects tradition with its extremely flexible and adjustable steel tube that ends in a polygonal cone-shaped diffuser, with a polycarbonate lens, focusing the beam of light with great intensity. The aluminium diffuser, covered in a transparent platinic silicone sheath, is micro-perforated, so countless sparkles of light emerge from the sides of the lamp, embellishing its otherwise utilitarian appearance. Mid-priced, the lamp is a highly desirable solution for a spotlight that serves its purpose while seeming stunningly ethereal at the same time. Jacques Herzog and Pierre de Meuron, two of the most celebrated architects in the international scene, designed and first used the Pipe Suspension Lamp for their 1999–2004 Helvetica Patria office in St Gallen, Switzerland. The pair's way of working, a permanent search for innovation and excellence, led them to collaborate with Artemide, a world leader in innovative lighting design. The potency and success of the Pipe Suspension Lamp have granted it immediate status of superiority. It was awarded the prestigious Compasso d'Oro prize in 2004 for its flexible, thin and elegant appearance.

PAL RADIO (2002)
Henry Kloss
(1929–2002)
Tom DeVesto (1947–)
Tivoli Audio
2002 to present

The PAL (Portable Audio Laboratory) is a small portable and rechargeable AM-FM radio. It was the last project that engineer Henry Kloss worked on before he passed away. It is based on the Model One Radio, another acclaimed product by Tivoli Audio – a company set up by Kloss's long-time associate Tom DeVesto. Made out of a special waterproof plastic, the PAL produces a good sound – surprising for a box measuring only 15.88 cm (6.25 in) high, 9.37 cm (3.67 in) wide and 9.86 cm (3.88 in) deep. It can also be connected to any audio device via Bluetooth or through an auxiliary input. To ensure the length of the playback,

the PAL comes with a Li-Ion battery pack, which fully charges in just three hours and provides the system with sixteen hours of autonomy. Its success lies in its ability to tune to stations accurately and quickly, using an innovative AM/FM tune, as well as being the perfect companion for smart phones. For its understated class and high performance, the PAL Radio is the culminating achievement of Kloss's long career.

TIME AND WEATHER CLOCK (2003)
Philippe Starck
(1949–)
Oregon Scientific
2003 (now ceased)

Starck's Time and Weather Clock, which comes in three sizes, is a triumph over button-laden, high-tech gadgetry in favour of thoughtful structure, grouping and communication of information and function. Through a series of permanently displayed read-outs that are each visually distinct, a compendium of information is available: the weather; indoor and outdoor temperatures; the day and date in any of five languages; humidity, expressed both numerically and through a comfort level of wet, normal and dry; high, medium and low tides; together with eight phases of the moon. In accessing this information or adjusting the various readings according to its location, the clock incorporates hidden technology. Despite the absence of dials and buttons, adjustments can be made by touch navigation across a grid of flexible polymer. The clock has attracted enormous sales. Starck's unusual box, striking colours and stylized graphic design bear witness to his enduring ability to transform overlooked everyday objects and information into desirable commodities.

CHAIR_ONE (2003)
Konstantin Grcic
(1965–)
Magis
2004 to present

Chair_One is manufactured by the Italian firm, Magis, typically associated with producing adventurous plastic products, but is the creation of the German designer Konstantin Grcic who trained in England. In many ways the chair is a hybrid of the different characteristics of these three different nations, with its initial impression of being uncompromising and cold, while simultaneously offering surprising comfort. The design is significant because it is the world's first die-cast aluminium chair shell. Cast aluminium has since become a staple of the furniture industry, yet a closer relative to Chair_One

is the Victorian cast-iron garden chair. Aside from the differences in material and weight, the most apparent difference is the uncompromisingly computerized form of this chair. Its spare, linear structure looks like something from a sci-fi film, yet it is ergonomically determined and perfectly embraces the shape of the body. It forms part of a collection called Family_One, which consists of a four-legged version as well as tables and bar stools. The chair pictured is a dedicated public seating version, using a very similar geometric die-cast shell but mounted on a conical cast-concrete base.

**BRUNCH SET
KITCHENWARE
(2003)**
Jasper Morrison
(1959–)
Rowenta
2004 (now ceased)

The kitchen appliance has long been promoted and purchased anew with each rising trend and fashionable innovation. Manufacturers have relied on marketing and styling both to distinguish their products and to ensure their respectfully short life. The Jasper Morrison Brunch Set by the German premium home appliance manufacturer, Rowenta, is different. Here, surface and structure merge as the basis of communication, with subtle gestures and inviting curves. The cordless automatic kettle, with a concealed, polished stainless-steel heating element, is as dignified in its use as in its appearance. The

notion of concealment is carried on to the coffee maker, which has an all-in-one concept with the combined storage for the paper filters, the filter itself and the serving spoon. The toaster includes instructions situated on the front, instead of the usual side location. It is a mistake to tag these clean lines with a misleading label, whether it be Minimalism, Modernism or Functionalism. While others have toyed with similar endeavours, none has achieved such warm modesty and timeless typology. The Brunch Set is of course a designed object, but its lasting success will be as kettle, coffee maker and toaster.

**IMAC G5
COMPUTER (2004)**
Apple Design Team
Apple
2004 to 2006

Where did the computer go? The computer is in the display, proclaimed Apple's marketing campaign for the iMac G5. A translucent white plastic box, roughly 5 cm (2 in) thick, surrounds either a 17 or 20 inch LCD display and encloses a G5 processor of up to 2.0 GHz. Behind, a one-piece anodized aluminium pedestal is screwed to the case, making the computer lean slightly forwards. With the addition of wireless technology, the power wire is the only cable; all the rest – keyboard, mouse, Internet and mobile connection – can be linked through the AirPort Extreme Card. The idea of anchoring the design of the iMac G5 to the iPod was a clever stunt from Apple's marketing division. By doing so, it created a powerful identity, and was able to win over those PC users who had fallen under the spell of the sleek lines of the famous mp3 player. But above all these factors, the idea of the computer – with its several separate components – has been transformed into a unified system for the first time, established within the beautiful design of a translucent, thin rectangle that sits elegantly, appearing only as a screen.

SOLID C2 CHAIR (2004)
Patrick Jouin (1967–)
.MGX by Materialise
2004

The Solid C2 has the distinction of being the first ever 3D-printed piece of furniture to be made in a single piece. Its designer, Patrick Jouin, one of France's foremost creative minds, first became aware of 3D printing in 2004, which up until that point had only been used for creating smaller-scale plastic models. He set out to create a full-scale chair using a generative design process in which software, working within given parameters, tried out multiple shapes and structures. These were later finessed before the chair was printed from stereolithography-formed epoxy resin. Generative design and 3D printing can result in some extraordinarily complex forms that would not have previously been possible with a piece of furniture; the C2 Chair appears as though constructed from blades of grass entwining in a breeze, and its name 'Solid' is an ironic nod to its impossibly light and open woven form. Jouin has gone on to create other 3D-printed furniture such as the TAMU Chair and the One_Shot. MGX collapsible stool. Confirming its importance to design history, Swiss furniture designer and maker Vitra marketed a limited-edition miniature version of the Solid C2, which was exactly one-sixth the size of the original.

KANTO MAGAZINE RACK (2004)
Pancho Nikander
(1981–)
Artek
2004 to present

Formed of a single piece of birch plywood, the Kanto is Pancho Nikander's stylish take on the magazine rack. As a boat designer and builder, Nikander has used his intimate understanding of the way wood can be bent and manipulated to inform his sleek and practical design. Unlike narrower racks, where magazines that are placed spine upwards can slip down, the U-shaped Kanto is generously proportioned, with enough width to stack reading matter and papers stably. The container's broader dimensions also mean it can store firewood, kept neatly in place by the top of the container, which angles over and doubles as a useful carrying handle – another benefit of the rack's shape is that it remains perfectly balanced when lifted. The Kanto is manufactured by Artek in Finland, the legendary company founded by Aino and Alvar Aalto, Maire Gullichsen and Nils-Gustav Hahl in 1935. Made in the same way as much of the Aaltos' furniture, by gluing thin layers of birchwood together and compressing them into a flowing organic shape, the Kanto is a design classic that pays homage to the Aaltos' unique aesthetic while retaining its own particular early 2000s Minimalism.

LUNAR BATHROOM RANGE (2004)
Barber Osgerby
Authentics
2004 to present

Since the mid-nineties Edward Barber (1969–) and Jay Osgerby (1969–) have produced a string of beautiful, rational pieces of furniture, predominantly created from plywood. Although it still contains the pair's characteristic style, the Lunar Bathroom Range, introduced by German manufacturer Authentics in 2004, is something of a departure, as it leaves the top end of the market. When Barber Osgerby began their research into a range of bathroom fittings, they noticed that there was no full collection available on the market. Made from ABS, Lunar consists of a toothbrush tumbler, soap dish,

a container with lid for cotton buds, waste-bin and toilet brush. On the outside each product has a clean, clinical look. However, inside there is an unexpected flash of colour that, apart from making them look rather fetching, helps hide dirt or dust. The range comes in combinations of white with red, light blue, dark blue, grey, orange, beige or green. It is what good product design should be about: honesty, detail and innovation. The collection is one that is intended to grow, with additions to the variety of items and colour palette.

XO LAPTOP (2006)
Yves Béhar (1967–)
Quanta Computer
2006 to present

Dubbed 'the laptop that would save the world', this little green-and-white computer was designed to empower children from the poorest countries through education and technology. The non-profit One Laptop Per Child was set up by Nicholas Negroponte, co-founder of MIT's Media Lab, aiming to sell low-cost machines direct to the governments of the developing world. The size of a textbook and lighter than a lunchbox, the XO is simple to use and hugely robust: its tough plastic casing and sealed, rubber-membrane keyboard can withstand heat, humidity and rough treatment, and it folds into a chunky e-reader or gaming console. The Linux-based operating system has no hard drive to crash and its mesh networking provides a single point of Internet access available to others. The XO scheme has been supported by the United Nations Development Programme and, though not without its critics, it has reached more than 2 million children and their teachers worldwide, mainly across South America, but also in Rwanda, Gaza, Haiti, Afghanistan, Ethiopia and Mongolia.

ALCOVE SOFA (2006)
Ronan Bouroullec
(1971–)
Erwan Bouroullec
(1976–)
Vitra 2006 to present

The Alcove Sofa, with its remarkably high sides and back, creates an intimate box-like space in a stylish response to the hectic and noisy environment of open-plan offices. Invoking the same sense of privacy and freedom from interruption as a church confessional, Alcove offers a soft and sheltered nook for small informal meetings, focused, break-out working or, at home, simply a quiet place to read. The sofa comes in one, two, three or four-seater versions and these can be arranged in infinite combinations to create mini rooms within larger spaces, or 'microarchitecture', as the sofa's designers, the

brothers Ronan and Erwan Bouroullec, refer to it. In a nod to Bauhaus design, the sofa has a tubular chrome frame and legs, while a smaller, frameless, lower-backed model has been produced for domestic spaces; some versions have built-in tables for laptops or drinks. The bolt-upright back means this is not a sofa for slouching in, although the padded backrest ensures comfortable support for working. Alcove is intended to be a rebellion against boring office furniture and an indicator of the need for flexibility in twenty-first-century working life.

iPHONE MOBILE PHONE (2007)
Apple Design Team
Apple
2007 to present

The launch of the iPhone in 2007 was the result of several years spent investigating the merits of touch screen technology. Steve Jobs, co-founder and CEO of Apple at the time, saw that mobile phone technology was dictated by the keypad, and while the range of programmes and functions of the phones developed, they became difficult to use, restricted by the limitations of the keypad. By eschewing the keypad for a touchscreen the iPhone set a benchmark for modern devices. The first generation had only three buttons on the sides and one on the front and later models did away with the 'Home' button entirely, replacing it with finger-print or facial recognition technology to access the menu. As well as with its sleek and minimalist design the original iPhone also broke new ground with its high-resolution screen and automated processes for screen rotation and brightness adjustment. By positioning itself as an easy-to-use product that was at once a phone, an iPod and an Internet communications device, the iPhone forced Apple's competitors to rise to the challenge of rethinking the functions of a phone.

TAB LAMP (2007)
Barber Osgerby
Flos 2011 to present

British designers Edward Barber and Jay Osgerby create sleek, simple designs that are the fruit of a highly demanding development process. Trained architects, many of their early projects involved folding sheet materials influenced by the white card used in architectural model-making. Their Tab Lamp, made in collaboration with the Italian lighting company Flos, returns to this concept, and hinges on the idea of folding a simple piece of die-cast aluminium to create the perfect lampshade. Starting with a quick sketch of the lamp's tent-like shape, the stem, base and finally the eponymous tab were added to the design, but the Tab's refinement took another four years. The lamp's visual simplicity belies its high-spec technical characteristics, which include a ceramic reflector that creates a pure and controllable light, and an integrated multi-LED diffuser in PMMA – a rigid and transparent plastic – to reduce glare and shadows. Produced in both desk and floor models, Tab is slender, functional and has a tactility – thanks to the tab and its manufacture in pressofused aluminium – that invites engagement.

SPUN CHAIR (2007)
Thomas Heatherwick
(1970–)
Haunch of Venison
2007
Magis
2010 to present

Like an oversized spinning top, cotton reel or teacup, Spun defies expectations of what a chair can be. British designer Thomas Heatherwick was inspired to create this decidedly unusual seat by the industrial process of metal spinning, commonly used to make objects like timpani drums and kitchenware; he wondered whether it was possible to create a chair that was rotationally symmetrical while maintaining stability. Heatherwick's studio produced prototypes in clay and plywood exploring different geometries, and eventually all traditional elements of a chair – seat, back, arm, front legs, back

legs – were ruled out. Even without these seemingly crucial features, the chair's unique design means it cannot tip over, and grooves, like those on a vinyl record, not only stop the sitter from falling out, but also catch the light as the chair spins. London's Haunch of Venison gallery initially launched a spun-steel-and-copper limited edition, and Heatherwick later worked with Italian company Magis to roll out mass production of a version made of rotational-moulded polyethylene. Suitable for both indoor and outdoor use, Spun playfully disrupts public and private spaces with its deceptively simple design and sense of fun.

CABBAGE CHAIR
(2008)
Oki Sato (1977–)
nendo 2008 to 2009

This unusual piece of furniture has humble origins that belie its intricate, multi-layered form. Made only from a roll of waste paper, the chair is Oki Sato's response to a challenge issued by fashion designer Issey Miyake to create a piece of furniture using the paper left over from the mass manufacturing of pleated fabric. Sato demonstrated his unique eye for repurposing by simply taking a roll of the paper, cutting each of its layers one by one and peeling them back to create the Cabbage Chair. The pre-resinated crêpe-like paper is soft and springy enough for comfort, but robust enough to bear a person's weight. Needing no other components such as screws or nails, the chair is elegant, organic and fun – typifying Sato's work. In addition to white models, Sato also made blue, red, orange and green versions, while a later edition of white, black and mixed black-and-white chairs was exhibited in 2009 at Friedman Benda, New York. The Cabbage Chair now features among the collections of the Victoria and Albert Museum in London, the Art Institute of Chicago and New York's Museum of Modern Art; and what started as a clever piece of recycling now fetches enormous sums when sold at auction.

KELVIN LED (2009)
Antonio Citterio
(1950–)
Flos 2009 to present

Antonio Citterio's elegant Kelvin LED Lamp combines aesthetics and high performance in a lighting piece that is both energy-efficient and technically innovative. Thirty bright and long-lasting LEDs set behind a specially developed diffuser cast a warm, soft glow, far removed from the harsh, cold light associated with other LED lamps. The fully rotating head and sleek pantograph arm of fused aluminium alloy mean that it can be positioned to light almost any space. The on/off switch is a sensor placed in the back of the lamp head, employing technology that allows the user to activate the lamp simply by touching it:

unlike traditional lamps that use halogen bulbs the LEDs ensure that the Kelvin remains cool to the touch. Available in a white, anthracite, black or chrome finish, Flos have produced various models including a wall-mounted version and another with a clamp base that can be attached to a desk. Founded in 1962 in Merano, Italy, specifically to produce modern lighting, Flos have been developing new lighting concepts ever since and collaborate with many internationally renowned designers. The beauty and innovation of the Kelvin lamp have ensured that it has already established itself as one of the 'classics' of their range.

DYSON AIR
MULTIPLIER (2009)
James Dyson (1947–)
Dyson
2009 to present

Famous for revolutionising the vacuum cleaner market in the early 1990s, James Dyson turned his attention to the desk fan in 2009 with the release of the highly original Air Multiplier. Unlike conventional fans that use blades to circulate air, the Dyson fan directs a constant flow through a large hollow ring: a process that results in a stream of air that feels continuous, and avoids the buffeting associated with traditional fans. The technology behind the design is complex but essentially the fan uses an impeller to suck air in through a grille in the base and then blasts this air through a thin gap that runs around the inside of the ring. Surrounding air is then drawn into the airflow in a process known as inducement and entrainment, resulting in the fan expelling 405 litres of air every second. The Air Multiplier can be tilted to various angles, has a rotate function, and rather than the standard two or three fixed settings offered by conventional fans, air speed is controlled with a dimmer-switch. Dyson also released a floor-standing version of the fan in 2010. The Air Multiplier completely reimagined both the image and the function of the desk fan and sets the standard for future devices.

28 (2009)
Omer Arbel (1976–)
Bocci
2009 to present

Canadian company Bocci, founded in 2005 by Omer Arbel, has become synonymous with quality, innovation and technical excellence. Like many of its boundary-pushing designs, the 28 range sits somewhere between sculpture and product design. Each one of 28's globes is unique and hand-blown in Bocci's Vancouver factory; during the manufacturing process, temperature and airflow are carefully manipulated to create subtly distorted forms. Smaller spherical recesses are introduced into the surface of each bulb, before an opaque, milk-glass diffuser, housing either a low-voltage xenon or LED lamp, is inserted inside the globes. The result is a celestial 3D landscape inside every piece that catches and reflects light. There is vast scope for customization as the 28 is available in ninety different shades of coloured glass, ranging from muted metallics to vibrant jewel tones, and in myriad configurations: bulbs can be fixed to a stem to form a standard lamp, attached to a metal armature, or bunched in clusters as a pendant. In its pendant form, globes are grouped in hexagonal clusters of seven, nineteen, thiry-seven or sixty-one, suggesting the natural geometry of honeybees' cells.

BRANCA CHAIR
(2010)
Industrial Facility
Mattiazzi
2010 to present

Nevio and Fabiano Mattiazzi founded their wood workshop in 1979 and, over the years, the company has evolved into a cutting-edge furniture manufacturer. In 2009, the company commissioned Sam Hecht and Kim Colin of London-based studio Industrial Facility to design a dining chair, and the result, Branca, is a sinuous, sylvan classic made from European ash. Despite its decidedly minimal outline, the chair wraps the human body elegantly and organically. Manufacturing begins with machine tooling before the wood is milled by CNC (computer numerical control) robots,

finessing the ash until it seems to evolve into a new material. Finally, the chair is finished by hand. Branca is made from just seven parts: two back uprights form a single piece with the back legs; two armrests that unite with the front legs; then a back-rest, seat and seat-support. Winning multiple awards, the chair has been acquired for the permanent collections of the Design Museum in Helsinki and the Victoria and Albert Museum and the Design Museum in London. It is an example of how twenty-first-century design and manufacturing technology can combine to create new forms with wood.

TOOLBOX (2010)
Arik Levy (1963–)
Vitra 2010 to present

This bright and compact toolbox achieves an appeal that is unusual for an object that is more generally thought of in purely functional terms. Although it abandons the heaviness of traditional toolboxes, it retains aspects of the conventional design – such as its robust, yet lightweight ABS plastic, various compartments and carry handle – and transforms them into something both practical and desirable. An imaginative response to the need for home organization, Arik Levy's toolbox for Vitra is slim, meaning that it can fit easily onto a shelf, desk or tabletop. Yet it is more than a desk tidy, as the ergonomic carry handle transforms it into something that can easily transport paraphernalia around the house. Cleaning, gardening or DIY equipment can fit into the multi-sized recesses, and its lack of a lid means that it is always open for quick access. The toolbox offers a ray of cheeriness in tones taken from Vitra's Colour Library, a range of seven mid-century and acidic colours that coordinate with other products from its collection.

PLUMEN 001 (2010)
Hulger
Samuel Wilkinson
(1977–)
Plumen
2010 to present

The Plumen 001 transformed the lighting industry, reinventing and rebranding the Compact Fluorescent Lamp (CFL) into something covetable. CFL bulbs were used widely in the 2000s as low-energy alternatives to incandescents, in response to growing concerns about sustainability. Yet, although they had strong green credentials, their rigid gas-filled tubes favoured functionality over aesthetics. In 2010, Plumen, a London company set up by Nicolas Roope and Michael-George Hemus, working with designer Sam Wilkinson, created the world's first designer CFL bulb, the Plumen 001. It retained the

CFL's twin glass tubes but these were hung in two loops that that twisted together in three simple, yet beautiful variations. It also used 80 per cent less energy than a standard light bulb, compared to the average one-third reduction of previous CFL bulbs. A commercial and critical success, Plumen 001 won Design of the Year and Product of the Year from London's Design Museum just a year after its launch, as well as the highly coveted 'Black Pencil' from D&AD. The company created an LED model of the 001 in 2018, but the range's unique aesthetics continue to stand out in a market dominated by retro styling.

TIP TON (2011)
Barber Osgerby
Vitra 2011 to present

In 2008, British design duo Edward Barber and Jay Osgerby were approached by the Royal Society of Arts to design chairs for their new academy in Tipton near Birmingham. In collaboration with Vitra, the designers assimilated the results of cutting-edge research from the Swiss Federal Institute of Technology on chair design and its impact on the body to develop the Tip Ton. The research confirmed the benefits of 'dynamic sitting' and concluded that using a tilting chair is healthier for the spine, helping circulation, reducing back problems and improving concentration. Accordingly the chair's key feature is a kinked bottom rail that allows the user to tilt forward by nine degrees, angling the pelvis gently and straightening the spine. The chair is made of robust, wipe-clean 100 per cent recyclable polypropelene, without moving parts that can work loose or squeak. Finally complete after the creation of thirty prototypes, development took too long for the chair to be used at the academy, but it was still named in the school's honour. Tip Ton is now used widely in schools, offices and homes and, coming full circle, was chosen for classrooms at London's Royal College of Art, where Barber and Osgerby studied.

REVOLVER COUNTER STOOL (2011)
Leon Ransmeier
(1979–)
Established & Sons
2011 to 2012
HAY 2012 to present

This 360-degree revolving bar stool designed by New York-based Leon Ransmeier is a fundamental rethink of the traditional design in which a rotating seat is fixed on top of a tall stem – fun to sit on but not always particularly stable. In the Revolver, the stool is supported by a bearing mechanism contained in the footrest and, because the overall design is an A-shape, the sitter's weight is far more evenly distributed. The heavy base keeps everything balanced, ensuring the sitter does not teeter on top of a wobbly platform, and the seat is slightly dished, with curved edges for added comfort. Available in three heights – low, counter height and bar-stool height – there is no need for an ugly gas-lift mechanism either. Having dispensed with the old-style rotating seats, the stool instead relies on its slick aluminium bearing to make spinning around a simple matter of pushing off the ground with a foot. Made of powder-coated steel and available in grey, red or black, the Revolver has an edgy industrial aesthetic, which means it looks equally at home in bars, restaurants and urban homes.

OSSO CHAIR (2011)
Ronan Bouroullec
(1971–)
Erwan Bouroullec
(1976–)
Mattiazzi
2011 to present

The word *osso* means 'bone' in Italian and it is not hard to see why both the form and the surface of this chair, designed by French brothers Ronan and Erwan Bouroullec, could be compared to such a strong, smooth and organic substance. Made by Mattiazzi in Italy, who combine robot-operated milling methods with traditional hand-finishing, the ash, maple or oak that is used to make Osso is sculpted into gently curving panels that almost become an extension of the human body. The quality of the wood is at the heart of this design – cut from the forests of Udine, an area famous for its chair production, it is free from

chemical treatments, and the Bouroullec brothers liken its selection to the sourcing of the finest ingredients for a gourmet dish. Constructed of eight sublimely crafted parts, the chair's four curved panels lend it great strength while also creating a pleasing symmetry. A dining chair, armchair, child's chair and a variety of tables in natural wood or muted pastel colours make up the Osso range, which demonstrates a seamless fusion of technology and the natural world that is typical of the work of both Mattiazzi and the Bouroullecs.

FARMING-NET LAMP (2012)
Oki Sato (1977–)
nendo
2012 to present

These lampshades by nendo are a quintessential example of founder Oki Sato's talent for transforming dull, everyday materials into something new and beautiful. Made from the functional polypropylene nets used by farmers and gardeners to protect their crops from animals and bad weather, the material is rigid enough to be fashioned into a shape, yet still very light and permeable. With the application of some heat, it can be moulded into spherical forms that do not need supporting frames; and once an electric cord, light fitting and bulb have been added, the nets transform into ethereal, gauzy lampshades that cast a soft, welcoming glow like that of a paper lantern. The exact hand-crafting and shaping used to form these delicate shades recalls the traditional Japanese art of *furoshiki*, where material is carefully folded and wrapped around gifts, and is typical of nendo's considered approach. Sato designed a whole series of household items with the farming nets, including vases, bowls, plates and even tables. The range is a testament to how design can respond innovatively to growing concerns about the environment in the twenty-first century.

LITTLE SUN (2012)
Olafur Eliasson
(1967–)
Frederik Ottesen
(1967–)
Little Sun
2012 to present

This cheerful floral solar lamp was designed by artist Olafur Eliasson and engineer Frederik Ottesen as a solution to the problem that millions of people in the world still live without easy access to electricity. Launched initially in Ethiopia (its form is inspired by the country's meskel flower), its reach has since extended to provide clean, reliable and affordable lighting to 2 million people worldwide, mainly across sub-Saharan Africa. Its light and compact design could not be simpler: the recyclable body is made of weather- and UV-resistant ABS plastic, holding a 0.5-watt solar panel, rechargeable battery and LED light. To charge the lamp, the user simply leaves it in the sunshine for five hours with the solar panel facing upwards. Little Sun also helps to reduce reliance on kerosene lamps, which are a fire risk and give off fumes that harm both people and the environment. Its designers claim it can power social and economic change by providing more than just safe, sustainable lighting; it enables extra study hours for children at night, as well as jobs and businesses for local sales agents.

KALEIDO TRAYS (2012)
Clara von Zweigbergk (1970–)
HAY 2012 to present

While the household tray might more usually keep a fairly low profile compared to other objects around the home – its very purpose to keep clutter inconspicuous – these colourful examples have evolved the form into a cool and chic way to maintain order. Kaleido is a modular tray system designed by Clara von Zweigbergk for Danish homeware company HAY. Her quirky salvers come in a range of geometric shapes and jewel colours reminiscent of the fragments found inside a kaleidoscope, and are fashioned from powder-coated steel. The six- and four-sided trays tessellate in limitlessly satisfying ways, encouraging the user to collect the whole set. The larger versions can be used for serving coffee or drinks, while the smaller ones are perfect for gathering tiny items such as jewellery or stationery. Von Zweigbergk is a Swedish art director and graphic designer, known for her expertise in colour awareness, and this has been skilfully applied to these joyful, sleek and vibrant trays that turn tidying into an art form.

TESLA MODEL S (2012)
Tesla Design Team
Tesla 2012 to present

Although electric cars have a surprisingly long history – the first were prototyped in the early nineteenth century – it wasn't until Tesla's Model S that they became a viable option for sustainable travel. Aiming to prove that an electric car could truly match – or even better – a petrol one, the world's first premium electric saloon car was equipped with incredible acceleration, reaching 96 kph (60 mph) in 4.4 seconds and a top speed of 210 kph (130 mph). It also surpassed the electric competition with its 85-kilowatt battery option, which gives the Model S a drive range of 480 kilometres (300 miles), supported by Tesla's impressive network of super-charger stations where charge times are three times quicker than those of other electric brands. The Model S includes a luxurious interior, a large touchscreen display for everything from navigation to climate control, 3G connection, Internet radio and top-quality in-car sound. Its curving roofline, rounded bumpers and chrome fake radiator give it an edgier look than many Japanese or American cars. These factors combined to make it the 2013 Motor Trend Car of the Year, achieving one of the US car industry's highest awards.

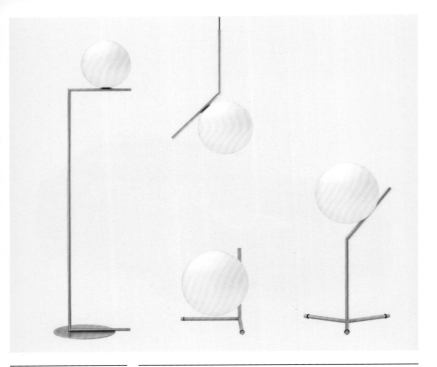

IC LIGHT FAMILY (2013)
Michael
Anastassiades (1967–)
Flos 2014 to present

Michael Anastassiades's IC Light family is elegant, playful and slightly surreal, intended by the designer to capture the sense of impossible balance and suspense found in contact juggling, where balls appear to float and glide over a performer's body. The frosted glass spheres hang, perch or hover on steel rods in different configurations in a range that includes wall lights, table lamps and pendants. The range's simple Modernist shapes and use of brass, chrome and glass imbue it with an Art Deco sensibility, albeit with a contemporary edge. Anastassiades originally trained as an engineer before becoming a

designer, and he uses this keen understanding of physics and materials to brilliant effect in all his work. This is especially evident in the IC family, in which the connection between glass sphere and steel rod is all but invisible. The hand-blown globes are made from milky-white opal glass, which gives excellent light diffusion, and they retain a soft moon-like form when lit. Anastassiades has collaborated extensively with Flos since 2013 on several successful product lines. The IC range stands out, however, for its beautifully poetic, even enigmatic qualities.

JUMP BIKE (2013)
JUMP Design Team
JUMP
2013 to present

The earliest bicycle-sharing schemes date back to the 1960s, but by the 2000s the idea had really taken off worldwide as a quicker, healthier and greener way to navigate traffic-clogged cities. JUMP's foray into this burgeoning market was the launch of a dockless, electric 'pedal-assist' bike – perfect for whizzing up the steep hills of San Francisco, where the start-up, founded by Ryan Rzepecki, is based. The bike's eye-catching cherry-red exterior is tough enough to withstand sun, rain and rider damage (mistreatment and vandalism are the greatest challenges of bike schemes), and stress-tested rubber seats and handlebars allow it to cope with heavy use by large numbers of cyclists. Unlike many clunkier rideshare bikes, JUMP's model has a lightweight aluminium frame, and is designed to give a comfortable ride experience for people of all sizes from 1.5 m to 2 m (4 ft 11 in to 6 ft 6 in). Plus, with a 250-watt motor and battery lasting up to 48 kilometres (30 miles), there is no need to pedal quite so hard. As the bikes continue to evolve, updated features include swappable lithium batteries – removing the need for overnight charging – and retractable smartphone-mounts for safer map-reading.

CLOSCA HELMET (2013)

Closca Design Team
Closca
2013 to present

The arrival of the Closca cycle helmet in 2013 radically challenged a design that had not greatly evolved since the first mass-produced version appeared in the 1970s. Sleek, curving and shell-like, Closca's clever collapsible design is light years away from the bulk and clunkiness of traditional rigid plastic helmets; it compresses to 55 per cent of its size in a second, meaning it can easily fit inside a backpack. Its collapsibility is also an important safety attribute as the helmet's flexible, ridged surface absorbs the shock of an impact more evenly than traditional models. The helmet also contains an integrated NFC

(Near Field Communication) chip that connects wirelessly to the user's smartphone so that, in an accident, the wearer can call a chosen emergency contact or share their location with a single tap on their phone screen. Closca, based in Valencia, Spain, used crowdfunding to launch a fabric-covered version in 2013, and the more rigid recyclable plastic model of 2015 has seen extraordinary success. The helmet's unique design has combined elements of style and safety, to encourage more people to take to their bikes, reducing congestion and carbon emissions in cities worldwide.

BEE BRICK
(2014)
Green & Blue
2014 to present

The Bee Brick is a simple but ingenious design that provides a safe nesting place for non-swarming solitary bees. Green & Blue, the Cornwall, UK-based company responsible for the Bee Brick, are passionate about helping to protect the more than 250 bee species in the UK, especially solitary bees who are vital for pollination. The Bee Brick is solid at the back and features moulded cavities where bees can lay their eggs, before sealing the entrance with mud or chewed up vegetation. The new bees emerge in Spring and begin the process of nesting again, repeating the yearly cycle. Unlike other designs that serve a similar purpose, the Bee Brick, which is made from concrete using up to 75% waste material from the Cornish China clay industry, has been designed to be used in place of standard bricks in construction and so can be used either as a standalone design feature in a garden, terrace, balcony or allotment, or integrated into a larger structure. The Bee Brick, which comes in a variety of sizes, colours and formats including blocks, posts, single cell and planter pots versions, has won a number of high profile sustainability and traditional design awards.

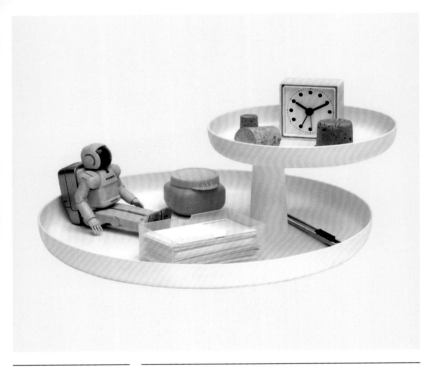

ROTARY TRAY
(2014)
Jasper Morrison
(1959–)
Vitra 2014 to present

The consummately elegant Rotary Tray is British designer Jasper Morrison's interpretation of the classic étagère, a multi-tiered tray traditionally used for displaying knick-knacks and especially popular with the Victorians. Morrison's two-level version is decidedly minimalist, responding to the 2010s trend for tidiness and simplicity, and features a handy rotating top tier for accessibility. The lips of both of its trays curve gently upwards to keep items in place, and its rounded forms create a friendly and appealing aesthetic. Made of ABS plastic, the Rotary Tray comes in eight colours, including poppy red, mint green and ice grey, and its unassuming neutrality means it looks equally at home in a kitchen, bathroom, hallway or study. Morrison, whose highly fruitful partnership with Vitra dates back to 1989, espouses a particularly painstaking approach that once resulted in taking four years to design a fork. He aims to achieve what he calls the 'super normal': rather than seeking to create an avant-garde object, he prefers to reinterpret existing design icons, refining and evolving them into something new – a rationale that is exemplified by the Rotary Tray.

NEST PROTECT (2014)
Nest
Nest 2014 to present

This combined smoke and carbon monoxide detector was designed specifically to address the often-infuriating downsides of conventional devices: false alarms caused by burning toast, interminable beeps when the battery runs low, as well as the aesthetically uninspiring design. As the first smoke detector to be compatible with a linked smartphone app, the Nest Protect allows for a higher degree of user-control: it signals low batteries silently via the app, avoiding unnecessary night-time disturbances, and the app can be used to deactivate the alarm, whether the occupier is at home or not. Taking the idea of a 'smart' smoke detector further still, a humidity sensor detects the difference between steam and smoke, while light sensors can distinguish between slow and fast-burning fires. The Protect can also synchronize with the entire Nest smart-home system of devices, including other smoke alarms or a thermostat to control temperature. Far more visually appealing than traditional models, Protect has a slim profile and rounded corners, making its unobtrusiveness and integration into daily life an aesthetic, as well as technological, advantage.

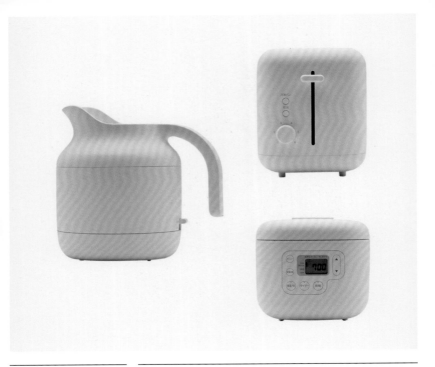

ELECTRIC KETTLE, TOASTER AND RICE COOKER (2014)
Naoto Fukasawa (1956–)
MUJI 2014 to present

Naoto Fukasawa is probably Japan's most significant industrial designer, whose design philosophy proposes that household objects create a profound sense of well-being when they are 'just right', and the role of the designer is to refine them until they reach that point. Fukasawa achieves this by solving everyday problems with 'microconsiderations' – rigorously designed details that make all the difference – and this hugely successful kitchen range for MUJI follows these principles to the letter. Each appliance features gently rounded curves rather than sharp corners, which Fukasawa says are more in tune with the human body; and the ergonomic handles, easy-to read displays and big buttons further adapt the products for ease of everyday use. Simple yet ingenious technological developments also demonstrate a real zeal for efficiency: the kettle boils water in just eighty seconds and the rice cooker has a handy spoon nestling in its lid. The toaster slots are minutely engineered to maintain an equal distance from the heating element on all sides of the bread, ensuring optimal toasting. Each detail is intended to create efficient products that are pleasurable to use, while their affordability has truly democratized good design.

ALUME CUBE CLOCK
(2014)
Natalie Sun (nd)
Gingko
2014 to present

The Alume Cube Clock may look like a simple blank aluminium cube, but it reveals its true identity with a snap of the fingers, clap of the hands, or a tap on top. When summoned this way, the cube illuminates the time, date, and temperature as if by magic. The sleek and minimal design is housed in a 68 × 68 × 68 millimetre (2.75 × 2.75 × 2.75 inch) cube made from MDF wood with a brushed aluminium veneer finish. The designer of the Cube Clock, Natalie Sun, is the co-founder of Gingko, a design-led, technology-centred company based in Warwickshire in England. Founded in 2011, the company is focused on creating high-end yet practical and stylish products for home and office environments. Sun's belief that technology can often be too intrusive and too complicated has led to a focus on super simple products that are engaging, aesthetically pleasing as well as being sustainable. The ethos at Gingko, 'escape the boring – design for a better life' – is perfectly encapsulated in the beguiling simplicity of the Alume Cube Clock.

COW, BAMBI AND SHEEP CHAIRS (2014)
Takeshi Sawada
(1978–)
EO 2014 to present

Animals often inspire the design of furniture for adults in an abstract way, but these children's chairs by Takeshi Sawada are far more literal. Sawada, a former fashion designer who created these Cow, Bambi and Sheep Chairs for Danish furniture company EO (Elements Optimal), understands the way animals can become benevolent miniature friends to a young child, and the tactile and diminutive chairs certainly evoke an emotional response. Beautifully made of wood and faux fur, they respect the natural world from which they draw inspiration. The Bambi is fashioned from oak and walnut;

the Sheep, beech and oak; and the darker-toned Cow in smoked oak and walnut. Wool and animal 'fur' is beautifully crafted, especially on the Bambi, whose dappling spots are highly realistic. With splayed legs, and horns or antlers serving as back rests, the chairs' forms aim to take on the essence of each animal. The genius of the range, one of Sawada's most successful projects, lies in the chairs' loving craftsmanship and tender vision of childhood innocence.

RABBIT CHAIR (2016)
Stefano Giovannoni (1954–)
Qeeboo
2016 to present

The Rabbit Chair was one of the star pieces in the 2016 launch of Stefano Giovannoni's furniture brand Qeeboo. The Italian designer's animal-inspired chair has a playful Pop sensibility, and its simple, smooth rabbit form reduces all detail to an archetypal level that makes it a symbol for all kinds of positive associations – which, says the designer, include childhood, fertility, love, springtime and *Alice in Wonderland*. Giovannoni's design is intended to be used flexibly: the sitter can lean back using the rabbit's ears as a backrest, or choose to face the other way, resting the arms on the ears, and the solid plinth formed by the rabbit's abstracted 'feet' gives the chair stability. The Polyethylene bunny comes in a range of colours and finishes, including velvet, high-gloss plastic and metallic silver and gold. To appeal to children there is also a miniature version, the Rabbit Chair Baby, and a rabbit-shaped lamp completes the range. The chair perhaps also alludes to Jeff Koons's famous *Rabbit* sculpture of 1986; but where Koons's piece was pure conceptual art, Giovannoni's chair remains highly functional.

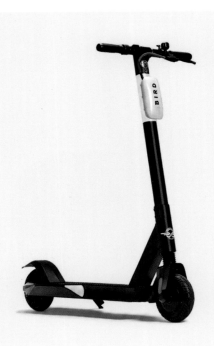

BIRD ZERO (2018)
Bird Design Team
Bird 2018 to present

Launched in 2018, the Bird Zero was the world's first electric scooter to be created and engineered specifically for the dockless rideshare market. Californian start-up Bird had been founded just one year before by Travis VanderZanden, formerly of Lyft and Uber, and the company introduced the Bird Zero to address failings in existing scooters that made them unsuitable for commercial use. The technology was updated to make the Bird Zero more suited to ridesharing, creating a steel-reinforced aluminium frame to be stronger and more hard-wearing than traditional models, making it

capable of withstanding heavy use and vandalism. Two features also improved ride stability: solid tyres instead of air-filled ones, and a longer wheelbase with a lower centre of gravity. The battery life is 60 per cent longer than previous models and it is equipped with better lighting for improved visibility and safety, battery indicators and speed indicators. These innovations gave Bird an edge on its competitors and, after just one year of trading, the company had operated 10 million scooter rides across the world.

KVADRAT SHADE (2019)
Ronan Bouroullec
(1971–)
Erwan Bouroullec
(1976–)
Kvadrat
2019 to present

Roller blinds have traditionally been valued for low cost and practicality over any aesthetic considerations, but Danish textile company Kvadrat and French design duo Ronan and Erwan Bouroullec set out to change that with this covetable and plastic-free blind. The Bouroullec brothers perfected the hardware, meticulously engineering metal pulleys, roller mechanisms and cassettes, while Kvadrat refined the textile element, creating a range of designs in premium fabrics and monochrome colour schemes. The result is totally PVC-free and has been called the 'Swiss watch' of blinds. The shades come in motorized and manual models, and have a sleek, elegant aesthetic that perfectly complements modern architecture and interiors. An aluminium-coated version reflects the sun's heat to keep buildings cool in summer, yet retain warmth in winter, reducing bills and CO_2 emissions. Kvadrat is renowned for taking a highly engineered approach to manufacturing and constantly innovates with its production processes. Working with renowned designers like Patricia Urquiola and Raf Simons, the firm creates simple yet expressive textiles that are emblematic of the Scandinavian design tradition.

INDEX OF PRODUCTS

Page numbers in bold refer to main entries

Index by Product

INDEX OF DESIGNERS

Page numbers in bold refer to main entries

Rohde, Johan **52**
Rolex Design Team **77**
Rosati, Dominick **86**
Rossi, Aldo **388**, **410**, **428**, **437**
Rotring Design Team **206**
Rowland, David **295**

S

Saarinen, Eero **138**, 151, **163**, 178, 212, **223**,
  245, 284, 308
Sapper, Richard **255**, **296**, **298**, **347**, **349**,
  364, **375**, **396**, 400, 407
Sarfatti, Gino **252**
Sargiani, Franco **348**
Sarpaneva, Timo **265**, **370**, 460
Sato, Oki **508**, **518**
Sawada, Takeshi **530**
Scarpa, Carlo **104**
Schärer, Paul **285**
Schild (A.) S. A. Design Team **108**
Schlumbohm, Peter J **142**
Schmidt, Herbert **118**
Schultz, Richard **283**
Scolari, Carla **316**
Segway Design Team **488**
Seth Andersson, Carina **465**
Severen, Maarten van **436**, **444**, **492**
Silver, Spencer **383**
Slingsby Design Team **299**
Sørensen, Johnny **359**
Sottsass, Ettore **378**, **381**, **389**, **455**
Starck, Philippe 149, **391**, 411, **414**, **425**,
  430, 466, **496**
Stave, Sylvia **68**
Stoppino, Giotto **341**
Stumpf, William **445**
Summers, Gerald **114**
Sun, Natalie **529**
Sundback, Gideon **44**
Swann-Morton Design Team **134**
Swatch Lab **395**

T

TAG Heuer Design Team **332**
Tayar, Ali **438**
Teodoro, Franco **317**
Terragni, Giuseppe **119**, **129**
Tesla Design Team **521**
Thonet, Michael 8, **18**
Thonet (Gebrüder) Design Team **85**
Thygesen, Rud **359**
Trey, César de **102**
Tupper, Earl Silas **152**

U

US Navy Engineering Team **149**

V

Vaaler, Johan **29**
Vacheron Constantin Design Department **219**
Vale, Gino **297**
Velde, Henry van de **28**
Vender, Claudio **128**
Venini, Paolo **104**, **174**
Vignelli, Massimo **294**
Visser, Arnout **474**
Volther, Poul **269**
von Zweigbergk, Clara **520**

W

Wagenfeld, Wilhelm **59**, 76, **87**, **218**
Wagner, Otto **36**, 40
Wanders, Marcel **459**, 479
Wedgwood, Josiah & Sons **8**
Wedo Design Team **367**
Wegner, Hans 115, **165**, **172**, **173**, **175**, **180**,
  264, 282, 302
Wienke, Karl F. A. **22**
Wilkinson, Samuel **514**
Wirkkala, Tapio **162**, **324**, **354**, 460
Wüsthof (Ed) Dreizackwerk **23**

Y

Yale, Linus Jr **19**
Yamada, Komin **392**
Yanagi, Sori **213**, **228**, **267**, **390**

Z

Zanuso, Marco **192**, **255**, **296**, **298**, **325**,
  343, 364
Zhang Xiaoquan **4**

AUTHOR LIST

PICTURE CREDITS

Phaidon Press Limited
2 Cooperage Yard
London E15 2QR

Phaidon Press Inc.
65 Bleecker Street
New York, NY 10012

phaidon.com

First published 2013
Reprinted 2016, 2017
This edition published 2020
Reprinted 2021, 2023
© 2013 and 2020 Phaidon Press Limited

ISBN 978 1 83866 143 4

A CIP catalogue record for this book is
available from the British Library and the
Library of Congress.

Commissioning Editor: Emilia Terragni
Project Editor: Emma Barton
Production Controller: Gif Jittiwutikarn

Cover Design by Julia Hasting
Interior Design by Hans Stofregen based on
original design by Sandra Zellmer

Printed in China